PRIVATIZING THE STATE

BÉATRICE HIBOU
editor

Privatizing the State

translated from the French by
JONATHAN DERRICK

Columbia University Press
New York
in association with the Centre d'Etudes et de
Recherches Internationales, Paris

Columbia University Press
Publishers Since 1893
New York
Copyright © 2004 Béatrice Hibou

Library of Congress Cataloging-in-Publication Data
Privatisation des Etats. English
  Privatizing the state/edited by Béatrice Hibou.
    p. cm.—(The CERI series in comparative politics
  and international studies)
  Translation of: La privatisation des Etats.
  Includes bibliographical references and index.
  ISBN 0-231-13464-9 (alk. paper)
  1. Privatization. I. Hibou. II. Title. III. Series.
  HD3854.P7413 2004
  338.9'25—dc22

                                                        200445479

Columbia University Press books are printed on permanent and durable
acid-free paper.

c 10 9 8 7 6 5 4 3 2 1

Printed in India

CONTENTS

PREFACE TO THE ENGLISH EDITION

Recent events, starting with 11 September 2001 and the invasion and on-going occupation of Iraq, remind us that the discourse on the legitimacy of state intervention continues on a massive scale in the public arena. Today, more than ever, there are calls for the state, for public policies, for regulations. And those calls do not come only from the 'have-nots' and people longing for the days of the Welfare State; they are also voiced strongly by those 'private' actors who are supposed to be challenging state interventionism. In the countries analysed in this book, all the policies of reform, liberalisation and privatisation implemented since the early 1980s have been public policies in the true sense of the term, and as a result have been rehabilitated by international institutions and states, despite their constant talk of disengagement by the state. This trend towards interventionism has recently been given new emphasis by aid donors' placing of social policies on the agenda—notably the struggle against poverty, sustainable development and promotion of civil society.

These observations would be trite if they did not fit into reflections on privatisation; they are intended essentially to underline that there are many modes of intervention and not just one single model. They also underline that ideas, concepts and the very way of understanding public action and interventionism are constantly changing. At any rate, looking at the long term it is not possible in any instance to talk of a retreat of interventionism or disengagement by the state—on the contrary, what is happening is a widening range of forms of state intervention. So why talk of 'privatising the state'?

The expression may have caused some confusion. It has sometimes been understood in one of its more restrictive and marginal senses, namely corruption, appropriation of national economic resources by wielders of state power: Russian state enterprises taken over by 'oligarchs', the Ben Ali clan in Tunisia securing the most lucrative contracts, the diversion of social policies and public aid by cronies of Suharto in Indonesia, etc. But basically this book does not deal with that, even though corruption is not alien—far from it—to the new ways of exercising power that the term 'privatisation of the state' seeks to convey.

It should be clear that in our understanding privatisation does not concern only state enterprises, public services (with Build-Operate-Transfer, public service concession, public work contracting, delegations and other private management contracts) or economic actors (working to 'promote the private sector'). That orthodox aspect of reform—at the heart of the dominant discourse of the international community—represents only one element of the 'building'[1] of economic policy. But privatisation has also spread to other domains and other interventions by the state. It also concerns—perhaps above all—development, economic resources, regulatory functions and the state's sovereign functions. As diverse as they are, these privatisations have several things in common: they all find approval in the prevailing liberal discourse, they all make increasing use of private means for governing, they all alter not only the forms of economic regulation but also the forms of political regulation and the forms of sovereignty. In other words, they all displace, relativise and re-draw the borders between 'public' and 'private'. This process of 'vulgarisation'[2] of privatisation is today one of the dominant modes of government in Southern countries, the 'formation' of privatisation having largely overtaken its 'building'.

One point should be made clear: talking of privatisation of the state is not a semantic slip, a play on words; it denotes two concomitant processes—the spread of use of private intermediaries for an increasing number of functions formerly devolving on the state, and the redeployment of the state. In this book, in attempting to pin down as narrowly as possible the 'privatisation' practices now being constructed, we have tried to analyse the *imaginaires* surrounding the distinction between public and private, economic and political.

Our statement of the *problématique* in terms of privatisation is thus directly derived from the fashionable rhetoric about the state (the crisis of the nation-state, the future of the state in increasingly privatised international relations, the difficulty of achieving state mastery over the economy, the evanescence of the state amid globalisation, etc.): a rhetoric that emphasises the rise of the private, the free market, transnational actors and networks, and commodification. But we have adopted that vocabulary so

---

[1] The distinction between 'state-building' and 'state-formation' was put forward by B. Berman and J. Lonsdale. State-building is 'a conscious effort at creating an apparatus of control' while its formation is 'an historical process whose outcome is a largely unconscious and contradictory process of conflicts, negotiations and compromises between diverse groups whose self-serving actions and trade-offs constitute the 'vulgarisation' of power': B. Berman and J. Lonsdale, *Unhappy Valley*, Harlow: Longman, 1992, p. 5. For a systematisation of this distinction, see the review of that book by J.-F. Bayart in the *Revue Française de Sciences Politiques*, vol. 44, no. 1, February 1994, pp. 136–9.
[2] Berman and Lonsdale, op. cit.

as to deconstruct its logic better: to prove that it is a matter of a discourse above all; to show that the facts are much more complex and ambivalent than a simple readjustment between public and private actors that would be easy to identify; and to bring out the methodological biases that underlie those interpretations. Among those biases are the liberal illusion; under-estimation of the processes of reappropriation, overturning of logics and conflicts among concepts of power; the adoption of narrow, confined definitions of the state, and ignoring of historical trajectories.

There is no need, then, to dwell on the fact that our use of 'privatisation' is above all ironical; the idea is to suggest that the forms of discourse conveyed by aid donors, the 'world community' and organic intellectuals of liberalisation and privatisation authorise very varied practices, sometimes poles apart from the expected effects, sometimes totally at variance with the pursued objectives. But irony does not stop us taking seriously a liberal discourse that to a great extent is part of the rhetoric of state powers; it therefore informs us about those powers' intentions and strategies, but also about those of non-state actors that also refer to it, and more than might appear.

A book published in France in 1999, whose field of study, reflections and ideas go back to 1996–7, can still be usefully presented to English-speaking readers today. When first published the reflections were relatively new, while today a number of works on the subject have been published. Now even believers in the retreat of the state acknowledge that the state is not endangered by the rise of the private sphere and globalisation. However, it seemed to us that our book was still topical: it sprang inevitably from a French way of thinking, notably through its approach based on in-depth empirical fieldwork and on sociological and historical theoretical reflections, and was clearly distinguished, on a number of points, from most political science and political economy writings published in Britain or the United States; that tradition seemed to us to be poorly represented in those countries.

All the authors in this volume, except for William Reno, share a non-normative vision of current transformation of state power: for us it is not a question of either the survival or the resistance of the state. This is essentially because we do not analyse current change in terms of anomie, destructuration, or pathological situations. We are influenced by works on the historical sociology of the state, particularly by the methodological essays of Max Weber, and by some writings of Michel Foucault, and not by internationalist writings in the tradition of theories of 'diffusion' or 'dilution' of power (following Strange, Hall and Biersteker) or certain works of international sociology or global studies (represented by Sassen, for example). Our concern was to understand the internal changes in societies, the dimension of those societies' international integration being only one of several dimensions to the changes. In no case did we seek to know whether there was more 'private' or whether the 'public' was resisting; whether non-state actors were taking over leadership or not in the definition of rules and norms; how the state was behaving when faced with the rise of rival powers (market authorities, moral authorities and illicit authorities, to use Hall and Biersteker's classification); how the state was changing under the effect of globalisation and the rise of non-state actors in the international sphere.

In our approach we evaded from the outset the question of the essentialist definition of the state (or of the public and private simultaneously). For that debate, it seems to me, is simply a resumption of older discussion on the introduction of the notion of the state in Western societies, the problems of continuity or discontinuity with preceding forms of power, the emergence of the nation-state and the possibility or impossibility of describing non-Western configurations as nation-states. It has long since been shown that the question of whether the state has always existed or not depended for an answer solely on the definition of the term 'state', and that the choice of a definition depended on criteria of expediency rather than truth.[3]

Our idea was therefore to go beyond lexical differences and moods so as to describe and interpret the changes that have marked the passage from one modality of government to another; to avoid positing *a priori* the distinction between state and non-state, political and economic, public and private, so as to avoid eliminating from our analysis elements considered *a priori* not to belong to the state, political or public field. At the same time, adopting Foucault's concept of power and government, we aimed to reinstate the historicity of states but also to emphasise the multiplicity of relations between the social and the political. In other words, we aimed to demonstrate the changes in the forms and points of state intervention and the remodelling of different values and norms. In that sense the 'privatisation of the state' does not only mean alteration in the ways of behaving in the economic and political fields. It also means alteration in the ways of being and understanding in those fields.

---

[3] See, obviously, the development of this theme in the Introduction to the book, based on methods of analysis of the political inspired by Foucault (for example in *The History of Sexuality, vol. I: An Introduction*, New York: Vintage Books, 1990 (French edition 1976)). But historians and sociologists of the state have also brought to light such a posture; thus I have been considerably inspired by Max Weber, but through non-literal and essentially methodological understanding (see the numerous quotations in the Introduction). See also the writings of N. Bobbio, for example in his *L'Etat et la démocratie internationale*, Brussels: Complexe, 1998.

This proposition requires a bit of explanation.[4] When I say that some present-day configurations are allied to what Weber analysed as forms of non-bureaucratised states and non-permanent intervention, which I have called 'discharge' situations using the French translation of the German terms *Verpachtung* and *Überweisung*,[5] and when I criticise the Weberian conception of international organisations, that does not mean that I intend to deny the existence of a rational, bureaucratic legal state in the Southern societies analysed in this book. But that existence is very specific: it is confined essentially to the *imaginaire*, to an unattainable ideal, emblem of modernity, or else it is present in certain administrations and through certain techniques of power, like Protocol or the security services (the political police). More precisely, it belongs even to a certain sort of *imaginaire*, since there are other *imaginaires* of the state, such as the Makhzen *imaginaire* in Morocco. The rational legal state emerged in the West in reality but above all in the *imaginaire*; this is often forgotten in popular understanding of Weber, which tends to identify the historical experiences of European states with an ideal-type. And 'Westernisation' has essentially occurred in that sphere; the rational, bureaucratic legal state now exists everywhere, but essentially as an *imaginaire*.[6] Current debates also feed on this confusion between the reality of historical experiences and the *imaginaire*. That is what I meant to show by underscoring the form I called 'discharge'.

Contrary to what most writing about globalisation tends to show, the chapters of this book emphasise the banality of political phenomena at work in our days, a banality displayed in at least two respects. There is, first, banality in the fears regarding threats to the state from international constraints. The political history of the modern age can indeed be read as a reflection on the crisis of the state,[7] on the tension between the nation state and the international dimension, a tension which is most often

---

[4] For this criticism of the non-universality of the legal-rational and bureaucratic form of state, see for example J.-P. Olivier de Sardan, 'Compte-rendu de B. Hibou (dir), *La privatisation des Etats*', *Revue Tiers Monde*, vol. XLI, no. 161, January–March 2000, pp. 217–21.

[5] I thank Denis Tull of the University of Hamburg for finding Weber's original terms for me.

[6] *Imaginaire* in the sense not of unreality, but of non-distinction between real and unreal; not constituted once for all, but a constituent part of reality. See J.-F. Bayart, *The Fictions of Cultural Identity* (who cites P. Veyne and G. Deleuze on that subject), London: Hurst, forthcoming.

[7] On the misuse of the notion of crisis of the state and difficulties of thinking of transformation of the state, see L. Hont, 'The Permanent Crisis of a Divided Mankind: "Contemporary Crisis of the Nation State" in Historical Perspective', pp. 166–231, in J. Dunn (ed.), *Contemporary Crisis of the Nation State?*, Oxford and Cambridge: Basil Blackwell, 1995.

analysed as a challenge to the state from external phenomena—war, imperialism, international markets, free trade—but which recent research tends rather to analyse as a phenomenon of entanglement of the two phenomena, the state being largely a product of globalisation.[8] That dimension is not, strictly speaking, analysed in *Privatising the State*, but it underlies our research posture which refuses to consider *a priori* that the state is in special danger or crisis.

Then, above all, there is banality in modes of government and rearrangements between public and private. One object of this book is to emphasise the recurrence, both geographical and historical, of private, indirect modes of government. One of our arguments is to show that far from yet another crisis of the state occurring, modes of government are being modified, 'as usual' one might say; we are only witnessing an additional transformation of modes of state intervention in the economy (as well as in the political and the social, which is less illustrated in the book but sometimes suggested). This transformation is at the same time an alteration in relations between public and private, economic and political, licit and illicit and legal and illegal, because of the growing importance of contracts. That last point can illustrate our proposition: Weber and Locke before him already stressed that the essential characteristic of life under the modern law was the central position of legal transactions, especially contracts.[9]

More generally, reading of analyses of non-modern societies suggests the extreme banality of these modes of government, from the publicans of Rome[10] to the delegations of feudal societies and the tax farming under European monarchies, but also the Ottoman Empire. Conversely, it helps us understand how the ordinary conception of the state and modes of government is influenced by idealising of a very recent and limited experience.[11] The point must be made clear: those historical experiences, often magnificently documented and analysed by leading historians and sociologists, are interesting only in suggesting the possible multiplicity of modes

---

[8] This is the central thesis of J.-F. Bayart, *Critique politique de la globalisation*, Paris: Fayard, forthcoming in 2003; it is also studied in *The Fictions of Cultural Identity* (note 6) and, for Africa, in J.-F. Bayart, 'Africa in the World: a History of Extraversion', *African Affairs*, vol. 99 no. 395, April 2000, pp. 217–67.

[9] Analysed and quoted by C. Colliot-Thélène, *Etudes wéberiennes, Rationalités, histoires, droits*, Paris: PUF, 2001.

[10] C. Nicollet, *Censeurs et publicains. Economie et fiscalité dans la Rome antique*, Paris: Fayard, 2000.

[11] For example T. Mitchell ('Nationalism, Imperialism, Economism: a Comment on Habermas', *Public Culture*, 25, 1998, pp. 417–24) criticises Habermas when the latter, as a principle, identifies economic policies with the nation state. That coincidence, he says, is very recent and contingent; it dates essentially from the nineteenth century.

of government—never in making any of them models, or backing interpretations (with overtones of racism or condescension) in terms of 'a return to the Middle Ages' or some other rediscovery of 'darkness'. It goes without saying that configurations and arrangements are specific to each historical situation (precisely because of the globalisation which has been so much studied) and each national or regional situation (because of the historicity of trajectories of the political).

Re-reading this work and especially its introduction suggests that some explanations could be useful. First of all, in trying too hard to convey the message that what is occurring is not a crisis of the state but its continuous formation, I let one aspect of my analysis be slightly de-emphasised, though it is a fundamental one: the importance of diversity in modes of government and the incomplete, unachieved nature of these arrangements. Of course there are historical configurations, and the weight of national trajectories is constantly stressed in the following pages. But this must not be understood in terms of regimes or systems,[12] given that the approach followed by me and my colleagues, who all give priority to empirical field work, has sought in contrast to bring out processes, the political in the course of formation, and hence, necessarily, the incomplete, unachieved and hybridised forms of the political. That is why interpretation of 'privatisation of the state' as an ideal-type or as a model is to some extent a misconception. That point has probably not been expressed clearly enough in the book, but it is a fundamental aspect that I am still exploring today in my works on the Maghreb and Europe.

If one sticks to the interpretation of 'privatisation' in the historical and sociological sense that is presented here, present-day situations must be understood not as an illustration of a new paradigm, but as an illustration of a multiplicity of allegiances, a multiplicity of registers, of management of complexity; or else, to use Janet Roitman's expression used in this book, of pluralisation of referents, norms and modes of regulation, of which 'discharge' is one form among others. In all configurations there is, of course, always a multiplicity of modes of government. Privatisation is only one modality among them, certainly a prominent and sometimes dominant and outstanding one, 'new' or more precisely rediscovered, but certainly not unique.

Certain criticisms, notably by authors who highlight challenging of the state in its traditional forms of intervention,[13] have regretted that the

---

[12] Contrary to what such schools of thought as 'Régulation' in France and 'Diversity of Capitalism' in the United States want to bring out.

[13] See for example C. Chavagneux, 'Une maîtrise politique de la mondialisation économique', *Revue du MAUSS* no. 20, second semester 2002 ('Quelle "autre mondialisation?"' special issue), pp. 54–64.

theme of private actors' capacity to obtain autonomy—a process mentioned but not always examined in the texts forming this book—was not further developed. That is probably true, but the explanation lies in the objective of the project: it was not our intention to say who was 'winning' between well determined public and private spheres. *Privatising the State* is not a book about some claimed change in hegemony, or an alteration in power relations (*rapports de force*). We rather set out to show that the very notions of private and public are changing, today as yesterday, according to changes in modes of government but also to changes in representation (of power especially) and processes of subjectivation.

That said, my introduction and all the papers in this volume have one thing in common—they show that, contrary to what theorists of 'diffusion' or 'dilution' of power assert, the keys to the changes and transformations described are to a great extent in the hands of state power. Of course that does not mean that state power orchestrates those transformations and is in control of their progress—quite the contrary. By adopting the term 'formation' (rather than 'building'), we have rather stressed the unforeseen processes of circumventing, appropriation and reinterpretation, the largely unconscious and contradictory historical process of conflicts, negotiations and compromises among various groups and actors. This fundamental aspect has often been obscured in commentaries on the privatisation processes; if one interprets the results of actions in terms of privatisation, one should not on that account forget the many conditions that caused it to emerge and then develop, nor underestimate the debates and conflicts among differing positions, among norms, among concepts of state power that inspire all the actors involved in this process—public and private, state and non-state.

Analysis of the transformation of the very notions of 'public' and 'private' would be a subject for a book on its own. But the succession of examples through the various chapters of the book, and above all the highlighting of ambivalence and misunderstanding between actors about these notions, suggest that privatisation, in this historical and sociological sense, reflects also an alteration in the very definitions of what is private and what is public. That is nothing new, of course, as Hannah Arendt's works argue: those notions—public, private, national, sovereignty, on the lines of state power—have never been static. While political economy is today one of the most important approaches to understanding of modes of government and the exercise of state power, it is interesting in this connection to recall that among the Greeks it was unthinkable to speak of political economy, insofar as everything that was economic and concerned the life of the individual was by definition not political because it was a private, family affair. It is, for example, only since the accession of society to the public domain that the economy and all the problems that were previously matters for the family have become collective, public preoccupations.[14]

The history of political ideas and theories is also a history of transformation of those notions that are necessarily influenced by the context that saw them emerge, and then by the various historical events that accompanied their progress. Since the modern era there has been, as Hannah Arendt put it, a hybrid situation in which private interests take on public importance, going so far as almost to end the distinction: 'both the public and the private spheres are gone, the public because it has become a function of the private and the private because it has become the only common concern left.'[15] But that does not mean, even so, that those domains have seen their contours fixed rigidly. All the chapters in *Privatising the State* have aimed to put forward, often implicitly, both the importance of those changes in meaning and the growth of 'zones of indifference'[16] between public and private—within which 'corruption', of which I spoke at the beginning of this Preface, is built up and deployed.

The authors of this book have not paid attention to the differentiated political and economic effects of 'privatisation of the state', even though that process means not only a moving of the borders between political and economic, public and private, but also a transformation of the points of intervention by state power and differentiation of the economic and social consequences of these new modalities of intervention. That very important dimension could be the object of later research. In this comparative book, it seemed to us that research should above all be centred on a better understanding of a global phenomenon (the appearance of those indirect interventions that pass through private intermediaries) which has meaning and interpretation only at the local level. As Yves Chevrier suggests in conclusion, there should be numerous case studies to refine the analysis of these differentiated consequences, and bring out the specific features— in relation to the Western trajectory particularly—of the trajectories of the political and the continuous formation of forms of state power and their modes of intervention in other situations.

---

[14] See especially Hannah Arendt in *The Human Condition*, but also Michel Foucault in '*Il faut défendre la société: Cours au Collège de France, 1976*', Paris: Gallimard/Seuil, 1997 and Jürgen Habermas in *The Structural Transformation of the Public Sphere: An Inquiry into a Category of Bourgeois Society*, Cambridge: Polity Press, 1989.

[15] Arendt (note 14), p. 69.

[16] G. Agamben, 'Dans cet exil. Journal italien 1992–1994' in G. Agamben, *Moyens sans fins. Notes sur la politique*, Paris: Rivages Poche 2002, links the phenomenon of the public sliding into the private with the spectacular publicity of the private.

Finally, as a conclusion I would like to clear up a misunderstanding. The 'privatisation of the state' has often been interpreted as the presentation of a new theory, a new ideal-type; hence the systematic nature of the argument has been criticised on the basis of continuation of some forms of traditional interventionism, the existence of wholly autonomised actors, and differentiation among geographical or sectoral situations. That model was perhaps convincing for some situations (especially in Africa), but much less for others (the Western world in general). Those considerations in reality showed an excessive interpretation of the ideas I sought to put forward in my Introduction and in the designing of this book. Let it be clearly understood: in no case did I intend to build a theory of a new configuration. My determination to persuade probably oriented the presentation of the argument, with some other dynamics and other modalities of public action obscured. Above all I aimed to show, on the one hand, that what some interpreted as a crisis of the state, its retreat, its erosion or its decay should on the contrary be seen as a different way of governing and of understanding the exercise of state power. On the other hand, my intention was more methodological than descriptive, and in no case a normative analysis: it was to reintroduce a historical sociology of the state and the economic in the recurrent debates on globalisation that have a tendency to forget it, to avoid talking of crisis and thinking in terms of abandonment and loss.

At all events, at no point did we mean, in this collective book, that the world was now witnessing the emergence of a new paradigm, a new *problématique* that would serve as a referent for the years to come. 'Privatisation of the state' is certainly not the new norm asserting itself as a model of interpretation and giving meaning to current changes. It is just one modality among many others, but now an influential and sometimes structuring one.

Paris, May 2003   B.H.

FOREWORD

Since the 1990s liberalism has been on the up, or so commentators tell us: Reaganism, Thatcherism and the end of the Welfare State in European countries, the establishment of structural adjustment programmes in developing countries, the transition to a market economy in the former Socialist countries, etc. There has also been a challenging of the economic sovereignty of states, which are even reduced to impotence in the globalised economic scene. It is in this context of liberalisation that privatisation has developed—supposed to represent reassertion of the free market and the rise in the power of private actors rid of political constraints. The movement towards privatisation of state-owned enterprises has been the most visible part, the most commented on; today it extends over the whole planet, developed and developing countries alike.

In some societies, however, the privatisation process is a much broader one, which also includes public services (with concessions and delegations); economic resources (appropriation and private exploitation of forests, mineral ores and precious stones, for example, but also unbridled privatisation of the state domain); certain functions formerly belonging to the state—management of labour relations and social security, for example, or economic regulation, especially in times of crisis and instability; and even some of the state's sovereign functions (taxation, security and the monopoly of violence—with the development of mercenary activity and private security companies). In other words, privatisation now affects modes of governing. This wide spread of privatisation is no accident; it is the product of generalised criticism of bureaucracy, ever louder rhetoric about the virtues of the free market and private enterprise, and generalised discourse about globalisation and transnational flows and networks.

This wider spread of privatisation is the subject of this book, based on experiences in Africa, the Maghreb, Asia, Russia and Eastern Europe. The aim is to offer not an exhaustive analysis of a worldwide phenomenon, but a general examination of the issues involved in processes that are both similar in their forms and different in their meaning. From the outset, one ambiguity must be cleared up: the very term 'privatisation' is not taken for granted; on the contrary, we have made our starting point the ambivalence and complexities of concrete situations, to define their development better. Beyond common appearances and commonplaces on the supremacy of the economic—of economic and financial constraints and opportunities—we have sought to attain a better understanding of, on the one hand, the development of the forms and qualities of the state and its regulatory capacities, and on the other, changes in the relationships between the economic and the political,* public and private, licit and illicit.

Our main hypothesis is that far from becoming impotent in the economic field, the state is adapting not only to external constraints, but to internal ones also. This adaptation takes the form of privatisation of states, a privatisation that is not so much a loss of control as an option for indirect government, using private intermediaries on an increasing scale. This option is not necessarily a choice (forced or otherwise); it results from the entanglement of multiple strategies and reactions by public and private actors. The privatisation of the state is not synonymous with the domination of private interests and the supremacy of economic causality within it; however, it corresponds closely with changes in relations between the public and private spheres and between the economic and the political.

In sub-Saharan Africa and the Maghreb, for example, the political sphere has been based, at least since the colonial period, on straddling practices between positions of power and positions of wealth accumulation, between the public domain and the private realm, between legal and illegal practices and behaviour. However, while these features are permanent, that does not exclude major changes. From the 1930s until the end of the 1970s what lay behind state action was on the one hand an emphasis on the 'publicness' of political sovereignty and economic regulation, together with the territorialisation of state authority, and on the other, the subordination of the economic to the political. Even though practice did not correspond to these principles in reality, nonetheless legitimate institutions were, during this period, represented by state-owned enterprises and banks, the administration, stabilisation or compensation funds, and other government agencies. Today, by contrast, there is no doubt that principles of liberalisation and privatisation, of the state's disengagement from the economic and social spheres, of autonomy being given to the economic in relation to the political are gaining acceptance. This is in line with the liberal norms adopted by the international community and expressed in the declarations—and the cash disbursements—of the developed countries. The legitimate institutions are now 'market forces', the 'private sector' and

---

* 'The political' is more than public institutions and the public agenda. It is a 'set of social and normative relations, some of which make it very specific in the range of social actions because they are power relations encompassing the whole social body and meant to address the collective needs of the whole community.' (Chevrier, Postface to this book)

'civil society'. Even if practice often remains the same—talk of privat-isation of the state by ruling elites, the power of 'uncontrolled' regional flows, the end of the state monopoly of legitimate violence, etc. was pre-mature—the norms used as a standard for judging that practice have altered radically. The same change can be observed in China since the late 1980s and in Central and Eastern Europe since 1989; everywhere can be seen a reorienting of state action, now centred around economic objec-tives, and a predominance of economic and financial discourse.

That breach with the past is what led us to analyse these changes in terms of 'privatisation'. Of course the phenomena described above are dif-ferent in kind: the privatisation of state enterprises has to do with the application of orthodox principles of management; privatisation of cus-toms services reflects, in a sense, the displacement of national authorities by aid donors; privatisation of violence reveals the state's incapacity to finance expenditure that is nonetheless considered necessary; and so on. However, all these practices are legitimised in one way or another by the prevailing discourse. In these circumstances even the term 'privatisation of the state' is an ironic wink at international institutions and the kits of ideas going around in the 'world community', emphasising the 'free mar-ket' and 'private enterprise' and disengagement by the state. But it is also a critical analysis of those dominant ideas: the Weberian concept that inter-national institutions have of the state affects comprehension of reality and confuses thinking. Privatisation should not be understood as the objective rise of private actors, the hegemony of a well defined private sphere over a public sphere with similar defined limits, or the emergence of new actors in competition with the state. It simply reflects breaches with the past: with the references and norms of the preceding decades, even though this breach occurs in line of continuity with various historical trajectories; and with the international environment and the overall management of its con-straints and opportunities.

This book aims also to challenge received ideas on the ongoing glo-balisation and uniformisation processes, caused by the rise of transna-tional actors, the supposed inefficiency of states in regulating capitalism, and the domination of economic and financial considerations. All the examples presented here show that in fact states and societies faced with worldwide phenomena (internationalisation, the rise of constraining fac-tors and of economic and financial considerations etc.) react in very different ways, depending on their own trajectories. In other words the 'privatisation of the state', while it involves identical practices, has differ-ent meanings from one continent to another, from one country to another, even from one region to another within a country.

'Privatisation of the state' is neither a concept nor a new theory of the state. Research on the generic term 'privatisation' claims no aim beyond bringing out the great variety of *gouvernementalités*—both really new ones and others for whom only the appearance or the way of perceiving them has changed. It seeks to pinpoint the current breaches with the past in modes of governing, hence in the nature of the state and its intervention, and also in relations between the public and private spheres in political institutions and in relations and new spaces of power.

This book is the fruit of two years of collective research punctuated by two days of study organised at the Centre d'Etudes et de Recherches Internationales in Paris (5 December 1997) and the Centre d'Etudes d'Afrique Noire in Bordeaux (22–23 October 1998), in collaboration with the scientific directorate of the Fondation Nationale des Sciences Politiques and the Institut d'Etudes Politiques of Bordeaux. I must express my thanks to the directors of all four bodies for the warm support they gave me. Hélène Arnaud keenly followed the work on this book and deserves all my thanks.

B.H.

THE CONTRIBUTORS

Béatrice Hibou is a researcher with the CNRS-CERI, Paris and a member of the editorial board of *Critique internationale* from 1998 to 2003. She has conducted research on the dynamics between public and private practices in political economy and the reconfiguration of the state. She is now studying the transformation of economic regulation in North Africa and in Southern Europe. Her publications include: *L'Afrique est-elle protectionniste?* Paris: Karthala, 1996 and (with J.-F. Bayart and S. Ellis), *The Criminalization of the State in Africa*, London: International African Institute in association with J. Currey (Oxford) and Indiana University Press (Bloomington and Indianapolis), 1999.

François Bafoil is a researcher with CNRS-CERI, Paris. He has published *Après le communisme*, Paris: Armand Colin, 2002.

Romain Bertrand is a researcher with the Centre d'Etudes et de Recherches Internationales (CERI, Paris). He has published *Indonésie, la démocratie invisible. Violence, magie et politique à Java,* Paris: Karthala, 2002.

Yves Chevrier is director of the Centre Chine, Paris, EHESS. He has published *Mao et la révolution chinoise*, Paris: Casterman, 1993, and articles on reform in China.

Gilles Favarel-Garrigues is a research fellow with CERI. He has recently edited *Criminalité, police et gouvernement: trajectoires post-communistes*, Paris: L'Harmattan, 2003.

Antoine Kernen teaches in the Graduate Institute of Development Studies in Geneva, and in the Institute of Political Studies at the University of Lausanne (Switzerland). He has published *Le processus de privatisation à Shenyang, République Populaire de Chine*, Paris: Karthala, 2003.

Françoise Mengin is a research fellow at CERI (Sciences Po, Paris). She is the author of *Trajectoires chinoises: Taiwan, Hong Kong et Pékin*, Paris: Karthala, 1998, and has co-edited with Jean-Louis Rocca *Politics in China: Moving Frontiers*, New York: Palgrave, 2002.

William Reno is Professor of Political Sciences at Northwestern University, USA. He has published *Warlord Politics and African States*, Boulder, CO: Lynne Rienner.

Jean-Louis Rocca is a research fellow at CERI. He has co-edited, with Françoise Mengin, *Politics in China: Moving Frontiers*, New York: Palgrave, 2002.

Janet Roitman is a researcher with CNRS-MALD, Paris. Her book *Fiscal Disobedience: Governing Citizens in Central Africa* is published by Princeton University Press.

1

FROM PRIVATISING THE ECONOMY TO PRIVATISING THE STATE: AN ANALYSIS OF THE CONTINUAL FORMATION OF THE STATE*

Béatrice Hibou

Today analyses of economic globalisation or internationalisation observe that the ways in which the state intervenes in the economy have changed. At the international level Susan Strange speaks of the 'retreat' of the state;[1] this process, she suggests, is the result of a 'diffusion' of power, hence of authority, to private agents and institutions; this rise of private actors at the international level, it is suggested, leads not only to loss of legitimacy and effectiveness for state action, but also to a gap in responsibility. At the national level the emphasis—varying according to countries and authors—is on a loss of legitimacy, sovereignty and authority by the state, or its decline. The most widespread idea is that the economic role of nation-states is now an outdated function, or at least that this function has been largely marginalised.[2]

* I thank my 'sister' Janet Roitman, whom I burdened by asking her to 'structurally adjust' the English version of my chapter. As a good *douanière-combattante*, she considerably contributed to its final form and to its surplus value.

[1] S. Strange, *The Retreat of the State: Diffusion of Power in the World Economy*, Cambridge University Press, 1996.

[2] The best known authors expressing these ideas are M. Porter, *The Competitive Advantage of Nations*, New York and London: Macmillan Press, 1990; Robert B. Reich, *The Work of Nations: Preparing Ourselves for 21st-Century Capitalism*, New York: Simon & Schuster, 1991; P. Drucker, *Post-capitalist Society*, Oxford: Butterworth-Heinemann, 1993. See also C. Chavagneux, 'Peut-on maîtriser la mondialisation?', *Economie et Sociétés* 4, série P, 1998. For an explanation of the spread of privatisation of state enterprises in the world through internationalisation of markets and the international environment, see G. J. Ikenberry, 'The International Spread of Privatization: Inducements, Learning, and "Policy Bandwagoning"', pp. 88–110, in E. Suleiman and J. Waterbury

By comparison with the preceding period, what can be seen in most
parts of the world is indeed a crumbling, even a break-up of power;
numerous breaks with the tradition of centralisation of political and
bureaucratic authority, especially in economic matters; the loss of total,
direct control by the state over the national economy and most of its interventions; a rise in external constraints, and hence an apparent supremacy
of market forces; increasingly inept administrations, which sometimes
actually become dysfunctional. These observed facts are interpreted as
revealing the impotence of the state: its inability to manage the territory or
the economy of a country as a whole, the crisis of legitimacy of a state progressively less able to assert itself as a reference. This view of present-day
trends poses a problem, however, because it is a negative one. The decline
in effective intervention by the state is what is noted, together with the
reduction in its direct and comprehensive controls, the reduced centralisation of its presence, and erosion of administrative action. The idea of the
retreat of the state, or of its decline, at any rate of some 'loss'—of the
state's sovereignty, its legitimacy, its capacity or its authority—is based on
a normative analysis. In developing countries, this refers to the norms of
the developmentalist ideology proclaimed from the 1950s onwards.

But if one tries to get away from those outdated and limited references,
it is not so certain that we are witnessing a trend towards retreat, or reduced interventionism. Today the state* is certainly going through a meta-
morphosis, especially because of the internationalisation of economies
and changes in productive structures. But before going as far as Strange
and saying that the state is now something ordinary, no longer exceptional
and no longer the source of supreme authority, an attempt should be made
to grasp the precise means of intervention and economic influence that the
state employs today.

In reflecting on the hypothesis of 'privatisation of states', one may be
able to consider the possibility of new ways of exercising power and government, and foresee new representations of the political. One can also

---

(eds), *The Political Economy of Public Sector Reform and Privatization*, Boulder, CO:
Westview Press, 1990. For developing countries, see I. Zartman (ed.), *Collapsed States.
The Disintegration and Restoration of Legitimate Authority*, Boulder, CO and London:
Lynne Rienner, 1995; and R. D. Kaplan, 'The Coming Anarchy', *The Atlantic Monthly*
273/2, February 1994, pp. 44–76.

* I distinguish between government (*gouvernement* in French), state (*état*) and central
power (*pouvoir central*). These terms are neither synonymous nor equivalent. 'Government' is meant in the strict sense of government institutions, ministries and administration. The 'state' is the ensemble of actors and social practices of power as understood by
the term *gouvernementalité* ('governmentality'—a rarely used term in English, however)
proposed by Michel Foucault, or the integral state described by Gramsci. 'Central power'
is the complex process for concentration and relative autonomisation of power through the
straddling of administrative practices, high-level political elites and social practices.

discern state strategies that appear to be in retreat, in decline, even in a state of decay, as part of the process of continual formation of the state, as a new modality for producing the political. While the term 'privatisation' is an explicit allusion to the dominant liberal rhetoric, to speak of 'privatisation of the state' is not at all a semantic slip or a play on words; the term describes parallel processes—extended use of private intermediaries for an increasing number of functions previously devolving upon the state, and redeployment by the state. For the privatisation of state enterprises and public services has been extended to other domains, to other areas of state intervention, and this has occurred not at the instigation of the bureaucratic apparatus and political authority, but through the operation of at least two movements, difficult to separate from each other.

On the one hand, the reforms themselves have had unforeseen and often unwanted side effects that have made such diffusion possible:[3] reduction in budget revenue and corresponding financial difficulties for administration; reduction in expenditure and in the quality of services, and hence loss of legitimacy by the state administration and public authorities; fragmentation of decision-making powers; and the primacy accorded to external rather than internal legitimacy, to speed rather than modes of action, to results rather than means. On the other hand economic and political actors, whoever they are, have contributed both to the transformation of the reforms and to changes in the environment in which they have occurred, besides helping—through their strategies, also through the conflicts, compromises and negotiations among different groups within society—to lay down the new outlines of the state and methods of governing.[4] Today, as a result, privatisation also concerns—perhaps especially— development, economic resources, regulatory functions and even the sovereign functions of the state. Numerous as they are, these privatisations— whether unbridled or planned—have several things in common: they receive favourable comment in the prevailing liberal discourse, they spread the use of private go-betweens in governing, and they alter not only the forms of economic regulation but also the forms of political regulation

---

[3] J. Linz and A. Stepan, *Problems of Democratic Transition and Consolidation. Southern Europe, South America and Post-Communist Europe*, Washington: Johns Hopkins University Press, 1996; B. Hibou, 'The Political Economy of the World Bank's Discourse: from Economic Catechism to Missionary Deeds and Misdeeds', *Les Etudes du CERI* 39, January 2000.

[4] The alternative paths of liberalisation are now well known; they have involved major economic and political actors playing with reforms so as to displace their rents, come to terms with political fragmentation and the financial crisis of the state, externalise the costs of economic change and increase their economic resources. See B. Hibou, *L'Afrique est-elle protectionniste? Les chemins buissonniers de la libéralisation extérieure*, Paris: Karthala, 1996, and 'Les enjeux de l'ouverture au Maroc. Dissidence économique et contrôle politique', *Les Etudes du CERI* 15, April 1996.

and the forms of sovereignty. In other words they all displace and blur the frontiers between 'public' and 'private', between 'economic' and 'political' and between 'licit' and 'illicit'.

Extending indirect methods of government

African configurations. A few examples can show that this is an interesting approach. Because of the worsening conflicts, the gravity of the economic crisis and the extent of socio-political tension, sub-Saharan Africa today is certainly one of the regions best fitted to help us understand the importance of these new forms of government. But for that it is necessary to go beyond the image of disorder, anarchy and 'heart of darkness' (Joseph Conrad) which appears to characterise most African societies, and to try to bring out what goes on behind the appearance of 'dissolution', 'implosion' and disappearance of the states of the continent. In particular, attention should be paid to behind-the-scenes relations, the operation of differing networks of belonging (regional, religious, ethnic, education-related etc.), and the realm of the invisible.

Mozambique is an example of almost complete privatisation of modes of government, a privatisation affecting both economic resources and almost all the sovereign functions of the state.[5] It concerns first of all the administration. As in several African countries customs services have been privatised and placed in the hands of a surveillance company (first the SGS, then Inskape); but that privatisation of the customs has today been extended to the work of assessment and collection of duties (a task handed to the Crown Agence company); in addition, foreign private companies have negotiated for control of Mozambique's maritime borders. Privatisation of overseas representation was in progress, with the sale by the director of emigration (who happens to be someone close to the President) of genuine but fraudulently delivered diplomatic passports. Major private enterprises, often foreign, enforce laws and regulations themselves, sometimes employing strong methods and resorting to use of private police forces. However, there should be no illusions about this systematic call on foreign actors: it indicates not a loss of sovereignty by the state and a process of recolonisation,[6] but rather the indirect exercise of those administrative functions by the ruling elites, through contracts kept secret

---

[5] Sources: essentially interviews, the specialist press (*Marchés Tropicaux et Méditerranéens, Nord-Sud Export, La Lettre du Continent, Africa Confidential, Africa Analysis*) and the local press (*Médiafax, Noticias, Savana*) and personal observation (January–February 1997).

[6] For an interpretation of these events in terms of recolonisation, see D. Plank, 'Aid, Debt and the End of Sovereignty: Mozambique and its Donors', *Journal of Modern African Studies* 31/3, 1993, pp. 407–30.

and constantly renewed. Similarly, the delegation of sovereign functions to national private actors remains well under control, because of the controls over the hierarchical structure of networks, and the shrinking of the political space.[7]

Because of the glaring inadequacies of the administrative apparatus,[8] privatisation has spread rapidly, since the end of the civil war, to development operations and policies. The massive influx of aid[9] heightened this propensity to elusive management: faced with multiple proposals by NGOs and aid donor states, the Mozambican authorities and administration were incapable of coordinating, managing and ordering priorities. However, this incapacity to retain control was, once again, often only apparent, and anyway it was frequently superficial: external financing was in fact appropriated by national elites and their local men of straw.[10] That appropriation could take place directly—this has happened, for example, with school and hospital building projects or gifts of vehicles for the police or the civil administration. But for most of the time it has taken place indirectly—by oiling the wheels of a rentier political economy, now privatised, the ruling classes strengthen their position, with the complicity of big private companies which are often considered by aid donors as the only reliable negotiating partners.[11] These abuses are encouraged by the lax attitude of aid donors, who do not follow up carefully on their funding, do not check the precise use made of the funds, and impose conditionality only on increasingly weak public actors.[12]

[7] On the tightening of power around certain sections of Frelimo, see C. Messiant, 'La Paix au Mozambique: un succès de l'ONU', pp. 49–105, in R. Marchal and C. Messiant, *Les chemins de la guerre et de la paix. Fins de conflit en Afrique orientale et australe*, Paris: Karthala, 1997 ('Les Afriques' series).

[8] Of the 487 technicians employed in the Ministry of Finance by the Portuguese administration, only 13 remained in Maputo and none in the provinces after independence. Today, the mechanisms for planning, budget making and control of public expenditure are still disastrously inadequate, and the staff unqualified. See especially L. S. Graham, 'The Dilemmas of Managing Weak States: the Case of Mozambique', *Public Administration and Development* 13, 1993, pp. 409–22, and J. Hanlon, *Peace without Profit: How the IMF Blocks Rebuilding in Mozambique*, London: Irish Mozambique Solidarity and International African Institute with James Currey and Heinemann, 1996.

[9] Grants increased from $56 million in 1980 to $213 million in 1986 and $304 million in 1987, to reach $565 million in 1994; aid reached up to 70 per cent of GDP in 1993. See the internal documents of the international institutions (the World Bank and IMF) and Hanlon (note 8).

[10] See for example J. Hanlon (note 8); J. Hanlon, *Mozambique: Who Calls the Shots?* London: James Currey, 1991; and M. L. Bowen, 'Beyond Reform: Adjustment and Political Power in Contemporary Mozambique', *Journal of Modern African Studies* 30/2, 1992, pp. 255–79.

[11] These reflections arose from a project evaluation that I did personally for an aid agency.

[12] See B. Hibou, 'The Political Economy...' (note 3), for an analysis of aid recipients' 'tricks' and the unintended consequences of conditionality imposed by the aid donors (arguing implicitly against the interpretation in terms of recolonisation).

Meanwhile, most of the country's economic resources are being appropriated today by private actors. Exploitation of the sea (fish, shrimps and
coral) is now in the hands of foreign companies (mainly South African,
Japanese and Spanish) linked to military personnel and to important politicians or political factions; neither the volume nor the exact revenue from
these exports is known, though they are the country's leading resources.
This privatisation of maritime activity—and of other activities too—has in
addition led to the privatisation of port facilities. Timber concessions are
sold to private buyers, notably foreign ones, who are close to the regime (an
example being the Mosaflorestal project, sold to M. Blanchard, financial
backer of Renamo during the civil war, switching to the Frelimo side not
long ago). Appropriation of land around Maputo (by people close to the
President of the Republic, the mayor of the capital and influential ministers) and in the rest of the country (later ceded to Afrikaners from South
Africa, Zimbabweans and Portuguese) has been a strictly private operation: in the absence of clear rules and definitive choices concerning the
policy to follow, the land is occupied by actors who have particularly close
relations with the local authorities.[13]

Last but not least, the rise of criminal activity and various parallel markets is largely the work of the ruling elite in search of new economic
opportunities, even if it is men of straw and middlemen (often of foreign
origin, especially Indians and Pakistanis) who appear in the foreground:
the niches of activity are divided among the various factions, there is constant negotiation over toleration, and operations to tackle crime (drug trafficking, stolen car and cigarette rackets etc.) are carefully calculated. At
the same time the proliferation of private security agencies, controlled by
former senior military personnel, ministers and heads of big private companies, has benefited from the demobilisation of Frelimo and Renamo
fighters; they are both a substitute for an incompetent police force and
undisciplined army and a very big economic resource.

Cameroon presents a similar profile.[14] Privatisation of the customs is
complete there (in the hands of the SGS), and since 1997 indirect taxation

---

[13] Besides national newspapers, see Bowen (note 10) and G. W. Myers and H. G. West,
'Land Tenure Security and State Farm Divestiture in Mozambique', Maputo, 1993 (LTD
Research Paper 110, University of Wisconsin, Madison, for USAID).

[14] Sources: essentially interviews, the specialised press mentioned in note 5, the local press
(*Le Messager, Challenge Hebdo, Elimbi, Dikalo, L'Action, L'Estafette, Le Patriote, La
Nouvelle Expression, Cameroon Tribune*) and personal observation (May 1993 and April
1996). See also B. Hibou, 'The "Social Capital" of the State as an Agent of Deception, or
the Ruses of Economic Intelligence', pp. 69–113 in J.-F. Bayart, S. Ellis and B. Hibou,
The Criminalization of the State in Africa, London: International African Institute in
association with J. Currey (Oxford) and Indiana University Press (Bloomington and Indianapolis), 1999; A. Mbembe, 'Crise de légitimité, restauration autoritaire et déliquescence
de l'Etat', pp. 345–74 and J.-F. Bayart, 'Conclusion', pp. 335–44, in P. Geschiere and
P. Konings (eds), *Itinéraires d'accumulation au Cameroun*, Paris: Karthala-ASC, 1993.

has been delegated to a private company (Revenue Management Associates Ltd, RMA, branch of the Lazard Brothers bank, responsible for collecting turnover tax). An increasing amount of exploitation of the forest is being handed over, under arrangements that are kept secret, to foreign private interests (French and Lebanese, but increasingly often Asian, especially Malaysian and Indonesian), which have also had sections of ports allocated to them. Of course the taxation of these activities is now entirely privatised: the national accounts do not record either the volume or the value of the exports, nor the tax and customs revenue. The administration is being privatised in segments—for example, a civil servant has to resort to bribery to receive his salary, and a minister must pay to be able to use his budget allocation. Privatisation of violence serves political functions but also economic ones, to the benefit of the political class; numerous security services belong to ministers (like the minister of Defence) or senior dignitaries; and there are the *feymen*,[15] swindlers tolerated by and even linked—if only intermittently—with the government.

Côte d'Ivoire is interesting because it offers another variant of this phenomenon. The façade of controlled liberalisation and reduced intervention, in a context of effective and traditional functioning of the state's management apparatus, conceals very different practices in reality.[16] Alongside the traditional bureaucratic apparatus there is a real parallel administration: civil servants fulfil two roles, one public but not very active, the other private and often highly lucrative. The administrative fiefs carved out in this way are indirectly held by 'barons' of the regime in permanent political competition. For example, the police cannot make investigations at Abidjan's autonomous port or its airport, where the customs officers' hierarchy can engage with impunity in rackets of all sorts (drugs, smuggling etc.). Like business enterprises, the state has double bookkeeping, and aid donors are unable to find out the exact situation of the state finances. In addition, tax collection is now delegated to the big companies in the formal sector, which are almost exclusively foreign private firms. It is they that centralise not only employers' contributions, company taxation and trade licenses, but also payroll taxes, VAT and various indirect duties, property taxes, etc. And tax reform has made this function official by concentrating the taxation system still more on economic actors.

[15] The word 'feyman' comes from Pidgin; it denotes an ability to attain wealth through witchcraft, trickery and devilish intelligence (but not through violence); it suggests also the ability to falsify, to take on different skins and to disappear. *Feymen* organise confidence tricks, frauds and financial swindles. See the press mentioned in note 14 and B. Hibou, 'The "Social Capital"' (note 14).

[16] Sources: essentially interviews, the specialised press mentioned in note 5 and personal observations (April 1993, May 1996 and November 1997).

The appearance of liberalisation should not deceive anyone. The links between political power and the private sector, already very close, have been made closer still since then;[17] with the decline in direct intervention by the state in the economy, the private sector is increasingly called upon to play a part, through front men, in the social and economic life of the country. The classic extraction of levies (from the revenue of the Stabilisation Fund for coffee and cocoa, from the resources of banks and state enterprises) has not really ended; it has simply been transformed and transferred. It is now scattered among various patronage networks and numerous economic channels, licit and illicit. But the previously dominant actors in the public sector are today very active in the private sector (this is true notably of the coffee and cocoa marketing channels). Above all, no new economic actor independent of the political sphere and acting according to considerations of long-term economic and financial profitability has established itself successfully; this is suggested by the difficulties encountered by some leading lights in the Ivorian business world— the Usher group, and François Bakou's Octide group—and, on the other hand, the rise of the SIFCA-SIFCOM group, directly linked to Konan Bédié, then President of the Republic.

These are not isolated cases; indirect government practices are found, in widely varying forms, in all countries of Africa. In the Congo (Brazzaville) it is the oil company Elf that is in charge of the state treasury and pays the state's debts, and use of militias is now part of the political landscape.[18] In Angola some social and economic functions—health, education, infrastructure—are carried out by the Eduardo Dos Santos Foundation, called after the President of the Republic; these acts of charity display both competition with state-run activities and collaboration with

---

[17] For the ties between the two power centres, see J. Rapley, *Ivorian Capitalism: African Entrepreneurs in Côte d'Ivoire*, Boulder, CO: Lynne Rienner, 1993 (for the theory of the intrusion of the economic world into the political); Y.-A. Fauré and J.-F. Médard (eds), *Etat et bourgeoisie en Côte d'Ivoire*, Paris: Karthala, 1981 and L. Gouffern, 'Les limites d'un modèle? A propos d'Etat et bourgeoisie en Côte d'Ivoire', *Politique Africaine* 6, May 1982 (for the theory of supremacy of the political sphere). For the strengthening of those ties in the present period, see Y.-A. Fauré and P. Labazée (eds), *Petits patrons africains: entre l'assistance et le marché*, Paris: Karthala, 2000; B. Losch, 'Le complexe café-cacao de la Côte d'Ivoire. Une relecture de la trajectoire ivoirienne', doctorate thesis, University of Montpellier, 1999; B. Losch, 'Coup de cacao en Côte d'Ivoire: économie politique d'une crise structurelle', *Critique Internationale*, no. 9, October 2000, pp. 6–14; and B. Contamin and H. Memel-Fotè (eds), *Le modèle ivoirien en question? Crises, ajustements et recompositions*, Paris: Karthala, 1997.

[18] On the privatisation of violence in the Congo, see R. Bazenguissa, 'Milices politiques et bandes armées à Brazzaville. Enquête sur la violence politique et sociale des jeunes déclassés', *Les Etudes du CERI* 13, April 1996, and the special feature 'Les deux Congos en guerre' in *Politique Africaine* 72, December 1998, pp. 5–109.

them, because this expenditure is passed on to the public.[19] In Kenya President arap Moi and the party then in power played with private and ethnic violence, notably for the purposes of economic control and appropriation of wealth.[20] In Senegal, despite permanent tension between the two parties in the 1990s, the Sufi brotherhoods are the privileged intermediaries for the government, both for political control over the population and to control its economic activity; meanwhile, the state's economic strategy is largely conducted through so-called informal networks.[21]

In Sierra Leone the 'shadow state' exerted influence through the intermediary of private actors: Lebanese enterprises and financiers, private security companies—notably Executive Outcomes—foreign mining companies, etc.[22] In the former Zaire, certain public services—building of infrastructure, education, police—had been handed over to big companies (especially mining companies) and to the ordinary people even before the rout of the army (the FAZ, Forces Armées Zaïroises) and the war of 1996–7, at the same time as natural resources were divided up among foreign companies (starting with De Beers) and the elite surrounding Mobutu.[23] In Tanzania liberalisation and the decline in direct intervention did not mean withdrawal by the political sphere and the end of 'parasitic capitalism'; the rents were transformed (especially into plunder of mineral and

[19] C. Messiant, 'La Fondation Eduardo Dos Santos: à propos de l'"investissement" de la société civile par le pouvoir angolais', *Politique Africaine* 73, March 1999, pp. 82–102.

[20] Africa Watch, *Divide and Rule. Sponsored Ethnic Violence in Kenya*, New York: Human Rights Watch, 1993; C. Thomas, 'Le Kénya d'une élection à l'autre: criminalisation de l'Etat et succession politique', *Les Etudes du CERI* 35, December 1997; and F. Grignon, 'Touche pas à mon khat. Rivalités meru-somali autour d'un commerce en pleine expansion', *Politique Africaine* 73, March 1999, pp. 177–85.

[21] See C. Coulon, *Le Marabout et le Prince: Islam et pouvoir au Sénégal*, Paris: Pédone, 1981; D. Cruise O'Brien, *Saints and Politicians. Essays on the Organization of a Senegalese Peasant Society*, Cambridge University Press, 1975; J. Copans, *Les marabouts de l'arachide. La confrérie mouride et les paysans au Sénégal*, Paris: Le Sycomore, 1980. Contrary to the impression given by C. Coulon in 'Touba, lieu saint de la confrérie mouride', pp. 226–38 in M. Ali Amir-Moerzi (ed.), *Lieux de l'Islam: cultes et cultures de l'Afrique à Java*, Paris: Ed. Autrement, 1996 (Mondes series HS no. 91/92), the 1990s crisis in relations between the brotherhoods (especially the Mourides) and the state power do not seem to us to cast doubt on this interpretation; on the contrary, it underlines the importance of intermediary activity and negotiation in this way of governing. On the importance of informal relations in the pursuit of economic policies, cf. C. Boone, *Merchant Capital and the Roots of State Power in Senegal, 1930–1985*, Cambridge University Press, 1992.

[22] See W. Reno, *Corruption and State Politics in Sierra Leone*, Cambridge University Press, 1995.

[23] See J. MacGaffey (ed.), *The Real Economy of Zaire. An Anthropological Study*, London: James Currey, 1991; *Les Cahiers du CEDAF* 2 (1/2); and Zairean newspapers such as *Le Soft de Finance, Le Potentiel* and *La Semaine*.

other natural resources) and continued to benefit the 'container bourgeoisie' which exercised power in an increasingly informal, non-institutional way.[24] Even in South Africa the policy of black empowerment has not followed the path of jobs in the administration or nationalised enterprises; it has mainly been financed by the big private groups, both English-speaking and Afrikaner, and has been carried out through stock exchange investments, most commonly financed by borrowing from banks, insurance companies and major private groups.[25]

In addition, the foreign policy of African countries is today more than ever in the hands of private interests—as a result of the personalisation of power, of course, but also, more profoundly, of de-institutionalisation, the local importance of private international actors, and social dynamics.[26] Generally speaking, the economic liberalisation imposed by aid donors leads not so much to the 'minimum state' of the neoclassical Utopia as to a redefinition of new state regulations, dispersal of decision making centres, and the primacy of mediations.[27]

North African configurations. The situation in the Maghreb, though more differentiated and less massive in its manifestations, reveals the extension of this indirect mode of government.

In Algeria, Martinez has shown particularly well how the state and the armed groups became 'complementary enemies' (Braudel's phrase) because of the economic interests and stakes in the civil war.[28] From the early 1990s, the splintering of centres of power opened the way to both privatisation of violence for economic purposes and privatisation of economic resources through violence. Far from being proof of the weakness of the state, this dual process of privatisation can be interpreted as a

---

[24] See P. Gibbon, 'Merchantisation of Production and Privatisation of Development in Postcolonial Ujamaa Tanzania', pp. 9–36, and C. L. Chachage, 'The Meek Shall Inherit the Earth but not the Mining Rights: the Mining Industry and Accumulation in Tanzania', pp. 37–108, in P. Gibbon (ed.), *Liberalised Development in Tanzania. Studies on Accumulation Processes and Local Institutions*, Uppsala: Nordiska Afrikainstitut, 1995.

[25] J.-F. Bayart, S. Ellis and B. Hibou, 'L'Afrique du Sud à la veille d'une élection décisive', *Politique Africaine* 73, March 1999, pp. 137–45.

[26] F. Constantin, 'La privatisation de la politique étrangère: à partir de la scène africaine', *Pouvoirs* 88, 1999, pp. 43–64.

[27] J. Coussy, 'Les ruses de l'état minimum', pp. 227–48 in J.-F. Bayart (ed.), *La réinvention du capitalisme*, Paris: Karthala, 1994.

[28] L. Martinez, *La guerre civile en Algérie*, Paris: Karthala, 1998 (Recherches Internationales series), translated as *The Algerian Civil War* (London: Hurst, 2000). See also by the same author, 'Les groupes islamistes entre guérilla et négoce. Vers une consolidation du régime algérien?', *Les Etudes du CERI* 3, August 1995, and 'L'économie de guerre: un obstacle à la paix', *La Revue des Deux Mondes*, September 1997, pp. 29–30. See also A. Roussillon, *L'Egypte et l'Algérie au péril de la libéralisationa,* Cairo: CEDEJ, 1996.

particularly astute way of managing conflict. Indeed, through it the state ensured both direct control (via the army) and indirect control (via private security companies) over strategic points of the Algerian economy, especially the oil and gas producing zone. Also, through indirect backing of the militias, it allowed for delegation of power to local people over other zones. Likewise, this process partially contributed to the dissolution of social barriers by fostering social mobility—war and violence having been an instrument for the accumulation of resources and access to power for the protagonists.

Economically, this mode of indirect government of the state favours everyone. The leading personalities and elites in power have benefited from the redistribution of former state monopolies to the private sector, and from the opportunities provided by the process of liberalisation and modernisation of infrastructure (notably by housing construction); in addition, they have favoured the privatisation of administrative services, especially of the customs and taxation, which provides them with extra resources, both political and economic. The state benefits from an unexpected acceleration of liberalisation policies, owing to the armed groups' attacks on loss-making or already bankrupt state enterprises as well as the forced privatisation of many sectors such as transport, cement and food. Its material foundations are strengthened through its policy of making an enclave of the oil and gas sectors. And by the same process its relations with international financial institutions have never ceased to improve. The armed groups, lastly, see expanding opportunities to survive—and, for some, to become rich—thanks to the implicit tolerance of their trafficking and extortions and, above all, freedom of trade (which allows them to redeploy and launder money through trading companies). In view of all this one can say, paradoxically, that by manipulating the violence and keeping it going, by favouring international firms' penetration of the oil and gas sector, and by providing opportunities for enrichment and prestige for the parties to the conflict as a whole, the state is able to proceed with its ongoing consolidation.

In Morocco the privatisation of patronage and allegiance goes back further, to the end of the French protectorate and especially to the reign of Hassan II.[29] Distribution of rents—exploitation of mines and quarries,

[29] Interviews and personal observation (February 1996, January and March 1997, June 1998); see also B. Hibou, 'Les enjeux de l'ouverture au Maroc. Dissidence économique et contrôle politique', *Les Etudes du CERI* 15, April 1996; C. M. Henry, *The Mediterranean Debt Crescent. Money and Power in Algeria, Egypt, Morocco, Tunisia and Turkey,* Gainesville, FLA: University Press of Florida, 1996. On the system of allegiance in general, see J. Waterbury, *The Commander of the Faithful: the Moroccan Political Elite—A Study in Segmented Politics,* London: Weidenfeld and Nicolson, 1970 and R. Leveau, *Le Fellah marocain, défenseur du trône,* Paris: Presses de la FNSP, 2nd ed., 1985.

issuing of licenses, etc.—and possibilities for access to economic activity were, from this period on, 'debureaucratised' and delegated to people close to the sovereign. But that process of delegation spread over time to the economy as a whole. Today, the explosive growth of criminal activities (counterfeiting, drug trafficking, stolen car rackets, illegal emigration, prostitution) and of the informal economy (smuggling, unrecorded production) is perhaps the 'revenge' of the 'market economy', as some claim. But in no way does it lead to the impotence of the state or the political more generally. Even if certain aspects of state power are in decline in some instances, the central power has contributed to the development of those activities, by its tolerance towards illegal activity and by the active involvement of some of its members.

Similarly, the tax system is noted particularly for fairly large-scale evasion; but at the same time it is characterised by impromptu and arbitrary interventions by the central power (for example, the drought solidarity tax and the forced contributions for the building of the Hassan II Mosque in Casablanca) and by little-known and sometimes abusive local taxes. Lastly, alongside the plethoric administration, inefficient and without apparent political control, there is a parallel administration managed by senior personalities, apparently without any political or administrative standing, but close to the Palace. The 'clean-up campaign' (*campagne d'assainissement*) launched in February 1996 illustrates perfectly the subtlety of this way of exercising state power. The people called in for questioning for corruption, tax evasion, drug trafficking and smuggling were not marginal figures: they had enjoyed high-level protection. Furthermore, the condemned activities were not at all proscribed as such, since they continue today, enjoying the same benevolent tolerance. But the arbitrariness of that campaign enabled the state to reassert its power, its primacy in the definition of norms and rules, its initiative in the renegotiation of relations with society and its ability to intervene in the political and economic fields.

The case of Tunisia is especially interesting for its tax system, characterised both by tolerance of evasion and by great difficulty in modernising the taxation apparatus. But one should not conclude that the state's capacity for control, or even that of the administration, is thereby eroded. In fact, since the end of 1992 a real private taxation system has been set up.[30]

---

[30] Interviews and personal observation (May 1997 and April 1998). On the state and the political sphere, see S. Benedict, 'Tunisie, le mirage de l'Etat fort', *Esprit*, March–April 1997, pp. 27–42; M. Camau, 'D'une République à l'autre: refondation politique et aléas de la transition libérale', *Monde Arabe, Maghreb-Machrek* 157, July–September 1997, pp. 3–16; and M. Camau (ed.), *Tunisie au présent, une modernité au-dessus de tout soupçon?* Paris: Editions du CNRS, 1987. On political control over economic and social activity, see I. W. Zartman (ed.), *Tunisia. The Political Economy of Reform*, Boulder, CO

The National Solidarity Fund (whose account number is the now famous 26.26) is supplied by 'voluntary' contributions from businesses and influential individuals, and is never accounted for in the national budet. That fund, which belongs to the President (who manages it in person and is in sole charge of it) is theoretically destined for social projects (electrification, housing, social welfare) and, secondarily, for the glory of the benefactor. As such the 26.26 account truly constitutes an example of privatisation of taxation. But it reveals great mastery over society and a particularly impressive capacity for the consolidation of central power. In fact contributors are listed and are given receipts when they make their donations. Any businessmen or influential personalities who fail to make the voluntary contribution are denied access to state contracts or even to private economic opportunities. Similarly, tax evasion is tolerated and widely known. In case of untimely behaviour or excessive ambition, arbitrary tax checks—or demands for payment of back taxes—are always possible. As in Morocco, abritrariness and fluidity of distinctions—for example between legal and illegal, public and private—constitute a mode of governing in themselves. Again, they are not necessarily indications of state weakness.

Mercenaries and private security companies. The final example that can serve to illustrate my point is the development of the mercenary and private security market all over Africa.[31] On the lines of Executive Outcomes, the best known, security companies have flourished across the continent since the mid-1980s: Sandline, MPRI, Africa Security, Eagle, Sagan, Dak, Wackenhut and others offer to ensure the security of the suburbs and smart districts of capital cities and airports, and mining concessions and oil fields, as well as offering military training. The rich and productive enclaves of the African economic scene are now protected by private companies which have succeeded in turning the problem of

---

and London: Lynne Rienner, 1991. On political control over financial activity, see Henry (note 29). On '26.26' see K. Zamiti, 'Le Fonds de solidarité nationale: pour une approche sociologique du politique', *Annuaire de l'Afrique du Nord* XXXV, 1996, pp. 705–12.

[31] For the special case of Sierra Leone, see W. Reno (note 22); for the special case of South Africa see S. Ellis, 'Africa and International Corruption: the Strange Case of South Africa and Seychelles', *African Affairs* 95, no. 379, April 1996, pp. 165–96. For a general analysis, J. Harding, 'The Mercenary Business', *London Review of Books*, 1 August 1996, pp. 3–9; R. Banégas, 'De la guerre au maintien de la paix: le nouveau business mercenaire', *Critique Internationale* 1, autumn 1998, pp. 179–94; P. Chapleau and F. Misser, *Mercenaires S.A.*, Paris: Desclée de Brouwer, 1998; D. Shearer, *Private Armies and Military Interventions*, Oxford: International Institute for Strategic Studies, 1998 (Adelphi Paper 316); R. Marchal, 'Terminer une guerre', pp. 5–48, in R. Marchal and C. Messiant (note 7); G. Mills and J. Stremlan (eds), *The Privatisation of Security in Africa*, Johannesburg: South African Institute of International Affairs, 1999.

political and military instability into a particularly lucrative economic opportunity (the companies being paid in cash or minerals). However, contrary to appearances and the views of most commentators, it is difficult to interpret this development in terms of laxity on the part of African governments and a 'threat to national sovereignty', as a UN spokesman put it.

First, relations between public and private actors are very close for most of the time: local governors, ministers and district police commissioners for the security companies, and the highest state authorities for the mercenary companies, are privileged contacts for the leaders of these private firms and in fact often closely related to them. When a police chief is replaced, not uncommonly certain companies go bankrupt and others prosper rapidly; Africa Security had difficult moments after the fall of Jean Fochivé in Cameroon. People close to former President arap Moi in Kenya and President Museveni in Uganda have had direct interests in profits of Executive Outcomes. In the case of that company (and its numerous front companies) the links with the official security apparatus extend to the recruiting of its personnel; mercenaries are often former members of the secret service or the elite units of the South African army. It is not uncommon to find former ministers at the head of such companies (in Cameroon, a former minister of Defence heads the Société d'Intervention Rapide) trying to control the entire sector, by getting laws passed to that effect (in Cameroon, a 'nationalisation' law has been passed in this way; in Côte d'Ivoire, the all-powerful General Tanny, head of the National Security Council, accredited and controlled these companies). Generally speaking, the heads of private security firms are most often former or present members of the security forces—the army, the police, former warlords.

Secondly, the contacts with the official authorities of these companies' countries of origin are informal but very real. The despatch of Serb mercenaries to Zaire at the beginning of 1997, and of South African mercenaries to Sierra Leone in mid-1998, is said to have been approved by, respectively, certain French politicians and certain members of the British government.[32] The Strategic Resources Corporation—a loose conglomerate which comprises about twenty companies, including the now famous Executive Outcomes and Sandline—has links to South Africa and Britain, MPRI and Wackenhut to the United States, and Africa Security and Secrets to France. This delegation of military or security work has more than one advantage; it enables the Western powers (France, the United States, Belgium, Britain, Israel) and regional ones (like South Africa) to conceal practices that do not fit in well with the principles of good governance being glorified in the meantime; it dilutes responsibility, and reduces the

[32] *Libération*, 12 May 1998; *La lettre du Continent*, no. 310, 23 July 1998.

costs of intervention. In addition, in the search for respectability and international legitimacy, private security companies outwardly display a commitment to respect the priorities, values and options of the great powers.

Lastly, these private security companies are involved in one of the determining factors in the changing face of the African continent: today, war and violence are in fact among the principal vehicles for emergent social, political and economic arrangements in African countries; by that very fact they contribute to processes of state formation. Not only are these private companies incapable of providing political solutions to conflicts, they also live off the conflicts; while they may create illusions in the short term, in the medium and long term they perpetuate violence which thus becomes entrenched as the dominant modality for state formation.

Negotiations and unstable arrangements

As I have attempted to show, privatisation is in no way synonymous with the retreat of the state, or even the primacy of private over public. As these various examples show, beyond the expanding role of so-called private bodies, privatisation entails constant negotiation between dominant actors (whether they be public or private); the constant redrawing of the frontiers between public and private; and the persistent hold of political relations and power more generally. Negotiations are always at the centre of this process of delegation and control which characterises this mode of increasingly private indirect government.

Privatisation seems today to be one form of negotiation and formalisation of power relations, if not the dominant form. Certain characteristics of the delegation process allow us to understand better the political function of private mediation. The concrete examples mentioned above show that contracts or agreements, whether formal or informal, made between the state and private actors are far from being permanent or even long-lasting. On the contrary, they are deliberately unstable, even volatile, and secret and up for renegotiation all the time. This is the case with lease-farming, subcontracting, contracts with national or foreign private security companies, or toleration of private appropriation and illegal and criminal acts. In Cameroon, for instance, President Biya, who himself signed the contract farming out the management of indirect taxation to the RMA company, came into conflict with other members of the government (most notably the Minister of Finance, who was not satisfied with the performance of the private firm), while the contract expired in 1998. The same went for the contract signed, in similarly opaque fashion, between certain political personalities and the SGS. One constant fact is that in these conditions fortunes are made and unmade very rapidly—proof, if any were needed, of the political games involved in the procurement of contracts. This instability is not the result of poor management or other inadequacies. Nor is it the expression of external dependency. It is rather at the heart of politics:[33] creating and maintaining conditions for the exercise of power.

This is not peculiar to Africa. The same tendency is found in China, for example, where the instability of policy towards the private sector is also a means for control of wealth. It leads actors in the private sector to 'insure themselves' by strengthening networks (which are a mix of public and private actors), multiplying contacts and relations with the public sector.[34] Similarly, in Russia, the proliferation of competing rules, and the vagueness and blurring of norms, are a way to tighten the links between the economic sphere, the criminal underworld and state power.[35] Montesquieu in fact noted earlier, especially in Book XIII of *L'Esprit des Lois*, the privileged relationship between tax farming, political negotiation and instability: the state chose its general tax farmers and the central power maintained the right to control finances, the farmers' profits and, last but not least, their downfall. Sustaining an element of uncertainty in the process of delegation arises from the same concern. The lack of a precise boundary between what is punished and what is allowed, between what is authorised, tolerated and condemned, between licit and illicit, and the games surrounding conflicts of principles—all this creates the space for political intervention and the exercise of arbitrary power at all times, and also leads to permanent negotiations among actors. That is the case, for example, in Morocco, where the blurring of referents is a mode of government.[36] In the absence of bureaucratised, continuous control over society and its leading actors, discontinuous control has emerged as an efficient mode of power. This is the reason for the multiplication of rules and norms, which allows for unending negotiations and transactions, and hence provides the means to control activities, especially economic activities.

In sub-Saharan Africa and the Maghreb—and the same thing is found in Asia and eastern Europe—practices of straddling[37] between positions

[33] S. Berry, *No Condition is Permanent. The Social Dynamics of Agrarian Change in Sub-Saharan Africa*, Madison: University of Wisconsin Press, 1993, highlights the central, even founding role of negotiations in both the economic and the political fields.

[34] See A. Kernen, 'Les privatisations dans un ancien bastion de l'industrie d'Etat chinoise: Shenyang', doctoral thesis, IEP, Paris, 1998.

[35] See Gilles Favarel-Garrigues' paper in this volume.

[36] M. Tozy, *Monarchie et Islam politique au Maroc*, Paris: Presses de Sciences-Po, 1999.

[37] See the Kenyan debate stimulated by M. Cowen and G. Kitching (for example, G. Kitching, *Class and Economic Change in Kenya: the Making of an African Petite Bourgeoisie, 1905–1970*, New Haven: Yale University Press, 1980). For a systematic view see J.-F. Bayart, *The State in Africa: the Politics of the Belly*, London and New York: Longman, 1993.

and practices of power and economic accumulation make it difficult to distinguish clearly between public and private, between state and market, between networks of power and networks of accumulation, etc. Private intermediaries who are called upon, both national and foreign, are rarely without any state connection. The case of security companies is exemplary in this respect. While it is not formalised, the largest security companies maintain close relationships with Western countries. In particular, delegation—through an explicit or tacit contract—creates mutual dependence between public entities and private intermediaries. The state needs such intermediaries to secure revenue or to maintain economic or political order; but they are directly dependent on the political power to carry out those functions. Of course, there can be movement towards effective autonomy, and control is never complete. But in a situation of political fragmentation, which is to a great extent the condition of these societies, movement towards relative autonomy can be a means of exercising power. The central power can do without controlling all its administrative organs and (to use the colonial term) its 'auxiliaries', so long as it is master of local go-betweens; it can show its presence by fits and starts only, often in an arbitrary way, while remaining distant, so long as it is master of the rules of the game or is the source of the prevailing norms and values; it can even face competition from various actors, so long as it manages to include them in its political economy, in its strategies of accumulation, redistribution and social mobility.

In this sense privatisation can be considered as a new form of state interventionism. Contrary to expectations, privatisation does not hamper mastery over society and, sometimes, a capacity for consolidation of the central power. Again, this mastery should not be equated with total and exclusive control; still less does it mean establishing uniformity. There is no question of denying the possibilities of autonomisation, or adopting the voluntarist illusion which involves assuming the capacity of the state or leaders to give practical effect to the policies they devise. Above all, the state is not univocal: the relations between state power, which is in a constant process of formation, and actors, social groups and local communities are highly diverse and complex. Not only is it always possible for private actors to invent ways to circumvent obstacles; in addition, the use of intermediaries and collusion between public and private interests are not synonymous with harmonious and symbiotic relations: they do not prevent tense and conflictual relations among the parties. Indeed, I have stressed how such conflictual relations and uncertainties are at the very heart of these arrangements. Everywhere there are slip-ups and spaces where freedom can slip in, and if there are none of these, for astute actors it is always possible to invent ways of circumventing. The conflicts, negotiations and compromises all go together to model the forms taken by power and its way of operating. Above all, ambivalence is characteristic of political action;[38] political and economic strategies often produce unforeseen effects, which sometimes turn out the opposite of what was intended; and their influence can only be oblique. In Morocco, it is certain that the clean-up campaign mentioned earlier corresponded effectively with a feeling, and probably with a reality, of loss of control over economic actors; and in sub-Saharan Africa, many activities—drug trafficking, for example—are protected without being totally controlled, and a certain number of economic networks and actors undoubtedly undermine the regulatory capacity of states.

However, beyond the conflicts, the manoeuvring and the rivalries there are often possibilities of accommodation and negotiation, and, through that, of indirect government and control. The importance of each state's or region's historical trajectory is clearly apparent here. In Africa south of the Sahara, the delegation of sovereign powers remains relatively under control, or at least known and tolerated, because of the control and the hierarchical structure of networks, as well as the narrowing of the political space. Appropriation of state property, or public and collective goods, for the benefit of a minority is not synonymous with mere *laissez-faire*: it is a power strategy, even if only *a posteriori*, that excludes actors who cannot be coopted and political entrepreneurs who are too ambitious. In addition, control by African central powers is also exercised through the possibility (very often used) of making and unmaking contracts. In Tunisia, the '26.26' account and the new Banque Tunisienne de Solidarité (which operates according to the same principles, that is, 'voluntary' private contributions and public management by the leading private operator, Ben Ali) cannot be seen as merely the appropriation of wealth, even for social purposes. Rather they are, so to speak, an 'exchange', in which real services are exchanged for political control and co-optation: the 'shadow areas' (*zones d'ombre*) are under tight control by the RCD, the ruling party (which in fact defines them for the President); and the donors are known.

Privatisation as 'discharge' and 'gouvernementalité'

The examples quoted above raise inescapably the question of the 'state'. For many observers, these negotiations, modes of management and methods

---

[38] On the ambivalence of the political, cf. J.-F. Bayart, 'L'invention paradoxale de la modernité économique', pp. 9–43, in J.-F. Bayart (ed.), *La réinvention du capitalisme*, Paris: Karthala, 1994, and J.-F. Bayart, *The Fictions of Cultural Identity*, London: Hurst, forthcoming. On the overlapping of the state and the community, cf. P. Geschiere, 'Le social standardisé: l'Etat contre la communauté?', *Critique Internationale* 1, autumn 1998, pp. 60–5.

of renewal are proof not so much of the vitality of states as of the ruses of those in power. This is the viewpoint of Zartman, for example, who argues that inept leaders are responsible for state collapse.[39] This is also one of the arguments put forward to refute the idea of the 'transplant' of the state in Africa and Asia. While some actors (especially import-oriented elites) succeed in responding to foreign models of the state, the historical culture of those countries, it is argued, prevents it from taking root in society.[40] But here again, one has to reject such a view which misunderstands the nature of the state and is flawed by its normative stance. In those interpretations, indeed, the state is defined in advance; all the studies that emphasise loss of sovereignty or legitimacy by the state, or even its retreat, implicitly share a substantialist and normative view of state power.

To avoid this pitfall, a return to the great classical masters of historical sociology is especially enlightening. The work of Max Weber on the one hand, and that of Foucault on the other, provide us with the theoretical and analytical tools for our approach. The term 'the Weberian state' is always used to describe the specific form of the rational-legal and bureaucratic state; Weber is primarily cited as the theorist of this ideal form.

However, Weber himself worked on other, non-bureaucratic forms of state, with non-permanent intervention. In particular, the idea of 'discharge' which he advanced to describe feudal situations could be interesting to round off our analysis of these modes of governing;[41] this modality of exercising power, which in particular avoids the cost of a major administrative apparatus, was historically common, he tells us. In no way did it indicate the absence of a state or a government; it was rather characteristic of situations or moments in history that were much less bureaucratised, relying little or not at all on an apparatus of management. In the same line of thought, the works of Fernand Braudel and Charles Tilly recall that war, extraction and economic accumulation, often private, interacted to shape the European states.[42] They stress in particular that brigandage, plunder,

[39] I. Zartman (note 2).

[40] B. Badie, *L'Etat importé. Essai sur l'occidentalisation de l'ordre politique,* Paris: Fayard, 1992.

[41] M. Weber, *General Economic History* (trans. F. H. Knight), London: George Allen & Unwin, 1927. Weber also speaks of it indirectly in *Economy and Society: An Outline of Interpretive Sociology* (trans. E. Fischoff *et al.*), ed. G. Roth and C. Wittich, New York: Bedminster Press, 3 vols, 1968 in connection with the ideas of appropriation (Vol. I, pp. 122 ff), forced loans (vol. I, pp. 194 ff), tax farming (Vol. I, pp. 194 ff) and concessions (Vol. I, pp. 231 ff).

[42] See Fernand Braudel, *La Méditerranée et le monde méditerranéen à l'époque de Philippe II*, Paris: Armand Colin, 1949 (1990 edition, 3 vols); C. Tilly, *Coercion, Capital, and European States, AD 990–1992*, Cambridge, MA: Blackwell, 1992; and C. Tilly, 'War Making and State Making as Organised Crime', pp. 169–91, in P. B. Evans,

piracy and gang rivalry belong to one and the same continuum and all contribute to state formation.

In this tradition of historical sociology of the state (revived more recently Anderson, Tilly, Skocpol and, in terms of the historicity of the state, Bayart) the substantialist view of the state is rejected: it is not presupposed and defined in advance. Similarly, what such studies seek to make out is continuity and, especially, historical breaks in forms of political and economic arrangement, and not recurrence of political and economic systems. That is why the taxonomic view of the state is not considered relevant (Médard's 'neopatrimonial' state, for example, or 'Sultanism' in the work of Chehabi and Linz[43]); that view makes it possible to emphasise that practices confusing public and private interests are commonplace, but not to discern the developments and breaks with the past currently taking place. At the same time the tradition of historical sociology of the state corresponds to a precise methodological approach: the political and the state are not defined *a priori*. Thus the chosen approach avoids excluding elements considered *a priori* as not belonging to a state-related field. Similarly, it avoids laying down a clear *a priori* separation between economic and non-economic, political and non-political, public and private.

Michel Foucault's work on the notion of power[44] and on the ways in which it is exercised refines this approach. Through Bayart's interpretation of power, some necessarily circumstantial, normative and reductionist definitions can be avoided, so as to observe the original processes of power. *'Gouvernementalité'* denotes 'a given configuration or historical sequence…whose "government" one intends to analyse as a mode of structuring of the field of action of individuals or groups.'[45] With this idea it is possible not only to recognise the historicity of particular states, but

---

D. Rueschmeyer and T. Skocpol (eds), *Bringing the State Back In*, Cambridge University Press, 1985. See also W. G. Hoskins, *The Age of Plunder. The England of Henry VIII, 1500–1547*, London and New York: Longman, 1976.

[43] J.-F. Médard, 'La spécificité du pouvoir en Afrique', *Pouvoirs*, No. 25, April 1983; H. E. Chehabi and J. J. Linz (eds), *Sultanistic Regimes*, Baltimore and London: Johns Hopkins University Press, 1998.

[44] Power 'is not an institution, it is not a structure, it is not a certain power with which certain people may be thought to be endowed; it is the name given to a complex strategic situation in a given society': quotation from Foucault taken from J.-F. Bayart, 'Le concept de gouvernementalité et l'analyse de l'historicité du politique', paper delivered to seminar 'Pratiques politiques et usages de Michel Foucault', Centre d'Etudes et de Recherches Internationales, Paris, 13-14 November 1997.

[45] J. -F. Bayart, 'Fait missionnaire et politique du ventre, une analyse foucaldienne', *Le Fait Missionnaire* (Lausanne) 6, 1998. See also J.-F. Bayart (ed.), *La greffe de l'Etat*, Paris: Karthala, 1996.

also to emphasise the multiplicity of relations between the social and the political. It sheds light on historical and political processes of subjectivisation. Thus the notion of *'gouvernementalité'* makes it possible to understand the privatisation processes currently underway both as a mutation in modes of government and—as a corollary—as the expression of subjectivation. The mutations undergone by the 'politics of the belly' in sub-Saharan Africa and by the Makhzen in Morocco are at the same time alterations in the forms and points of state intervention and remodelling of different 'life styles', values and norms linked to historically relevant registers—for example those of the Christian missions in sub-Saharan Africa or the *bay'a* in Morocco.[46] From a methodological point of view, the notion of *gouvernementalité* affords insight into an additional dimension of privatisation of the state: that is, ways of being and understanding, and not only acting, in the economic and political fields.

This approach, it goes without saying, can arouse a number of reservations. To answer criticisms concerning the fuzziness of the concepts used, the distinctions made (public vs private, for example) and the confusion in the use of terms (for example, the terms state, power and elites), four points can be put forward.

1. Analysis of concrete situations teaches us that, to apprehend and understand the state, it is impossible to separate state and power, state and ruling elite. In other words, to understand the state, it is necessary to understand the people in power and, equally important, their games, their strategies and their historical practices. This mutual dependence defines the outlines of the state. It is impossible to separate the economic from the political, private interests from public interests, the particular from the general. The political role of private interests, or the monopolisation of wealth by the elite or by a restricted group of political leaders, does not subvert or undermine the state, in so far as those private actors are also public and state actors. These practices of accumulation become political—in other words, a *gouvernementalité* in its own right.

   In sub-Saharan Africa, for example, it is impossible to understand state formation without taking account of the innumerable processes of negotiation between the elites and other actors, foreign ones included. These negotiations can take multiple forms, notably war and conflict. And the register of values known as 'belly politics' (which extends far beyond corruption) has become a mode of managing the public

---

[46] Ibid. for sub-Saharan Africa; for Morocco Mohamed Tozy, while he does not use the concept of *gouvernementalité*, demonstrates well that *bay'a* (allegiance) helps 'to fix the ideological, doctrinal and behavioral dimensions of power relations' (note 36, p. 78).

space.[47] Similarly, in Indonesia, the family register is an integral part of the state and has become, over time, 'a modality for managing the public space edified as an ethic'[48] on the same level as ethnic- and kinship-based registers. In Asia, several authors have shown how corruption (the site par excellence of this overlapping of public and private) contributed to economic growth and oiled the wheels of redistribution, in that way helping the state to take root thanks to its appropriation by an ever broader social mass.[49] In Morocco, the Makhzen's practices can be seen as the work of one man, the king, and his entourage, the palace. But they serve to model *gouvernementalité* in Morocco; the Makhzen, which 'is the object of negative and positive projection at the same time', is 'the order considered necessary and consolidated by unlimited recourse to violence'; it 'expresses the nakedness of the exercise of authority and political reason, stripped of all morality or sentiment'; in an even more profound way—because it relates to modes of subjectivation—Dar al-Makhzen, 'which is the sole provider of symbols of authority for the system', is 'the seat of reverential fear which constitutes the foundation of power.'[50]

Privatisations fit into this framework. Strengthening the power of this or that politician (or this or that faction) through appropriation of economic resources, or transfer of enterprises, obviously offers a personal opportunity for enrichment, or is a short-term tactic to give a base to contested or delegitimised authority. But, more than that, it traces the possible outlines of political action. It takes account of the interdependence of processes of economic accumulation and political control (and by the same processes maintains that interdependence); it is intrinsic to the negotiation of allegiances and loyalties. In Africa, it means gaining opportunities for indirect control over social capital, that is, over people—for example, gaining opportunities through resources derived from extraversion to show loyalty and generosity that go with political domination and state formation. In Asia, it means helping sustain the paternalism and patrimonialism characteristic of the authoritarian regimes in the region. Having recourse to violence, even war, for private economic purposes is also a way to help remodel power and take part, if only involuntarily, in state formation.

---

[47] J.-F. Bayart (note 37).

[48] R. Bertrand, 'La politique du FMI et l'Indonésie de Suharto', *Esprit* 242, May 1998, pp. 47–57.

[49] J.-L. Rocca, 'La corruption et la communauté. Contre une analyse culturaliste de l'économie chinoise', *Revue Tiers Monde* XXXVII (147), July-Sept. 1996, pp. 689–702, and K. Yoshihara, *The Rise of Ersatz Capitalism in South East Asia*, New York: Oxford University Press, 1988. It should be noted that this permanent straddling was also at the root of the recent Asian crisis.

[50] Tozy (note 36) pp. 42–3.

2. To understand the changes taking place, the different attributes and functions of the state must be distinguished: notably, a distinction must be made between state power and sovereignty, or between the state's capacity to exercise power and its capacity to master a regulatory authority (in concrete terms, to have mastery over an economic policy or to control wealth, or the economic productivity of a people, or the people as such). This distinction makes it possible, for example, to see how the regulatory capacity of the state can be formally eroded while its power remains and is constantly being redeployed. It also highlights how the new modalities of appropriation of resources—which sometimes operate through privatisation—can be compatible with state modes of intervention, and hence do not necessarily undermine the foundations of the exercise of state power.[51] It is because we define the state, for example, in terms of sovereignty, or as the sole holder of the monopoly of legitimate violence and levying of taxes, that we conclude that there is a decaying of the state or competition with the state from new powers (such as transnational networks, 'mafias' or major consultancy and evaluation multinationals, but also local eminent personalities or warlords). On the other hand, if one considers that the points of state intervention can extend beyond institutions and that the question of sovereignty is distinct from that of state power, the appearance of those actors, flows and powers apparently competing with the state can be considered as points—new or not—of state intervention.

For example, in sub-Saharan Africa as in the Maghreb, smugglers undermine the state's regulatory authority to some extent, by challenging the formally decreed foreign trade policy. But they do not challenge national sovereignty and do not undermine the state as such—insofar as the state succeeds in including the smugglers in its strategies for accumulation, management of rents and social mobility, redistribution, etc. Moreover, both contribute to the same political economy and share the same values, the same methods and representations of the exercise of power.[52] This distinction between power and sovereignty, between the exercise of power and regulatory capacity, relates—once again—to *gouvernementalité*; it demonstrates that 'privatisation of the state' does not mean dilution of the political in the economic, nor domination of

---

[51] See Janet Roitman's chapter in this volume.

[52] B. Hibou in *L'Afrique est-elle protectionniste?* (note 4) shows how fraud and smuggling finish up as part of commercial policy itself. J. Roitman, 'Objects of the Economy and the Language of Politics in Northern Cameroon', PhD thesis, University of Pennsylvania, 1996, shows how the epistemological foundations of *douaniers-combattants*— 'fighting customs officials' extorting rents from trade—are coherent with those of the nation-state.

public logic by private logic, but multiplication of the points of exercise of state power.

3. Redefining public/private relations and modifying *gouvernementalité* are two aspects of the same process. Changes in taxation necessarily lead to modifications in the logics of extraction and redistribution, and thus transform modes of unequal accumulation or redistribution that legitimise the political. They also correspond to renegotiation of the mix and the relations between differing values, norms and rules. In other words, they touch on modes of subjectivation themselves. In the privatisation process now underway there is a notable tendency towards monetarisation of social relations and the commodification of the political; the legitimacy of influence peddling and clientelism; widening of the spectrum of the forms of value and wealth; and acceptance of wealth as the basis of the political, even if perceptions of it remain extremely ambivalent.[53] Similarly, Roland Marchal and Achille Mbembe have shown how the development of violence (war, plunder, rioting) for economic purposes transforms notions of property through this process of unbridled private appropriation, thus participating in the renegotiation of public and private space and, ultimately, in state formation. The examples of conversion of public debt into investment, shares or natural resources (especially petroleum) are also eloquent.[54] They suggest that the value guaranteed is no longer the capacity of the state to extract funds, but its privatised collective heritage; that state enterprises, installations and fixed assets, and natural resources are alienable; that financial obligations are transformed into alienation of the private domain; and that the public debt is transformed into a private asset and has generated a new market.

The analysis of 'privatisation of the state' which I put forward in these pages, in emphasising these forms of redefinition and remodelling, cannot be the occasion for an overall, uniform interpretation; on the contrary, it pays great attention to the special forms taken by the dispositions and new relations among these various values, norms, rules and principles of acting and being—and, by the same token, to

---

[53] See for example R. Banégas, 'Bouffer l'argent: politique du ventre, démocratisation et clientélisme au Bénin', pp. 75–109 in J. L. Briquet and F. Sawicki (eds), *Clientélisme politique dans les sociétés contemporaines*, Paris: Presses Universitaires de France, 1998; J.-P. Olivier de Sardan, 'A Moral Economy of Corruption in Africa', *Journal of Modern African Studies* 37/1, 1999, pp. 25–52; Roitman (note 52).

[54] On these processes of debt and credit conversion, see L. Hernandez and S. Katada, *Grants and Debt Forgiveness in Africa*, Washington: World Bank, September 1996 (Policy Research paper 1653). For a problematisation in terms of privatisation, see O. Vallée, 'La dette publique est-elle privée?' *Politique Africaine* 73, March 1999, pp. 50–67.

the necessarily varied forms and meanings of this apparently global process.[55]

4. These phenomena of discharge and permanent negotiation are inscribed in the long term, and constitute a fundamental aspect of the historical trajectory—specific to each country or region—of the political entities involved. The process of delegation of state power to the private sector is a very old phenomenon. Today it appears to be a new technique because of the adoption in recent decades of normative representations (the rational-legal state, the welfare state, the development state) and the occultation—on the grounds that they are archaic?—of past forms, however efficient. The overlapping of state and elite strategies extends so far back in time that it is futile to try to distinguish between the two—especially as those practices are common to all political actors, as is shown by the continuity of African and Asian political economies after regime change and the establishment of multi-party politics.[56] The following pages explore the role of these historical trajectories in the present-day situation and in the process of differentiation through globalisation.

The historical specificity of privatisation of the state

Considering historical trajectories in order to understand contemporary privatisation of the state is important for two reasons. First, following those trajectories shows how 'discharge' and 'privatisation' are configurations that are both commonplace in principle and specific in their arrangements—in the disposition of relations between public and private, economic and political. Secondly, understanding these trajectories makes it possible to see how they influence the concrete shaping of various *gouvernementalités*—the 'privatisation of the state' is in part the fruit of globalisation, but it is just as much the product of local history.

The banality of private indirect government in history. The Ancien Régime in France is probably one of the best examples showing that indirect and private government is something historically normal, since France is seen as the 'Weberian state' par excellence. Tax administration, under the Ancien Régime, was privatised to a great extent; fiscal and financial

---

[55] R. Marchal, in his article 'Des contresens possibles de la globalisation: privatisation de l'Etat et bienfaisance au Soudan et en Somalie', *Politique Africaine* 73, March 1999, pp. 68–81, shows in a very concrete way how acts of charity or goodwill lead to very different exercises of state power.

[56] R. Banégas, 'La démocratie à pas de caméléon. Transition et consolidation démocratique au Bénin', doctoral thesis, Paris, IEP de Paris, 1998; and the chapters by Jean-Louis Rocca, Romain Bertrand and Gilles Favarel-Garrigues in this volume.

offices were bought and sold like private property, like an inheritance. Tax farmers (*fermiers généraux* and *traitants*, who were private actors) collected taxes for the state. This policy was due to a series of constraints, including deficiencies in the bureaucratic apparatus, the inadequacy of administrative staff, and the continued financial imperatives due to increasingly expensive and frequent wars. Privatisation in fact made it possible to resort to more imaginative, but also more coercive methods of recovering taxes. As a result the state apparently did not have control over tax revenue. But it is impossible to understand the political economy of the Ancien Régime if one sticks to that first impression.

Dessert's work has admirably demonstrated the mutual dependence that existed between the actors in a 'fiscal-financial' system characterised by two elements:[57] on the one hand, the private collectors of tax revenue were also those who made loans—voluntary or forced—to the king; on the other hand, they were obliged to make advances on revenue to the Treasury, because of the complex organisation of the tax system and, above all, the permanent deficit in the kingdom's public finances. This meant that the king depended to a great extent, for his revenue, on financiers who could always refuse him new loans; but general tax farmers and *traitants* depended on the protection of the court and the councils for access to coveted posts. They had necessarily to be affiliated to a man and to a political faction to obtain information, permits and opportunities for enrichment, and, above all, to be able to get tax advances for the amounts that they could not take from their own fortunes. Ultimately, the financiers were only a mediation; behind them were powerful people who accumulated privatised rights (senior officials and ministers such as Richelieu, Colbert and Fouquet, and the higher aristocracy, starting with the royal family) but who were an integral part of the state. The 'fiscal-financial' system of the kingdom made it possible to create finance capital on a large scale, but it remained closely linked to the centre of political power, so much so that the interests of private financiers, corporate groups (general tax farmers, *traitants*, bankers, *intendants*, receiving officers, but also munitions

---

[57] D. Dessert, *Argent, pouvoir et société au Grand Siècle*, Paris: Fayard, 1984. On privatisation as the preference for immediate financial returns (over any objective of equity or justice), see Montesquieu, *L'esprit des lois*, Book XIII, and M. Weber, *Economy and Society* (note 41), vol. I, pp. 194 ff. See also K. Norberg, 'The French Fiscal Crisis of 1788 and the Financial Origins of the Revolution of 1789', pp. 253–98, and P. Hoffman, 'Early Modern France, 1450–1700', pp. 226–52 in P. Hoffman and K. Norberg (eds), *Fiscal Crises, Liberty and Representative Government, 1450–1700*, Stanford University Press, 1984. On the economic aspect, see also J.-Y. Grenier, *L'économie d'Ancien Régime*, Paris: Albin Michel, 1996. All indirect taxes were managed by private receiving officers, and in accordance with the increase in financial constraints, other dues (including revenue from public domains) were also privatised.

makers, manufacturers and administrators) and the state were all merged. Delegation of power never meant loss of power: privatisation of the tax system corresponded to a strategy of almost non-stop negotiation of the power relations between the king and the powerful figures of the absolute monarchy regime.

Meanwhile the administration (through the ministers and senior finance officials) chose the general tax farmers; the central power retained a right of supervision over the financiers, over their successes and collapses. The Chambers of Justice were among the favoured areas of factional struggle. The meetings of those Chambers, and the ordering of compulsory levies and settlement of the kingdom's bankruptcies, were favoured moments for expression of this state control over the world of finance. Ultimately, the privatisation of taxation certainly reflected increased dependence of the state on the private sector and especially on financial auxiliaries, and an undeniable failure of the monarchical administration to adapt to cope with its growing needs. But privatisation never meant loss of influence by state power. That state power retained indirect control over the world of finance and was assured of fiscal and financial revenue; its intervention was fiftul and often arbitrary, but it was particularly effective. This choice of an indirect, partly privatised mode of management characterised the French absolute monarchy regime for about two centuries—a regime that cannot be described as impotent.

The Ottoman Empire between the seventeenth and nineteenth centuries illustrates another way in which this indirect but none the less efficient way of state management could operate. The formation of the Ottoman state took place through bargaining among the various elements of society, especially through the 'purchase' and distribution of patronage—bandits and mercenary forces being among the beneficiaries.[58] One must not be misled by the appearance of anarchy, dissolution of power and a chaotic society. Private violence did not express contesting of state power, but the managing of violence that the state had to a great extent manufactured to consolidate its power. Bandits and mercenaries are thus seen to be products of formation of the state, which over time delegated tasks to them, such as the maintenance of security and tax collection. Privatisation of violence and of part of the taxation system, far from signifying a loss of state control, was proof of the strength of a state handling its authority and influence with skill through its flexible and adaptable relations with various segments of society.

These two examples, among many others, are only put forward here to show how these practices of government by delegation and through

[58] K. Barkey, *Bandits and Bureaucrats: The Ottoman Route to State Centralisation*, Ithaca, NY: Cornell University Press, 1994.

private intermediaries are historically something normal. We are far from suggesting making them models and interpreting present-day situations in the light of past experience. But the detailed analyses devoted to them can enlighten us on the various mechanisms of discharge and delegation.

Different historical trajectories and their influence on privatisation today. On the margins of the Ottoman Empire every state was built, and found its own system of government, according to the degree and methods of mobilisation of allegiances by the central power.[59] In Tunisia, for example, central authority was limited to levying of taxes, protection of cities and peasants, defence of Islam and administration of justice.[60] The centralisation of the state was inseparable from the autonomy of the tribes, and modes of combined 'indirect exploitation' of property and assets and 'indirect development' spread through the entire society. 'The nation is entirely subject to the Bey of Tunis, but governs itself,' an eighteenth-century witness said.[61] But trade with the West, like the corsairs' operations, *Jihad*, piracy and the use of militias, constituted a principle as well as important government resources for the formation of the Tunisian state.[62] The major state manufactures and, above all, taxes, were farmed out.[63] In a parallel process, social and cultural activities were privatised by the *Ulema*, notably through *waqf* but also through administration of education and justice.[64] But the links between men of religion and the central

---

[59] On this subject see M. Camau, 'Politique dans le passé, politique aujourd'hui au Maghreb', pp. 63–93, in J.-F. Bayart (ed.), *La greffe de l'Etat* (note 45), and L. C. Brown, *The Tunisia of Ahmed Bey, 1835–1855*, Princeton University Press, 1974.

[60] L. Valensi, *Fellahs tunisiens. L'économie rurale et la vie des campagnes aux XVIIIe et XIXe siècles*, Paris: Mouton, 1977.

[61] Quoted by Camau (note 59), who himself took it from Valensi (note 60).

[62] Braudel (note 42) and Camau (note 59). With the upheavals which that caused in terms of taxation, trade with Europe had consequences reaching the furthest ends of the country. See Valensi (note 60) and M. H. Cherif, 'Document relatif à des tribus tunisiennes des débuts du XVIIe siècle', *Revue de l'Occident Musulman et de la Méditerranée* 33 (1), 1982.

[63] A. Hénia, 'Le Grîd, ses rapports avec le beylick de Tunis (1676–1840)', doctoral thesis, University of Tunis, 1980; A. M. Planel, 'Etat réformateur et industrialisation au XIXe siècle', *Monde Arabe, Maghreb-Machrek* 157, July–Sept. 1997, pp. 101–14; M. H. Chérif, 'Fermage (lizma) et fermiers d'impôts (lazzam) dans la Tunisie des XVIIe–XVIIIe siècles', pp. 19–29, in *Les Cahiers de la Méditerranée*, special issue *Etats et pouvoirs en Méditerranée*, Vol. 1, 1989, Nice: Université de Nice; and especially M. H. Chérif, *Pouvoir et société dans la Tunisie de Husayn bin 'Ali (1705–1740)*, 2 vols, Tunis: Publications de l'Université de Tunis, 1984.

[64] On this point see Khayr el-Din, *Essai sur les réformes nécessaires aux Etats musulmans*, Paris, 1868 (Aix-en-Provence: Edisud, 1987). In the course of time those ties were strengthened so far that the reform movement involved an initial submission of *waqf* property to the state, full state control over them being eventually imposed at the time of independence. See L. C. Brown (note 59) and A. Hourani, *Arabic Thought in the Liberal Age, 1798–1939*, Oxford University Press, 1962 and Cambridge University Press, 1983.

power were close: the former served as 'intermediaries' or 'liaison agents' between society and the state. Tunisia was then 'a society of private law whose activities were based on contractual agreements between partners, state interventionism remaining marginal'.[65]

In Tunisia today privatisation cannot be understood without reference to what can be called a reverse process—of centralisation and 'statisation'—carried out by reformers at the end of the nineteenth century.[66] Not that we are witnessing a sort of reversion to the past or entering a new phase in a cycle of alternating centralisation and privatisation. But, in order to interpret and understand present-day processes of privatisation, people refer to a register that is the product of that earlier history. At the end of the nineteenth century the reform movement was, in Tunisia as in Egypt, a challenge to that indirect mode of management, and was aimed at recentring state power on the administrative apparatus. Privatisation of the tax system and, above all, of social and cultural activity can be interpreted, today, as a refutation of this recentring and as a reinvention of institutions whose principles are taken from the *waqf* and other private institutions of the Beylicate. The return to privatisation of certain economic and social functions is not, in this case, synonymous with a loss of control; on the contrary, it allows for closure of the gap between the perception of the 'practical necessity' of state tutelage and the material possibilities for the exercise of central power. In the name of profitability and rationality, privatisation of the economy and the state enables the state authority to alter power relations and, most important, to avoid, through fragmentation, the constitution of strong poles of economic attraction. Likewise, it allows state authority to favour unofficial relations—not formalised or legal—in the hope of downsizing political and managerial power which might otherwise become autonomous.

Similarly, the current privatisation process in Morocco only makes sense in relation to the Makhzen power logic[67]—which had never disappeared,

---

[65] M. Morsy, 'Présentation' (1987), p. 61 in Khayr el-Din (note 64).

[66] See Khayr el-Din (note 64); Hourani (note 64); and Brown (note 59). The contemporary changes are without any doubt a 'new mode of existence for the nation-state' which challenges the reformist model characterised by 'three principles...capture of power into the hands of those managing the *res publica*, development of that power by establishment of administrative tutelage over the nation ('statisation'), and promotion of legislation as the special—and coercive—mode of relations between the citizen and the state': Morsy (note 65), p. 65. See also M. Camau, 'Tunisie au présent' in M. Camau (ed.) (note 30), especially pp. 32–7.

[67] On the permanence of the Makhzen logic and the impact of historical experience in Morocco, cf. M. Tozy, 'Les enjeux du pouvoir dans les "champs économiques désamorcés"', pp. 153–68 in M. Camau (ed.), *Changements politiques au Maghreb*, Paris: Editions du CNRS, 1991, and Tozy (note 36) (for the social and political dimension), and B. Hibou, 'Les enjeux de l'ouverture économique du Maroc' (note 4) (for the economic dimension).

but may have been covered over by the practices of the colonial state and then, after independence, by the developmentalist and interventionist ideology of the 1960s and 1970s. In reality, the role of the Makhzen had already been modified and extended under the impact of colonial rule (the inheritance and appropriation of the colonial organisation, especially with respect to the administration) and nationalism (the expansion of the Makhzen's intervention in the economic sphere). In the Sherifian kingdom the discontinuity in the Makhzen's exercise of power is another form of government out of harmony with the traditional model of centralised, permanent interventionism. The distinction between *bilad al Makhzen* (space of submission) and the *bilad al Siba* (space of dissidence) was characteristic of the kingdom's political organisation; while the former recognised the authority of the state, the latter recognised only the Sultan's religious authority. But numerous historical works have shown that the frontiers between those two spaces were unstable and fluid, and that in the space of dissidence, the presence of the central power, however irregular and often invisible, was none the less real, appearing from time to time through allegiance, negotiation or violence.[68] In a context where the central power was unable to permanently control all of Moroccan space, the sovereign encouraged, and even contributed to the construction of dissident spaces. The latter made it possible to preserve an internal status quo and to exert authority through both division and remote control. This 'controlled dissidence' or 'normalised dissidence'[69] was thus part of state engineering. It was manifested not only in the *harkas* and *mehallas* (according to whether troop movements had a military objective or a peaceful one), but also in constant conflict and confrontation with local elites.

This organisation of space through ruse and negotiation rather than through violence and command was not confined to the political sphere; it was extended to the taxation system and control over economic activity.[70] With the present-day policies of liberalisation and practices of privatisation, the contemporary relevance of the traditional Makhzen appears

---

[68] See, among others, J. Brignon, A. Amine, B. Boutaleb, G. Martinet and B. Rosenberg, *Histoire du Maroc*, Paris: Hatier, 1967; J. Ganiage, 'North Africa', in R. Oliver and G. N. Sanderson (eds), *The Cambridge History of Africa*, vol. 6. *1870–1905*, Cambridge University Press, 1985; and C. Geertz, *Local Knowledge: Further Essays in Interpretive Anthropology*, 2nd ed., New York: Basic Books Classics, 2000 (1st edn 1983).

[69] Tozy's words, used in *Monarchie et Islam politique au Maroc* (note 36).

[70] See for example P. Guillen, *Les emprunts marocains: 1902–1904*, Paris: Editions Richelieu, undated, and M. E. Mansour, *Morocco in the Reign of Mowlay Sulayman*, New York: Middle East and North African Studies Press, 1990. See also F. Zaïm, *Le Maroc et son espace méditerranéen: histoire économique et sociale*, Rabat: Confluences, 1990, and D. Schroeter, *Merchants of Essaouira: Urban Society and Imperialism in Southwestern Morocco, 1844–1886*, Cambridge University Press, 1986.

quite obvious. The blurring of referents is a mode of governing; maintaining fluidity between legal and illegal activity is an instrument of power (widely used in the realm of criminal activity and taxation), as is playing on the two criteria of government—legality and allegiance—which are contradictory but coexist. The palace's indirect control through protection, mediation, negotiation and 'arrangements' remains the rule.[71] Arbitrariness is still used as a non-continuous but particularly effective mode of governing. In this context contemporary 'campaigns' echo the *harkas* of the past which, as Mohamed Tozy reminds us, were formerly one of the most important moments of the exercise of power. They enable the government to express its strength and guide negotiations, as is evident in the case of the 'gentlemen's agreement' signed with the business community following the clean-up campaign of 1996. They give the state an opportunity to demonstrate its mastery over society, including the zones of dissidence (today consisting of certain economic activities, legal or illegal), and its ability to remain master of the rules of the game—it can, at any moment, 'break' a powerful figure, but it can also make social mobility possible. In no circumstances can one speak of a weak state in reference to the Makhzen. Its power is exerted in piecemeal and partial fashion; its presence is not always visible according to international norms, and its control is discontinuous; but it does not allow the emergence of other, potentially autonomous centres of power, even if that power remains confined to the economic sphere.

Similarly, the current privatisation of the economy and the state in Algeria can only be understood in relation to the *imaginaire* of conflict and violence shared by the various protagonists in the civil war.[72] Conflict and violence are seen as economic opportunities favouring the distribution of wealth and as vectors of social mobility. The models of the 'Emirs' today are the Raïs (the corsairs of the Ottoman Empire), the Caïds (indigenous officials of the colonial regime) and the officers of the Armée de Libération Nationale, all three being decisive actors in the building of the Algerian state. In the light of this history, the current situation reflects not so much a weakening of the state and political dissipation as the pursuit of their ongoing construction through 'de-bureaucratisation', militarisation (violence being managed with the aim of consolidating the regime in power), and delegation of sovereign functions (notably security but also taxation) and also economic development and redistribution functions to the private sector.

---

[71] See J. Waterbury (note 29); R. Leveau (note 29); and M. Tozy (note 36). For mediation in the Arab world generally, see J. Leca and Y. Schemeil, 'Clientélisme et patrimonialisme dans le monde arabe', *International Political Science Review*, vol. 4 no. 4, 1983, pp. 455–94.

[72] See L. Martinez (note 28).

In sub-Saharan Africa contemporary developments need to be understood and interpreted in the light of the experiences of colonial Indirect Rule and the slave-trading and import-export economy of the pre-colonial era. Today, privatisation of the economic and political spheres is an intensifying of the fertile *gouvernementalité* of the 'rhizome state'.[73] It is not insignificant that today the road to privatisation of the state takes certain detours that necessarily echo past experience. For example, the revival of war and violence as ways to social mobility and economic and political resources brings the warlike past of African societies into the contemporary era. In the pre-colonial period war and raids provided substantial economic and political resources for central authorities, which asserted their presence, extracted revenue (taxes and levies of men and goods) and gained prestige by judicious control of conflicts.[74] Colonial rule did not mark a digression in this respect; practices of coercion (forced labour, extortions by concessionary companies and by auxiliaries) were intensified and systematised by the colonial indirect administration.[75]

Another example is the dependence of the African continent and, a parallel development, the growth of ingenious practices of getting round external constraints, which are also characteristic of the 'new' configuration of state power. Calling on foreign private companies to administer the customs, exploit resources or impose security does not mean allowing recolonisation; it is a way of managing dependence according to very

---

[73] On the historicity of the 'rhizome state', see J.-F. Bayart, *The State in Africa* (note 37). On the importance of historical experience in present-day economic, social and political practices, see J.-F. Bayart, 'The "Social Capital" of the Felonious State, or the Ruses of Political Intelligence", pp. 32–48 in J.-F. Bayart, S. Ellis and B. Hibou, *The Criminalization of the State in Africa* (note 14), as well as A. Mbembe, *De la postcolonie. Essai sur l'imagination politique dans l'Afrique contemporaine,* Paris: Karthala, 2000, published in English as *On the Postcolony*, Berkeley: University of California Press, 2001; and A. Mbembe, 'Du gouvernement privé indirect', *Politique Africaine* 73, March 1999, pp. 103–21; P. Richards, *Fighting for the Rain Forest: War, Youth and Resources in Sierra Leone*, London: James Currey, 1996; W. Reno (note 22); and M. Diouf, 'Privatisation des économies et des Etats: commentaire d'un historien', *Politique Africaine* 73, March 1999, pp. 16–23.

[74] See in particular I. Kopytoff, 'The Internal African Frontier: The Making of African Political Culture' in I. Kopytoff (ed.), *The African Frontier: the Reproduction of Traditional African Societies*, Bloomington: Indiana University Press, 1987, and A. Mbembe, *La naissance du maquis dans le Sud-Cameroun (1920–1960)*, Paris: Karthala, 1996; J. Searing, *West African Slavery and Atlantic Commerce: the Senegalese River Valley, 1700–1860*, Cambridge University Press, 1993. For examples of that practice today, see C. Geffray, *La cause des armes au Mozambique. Anthropologie d'une guerre civile,* Paris: Karthala, 1990; Richards (note 73); R. Marchal and C. Messiant (note 7); J.-F. Bayart, 'La guerre en Afrique: dépérissement ou formation de l'Etat?', *Esprit* 247, November 1998, pp. 55–73.

[75] Bayart, 'The "Social Capital"' (note 73).

precise historical referents. Extraversion has always been, in sub-Saharan Africa, a state resource or even a rent.[76] Use of external resources to manage internal conflicts, alliances with foreign actors to strengthen the central power, the transfer of the burden of foreign conditionality to the mass of the people, the instrumentalisation of conflicts among the powers to extract more resources—all these things have for centuries been a means of insertion into the world scene, but also of domestic political action. Today, this management of extraversion increasingly takes on a private form. Thus one sees those countries playing on rivalry among foreign powers over privatisation of state enterprises, over the securing of management contracts, or over the control of free zones. This rivalry is seen in operation between France and the United States or between European and Asian countries for taking over of refineries, telecommunications or cement works; between the United States, Britain and South Africa for the choice of security companies; and between various 'mafias' for control over free zones or duty-free territories.

External constraints are loosened through appeals to private banks or firms, with respect to financial and technological resources alike. In Angola only private companies (private banks securing loans on oil, or oil companies directly) are today called upon to make new loans or renegotiate the debt.[77] In sub-Saharan Africa the weariness of traditional international donors and the personal interests of African leaders are such that transfers of technology are today made principally by private companies, both in management (with surveillance companies, consultancy firms and other subsidiaries of banks or insurance companies) and in the military arena (with private security firms). But this private management of insertion into the international scene expresses strong political preoccupations, as is suggested by the trading-post economy and, above all, the slave trade. Miller's research, centred on Angola, is one of the most important for understanding mechanisms of power in Africa.[78] The main reason for the well known expansion of the slave trade in this region was that it carried out an essential political function. In exchange for ivory and then slaves, African kings obtained, for their private use, European or Asian goods. Those imports offered the African leaders unprecedented opportunities for increased prestige and obligations; they strengthened and fostered subjects' dependence on the political authorities, and enabled the elites to

---

[76] See Bayart (note 37), who speaks of the 'resources of extraversion' and puts forward a non-dependency theory of the management of dependence. For a contemporary example of this management, in a private form, see William Reno's chapter in this volume.

[77] Olivier Vallée (note 54).

[78] J. Miller, *Way of Death. Merchant Capitalism and the Angolan Slave Trade, 1730–1830*, Madison: University of Wisconsin Press, 1988.

make their control over the people closer. That explains why the monopoly over the Atlantic trade was jealously guarded by those in power. That process was not peculiar to Angola;[79] it occurred also in West Africa, in the rest of Central Africa, and in East Africa. For example, the Sultan of Zanzibar, whose entrepôt-empire was very little developed administratively and politically, succeeded in governing all of its territory by monopolising foreign trade (slaves, cloves, ivory) and by allying himself with the emerging merchant class, the Indian traders and the chiefs of the interior.

Everywhere political domination and state formation operated, among other factors, according to loyalty and 'generosity', both of which were made particularly operational through imports and international trade. Like the organisation of the slavery economy, today privatisation and the development of the so-called informal economy are, for African states, another way of asserting their sovereignty and their power in a context of increasing dependence and economic crisis.

It should also be noted that domination through the agency of prominent personalities or local men of straw is today, in many parts of Africa, a modality of governing that has largely replaced intervention by administrative bodies. During the colonial period the administrators relied, for management of the local people, on auxiliaries who gradually acquired wide latitude in relation both to the colonial government and to the local societies. These 'traditional' chiefs, interpreters and other administrative intermediaries eventually became a sort of indirect and informal leading elite, possessing wealth and power. While they indirectly undermined colonial regulation by their own strategies, they nonetheless coexisted with the colonial government and shared the same political economy with it.

Similarly, it is not mere coincidence that executives of the big foreign companies that take over privatised enterprises and manage concessions of public services or security and surveillance companies are white people who often come from the former colonial countries. This configuration

---

[79] On other zones in Central Africa see in particular D. Cordell, 'Economic Crises and Demographic Dynamics in African History: Central and Eastern Central African Republic in the Precolonial and Contemporary Eras', paper delivered to Royaumont seminar on 'Crise économique africaine et dynamique démographique', organised by CEPED (Centre Français sur la Population et le Développement) 22–24 May 1995, and J. Cordell, *Dar al-Kuti and the Last Years of the Trans-Saharan Slave Trade*, Madison: University of Wisconsin Press, 1985. See also A. von Oppen, *Terms of Trade and Terms of Trust: the History and Contexts of Precolonial Market Production around the Upper Zambezi and Kasai*, Studien zur Afrikanischen Geschichte, Bd 6, LIT Verlag 1993. On West Africa, see J. Searing (note 74). On East Africa, see A. Sheriff, *Slaves, Spices and Ivory in Zanzibar: Integration of an East African Commercial Empire into the World Economy, 1770–1873*, James Currey, Heinemann, Tanzania Publishing House and Ohio University Press, 1987.

inevitably recalls the days of concessionary companies. Then the colonial governments, like governments today, delegated exploitation of wealth to private companies, under a regime of commercial concessions.[80] Commercial firms assumed responsibility for exploration, road building and a minimum of public services in return for concession of special privileges, monopolies, and exclusive rights to natural resources.' This dual delegation was illustrated in the realm of taxation: taxes were collected both by the concessionary companies and by intermediaries. Neither hesitated to use for that purpose violence that in fact ceased to be a 'legitimate monopoly' of the colonial state. This ambivalence and redefinition of tax relations is found again today; certain forms of levy exacted by the new intermediaries—local eminent personalities, officials extorting unofficial taxes from illicit trade (*douaniers-combattants*), warlords etc.—and considered officially as illegal and illegitimate by the state authorities (such as war booty and payments demanded for passage or protection, for example in Cameroon, Chad, the CAR and the former Zaire, but also in Côte d'Ivoire) are nonetheless legitimised both by the local people and, implicitly, by the state authorities.[81]

The behaviour of aid donors and NGOs similarly harks back to two colonial phenomena that remain particularly present in the memories of African societies. It follows the pattern, first, of the colonial administration: donors try today to get involved in local affairs with as much fervour, but also as much ineffectiveness, naiveté and unintended effects as their predecessors, the colonial officials. The value of this comparison is not so much objective—African states' room for manoeuvre is not so insignificant, and resort to coercion is a thing of the past—but subjective, as is suggested by the contemporary rhetoric of the great majority of African intellectuals about recolonisation of the continent. The second register of comparison is that of the Christian missions. The World Bank's catechism, for example, strangely recalls missionary preaching with its obsession with 'good' government, its determination to do 'good', its civilising ambition.[82]

---

[80] See especially Mbembe (note 74); C. Coquéry-Vidrovitch, *Le Congo au temps des grandes compagnies concessionnaires: 1898–1930*, Paris: Ecole Pratique des Hautes Etudes and Mouton, 1972; Laboratoire 'Connaissance du Tiers-Monde', *Entreprises et entrepreneurs en Afrique: XIXe et XXXe siècles*, Paris: L'Harmattan, 1983, 2 vols.

[81] As J. Roitman demonstrates particularly well for the region of the Lake Chad basin in 'The Garrison-Entrepôt', *Cahiers d'Études Africaines* 150–152, XXXVIII (2–4), 1998, pp. 297–329; see also, for Cameroon, K. Bennafla, 'Mbaiboum: un marché au carrefour de frontières multiples', *Autrepart* 6, 1998, pp. 53–72.

[82] B. Hibou (note 3); J.-F. Bayart, 'Fait missionnaire' (note 45); and D. Péclard, 'Ethos missionnaire et esprit du capitalisme: la mission philafricaine en Angola, 1897–1907', *Le Fait Missionnaire* (Lausanne), 1995 (Cahiers 1).

Two other historical experiences characterise the forms of contemporary indirect government. Today as yesterday, rights and rules are characterised by their multiplicity, their flexibility and their instability. Political power was and still is exercised less through fixed rules, universal and applicable to all in all circumstances, than through confirmation of flexible, separate and divisible rights. This has the advantage of allowing constant negotiation and dealing, and hence knowing and sometimes controlling activity, notably economic activity.[83] At the same time, the confusion between 'public' and 'private' does not date from the current privatisation and criminalisation; intermediaries had wealth and power; it was they who ultimately, and often without the agreement or even the precise knowledge of the colonial authorities, collected taxes, recruited men for forced labour, chose others for public works, etc. Mbembe spoke on this point of 'privatisation of chieftaincy': 'The diversion of resources of coercion to private ends eventually came to constitute a characteristic not only of the chieftaincy system, but of the whole colonial set-up also.'[84] Today as yesterday, access to the state is turned into private profit.

Similarly, Chevrier's impressive Chinese portrait helps to comprehend the current process of privatisation of the state in China by reference to 'the overstretched empire'.[85] Privatisation, as the offspring of a history in which institutionalisation was never a power strategy, cannot be interpreted as retreat by the state or by the political, but rather as the capacity of

---

[83] I. Kopytoff wrote notably: 'These sometimes baroque elaborations on rights focusing on sex, labor and progeny reflect a cultural readiness to allow for a great variety of very precise ways of securing various kinds and degrees of control over people. Most of the transactions involved the exchange of one or another kind of right-in-persons for wealth. And, indeed the greater the wealth in kin group, the greater was its capacity to expand its human "capital" and maximise its control over people' (Kopytoff (note 74) p. 46). For an example of this practice today, see S. Berry (note 33), and F. de Boeck, 'Domesticating Diamonds and Dollars: Identity, Expenditure and Sharing in Southwestern Zaire' in P. Geschiere, B. Meyer and P. Pels (eds), *Globalization and Communal Identities*, Oxford: Blackwell, 1998.

[84] Mbembe (note 74), p. 143.

[85] See Y. Chevrier, 'L'Empire distendu: esquisse du politique en Chine des Qing à Deng Xiaoping', pp. 265–395 in Bayart (ed.) (note 45): 'Corruption, wheeling and dealing, straddling between positions of power and positions of accumulation, and crumbling away of power and society are effects of a whole situation brought about by the logic of non-institutionalising of Chinese regimes and the forms of erosion resulting from that. This is the basis of the strategy of circumventing: the spaces of autonomy ("capitalism", the "market") and of informal activity are not only tolerated because the axes of power are not harmed by them; they constitute a structure which does not positively make them official in its institutions but functions only because of them. Far from being a residue or an oddity of identity, which might be "grafted" on to a different history from now on, the socialist nature of the regime is the pole which has made it possible for the reforms to raise the unofficial alongside the official in a distended configuration.' (p. 277)

the political to find a place for the non-institutional, the unofficial, the non-central. In other words, privatisation of the state is not a form of political de-construction or withering of the state, but a wholly separate form of state formation, borrowing, once again, from the circumventing strategy characteristic of the political in China. The de-concentration of power in favour of local authorities is not a process of pure loss; the central power and the public sphere remain decisive in the Chinese economy. They make it possible to earn legal and illegal profits (through public employment, granting of tax privileges, arbitration over professional careers, political relations, etc.) while remaining masters of the rules of the game (as shown by trials for corruption and the definition of rules governing the economic opening to the rest of the world). And even if the state is considered negatively—as a predator, especially—in words and even in some forms of practice, state norms penetrate society, helping to redefine the political.[86] Privatisation of the economy allows not so much control over the people as control over wealth, and especially possibilities of gaining wealth; it allows the renewal of bureaucratic power and moreover its conversion into economic power; it reflects investment by the government in the economy, and creates a fluid situation that has generated the economic miracle and new interests.

Continuity and breaks with the past. The forms of intervention described above share some characteristics: delegation and protection; the presence of the state in an intermittent, fitful way (arbitrariness being in that case a preferred mode of intervening); de-centring of the state administration to more scattered actors or institutions; use of intermediaries and go-betweens including, especially, unofficial and even illegal ones. However, this global trend towards privatisation and indirect modes of management has different meanings according to countries and regions, to the history of each state, each society and relations between state and society. That is the first lesson of the historical experiences recalled earlier; present-day situations, however similar they may look, only have meaning in relation to the past of each of the societies concerned. In all these societies, straddling cannot be seen as an anomaly, or as a transitional phenomenon. It is rather a specific feature of the political field. That is why private management is often the image of public management.

---

[86] J.-L. Rocca, 'La corruption et la communauté. Contre une analyse culturaliste de l'économie chinoise', *Revue Tiers Monde* XXXVII (147), July–September 1996, pp. 689–702; Y. Chevrier, 'Une société infirme: la société chinoise dans la transition modernisatrice' in C. Aubert *et al., La société chinoise après Mao. Entre autorité et modernité*, Paris: Fayard, 1986; J.-L. Rocca, 'La "mise au travail" des Chinois', pp. 47–72 in J.-F. Bayart (ed.), *La réinvention du capitalisme* (note 27), and the chapters by Kernen, Rocca and Chevrier in this volume.

In Tunisia, for example, the philosophy of the *mise à niveau* (modernisation and adjustment) programme, aimed at preparing businesses for the liberal environment arising from the free trade agreement with Europe, has an uncanny resemblance to the previous interventionist and planning period. In sub-Saharan Africa the 'plunder economy' has taken the form of privatisation after that of nationalisation. In Russia, the bureaucracy's way of operating has only changed slightly; even if the Party is no longer dominant, the administration is still accompanied by a parallel set of informal bodies and private and public local interests; civil servants still use their positions to financial advantage, and things still remain opaque. In Indonesia, the language of kinship structures the recent '*reformasi*' period, as it did the New Order before then and, earlier still, the colonial period. And in China the private sector has developed modes of social management (health insurance, unemployment benefit, payment in kind) close to those practiced by state-run enterprises.[87]

These various examples converge, suggesting that contemporary situations are both a global process of diffusion of indirect modes of government, acting through the intermediary of private actors, and a very particular process of continuing state formation in accordance with particular historical trajectories. In emphasising the historical referent we would not want to deny breaks with history, or changes, to declare that there has only been continuity; historical determinism based on that idea would be just as simplistic as the globalisation determinism rejected earlier. On the other hand, I consider that history can be a method of political economy itself; understanding processes of state formation over the *longue durée* can bring out specific processes and forms of construction, 'trajectories' and recurring features that may reveal the uniqueness of the contemporary situation.[88] If there is continuity, it is expressed more by

---

[87] See the chapters by Favarel-Garrigues (on Russia), Bertrand (on Indonesia) and Rocca and Kernen (on China) in this volume.

[88] For the long term perspective, see (obviously) F. Braudel, 'La longue durée', pp. 41–83 in F. Braudel, *Ecrits sur l'Histoire*, Paris: Flammarion, 1985. For a historical approach to analysis of the present, see C. Geertz, *The Interpretation of Cultures. Selected Essays*, New York: Basic Books, 1973 (which speaks of the 'cultural foundations' of the state); Y. Chevrier (note 85) (whose ambition is to develop historical comparative sociology of the political); J.-F. Bayart, 'L'historicité de l'état importé', pp. 11–39, in Bayart (ed.), *La Greffe de l'Etat* (note 45) (which envisages three ways of re-establishing the historically defined nature of the state: the 'becoming' civilisation put forward by Braudel, the structural concatenations through which social inequality develops, and the cultural configurations of the political). On the idea of a 'trajectory' as the historicity of each state formation, see Bayart, *The State in Africa* (note 37), and Bayart (ed.), *La Greffe de l'Etat* (note 45) in which he which adopts Perry Anderson's expression and, only in part, his analysis: '...the diachronic concept of a trajectory, which we have borrowed from Perry Anderson and which emphasises the peculiar historicity of the numerous routes to state

representation and discourse, by historical memory and *imaginaires*, by the transmission of a 'culture' (beliefs and values), than by the existence of stable structures or unchanging cultural, economic or political determinants. If Weberian political economy is adopted—the theory of concomitant formation of the political, the economic, the social and the cultural—the only way to grasp the true meaning of an identical economic reality (meaning, in this case, 'discharge' or private indirect government) is to go back to the history of that systemic construction. Learning only about the varying forms of private indirect government does not really teach us much about what we are trying to understand—that is, to what these new modes of state intervention in the economy correspond.

The place given to history in the interpretation of present-day situations does not mean underestimating breaks with the past, or changes at least, that have occurred. Even though we have related present-day meanings to the past in each society, all the examples quoted above have sought precisely to emphasise what is 'new' in privatisation of the state by comparison with the preceding period. Institutions, norms and legitimate values are no longer the same, as is suggested by the appearance of rhetoric on the 'market', the 'private' sphere and 'networks', and the disappearance of the rhetoric centred around state enterprises and official marketing boards and other bodies. The history which helps us to understand the present does not stop at the beginning of the last century: the idea of 'discharge' and the characteristics we have highlighted should not be understood as suggesting a simple return to the systems of government of the eighteenth and nineteenth centuries. The experience accumulated since that period and, above all, the economic changes that have occurred over a century have thoroughly shaken up both the forms of intervention and its effects. For example, with the opportunities offered by the internationalisation of economies and modernisation of means of communication it is no longer possible to exercise even indirect control as univocal as before over national economies and economic actors; but conversely, thanks to the numerous levers for intervention and increasing possibilities of coordination, these same opportunities can provide the central power with an improved capacity for reducing subordinate actors to submission.

Theorising about these changes is difficult because of the very ambivalence of their effects. However, it is obvious that discontinuities, the product both of international developments (the increased financial orientation

---

formation, directly opposed to the glossy and unhistorical comparative outlook underlying the idea of the "Third World", makes it possible to place the contemporary political sphere under the spotlight of "those layers of slow-moving history", "that depth, that semi-immobility" around which "everything gravitates"' (pp. 16–17).

of markets and their internationalisation, changes in production arising from technological innovation) and domestic ones (weakening of the state's regulatory capacity, or alteration in perceptions and demands in society) have consequences that are too important to neglect. But only through history can we understand how these 'novelties' of global changes produce specific effects and meanings.

'Privatisation' as the uncertain exercise of state power. This passage through history, and the recurrence of 'discharge' today, suggest that the normative value and supposedly universal model of direct government—bureaucratised, permanent and continuous, characteristic of developed countries and of the last few decades—should be relativised. Mediation, especially with private intermediaries, was and remains one method like any other of exercising power. But even so, this should not lead to an excessively functionalist and voluntarist interpretation; privatisation cannot be considered as the result of a deliberate strategy on the part of this or that state, as a choice of one way of governing rather than another. Certainly 'discharge' to private intermediaries may correspond to a gap between increasing demands and limited capacity on the state's part to respond to these in an institutional, formal way. It may also reflect the 'politics of survival' and 'dirty tricks' strategies characteristic of fragmented societies.[89] But more fundamentally, privatisation of the state is the result of multiple, sometimes contradictory strategies, which reflect especially a lack of confidence in state institutions and primacy of allegiance over functional relations.

Privatisation of the state arises not so much from a state strategy for survival or consolidation as from numerous actors or numerous logics of action. There are economic logics: the pursuit of profitability and efficiency in the productive sector and, still more, the search for new economic resources, for new opportunities for enrichment in a context of shrinking direct state revenues and, above all, of dwindling of rents and prebends available for distribution and indirect control over economic activity. Then there are political logics: management of opposed forces that are nonetheless indispensable to the state in a context of fragmentation of society and centres of power, renewal and reconversion of bureaucratic power as economic power dependent on the state, or a strategy of shifting responsibility in the face of social and political protests. And there are social logics: new relationships between states and citizens in a context of debureaucratisation. There are individual and collective logics of social mobility: upward mobility for a class associated with the state or a group of actors,

---

[89] J. Migdal, *Strong Societies and Weak States: State-Society Relations and State Capabilities in the Third World*, Princeton University Press, 1988.

but also possibilities of survival for marginalised groups. There are other logics as well: logics of creation of a new economic space for negotiation of social relations, even for bargaining over them; logics of insertion into the world economy with respect (or an appearance of respect) for conditionalities imposed by aid donors; logics of diversified management of dependence, notably to make the dependence less restrictive; administrative, financial and missionary logics of aid donors and, correspondingly, logics of resistance to those donors; logics of enrichment, logics of patronage, logics of war and conflict—and so on.

Today this tangled web assumes the form of privatisation, especially because of the diffusion of norms and modes (the minimum state, liberalism, privatisation of state enterprises, concession of public services, disengagement of the state, etc.) and of the objective factors of globalisation (the power of multinational firms, major consultancy and insurance companies, audit and evaluation firms, aid donors, the financial markets, communication technology). The very multiplicity of actors and their ambitions rules out a single strategy, even on the part of the state. And if these factors do not necessarily lead to weakening of the state, they nonetheless emphasise its de-institutionalisation.

Is 'discharge' a new form of state intervention?

It is only after this analysis that the varied significance of the processes of state enterprise privatisation can be understood. As Max Weber wrote, externally identical forms of economic organisation can be associated with very different economic ethics, and thus have greatly varying historical consequences according to the different ethics.[90] Historical trajectories on the one hand, and the global trend towards liberalisation and the dominant ideological climate on the other, work together to ensure that privatisation means very different things from one country or region to another.

Taking all the social and political processes mentioned above into consideration, the economic objectives of privatisation are shown to be usually secondary. A new manner of managing enterprises, primacy for criteria of efficiency and profitability, achievement of a true 'market economy', changes in relations between employers and employees, injection of fresh financing—all this is only rarely the most important aspect of transfer of ownership. On the other hand, the modalities and results of

---

[90] M. Weber, *The Sociology of Religion*, tr. E. Fischoff, London: Methuen, 1963 (German original 1922). For a portrayal of privatisation as ideology, see M. A. Bienefeld, 'Structural Adjustment and Prospects for Democracy in Southern Africa', pp. 91–128 in D. Moore and G. Schmitz (eds), *Debating Development Discourse: Institutional and Popular Perspectives*, New York: St Martin's Press and London: Macmillan, 1995.

privatisation of state enterprises are always a reflection of the political system,[91] the historical trajectory of a country and the way in which it is linked to the rest of the world. They reveal the nature of political and economic communities to the extent that the political game is also played—sometimes mostly played—in the economic arena. Privatisation of state enterprises can therefore be simply cosmetic, corresponding to organised resistance or strong entrenchment of political and bureaucratic power.[92] Conversely, it can symbolise a real attempt to break with the previously existing order.[93] But it can also be informal,[94] even unbridled,[95] or captured by parallel networks[96] or used as a channel and means of laundering

[91] Generally and on the level of theory, Linz and Stepan note this regarding various political regimes. According to them, for example, privatisations of state enterprises are capable of challenging a Sultanistic regime, while they only modify the modes of government of an authoritarian regime. See J. Linz and A. Stepan (note 3). For Western countries, H. Feigenbaum, J. Henig and C. Hamnett, *Shrinking the State. The Political Underpinnings of Privatisation*, Cambridge University Press, 1999, show that privatisation of state enterprises is above all a political phenomenon.

[92] As is the case in Iran (see on this point A. Rashidi, 'Privatization Schemes in Iran (1989–1996)', paper delivered to CERI research seminar, 21 March 1997); in Egypt (J. Waterbury, 'The Political Context of Public Sector Reform and Privatization in Egypt, India, Mexico and Turkey', pp. 293–318 in E. N. Suleiman and J. Waterbury (eds), *The Political Economy* (note 2), and J. Waterbury, *Exposed to Innumerable Delusions. Public Enterprise and State Power in Egypt, India, Mexico and Turkey*, Cambridge University Press, 1993); and in a number of African countries (see 'Les privatisations en Afrique subsaharienne: le regard critique du professeur E. Berg', *Marchés Tropicaux et Méditerranéens*, 13 May 1994; *Un continent en transition: l'Afrique subsaharienne au milieu des années 1990*, Washington: World Bank (Africa Region), 'A Continent in Transition: Sub-Saharan Africa in the 1990s' (mimeo, January 1995); *Private Sector Development in Low Income Countries*, Washington, DC: World Bank, January 1996.

[93] See for example François Bafoil's chapter in this volume, which shows how in certain contexts and on certain conditions privatisation of state enterprises can amount to adoption of a new order, new rules and new principles of production.

[94] For informal privatisations, on Mozambique see M. L. Bowen (note 10); on Africa in general, B. Hibou, 'The "Social Capital"' (note 14); on Russia, Favarel-Garrigues (in this volume); and on East European countries, A. Köves, *Central and Eastern European Economies in Transition: the International Dimension*, Boulder, CO: Westview Press, 1992, which speaks of 'privatisation from below'. On China, see J.-L. Rocca, 'L'entreprise, l'entrepreneur et le cadre. Une approche de l'économie chinoise', *Les Etudes du CERI* 14, April 1996.

[95] Unbridled privatisations have taken place above all in civil war situations. For Algeria, see Martinez (note 28); for Angola, M. E. Ferreira, 'Angola: la reconversion économique de la nomenklatura pétrolière', *Politique Africaine* 57, March 1995, pp. 11–26; for Liberia, S. Ellis, 'Liberia 1989–1994: a Study of Ethnic and Spiritual Violence', *African Affairs*, vol. 94 no. 375, 1995, pp. 165–97.

[96] The case of privatisation captured by informal networks is illustrated for Nigeria by W. Reno, 'Old Brigades, Money Bags and Ironies of Reform in Nigeria', *Canadian Journal of African Studies* vol. 27 no. 1, 1993, pp. 66–87; for Africa in general by Hibou, 'The "Social Capital"' (note 14) and H. Bernstein, 'Agricultural Modernization and the Era of

dirty money,[97] thus enabling diffusion of the principle of privatisation to the entire economy and the central power—in which case it reveals a change in modes of governing. This does not mean that when privatisation effectively takes place, these phenomena occur systematically; an interesting example of the contrary occurring is provided by East Germany.[98]

To resume briefly the analysis we have made of various countries: it can be said that in sub-Saharan Africa privatisation of state enterprises has corresponded to a change in the modalities of the 'plunder economy' and the strategy of 'dirty tricks' which has accompanied the changes—notably in the direction of more concealed, even illegal activities—in the economic opportunities of the political world; it has also corresponded to an exacerbation of factional struggles and a strategy of displacement of external rents (notably when, in the course of operations in favour of foreign investors, a portion is reserved for national shareholders or even for the state).[99] In Morocco, privatisation strengthens the Makhzen modes of governing and exercising power in the economic field, with increased concentration of the circle of influential actors.[100] In Tunisia, it has corresponded to a political strategy of fragmentation and division of potential rivals, in a context of hardening of the political regime and its criminalisation.[101]

Structural Adjustment: Observations on Sub-Saharan Africa', *Journal of Peasant Studies* 18 (1), October 1990, pp. 3–35.

[97] For examples of privatisation as means of money laundering, see for Africa, Bayart *et al., The Criminalization of the State in Africa* (note 14); for Russia, G. Favarel-Garrigues (in this volume).

[98] For real alteration in the rules of the game, see F. Bafoil, *Règles et conflits sociaux en Allemagne et en Pologne post-communistes*, Paris: L'Harmattan, 1997.

[99] See B. Hibou, 'The "Social Capital"' (note 14) and 'Political Economy' (note 3); B. Contamin, 'Entreprises publiques et désengagement de l'Etat en Côte d'Ivoire. A la recherche des privatisations', pp. 89–107 in B. Contamin and H. Memel-Fotê (eds) (note 17); P. M. Lewis, 'State, Economy, and Privatization in Nigeria', pp. 210–33, and J. Herbst, 'The Politics of Privatization in Africa', pp. 234–54 in E. Suleiman and J. Waterbury (eds) (note 2). A privatised enterprise is used as a resource, just like the previous state enterprises; the holdings remaining in the hands of the state or the employees (in Mozambique, for example, 20 per cent systematically remains directly in the hands of the leaders) allow for continued possibilities of political management; above all, the re-sale of those holdings to clients, to the Nomenklatura, provides for such management to be continued indirectly. When there is direct sale to the Nomenklatura, the latter can seize great opportunities, even use the business to cover other unregulated forms of commerce (often informal imports) or for money laundering. It is not uncommon to see the normal activities of a business stopping, and privatisation thus amounting to a simple property transaction.

[100] See B. Hibou, 'Les enjeux' (note 29); C. Khosrowshahi, 'Privatization in Morocco: Politics of Development', *Middle East Journal* 51 (2), spring 1997, pp. 242–55; and personal interviews and observation (January and March 1997, June 1998).

[101] Personal interviews and observation (May 1997 and April 1998); B. Hibou, 'Tunisie: le coût d'un "miracle"', *Critique Internationale* 4, summer 1999, pp. 48–56. On the

In East Germany, it has amounted to a process of institutionalisation (notably with apprenticeship for cooperation among actors and assertion of the principles of federalism) and forced integration into the economic and political space structured by West Germany (which included submission to the economic interests of the Western part).[102] In Russia, it has involved a strategy of manipulation, by the Nomenklatura and criminal actors, of their insertion into the state, a renegotiation of centre-periphery relations, and exacerbation of political and factional conflicts in the economic field.[103] Lastly, in China privatisation has been one of the ways in which the 'overstretched state' has taken shape (with continued blurring of legal distinctions between public and private, and the importance of 'intermediaries' or 'interfaces' between business and its environment).[104]

Debates among aid donors, solely centred around the pace and the best procedures for privatisation, reveal ignorance of the fact that any economic process is at the same time a socio-political process and, to use Max Weber's expression, 'The science of economic policy is a political science'.[105] While noting that privatisation favours the authorities in power and sometimes the world of crime, these advocates of 'reform at any price' neglect the perverse effects of privatisation in terms of political significance and in terms of legitimacy.

By emphasising the appearance, or reappearance, of indirect and discontinuous forms of government we have stressed also the changes underway in relations between the public and private spheres. These changes do not necessarily condemn public action, and do not necessarily mean loss of control by the holders of state power; rather, they emphasise the invalidity of the public/private or state/non-state dichotomy put forward in particular

financial side, see H. C. Moore, *The Mediterranean Debt Crescent: Money and Power in Algeria, Egypt, Morocco, Tunisia and Turkey*, Gainesville: University of Florida Press, 1996; and C. M. Henry (note 29).

[102] See F. Bafoil (note 98).

[103] See J. Linz and A. Stepan (note 3); Favarel-Garrigues (in this volume); and G. Favarel-Garrigues, 'La région de Sverdlovsk et le pouvoir de gouverner', *Nouveaux Mondes* 7, winter 1997, pp. 161–91.

[104] See Y. Chevrier, 'L'Empire distendu' (note 85) for the historical interpretation. For modalities of privatisation, J.-L. Rocca, in 'L'entreprise, l'entrepreneur et le cadre' (note 94), shows how all enterprises (public, collective and private) are in both the public and the private domains, and concludes—rightly, it sems to us, regarding other countries too—that it is impossible to pursue analysis in terms of 'ownership of the means of production'.

[105] M. Weber, "The Nation State and Economic Policy" (1895) in M. Weber, *Political Writings*, eds. P. Lassman and R. Speirs, Cambridge University Press, 1994, pp. 1–28.

by the aid donors who are such important actors in 'transitional' and 'developing' countries. Not only are the borders between one domain and the other always blurred, but concrete situations are characterised by practices of straddling and, above all, the multiplicity of forms of property, modes of regulation, legitimacies and interventions. In addition, concepts and representations of the public and the private differ from one society to another, and even from one actor to another. Thus, despite the liberal discourse, privatisation does not involve private actors gaining autonomy, or the mutual autonomisation of the economic and the political. It is a restructuring of ways of being, understanding and acting within political and economic spaces. In concrete terms, what we see here in economic and political practices is the plurality of mixed forms that obscure landmarks and borders, as well as multiple principles of legitimacy that characterise the current processes of economic liberalisation, reform and privatisation.[106]

In addition, as all the examples given above have shown, privatisation, this new way of governing, is not a return to 'the liberalism' of the era before the turn of the twentieth century, before the 'great transformation' described by Polanyi.[107] Privatisation should not be interpreted as an advance of the liberal strategy. In sub-Saharan Africa and the Maghreb (but contributions to this volume suggest that it is true of the other continents also) the private sector remains tied to state power; it does not respect either the rules of competition or free trade, and in a considerable number of countries it has not yet been 'privatised'.[108] This interpretation seems to be confirmed by contemporary research relating to other regions

---

[106] For a good example of this process in other countries than the ones analysed in this volume, see D. Stark, 'Recombinant Property in East European Capitalism', *American Journal of Sociology* 101 (4), January 1996, pp. 993–1027, and D. Stark and M. Bruszt, *Postsocialist Pathways. Transforming Politics and Property in East Central Europe*, Cambridge University Press, 1998.

[107] See *The Great Transformation: The Political and Economic Origins of Our Time*, first published 1944, Boston: Beacon Press, 1957. Polanyi writes particularly: 'Economic history reveals that the emergence of national markets was in no way the result of the gradual and spontaneous emancipation of the economic sphere from governmental control. On the contrary, the market has been the outcome of a conscious and often violent intervention on the part of government which imposed the market organization on society for noneconomic ends.' (p. 250).

[108] According to the observation by John Waterbury. See 'Le potentiel de libéralisation politique au Moyen Orient', pp. 95–128 in G. Salamé (ed.), *Démocraties sans démocrates*, Paris: Fayard, 1994, also published in English as *Democracy without Democrats? The Renewal of Politics in the Muslim World*, London: Tauris, 1994; and (in collaboration with A. Richards), *A Political Economy of the Middle East. State, Classes and Economic Development*, Boulder, CO: Westview Press, 1990.

of the world; economic studies emphasise, more than ever, the mixed character of capitalist economies;[109] political scientists have shown that states have constantly invented new rules of intervention;[110] political economy analyses challenge the principles of separation of state and market or state and society, public and private, official and unofficial, regulated and unregulated.[111]

Contrary to the doctrine of the minimum state, we are not witnessing, with privatisation and promotion of the liberal scriptures, a return to the state as referee; the state and the political in general remain decisive actors in the economy, but their influence is wielded indirectly. Privatisation corresponds not so much to a decline of the public to the advantage of the private as to a new combination of the public and private, and continued exercise of state power and•of the political generally. Similarly, analysing present-day situations in terms of privatisation of the state does not lead to proof of loss of state sovereignty and legitimacy, but contributes to challenging of the narrow and normative conceptions of these notions.

[109] See for example J. R. Hollingsworth and R. Boyer (eds), *Contemporary Capitalism: the Embeddedness of Institutions*, Cambridge University Press, 1997. These works reach the same conclusions put forward for a very long time by historians (like F. Braudel in *Civilisation matérielle, Economie et Capitalisme, XV–XVIIIe siècles*) and heterodox economists (starting with Polanyi).

[110] See the various contributions to J.-F. Bayart (ed.), *La réinvention du capitalisme* (note 27), especially Bayart's introduction, 'L'invention paradoxale de la modernité économique' (pp. 9–43); E. Cohen, *La tentation hexagonale*, Paris: Fayard, 1996; L. Weiss, *The Myth of the Powerless State*, Ithaca, NY: Cornell University Press, 1998; N. Spulber, *Redefining the State. Privatization and Welfare Reform in Industrial and Transitional Economies*, Cambridge University Press, 1997; L. Rouban, 'Les Etats occidentaux d'une gouvernementalité à une autre', *Critique Internationale* 1, Autumn 1998, pp. 131–49; and S. Sassen, *Losing Control? Sovereignty in an Age of Globalization*, New York: Columbia University Press, 1996.

[111] See for example, for Africa, G. Kitching (note 37); J. P. Warnier, *L'esprit d'entreprise au Cameroun*, Paris: Karthala, 1993 ('Les Afriques' series); E. Grégoire and P. Labazée (eds), *Grands commerçants d'Afrique de l'Ouest: logiques et pratiques d'un groupe d'hommes d'affaires contemporains,* Paris: Karthala-ORSTOM, 1993; J. Coussy, 'Les ruses de l'Etat minimum', pp. 227–48 in Bayart (ed.), *La réinvention du capitalisme* (note 27); S. Ellis and Y.-A. Fauré (eds), *Entreprises et entrepreneurs africains*, Paris: Karthala-ORSTOM, 1995; B. Hibou, *L'Afrique est-elle protectionniste?* (note 4). For Latin America, see B. Lautier, C. de Miras and A. Morice, *L'Etat et l'informel*, Paris: L'Harmattan, 1991. For China, see Chevrier (note 85) and Rocca (note 94). For Western countries, see H. Feienbaum, J. Henig and C. Hamnett (note 91).

Part I

THE PRIVATISATION OF PUBLIC ENTERPRISES

When 'privatisation' is mentioned, the first notion that comes to mind is naturally the privatisation of state enterprises. That reform is now so widespread that it has become one of the main symbols of the much vaunted globalisation process of modern times. To the extent that enterprises are the essential units of the 'market economy' which reforms are seeking to impose, changes occurring among them ought to inform us about the adoption or, alternatively, rejection of the market economy. Are we finally witnessing convergence of modes of management according to liberal principles? Or the autonomisation of the economic in relation to the political? Or the primacy of criteria of management, profitability, competitiveness? Or the domination of private norms over public ones, of economic referents over political ones, of neutral intervention over partisan intervention? In short, are we witnessing a break with the previous order, necessary for the spread of the market economy?

This is not clear, since there are so many facets of privatisation. Above all, it is difficult to analyse the privatisation of state enterprises in purely economic terms. Looked at more closely, privatisation is much more than the simple transfer of ownership, the alteration of the rules of management, the injection of new capital of a different sort, or the advent of new qualifications and modern technology. In reality, the ways in which privatisation takes place are very revealing of political situations and change— or, conversely, continuity—in modes of governing.

On the one hand, apart from the incidence of corruption and appropriation by political elites, privatisation is a stake in power relations. For that very reason, business enterprises are especially privileged sites for observing social and political change in 'transitional' or 'developing' countries. On the other hand, withdrawal by the state is, of course, neither homogeneous nor total; if the state disengages from direct management of productive enterprises, it is redeployed simultaneously in the management of the social realm, in modernisation policies, or in the management of external economic relations.

Lastly, privatisation is seldom synonymous with an abrupt break with the past; the most normal situations are rather typified by a variety of mixed forms (of ownership especially, but also of the exercise of power), by fluid situations and a multiplicity of rules or even of principles of legitimacy and authority. This underlines even more strongly the significance of overlapping between the economic and the political. Indeed, analysis of the privatisation of state enterprises serves not so much to describe a dimension of the economic globalisation process as to inform us about the social and political realities of the states where these operations take place.

2

FROM CORRUPTION TO REGULATION: POST-COMMUNIST ENTERPRISES IN POLAND

François Bafoil

In 1990, when Communism was collapsing in Central and Eastern Europe, privatisation of formerly collectivised economies was the cornerstone of the change of system. Radical transformation of property rights was supposed to lead to behaviour adapted to the new economic relations. Now, almost ten years after the initial decisions, the rules in force do not correspond really to what had been expected, the former behaviour has not disappeared, and, further, social relations in business matters often reveal a return to the former compromises.

This is seen widely in the structure of ownership in Poland. The state sector, at the end of 1997, was still employing nearly 45 per cent of workers, and above all, it still had majority control over the energy, chemicals, mining,[1]

---

[1] The mining sector undoubtedly poses, with agriculture, the most acute problem for Poland's entry into Europe. In 1990 it employed 320,000 people, which meant that more than a million depended directly on it. In addition, this sector is concentrated in a reduced area, 90 per cent of which is in Upper Silesia. After the failure of several reconstruction plans which, in the first years of the decade, led to major strikes, the new government, although dominated by the Solidarity coalition, drew up a reform programme providing for closure of 24 mines employing 40,000 miners. This plan was not made public, for fear of a general strike. By 2002 Poland was supposed to have carried out a programme aimed at reducing production from 121 to 112 million tonnes, but above all reducing the number of miners from 240,000 to 126,000. There are proposals to privatise the seven holding companies which own 57 mines and to give a 10 per cent share of capital to managers. This reform will cost 6.2 billion zlotys (about £1.2 billion); of this three quarters are

and steel[2] sectors. Many enterprises, still dependent on state power but required to reform in the medium term, had come under the public Treasury.[3] The transformation of ownership rights—former state enterprises are now Treasury companies—has not meant fundamental change, even though they are certainly obliged to adapt to the rules of the market. State subsidies remain vital for their survival. The private sector, for its part, is far from homogeneous.[4] It includes, firstly, small and medium enterprises, in fact microscopic in size, which show very active development but also great instability;[5] secondly, enterprises left in the hands of their former employees through Management Buy Outs (MBO);[6] and thirdly, enterprises acquired by foreign investors.[7]

How to explain this discrepancy between the expectations in 1990 and the results obtained today? First, it should be emphasised that changes in ownership rights alone are not enough to ensure necessary changes in behaviour, unless they are accompanied by establishment of external controls,

expected to go on social costs. The cumulative total of debts, social costs (social security) and tax arrears will cost the state 13.6 billion zlotys (about £2.7 billion). Cf. F. Bafoil, 'The Silesian Question: an Economic or a Political Solution?', pp. 81–116, in Collegium Budapest, *Strains of Postcommunism*, Budapest: Collegium Budapest, 1998 (Workshop Series no. 4).

[2] Only a few steelworks have been privatised, like the big enterprises in Warsaw sold to the Lucchini group of Italy.

[3] The enterprises coming under the State Treasury were liquidated as collective enterprises and turned into Treasury companies, as a preliminary to privatisation or bankruptcy and definitive liquidation. Among them must be included 15 National Investment Funds, whose portfolios include management of about 600 enterprises which they are restructuring with a view to privatisation.

[4] Except for the latter, the scarce data available on private enterprises speak of long working hours, wages below public sector wages, lack of respect for social laws, and, in several cases, dissolution of trade union organisations. See F. Bafoil, *Règles et conflits sociaux en Allemagne et en Pologne post-communiste*, Paris: L'Harmattan, 1997.

[5] The rate of bankruptcy in the year of their creation was about two-thirds. These businesses rarely have more than two employees; the domestic economy is dominant.

[6] These Management Buyouts, involving transfers of ownership either to the employees as a whole or to the executives, are widely criticised, on the grounds that ownership rights are very imprecise and open to manipulation. Some observers note that enterprises like these have nonetheless encouraged social peace and ensured productivity levels higher than those recorded in state enterprises. See M. Jarosz (ed.), *Management Employee Buy-Out*, Warsaw: PAN-ISP, 1995.

[7] Foreign direct investment passed the $10 billion barrier in Poland at the end of 1996, and this sector demonstrates very vigorous dynamism. At the end of 1997 it was providing about 20 per cent of total employment (compared with 35 per cent in Hungary). The sectors which attract foreign buyers are obviously the most profitable: the motor industry, telecommunications, building materials, agro-food industries, etc. In contrast, the sectors showing little dynamism, such as textiles and garments, remain in the hands of local investors. This is true of Eastern and Central Europe as a whole. See F. Bafoil (ed.), *Les stratégies allemandes en Europe de l'Est*, Paris: L'Harmattan, 1997 (Pays de l'Est series).

which alone can ensure respect for regulation. The imposition of 'harsh' budgetary restraint may turn out to be insufficient if managers responsible for enterprises can with complete impunity fix the rules of the game, rearrange resources accumulated before, and maintain their domination almost unchanged. In other words, without regulation from outside it seems difficult to imagine any real change. But on the other hand, where one sees former executives retaining their posts, does this mean that the balances built in during the last forty years are permanent, and there is no change?

The distinction between regulation from within and regulation from outside is a useful one both to mark out different periods and to isolate their actors, differing but still confronted by identical questions. Those questions have turned on adaptation of behaviour to local contexts. Questions about the nature of regulation applied in differing ways in post-Communist enterprises are thus included in reflection on 'institutional apprenticeship', in which the ideas of continuity, duration and complexity are most prominent. That is what the idea of 'path dependency', widely used in the study of post-Soviet economies,[8] involves.

Our contribution to this debate has two aims. The first is to determine the limits within which an approach of the 'path dependency' type can be applied and those within which, conversely, a theory of contract is possible. The former term relates to permanence of collective ties, the latter to a break in those ties through the establishment of more individual relations. The question is how far the rearrangement of previous resources can be continued, and what costs may be incurred, when an attempt is made to impose regulation of change from outside. That leads us to embark on an initial classification of post-Communist changes on the basis of behaviour which, in enterprises, is aimed either at respecting 'harsh restraint' or at getting round it. Several categories are important: corruption, uncertainty, compromise, violence.

The empirical basis for this work consists of the findings of investigations in April and July 1997 in three Polish cement works taken over by a French group in 1995.[9] The objective was to study the actions of various

---

[8] G. Grabher, 'Neue zur Rolle des historischen Erbes in der Reorganisation von Betrieben und Regionen in Brandenburg', WZB Paper, FS I 96–194, Wissenschaftszentrum Berlin für Sozialforschung (WZB) 1996; D. Stark, 'Recombinant Property in East European Capitalism', *American Journal of Sociology* 4, 1996, pp. 993–1927; B. Chavance and O. Magnin, 'L'émergence d'économies mixtes "dépendantes du chemin" dans l'Europe centrale post-socialiste', pp. 115–53, in R. Delorme (ed.), *A l'Est du nouveau*, Paris: Harmattan, 1996; A. Rona Tas, 'Path Dependency and Capital Theory: Sociology of the Post-Communist Transformation', *East European Politics and Societies* 12 (1), pp. 107–31; D. Stark and M. Bruszt, *Postsocialist Pathways. Transforming Politics and Property in East Central Europe*, Cambridge University Press, 1998; F. Bafoil, *Le post-communisme en Europe*, Paris: La Découverte, 1999 (Repères series).

[9] The first survey was conducted over seven weeks, in April and during the summer of

managers to cope with a number of constraints that became apparent before and after 1995. In one case, where the former directors retained their posts, the question facing them was how to get round the new owner-ship rights in order to keep their margins of power intact. In other cases, the question was radically different. There it was a question of knowing what costs might be incurred by a Western buyer who decided to impose the rules of the market. Questions focused on the strategies applied to re-duce or even end the uncertainty aroused by possible defection of part-ners. The concept of uncertainty is understood here in the most classic sociological sense: as a resource manipulated for the purpose of increas-ing the margin of play for a partner holding strategic information.[10] Hence the questions posed in terms of violence of intervention to impose the rules of the market, and the need to understand the market as a field of struggle among several actors, some being groups organised for mono-poly of resources while others are isolated individuals whose freedom of choice is very limited.

How has reinvestment of resources, combined with diversion of capaci-ties in enterprises, allowed some groups to ensure their capacity for action at the national level, and in fact to strengthen it, since 1990? To under-stand this, we should concentrate first on the idea of corruption. We shall then be in a position to understand the questions that have been faced locally by a Western purchaser. That purchaser, anxious to impose change,

---

1997. There were 82 individual interviews and six collective ones, with workers of the three teams of the K. enterprise. The three sites acquired from 1995 onwards by the L. group account for 20.5 per cent of the Polish national cement market. The first 'K.' enterprise consisted of three production locations (two quarries, a lime plant and a cement factory built in 1972); 1,300 were employed there at the end of 1996. Located 30 km from the big city of Bydgoszcz, it enjoys a monopoly position in northern Poland. Its technology is old, using the wet process. The management, closely linked to the trade unions, had powerful connections at the level of the regional and national political authorities. The second site is about 30 km from Radom, in a region particularly affected by unemployment (more than 33 per cent in July 1997) and distinguished by a particular social category: worker-peasants. This cement plant, the first built after the war, employs about a thousand workers since 1990. There too the technology is old—the wet process also—but above all, the management has not adapted to changes made necessary by privatisation. Corruption is considerable. The last site is the Malogoszcz site near Kielce, employing 750 people. The peculiar feature of this plant is less to do with its use of mod-ern technology—the dry process—than with the personality of its manager who has been able since 1990 to initiate a very major process of change. It was at his instigation that M. embarked on the road to ISO 9002 certification. In that respect it is the second enterprise in that sector in Poland. I have analysed the forms of paternalist and authoritarian domi-nation exerted by its manager and the managerial staff in an article in Polish: F. Bafoil, 'Zmiana w przedsiebiorstwie. Tradycja, Charisma czy Reguly w organizacjach', *Przeglad Socjologyczny* 1 XLVII, pp. 145–66.

[10] M. Crozier and E. Friedberg, *L'acteur et le système*, Paris: Seuil, 1977.

has had to reduce the effects of a dual heritage: the impediments peculiar to the Communist system and the obstacles arising from changes achieved since 1990. The concept of strategic uncertainty is essential here. On the basis of some conclusions drawn from our case study, in conclusion we shall try to make a preliminary classification of post-Communist industrial enterprises with varying national configurations.

Corruption as a social transaction

Corruption can be defined in the most general way as the use of a position of authority to ensure transformation of public resources into private assets. This definition is not very far from that of Palmier, who says corruption is 'the acquisition of forbidden benefits by officials or employees, so bringing into question their loyalty to their employers';[11] or from Jean-Gustave Padioleau's definition as 'the use of favours to make a politician or official act against his duty'.[12] But is it possible to distinguish corruption in the Communist system from corruption in the political system of the free market?

Before 1990. It seems that in both systems, Communist and capitalist, corruption illustrates a special case of a social transaction marked by obscurity. The uncertainty of the results comes from the very fragility of the dealings. The other side of the bargain, indeed, may never appear, and the resulting debt may remain unpaid with impunity. In both cases, too, corruption is defined in relation to established references, and to gaps appearing between norms no longer regarded as valid and others trying to assert themselves. This makes it possible to understand changes in representation and in attitudes to practices that were considered, until a certain moment, to go without saying, to be normal. Centralised systems can thus be described as entities dominated by a 'supernorm' whose extension leads in practice to efforts to get round it. Corruption is in the image of the bureaucratic vicious circle analysed by Michel Crozier: at the same time as it contradicts the existing order, it ensures continued functioning of that order by other means. If it becomes general, it stops the machine working. Granted all this, it seems that the phenomenon of corruption in the former Communist regimes reflects peculiar aspects related to the nature of the political system—in other words, to Soviet-type authority and organisation.

The very nature of the centralised Soviet economy accounts for the presence of informal elements within it; without them that economy, also

---

[11] Quoted in L. T. Holmes and W. Roszkowski, *Changing Rules. Polish Political and Economic Transformation in Comparative Perspective*, Warsaw: PAN-IPS, 1997.

[12] J.-G. Padioleau, *L'Etat au concret*, Paris: PUF, 1982 ('Sociologie' series).

called a shortage economy, would never have been able to function. Because centralised planning reigned supreme but, at the same time, planners could not foresee everything, an enterprise that wished to implement its plan needed to find by its own methods resources that were inevitably lacking. The development of informal networks met that need. For that reason a certain actor acquired a very special place in a Soviet enterprise: the Tolkash, whose task was to establish relations with suppliers to ensure supplies that were lacking. Because of the advanced degree of integration that characterised enterprises under that regime, in reality informal relations made it possible for the entire economy to function. In the absence of clear signals such as prices (they were fixed by the administration) or customers (who had no choice but took anything they could find) there remained barter, a more or less collective equivalent of individual resourcefulness. The Tolkash had the very precise task of exchanging goods that were not comparable, so as to ensure that things cohered generally. In short, that network of reciprocal giving stabilised economic and social transactions. It guaranteed supplies, kept relations going in the long term through proven practice of gifts and concessions, and, lastly, provided a basis for political stability by establishing networks of customers at the discretion of the authorities.

In these conditions corruption was the name given to what went beyond good sense—the good sense of dealings that were 'bent' but kept within the limits of non-ostentatious social practices. In other words, corruption was a label that the authorities could easily decide to apply as a convenient way to get rid of too visible signs of self-enrichment, through purges. The 'corrupt' and other 'rotten' elements were most often marked out for popular anger for having failed in their duty of discretion.

It has thus been possible to analyse the Soviet-type economy as a collection of markets of different colours, indicating levels of political tolerance and all, without exception, characterised by uncertainty about how far they really extended. In other words, while legality, in order to function, could not do without informal rules, on the other hand the use of those rules could face repressive action at any moment. The economist Katsenelinboingen identified, first, the 'red markets' whose prices were fixed by the state, in which sellers had important capacity for manipulation at their disposal, as they could put people further forward or back in the queue. Then there were the 'grey markets', informal networks par excellence, filling gaps left by the state but at the risk of interruption at any moment. The 'brown markets' indicated that the limits for individuals claiming a special right to use of public property were exceeded. As for 'black markets', they were illicit phenomena of exploitation and speculation.[13]

---

[13] A. Katsenelinboingen, 'Colored Markets in the Soviet Union', *Soviet Studies*, vol. 29 no. 1, January 1997, pp. 62–85; G. Duchêne, 'L'officiel et le parallèle dans l'économie

In short, in the Soviet-type economy, corruption was, from the organisational viewpoint, related to practices of barter and informal trading; regarding the foundations of domination, it related to practices of patronage and paternalism; lastly, as regards representation, it related to the uncertain, fluctuating character of the just and unjust, of what was permitted, tolerated or forbidden. So once the inherent constraints in this sort of system had disappeared, how were transactions conducted? More precisely, in view of the uncertainties linked to the innovative character of privatisation legislation from 1991 onwards, how were changes in ownership carried out?

Considering Poland alone, it seems that misappropriation of public property was massive towards the end of Communist domination. Many authors have exposed the process by which public resources were appropriated by the political authorities in charge under the last Communist government, that of Mieczyslaw Rakowski.[14] Taking advantage of economic liberalisation laws, and notably of the possibility of creating private enterprises, political leaders of the Communist Party, or others close to the Party, built up business enterprises from scratch with capital from public funds. Thus, in January 1990, several small companies were registered by the regional authorities in most of the big cities, all belonging to former leading figures of the Party, some with the objective of ensuring local economic development. Afterwards it was through them that some financial flows, notably from the European Union, transited. Similarly, several members of the former Nomenklatura set up banks whose portfolios included state enterprises to be sold later at favourable prices to their customers, also former members of the Nomenklatura. According to a number of observers, enterprises linked to foreign trade were the ones that lent themselves most to massive embezzlement by former senior officials who acquired them or else, again, disposed of them at favourable prices. People thus talked of 'hybrid capitalism'[15] to highlight both the combinations of private and public capital and the networks linking the new managers

---

soviétique', *Libre* 7, 1980, pp. 151–88. This recalls in some ways Arnold Heidenheimer's analyses showing that corruption markets can be distinguished according to the perception that citizens and those in authority have of them. In this analysis 'white' markets have some justification among both types of actor; 'black' markets are condemned by both; and 'grey' markets reflect divergent views between the two. A. Heidenheimer (ed.), *Political Corruption*, New York: Rinehart and Winter, 1970.

[14] J. Staniszkis, 'Political Capitalism in Poland', *East European Politics and Societies* 5, 1991, pp. 127–41; W. Roszkowski, 'The Afterlife of Communism in Poland', pp. 83–111, in L. Holmes and W. Roszkowski (ed.) (note 11).

[15] J. Staniszkis, 'Polityka postkommunistycznej institucjonalizacji w perspektywie historycznej' (Politics of post-Communist institutionalisation in historical perspective), *Studia Polityczne* 5, 1996, pp. 5–25.

with leaders of the post-Communist political parties, especially the Peasant Party. Insider dealing, though it was never called by that name, was very common. Scandals and bribery made the headlines on a large scale; the press sometimes went so far as to lump together the misappropriation of public property by the former Red Nomenklatura and the acquiring of positions of responsibility by the new leaders of Solidarity. Such phenomena of reproduction of elites have been analysed similarly in the cases of the Czech Republic[16] and Hungary.[17]

1990–1995. Let us consider now the results of our empirical investigations. The phenomena we discerned in the cement works do not contradict this general impression; quite the contrary, they complement it on many points. To make clearer the means used for reprocessing of resources existing before, we can distinguish three levels, which are three power networks varying according to their more or less organised aspect: the levels of political contacts and bureaucratic contacts, and one relating to the internal situation within the enterprise. In the post-Communist period it was the last-named that allowed the other two to get reorganised. The central organisations—of the Communist Party and administration type—may well have been liquidated, but their leading figures found a way to get a new form of value for their resources by posing as partners in business. In other words, for the leading office holders in various organs of power, change involved turning the ties of dependence organised and cemented within a centralised political system, in which business played only a minimal role, into less formalised ties of partnership around a pivot, the pivot being business in a free market economy. What is analysed in terms of informal networks or cronyism at the political level can be understood in terms of arrangements in the economic arena, and more widely in terms of a network on the social plane. The term 'network' on its own seems to refer more to something organised, whereas 'informal networks' relate rather to sentiment (corporate sentiment, notably) or alternatively to informal arrangements.

First, the political relations network. We shall hardly go into any detail on this point, except to highlight a fairly common phenomenon in the Communist economy: managers of major enterprises were strongly integrated into the political hierarchy. This integration had to do firstly with the Party organisation proper, with its regional representatives—devolved

---

[16] E. Hanley, P. Mateju, K. Vlachova and J. Krejci, *The Making of Post-Communist Elites in Eastern Europe*, Prague: Institute of Sociology, 1996 (Working Paper, 96/3).

[17] For Hungary, see E. Hankiss, *East European Alternatives*, Oxford: Clarendon Press, 1990; I. Szelenyi, *The Rise of Managerialism: the 'New Class' after the Fall of Communism*, Budapest: Collegium Budapest, Institute for Advanced Studies, 1995 (Discussion Paper).

grades of the central authority, and thus key elements in the equilibrium of the Communist system—and also its commune-level representatives; secondly, with the national political fora, in the image of the Central Committee. The leading executives of the three cement production sites were all, in one way or another, members of regional and local executive commissions, and in the case of the first, the general manager of the K. combine, a member of the Central Committee. In view of this, what sort of lucrative services were the political leaders whose organisations were dissolved in 1990 able to offer to their former protégés? In the absence of irrefutable proof, we have to be content with hypotheses and to suppose that the ties of comradeship woven through long experience of power allowed certain redundant Party officials to find new jobs in industrial units formerly coming under their jurisdiction. Meanwhile the renewed vigour which the Communist Party's heir, the SLP, was able to find after 1994, and its place as the leading party in the Voivodship from 1994 onwards, probably favoured reinstatement of the former elites.

The second network was the one represented by the central bureaucratic organisations. Making lucrative use of accumulated resources was much easier for them because of the material resources that could be put to use and turned into cash immediately by former officials. The creation of intermediary companies between enterprises and individual customers contributed to this considerably. How should one understand this? Within the Ministry of Construction the main cement site managers and senior officials of the administration formed the Cement Commission, which was responsible for fixing quantities to be produced and the allocating funds for investment. The heads of the Foreign Trade bureaux, on their part, had prerogatives related to the monopoly position they held in respect of exports, especially allocation of foreign currency. Indeed an enterprise could not sell its products itself without passing through those bureaux, except, of course, for barter deals whose ultimate aim was not making money. After 1990 these people profited widely from their positions acquired under the old regime and easily adapted to work as intermediaries or dealers, this time private ones. This was all the easier for them because they were the only ones who knew the state of distribution, the executives of the business enterprises, and, perhaps still more important, the customers. All this was without any major financial outlay—having an office, a telephone and a fax close to the cement products silos was enough. In the three cases studied these dealers were former senior officials of the pre-1990 cement administration.

The third network is the internal network in the enterprise. There the rearrangement of resources has taken place through a share-out of the enterprise among some people. Some departmental or workshop managers in fact privatised their sector of activity, taking machinery and staff with them, without leaving the site itself. In other words, there were units in differing situations side by side on the enterprise's premises, some of them not paying any dues, however small, to the mother enterprise. This happened on a massive scale in two sectors, road transport and mechanical and electrical maintenance. The advantage of such a procedure was considerable. It not only made it possible to talk of privatisation, it contributed to staff reductions—about 300 jobs were 'privatised' in this way; in addition, it enabled new contractual regulations to be drawn up. The contracts signed between the general manager of a site and the new managers of privatised units included preferential clauses for the first year following privatisation, on condition of maintaining jobs. These clauses were subsequently extended at the level of orders from the 'mother firm', though the reciprocal obligations were not always respected. It should be noted, lastly, that contracts drawn up in top secrecy in respect of the enterprise's employees laid down higher pay for those 'leaving', though that clause does not seem to have been maintained in the long term. Besides this share-out there was establishment of new enterprises. For example, a company entrusted with supplying cement powder to the K. cement works was established by three major shareholders—one third being held by the enterprise as a whole, another third by outside suppliers, and another by the six most prominent managers on the site.

These few data explain how positions acquired under the old regime were, in the absence of an external buyer, the main factor in the process of transformation of public ownership, and how this subsequently opened the way—in the absence, still, of a third party guarantor—to large-scale embezzlement. The concept of corruption—meaning, as defined above, the use of positions of authority for private acquisition of public property—was made easier by a legal framework that allowed for privatisation or else for the establishment of third companies. The process of transformation involved altering the nature of the relationships formed between the various political, administrative and economic departments, in the direction of greater flexibility of the organisations. Their more flexible and informal character did not however exclude contractual procedures. If it is possible to speak of corruption in this connection, it is because the procedures followed, besides being not at all public, made skilful use of the legal provisions in force. This happened with the partial 'privatisations'. It is also noticeable in the phenomenon of arrangements, as illustrated by the case of the cement powder supply company mentioned above. In that case the private suppliers, like the managers, had an interest in increasing prices so that the third shareholder, the enterprise itself, paid major costs and in that way increased the dividends of the other two. There was another type of arrangement also: directing orders to one single contractor for repairs, supplies or transport, whose managers were all former subordinate staff of the general manager who instigated the privatisation.

For this reason the form of domination peculiar to this first period of post-Communist change seems not to have been fundamentally different from that of the Communist period, except that the guarantee represented by political authority was successfully replaced by a legal guarantee. Within a framework that was in general a very relaxed one—the privatisation framework devised after considerable hesitation in 1990—these senior executives were able to fall on their feet well, so as to take advantage of their positions, make rearrangements regarding their foreign and domestic customers, and avoid touching the internal organisation completely. To understand this one should no doubt bear in mind the formidable spirit of change that was blowing then, and the determination to transform the public structure of ownership. That is what the 'old-new' managers did, while maintaining employment overall. This 'spirit' brought with it extreme respect for individual initiative and a rejection of decisions made at the centre, and that correspondingly encouraged the aims of local actors.

The varied forms of behaviour that were tolerated because of corruption under the old regime led also to a view of public property—the state or the state enterprise—as goods to be appropriated, something to be pocketed. Thus it was possible to gain the support of the workforce passively, without it being expressed openly, so long as the privatisation contracts for 'private' companies guaranteed jobs. In some case there was no strengthening of control measures for work discipline. Misappropriation of cement for private use did not stop. To sum up, at least in the first two cases studied, domination was maintained externally by perfection of arrangement procedures, internally by the sharing out of prerogatives.

What did the trade unions do about this? At first it seems they did nothing, or almost nothing, as they proved so incapable of playing any positive role. Should one go so far as to think that they actively backed management in its strategies of coping with the constraints of the free market? Yes, probably. On the first site, several people to whom we spoke mentioned a 'clan', meaning the senior administrative staff as a whole, including the unions. The latter expressed no opposition to transfers of jobs and did nothing to improve working conditions. Worse still, they allowed staff canteens to be abolished at the end of 1995 without a word of protest. On the second site studied, the trade unions were shoved aside, given no consideration either by management or by the staff, who were unanimous in emphasising their incompetence. As for the third site, the manager found a way to keep the unions at arm's length, acting in a quasi-autocratic fashion, and at the same time involve them in decision making, giving them prerogatives in management of the social side.

But given all this, to reduce their activity to corruption alone would be going too far. In the post-Communist period the unions retained powerful means of bargaining in public enterprises.[18] In the cement production facilities this meant that they were able to negotiate with a buyer a clause providing for maintenance of jobs for three years following signature, together with a second clause stating that in the fourth year job cuts could not exceed 10 per cent. That could be the explanation of the fairly high rate of unionisation, about 50 per cent on the three sites.

But it was precisely that job guarantee, voluntarily accepted by the foreign buyer, which was an intolerable constraint for him, one that he never stopped getting round—that, indeed, became the basic axis of his strategy for imposing of rules. The handling of uncertainty turned out to be decisive in his attempts to counteract the opportunism of the national partners—exposing the duality of regulation, which produced order and disorder at the same time.

Regulation and rational order

The new rules of the game were based at first on clarity of procedures, that is, on their intelligibility where pay was concerned; every employee could understand the information provided on his pay slip; at the level of different contracts (notably involving subcontracting) the expectations expressed were laid down. That meant that ideas of assessment and controls were considered important, as they alone could ensure checking of the procedures to which parties were committed—both at the level of maintenance (with follow-up after breakdowns and repairs) and at the level of establishment of ISO standards (with precise definition of tasks and responsibilities). Because of this the idea of coordination covered a double reality: individualisation of tasks and cooperation among the various employees of a department and among departments. With general contractualising of relations ties of allegiance, whether internal or external, disappeared.

But over this movement to impose clear and supervised imposition of regulations, corresponding to a logic of action widely accepted as valid because of its effectiveness in the West, was superimposed a second, radically different movement, which can be analysed in terms of a strategy of violence. To get round the constraints regarding staffing, though these had been initially agreed with the trade unions, the buyer of the enterprise did not hesitate to embark on a social plan whose consequences in terms of

[18] M. Jarosz, *Foreign Owners and Polish Employees of Privatized Enterprises*, Warsaw: PAN-ISP, 1997.

disorder and anxiety were considerable. The manipulation of uncertainty thus went together with strict respect for normative rules.

A gamble. Examining the strategies developed by the French group indicates how the search for compromise prevailed initially. Far from going for a complete sweeping takeover, which would have meant the immediate removal of the former executives, the French initially put their trust in cooperation. Ignorance of the language is obviously not enough to explain this, if only because other foreign investors, with equally little knowledge of Polish, preferred to proceed to immediate and radical replacement of the management. The decision to 'duplicate' the existing hierarchy with a small team of a few French people corresponded rather with the experience of the group itself, which had adopted such a strategy in East Germany.[19] It had a deeper significance also: local actors on each site were the ones to develop an enterprise, and not the group. In other words, while L. certainly had regulations for validity in matters of quality and control, there was no question of imposing a single organisation for all its enterprises. This preference for cooperation was also reinforced by the special ways in which the sites were acquired. There had been a good deal of hostility towards applicants for takeovers in general, and this explains why the French group, to win the contract, had to sign a guarantee of maintaining jobs mentioned earlier.

The idea of integrated apprenticeship—that is, gradual and smooth delegation of responsibilities—was thus predominant in an initial phase. But, little by little, this turned out to be a real gamble, difficult to maintain in the long term because of the lack of confidence displayed by some Polish managers. In the short term such a strategy was interpreted by the local actors as delegation to national managers, even as letting them get on with the job. Keeping the management in place meant encouraging a feeling of uncertainty which on this occasion seriously damaged the interests of the French, once a period considered reasonable for assessing a situation correctly had passed. Misappropriation of cement continued; the hostility of a certain section of the management was manifest; and meanwhile, the changes accomplished were not visible. The determination to impose clear rules of the game, based on dealings and communications among the groups, was threatened with failure if the French persisted in their reluctance to 'take the reins'. That was done in the spring of 1997. On the first site the two leading managers were removed and replaced by two French

---

[19] I have analysed the procedures for change installed by the same Western buyer in the enterprise that he took over in 1990 in Saxe-Anhalt in East Germany in F. Bafoil and O. Giraud, 'Les changements dans l'entreprise K', *Les Cahiers de l'Observatoire de Berlin* 9, 1991.

expatriates. On the second an indirect manoeuvre was used, since the management was subject to the authority of the manager of the third site, who was given the task of imposing the changes that he had already carried out in his enterprise.

Clarity and cohesion. The various reorganisation moves were aimed on the one hand at simplicity and functional autonomy, on the other at achieving coherence among the elements involved in intervention. As far as reform of pay agreements was concerned, the scales were clearly redefined and qualifications were made to correspond with jobs. Various additions to basic pay were abolished—a sign that the period when benefits in kind (such as coal tokens or butter) were dominant had ended. As well as technical points concerning income brackets and criteria (whose number was increased), and overtime pay and the consideration of experience in additions to basic pay, the new agreements sought to differentiate the categories of workers and executives, indicating the nature of responsibilities involved in the allocation of bonuses.

As for the internal organisation of an enterprise, the prevailing idea was to justify levels of competence and, accordingly, reduce the importance of hierarchical levels, to abolish intermediate grades, to decentralise responsibility to the level of operators and to strengthen cooperation. This implied giving more importance to the productive sector, always marginalised under the old regime, and admitting its senior manager to the plant management council. The autonomous management of mechanical and electrical maintenance was abolished and the workshops were shared out under the responsibility of the production sectors. This change has been considered one of the most important reforms, as that autonomous management had previously been so much a true 'fief', distinct from production but dominating it by forcing its executives to make constant demands to get satisfaction; similarly, the chief engineer of the mechanical and electrical sector had enjoyed considerable power of control. Quality control positions were also placed under the responsibility of the production manager.

At the level of financial and accounts administration, the nature of the elements making up costs and the ways of breaking down the various operations were the object of attention. For that purpose the methods of calculation had to be reversed. Previously, they started from the rock in the quarry and followed the various components at the level of cement production, up to sale. In calculation of energy it was not the calorific capacity expressed in joules that was considered, but the cost of coal per tonne (and it mattered little what might be added to that, straw or whatever). The rational approach, in this case, involved breaking down the various elements entering into calculations—which supposed a knowledge of operations at production level and an effective system of communica-tion—taking the physical measurement of energy into account, and, lastly, establishing points of exchange among the various offices. The lat-ter had previously been responsible for different functions, such as pro-duction of analytical accounts (that is, figures) and of accounts of results according to activity (economic analysis).

The same logic—knowing the elements of fields of intervention, search-ing for information and coherence of action—prevailed in the changes affecting sales departments. Previously confined to the basements of fac-tories, the sales staff sometimes had no cars for official travel, no files of customers and no operational strategy. Now they were obliged not only to become acquainted with products and markets but also to pass on custom-ers' demands to the production departments, to make enquiries about achievement of quality norms—in short, to take account of demands made.

The field of subcontracting was also tackled, starting with the establish-ment of procedures for contractual relations excluding any special rela-tionship with any partner. At the end of 1997 relations with 300 private transporters engaged in retail delivery to the enterprise had been placed on a contractual basis. This also led directly to the order to all the repair workshops that had previously been part of the enterprise to move out of the site. Having been 'privatised' in the first post-Communist years according to the rules examined earlier, they had obtained the right not only to stay within the perimeter of the combine but to enjoy guarantees of contracts for annual repairs, which were important contracts.[20] They were obliged to find premises outside, in a very short time. Meanwhile, con-tracts for foreseeable repairs (80 per cent of the total) were drawn up on the basis of tenders and submission of estimates showing very precisely all elements of the calculation. It was in this way that in 1998 a subcon-tracting enterprise, employing 300 workers and formerly a workshop within the combine, risked bankruptcy because of a higher estimate than that submitted by a competitor in another region. As for uncertain re-pairs—those which might not happen for various reasons—estimates were also demanded from subcontractors, but without any commitment on the part of the party wanting them.

---

[20] Identical relations were recorded in East Germany in 1990, when the law required enter-prises, former combines, to accord contracts of limited duration to their sections which had gained autonomy, allowing them to make the transition to accounting autonomy. But these contracts were part of a system of reciprocal obligations that reinforced the charac-ter of the law. In fact they were the counterpart of the obligation for the sections gaining autonomy to guarantee a year's employment to their workers. In other words, the former mother enterprise committed itself for one year to provide work for its former depart-ment which, in return, promised not to lay off the workers who all came from the former mother house. After one year, the rules of the market prevailed.

Lastly, the application of ISO standard certification on the third site seems to have epitomised these various demands and imposed discipline and order unknown until then. In this task efforts to define individual and collective procedures in matters concerning controls and checks were joined together; so it can be considered as a typical example of the rule of rational regulation. In this process there was proliferation of red tape, whose dimensions cause one to wonder, lastly, about the impulse behind the decision to impose ISO standards; its ultimate effect seems to be not so much the quality of the product as the strengthening of a system of order.

The reign of standards. The adoption of the ISO 9002[21] regulations is of considerable interest. Adherence to ISO standards was certainly one of the main sources of order in post-Communist enterprises, since it truly marked the end of Communist-style improvisation. There were quality standards before 1990, just as there was a formal organisational structure and definition of tasks, etc. But the centralised nature of planning, the presence of irrational elements such as the domination of the Communist Party in enterprises, and the subordination of economic sectors to the demands of quantity ruined all sources of order. General confusion prevailed. Results were measured in terms of breakdowns, incidents, patching-up and accumulation of spare parts and manpower. But now, imposition of adherence to ISO standards prevented any such ways of getting round the rules. If an operator could not decide on something, he could refer immediately to the book of instructions. Looked at from a strictly bureaucratic point of view, ISO was the source of collective action.

Regulation, in addition, was not just a simple imposition from above. Considered in the abstract, ISO 9002 proclaimed general principles. Valid

---

[21] Certification of the ISO 9002 standard was linked to the writing of a book, *The Book of Quality Reports (Ksiega jakosci)*, signed by the Chairman. This was the basic document, since by laying down everyone's responsibilities in matters relating to quality, it was geared to emphasising respect for ISO standards in the enterprise. In this document were found the description of the enterprise (the historical circumstances of its establishment, its product range), the organisation and departments, and an exposition of the process of checking, its area of extension, the controls and procedures, training and, finally, an organisational chart and a graph of the production sites. In the booklet on quality procedures, the operations are: elaboration, definition, checking, confirmation, duplicating, updating, conservation, record keeping. As for the areas of intervention, they relate to tenders, trade, documentation on construction, technical documentation, purchasing, production, control, research, reception, normalisation, training, and organisation of staff and customers. Every operation is then formulated precisely in the document. Then the procedure is laid down explicitly in a 66-line table which sets out instructions with, in nine columns, checking and control operations (elaboration, checks, confirmation, disclosure, etc.) that the various partners in the enterprise must carry out. In this way each section lays down the role of actors and their cooperation in a given field for an operation.

for all industries and all branches, it represented the most general form of quality requirement. Hence the way it was interpreted was essential. Executives interviewed were insistent on this point. In fact it was up to each department to accomplish its tasks in accordance with the standard's requirements—though in conformity with the process within which it was operating—and more precisely with the task to be done. Hence the multiplicity of procedures for one point of the standard, and, as a consequence, the multiplicity of instructions.

Let us take the example of the idea of 'product'. According to the 9002 standard, there was one single definition. But for the quality control management of the third cement production example studied, the definition covered two products, clinker and cement, but not additions such as gypsum, sand or—still less—machinery. And yet the general definition included these. Hence the manager was obliged to refer the matter to a consultancy firm outside the establishment, so as to bring his definition properly into line with what was expected. Thus a distinction was made between finished products (cement and clinker), products included in the course of production (stone) and additional raw materials such as gypsum. Interpretation was thus a dual process of examination and consultation, internally and externally, the differing definitions being aimed at adapting the enterprise to the expectations based on the standard.

The standard, being a source of discipline, generated a hierarchical order.[22] The chairman had to sign the final text that was supposed to be certified; the production manager had to confirm the various procedures; the head of each department had to set out each procedure; the foreman had to issue instructions.

The standard, lastly, was a work of coordination. Individuals' tasks were included in a chain of control which strengthened the cooperation programmed at the departmental level and among departments. Thus meetings were held after working hours of everyone involved in a department. From March to July 1997 two or three meetings per week brought the executives of various departments together to adjust procedures. The decentralising of controls and checks at the level of implementation thus went together with a test of collective coordination. While it was up to each department to define its own procedures, it was just as much its task to coordinate them with other departments, on the one hand, and with the quality control department on the other. The checking test was a test of compatibility. Collective efficiency could be measured in this way, since each operator's adherence to special instructions depended on the other operators following the same procedures. One of the sources of order was

---

[22] 'You don't argue, you show respect; it is very restricting perhaps, but very efficient', said a mechanical and electrical maintenance executive.

based on this point. What might have been interpreted elsewhere as a source of increased bureaucratisation, and for some actors (like the manager in charge of electrical maintenance) as extra useless paperwork, was nonetheless generally analysed as one of the very first sources of order in an enterprise, whose absence in the years before 1990 had penalised Polish enterprises considerably.

But that was where the shoe pinched. Imposition of the ISO standard reflected, very precisely, the suppression of the last acts of resistance against the domination of the third site's manager. The standard not only conferred appearance and procedures of the highest rationality on the manager, it gave his initiatives the blessing of an external authority all the more unchallengeable because German services were involved (TÜV). So one can understand that some observers in the West, on the basis of similar experiences, considered the two types of bureaucracy—the Communist and free market type—in parallel, so as to suggest that they were much the same. One can certainly reply to this that in the one system bureaucracy was the expression of totalitarian domination producing disorder, while in the other it was subjected to rules of rational calculation. The legality of procedures was the distinguishing element here. The growth of written standards of reference is inescapable, and its objective, in the opinion of everyone we spoke to, is supposed to be not the production of confusion, but that of its opposite—clarity. In so far as any change in organisation has to be recorded in a procedural document, it ought to follow that on that particular point arbitrariness is removed. But for precisely those reasons, this can lead to fear of the direct opposite of the legal-rational order, that is, formalism. The ISO standard could carry the seeds of irrationality within itself, through an overabundance of regulations.

These questions have been raised about some enterprises in the West.[23] In the post-Communist economies, at least in our example, it seems still to be rather a question of an imitation effect, a sort of initiative aiming to cling more closely to Western patterns, on the part of leaders concerned above all else to consolidate their margins of power and strengthen power that is to a great extent bureaucratic.

Uncertainty and violence in the post-Communist order

That the various modernisation movements encountered difficulties seems obvious. In addition to the strengthening of discipline accompanying the establishment of the new procedures, the changes at the level of the organisational chart aroused the most questioning—especially the abolition of

[23] D. Segrestin, 'La normalisation de la qualité et l'évolution des relations de production', *Revue d'Économie Industrielle* 75, 1995, pp. 291–307.

some hierarchical categories, such as the brigade members who were defined under the former regime as the first workers in the group (the brigade), and who had no Western equivalent. Almost all the brigade members became ordinary workers again, while on the third site the rationalisation effort was applied on a massive scale to the posts of foremen, the first category in the hierarchy. Discontent seems to have been profound, especially as many posts of assistant head of sector or department were abolished at the same time—in short, very many grades that had extended the hierarchical lineage to five or six levels of responsibility. In this particular case the abolition of these grades led to the departure of almost all the individuals concerned.

Strategic uncertainty. The extent of the changes introduced in the three cases studied raises questions about the procedures laid down to operate this rationalisation of jobs and hierarchical lineages. For while nobody disputes or could ever dispute the overstaffing of Soviet-type enterprises (the observation is valid for these three cases), it is still best to state precisely where this overstaffing was manifested, what posts had to be abolished, to give way to what type of new post on the basis of what technological modernisation. In other words, before severe cuts were started in all departments there was supposed to be an exact knowledge of the relations between tasks and posts, and a final plan, or at least a staged plan, for job rationalisation. To be effective, such a plan had to be coupled with a second, relating to modernisation of equipment. Separating those two logics of change would inevitably increase uncertainty and, as a result, the anxieties of the workers. In fact disorder increased precisely as a result of a time lag between different change procedures and lack of preparation for some measures, in the absence of a shared development vision.

When the modes of application of the social plan decided in the spring of 1997 are examined, the incoherence and disorder that occurred can rather be interpreted as elements of a strategy embellished with some more or less well founded arguments. First of all, that social plan was decided so as to reduce the constraints deriving from the initial purchase clause. In taking over the first two sites, L. promised not to modify the number of jobs at all for three years. It was only on that condition that it had had any hope of winning the contract. This was a difficult constraint to endure, one suspects, considering the initial staff of about a thousand workers on the Polish sites, while less than two hundred were needed to operate such a plant in the West. The only strategy that had a chance of avoiding the fury of the regional authorities, wary where jobs were concerned, was one based on voluntary departure of workers.[24]

---

[24] The labour office, at the Voivodship level, in fact guaranteed the validity of contracts made between the various partners in enterprises for collective bargaining and, more

To encourage this, the French team drew up a plan for bonuses reduced over time; the first bonus offer allowed a worker to pocket the equivalent of two years' gross salary, the second one year's and the third six months' salary. Anyone who wanted to take advantage of this offer had to inform his superior who had to countersign the application. In the absence of precise criteria concerning the age and qualifications of people leaving, there was considerable chaos in several departments, especially production departments. Very many workers, mostly young ones, took advantage of the windfall to leave the factory. They were followed by several older workers, who were favoured by a clause of the plan laying down that people near retirement could benefit by the plan's provisions while still applying for early retirement. There was considerable disruption for some departments that were forced to cope, in a few weeks, with the departure of almost half of their staff.[25] The voluntary staff retrenchment measures, then, were applied without being concerted with the hierarchy, and without any examination of posts that might be replaced at short notice.

Here one is tempted to interpret the place of uncertainty in the most classical terminology of organisational sociology—that is, as a resource at the disposal of purchasers, manipulated by them to impose their vision of the game, and used by them to destabilise partners, in other words, to force them to choose.[26] With our examples, what has uncertainty comprised? Basically, silence over the employment target to be achieved. The purchaser based his strategy of circumventing obstacles on that uncertainty. In short, uncertainty definitely bears the image, here, of a game between players of very uneven ability, of whom one kept the initiative while the other adjusted his decisions on the basis of limited representations of possible gains.

Two elements are decisive: inequality and time. The partners were certainly unequal, since the purchaser had more power in his hands than the workers, even if he was not sheltered from unforeseen reaction of a violent sort. The employment constraint, and group pressure over objectives to be achieved, were too important for irresolution to be tolerated for very long. Power in an enterprise going through restructuring is not exchanged, at the most it is acquired by certain groups of workers on condition of adapta-

---

widely, for everything relating to social law. From the moment when the French group decided to get round its initial commitment to maintaining staff strength, through application of a negotiated social plan, it had to obtain not only the agreement of the social partners but also that of the regional employment office.

[25] The disorder was all the greater because these measures took effect in the middle of the summer, the season when activity involving cement reaches its annual maximum. Besides this pressure there were the exceptional conditions due to floods during July 1997.

[26] M. Crozier and E. Friedberg (note 10); E. Friedberg, *Le pouvoir de la règle*, Paris: Seuil, 1993.

tion. In other words, the weight of a group is often measured by its capacity for strict adjustment to the desires of the purchaser. The ideas of a game played around regulation, appropriation, or autonomy do not seem relevant for analysis of this period of post-Communist change; on the other hand, the idea of control by the hierarchy is the widely dominant one. Finally, time is an essential resource for all the players, for calculation of the best opportunities; but there again, it has to be admitted that uncertainty is unequally shared according to one's position.

In response to criticism of this absence of criteria, senior French executives said that this was, on the contrary, a relevant method of identifying the workers who felt attached to the site and parting company with those who wanted to leave. This was a fallacious argument, since it is easy to understand that some could leave saying that it was better to do so immediately with the lump sum offered, rather than later under redundancy. In fact it was a doubly fallacious argument, considering that the purchaser had never made it clear himself which posts had to be maintained over the long term. In reality, beyond his stated justifications, the purchaser's strategy aimed at facing the workers with contradictory choices, for which they had only minimal information. On the one hand, the workers had to assess themselves and commit themselves at the risk of losing out. On the other hand, various senior executives had to find the necessary human resources in their departments. They were obliged to get to know the abilities of their workers, even if it was after all admitted, in private, that a burner could not be replaced immediately, any more than an electrician or a mechanic could.

Acquisition of status. This was a violent strategy, for it showed little regard for the immediate consequences at the workshop level. It makes it possible to understand an essential aspect of the very nature of the post-Communist transition. The way in which uncertainty was handled throws new light on the *sine qua non* condition for application of the new rules of the game: freedom. Individual workers were in effect called upon to be free, that is, forced to choose; that meant that they could either lose or gain. But they could only know what would happen after realisation of many possibilities which they were not in a position to weigh up. That was true of people who decided to leave, whose chances of opening a shop or a workshop in a more or less favourable environment depended on conditions that fluctuated a great deal;[27] also of those who decided to stay in the

---

[27] In the first years of the process of change, the risk involved in opening a worksite shop, a repair workshop or a drinking establishment was not very great, in view of the scarcity of such businesses before 1990. Eight years later the local Polish economic structure was saturated with these small trading or service units, production units being much rarer.

enterprise, whose jobs might be preserved, but certainly not in the existing state. Uncertainty obscured every stage of decision making and accordingly limited ability to make a judgment. However, this obligation to gamble was a foundation of social transactions, for it thrust dealings outside the enterprise. Individual freedom—even if it was constrained to a great extent—is an indicator of numerous possible social roles.

One can certainly argue that freedom was an illusion to the extent that people were forced to be free, that is, obliged to make a choice, all the more so as the risk of making the wrong choice was very high. One might conclude that here was a process of alienation, all the more profound because it was dressed up in the illusion of free choice. But such a view is contradicted by a very concrete phenomenon: very many people took advantage of the offer made. Almost 400 did so on the first site, nearly 300 on the second, 100 on the third. Unless one assumes that they were totally irrational—which would mean defining what 'true' rational behaviour would be in this case—it must be admitted that they made a choice in their own interest, even without sufficient knowledge. That is in fact the basis of the idea of contract, since those who stayed accepted the rules of the game, the new procedures and the principles of action. What matters is to recognise properly that in driving out of the enterprise some transactions formerly included within it, this strategy forced other actors to play their part. In this way the actors in public community institutions were now called upon to take charge of social policy or apprenticeship.

It should be recalled here that the redundancy scheme applied on the first two sites was accompanied by employment support and enterprise creation measures which had few equivalents in post-Communist Poland. By creating an employment cell out of nothing and transferring several workers to it, with the task of managing the files of people wanting to leave, the purchasing firm was not only seeking to reassure the state authorities, who were satisfied with the compensation measures but worried about the expected increase in the number of unemployed. It was seeking above all to take part, as far as possible, in the revitalising of an economy profoundly disrupted by collapses and bankruptcies of all sorts. Aid for new enterprises was an example; placing the employment cell at the disposal of local communities in the area was another. We would be inclined to think that these were cases—if surprising ones—of what is usually called 'institutional apprenticeship'; by transferring a procedure that was common in its relations with the environment in the West, the group joined in

---

What is lacking is rather intermediate units. Very few small and medium enterprises employ more than 200 people in rural areas. In addition, workers who choose to leave have few qualifications; those who want to start their own businesses are therefore very likely to try in sectors already full.

the creation of hitherto unknown forms of partnership. The paradox, of course, was that all this was based on the expulsion of a large number of people.

This process of expulsion seen in the enterprise was also found at the level of organisations responsible for employment, regionally and locally. Those offices were anxious to retain only the 'noble' part of 'active' policies of struggle against unemployment, and so widely favoured aid to enterprises, while aiming to pass on 'less profitable' aid (such as aid to local public works) to local self-management bodies. In so doing they contributed to the creation of a vicious circle in which enterprises wanting to take advantage of this aid sacked workers so as to employ better those covered by government aid.[28] Lastly, as the number covered was insufficient (about 50 per cent of the unemployed received unemployment benefit), a large number of them[29] were thrown onto public assistance, which for its part did not have sufficient means to take responsibility for them. So for the great majority of excluded people there was only one worthwhile remedy: using one's own resources and cheating the system, which the state authorities encouraged on a wide scale; probably one of the peculiar features of this in Poland, unlike Western societies, was the strong support it received from the domestic sphere in the form of moonlighting.[30]

Finally, widening the range of choice was evidence of departing from tradition with its limited possibilities for transactions. Instead of the representation of the individual's unshakeable attachment to his group, often identified with only one place, and the feeling of an unchangeable old order which was widely characteristic of the Communist order, there was now a representation of mobility, plurality and variety. On this point contracts formalised circumscribed relations linked to individual services and expected reciprocal gains. Contracts no longer represented a guarantee valid for all eternity, giving protection against all hazards. They were valid only for a certain time, whose limits were agreed between the contracting parties. It would be possible to break down the various elements con-

---

[28] There occurred then precisely what is called in the West the 'windfall effect', which helped to make some social benefits superfluous.

[29] People who had exhausted their entitlements were to a great extent unqualified people, single women and active older people.

[30] The second part of the inquiry, carried out this time in June and July 1998 in the environment of the cement works, analysed the generalised exclusion procedures followed by the state authorities and the creation of an economy firmly included in the domestic sphere—which therefore took care of a good deal of social control. It was there that the very strong development of 'shops' and other micro-enterprises, which fashion the Polish economic landscape today, took root (F. Bafoil, 'Les dynamiques sociales dans les PECO', pp. 115–35, in M. Frybes (ed.), *Les transformations en Europe centrale et orientale*, Paris: La Découverte, 1998; F. Bafoil, 'Contrats, règles et relations informelles en Allemagne de l'Est, Pologne et Bulgarie', *Revue d'études comparatives Est-Ouest* 3, 1998, pp. 85–110).

stituting employment relations and emphasise the guarantees given. Let it suffice here to stress that the two orders are radically different: as opposed—radically opposed—to lack of determination of priorities and lack of differentiation in people's status, both of which had led to generalised confusion in Communist enterprises, now there was distinction among the economic, political and social orders, precise criteria, and validity of various controls within the enterprise, developing in the free market.

But it is clear also that the freedom imposed by the purchaser could turn out eventually to be a fairly slender gain, by comparison with the guarantees provided under the former regime. Thus one can understand the mental processes through which an idealised comforting past comes to be reassessed.

Rejecting the past and bringing it back. This is all the easier to understand because production workers did not grasp the logic of action aimed at simplifying the various organisational or pay-related elements. The abolition of equivalents and other pay additions, now included in calculation of basic pay, was experienced as a loss. It was on that point that the trade unions were the object of sharpest recriminations on the part of the workers who felt they had been swallowed up and were victims of the changes. Many of them thought the unions had discredited themselves by not defending their own interests, rather giving in to the bosses' orders.[31] Together with reproaches against the unions there developed criticism of the whole new pay system, accused of favouring white collar workers above all, reducing the foremen's margins of manoeuvre, increasing the distance between overseers and workers and strengthening the power of the bosses.[32]

Behind these criticisms was denunciation and rejection of all the changes accomplished since 1990, in the first period and then in the second. The first changes were considered to have been carried out by corrupt individuals responsible for the decayed state of the installations and only concerned with their clan interests. On the basis of this sentiment one can understand better the expectations placed in the group taking over the enterprise—expectations of better working conditions, repair of the workshops, pay increases, technological investment, maintenance of jobs, etc. But in fact the changes introduced by the Western group were dominated by uncertainty over jobs. To this was added other uncertainty connected

---

[31] 'I was with Solidarity but I left it. While the unions are in charge of the factory they do nothing for the workers' (packing worker); 'The unions have very little interest in us. Of course you see them before the elections, but none of them show concern for us' (kiln burner). 'The union dances when the boss says' (kiln overseer).

[32] 'The executives who are in charge should earn more, but without too much difference. The office up there, what does it do? They drink coffee and they earn twice as much as us' (grinding worker).

with the time lag necessary for technological investment whose cost was often close to a billion francs. The regrading of certain jobs considered indispensable did not occur, and as the decline connected notably with voluntary departures accelerated meanwhile, all things together helped to encourage a feeling of rejection unpropitious for any mobilisation—and, in addition, a reassessment of some aspects of the former collective life, in the form of regret for the loss of social relations previously assured by the Communist Party.[33]

Conclusion: an initial classification

It seems that to identify the areas of true change in post-Communist enterprises, a fault line must be brought in, to separate an endogenous process, producing corruption especially, and an exogenous process, producing both integration within the enterprise and exclusion outside it. Two provisional conclusions can be drawn from our research.

The first is a fact established: it seems that major enterprises formerly subjected to the rules of centralised planning cannot embark on the road to restructuring without a contribution of foreign capital. In other words, only constraint from outside can make change possible. Conversely, without an external impulse the balances created during the Communist period tend to prove self-perpetuating, together with the phenomena of barter and corruption. The second conclusion concerns the radical break that the free market calls for. Domination by regulation implies destruction of the ties of personal loyalty and fidelity. Its basis lies in the individualisation of positions and functions, as the sole guarantee of cohesion of aims collectively accepted as rational.[34]

On the basis of this twofold observation, we can now attempt an initial classification of post-Communist industrial enterprises belonging to several countries. The criteria for differentiation relate to the varying ownership rights and to managers' capacity for adaptation to 'harsh constraint'. In some cases it has been possible to mitigate this constraint through revaluing of previous resources, in other words, reconversion of assets linked

---

[33] 'The contact between the overseer and worker has been broken. It was there before. The responsibilities were the same among us; before, he was our equal; sometimes it happened that he could come at night, now that no longer happens' (burner, night shift). 'Before, the worker had somewhere to complain to. The foremen, the overseer, there was always someone; the Party, even if it did not sort things out with words, gave some consolation. If you went to the union, you could get some help. But now? The unions don't help the workers.' (grinding worker).

[34] M. R. Lepsius, 'Die Institutionenordnung als Rahmenbedingung der Sozialgeschichte der DDR', pp. 17–30, in H. Kaelbe, J. Kocka and H. Zwahr (eds), *Sozialgeschichte der DDR*, Berlin: Klett Cotta, 1994.

to hierarchical positions occupied in the old system. In other cases, the former vertical or horizontal networks have been completely done away with.

In this study the first phase of transition has been identified as a time of rearrangement of resources at the disposal of the former elites, on the lines of private appropriation, through manipulation of legal methods. This rearrangement was accompanied by a limited reorganisation of the enterprise, leading to reconstruction of some former balances on the basis of personal relations. Spaces for exchange were organised, reducing the intervention of outside agents. The constraints of the market were made less severe in this way. The result was phenomena of corruption, prevarication, deception, and coming to arrangements.

Such observations, limited to the first period of post-Communist transition, are not far removed from those recorded for Hungarian and Czech enterprises; in both those countries the term 'mixed economy' has been widely used to describe the phenomenon of overlapping of public and private assets within the new forms of ownership.[35] That overlapping includes varied cross-shareholding among public and private actors, and central coordination through management of the accumulated debt, as well as the reproduction of a certain number of institutional blockages. In both cases the renewal of former links in fact led to a return to the institutional blockages of the pre-1990 period, which are the basis of interpretation in terms of 'path dependency': through them horizontal and vertical networks were revived, leading to forms of paternalist domination peculiar to the former system.

In the Hungarian case the processes of deconcentration and privatisation led, for example, to the creation of 'satellites', subcontractors of the main enterprise, dependent on it in accordance with the risks and shares that the managers granted to themselves. This process was accompanied by reconcentration of powers at the level of the state, which was able to control the debt accumulated by the enterprises through the establishment of new banks—and in that way to have powerful means of pressure on their managers.[36]

---

[35] G.-A. Dermott, *Renegotiating the Ties that Bind: The Limit of Privatization in the Czech Republic*, 1994 (WZB-Papers, Fs 94–101, Wissenschaftszentrum Berlin für Sozialforschung); D. Stark (note 8); J. Kornai, 'Paying the Bill for Goulash Communism. Hungarian Development and Macro-Stabilization in a Political Economy Perspective', Budapest: Collegium Budapest, Institute for Advanced Studies, 1996 (Discussion Papers, 23); B. Chavance and G. Magnin (note 8); R. Frydman, C. W. Gray and A. Rapaczynski (eds), *Corporate Governance in Europe and Russia*, vol. 1, 2, Washington, DC: World Bank, 1998.

[36] For David Stark (note 8), 'Recombinant property is a form of organisational hedging or portfolio management, in which actors respond to uncertainty in the organisational

In the Czech Republic case, overlapping of ownership favoured former local networks composed of managers and local communities, strengthening the ties of autarky developed in the days of the former Czechoslovakia. Companies thus remained confined within the complex of former relations, assuming collectively the risks attached to changes in ownership. Such coalitions were in a position to block the bankruptcy law which, if it had been implemented, would have inevitably led to the collapse of a very large number of enterprises. In 1991 total debts amounted to 66 per cent of GDP (compared with 46 per cent in Hungary and 30 per cent in Poland); 80 per cent of enterprises found it impossible to honour their debts. Because of the high degree of monopolisation, criss-crossing of inter-enterprise debts, and the considerable holdings of banks in enterprises, the bankruptcy law was quite simply suspended by the state. This rethinking had the effect of reasserting the power of the informal ties that typically linked enterprises among themselves in former times, as well as the intensity of formal ties within regional industrial unions. The crisis that broke out in 1997 had its origin in this confusion of private and public, to which Vaclav Klaus' rhetoric added, mixing liberal slogans with the maintenance of former balances.

Some studies carried out in Russia lead partially to the same conclusion. In fact, in the absence of regulation brought in from outside, the risks of institutional blockages are considerable: the overlapping of new ownership rights with hierarchical posts held under the old regime leads at the same time to reconstitution of the former power networks, blurring of differences between control groups within the enterprises and external to them, and the emergence of very numerous conflicts over areas of competence. The application of ownership rights was thus distinct from the exercise of real control in an enterprise.[37] Hence the exclusion of non-executive staff from the game and the primacy of managers, one of whose main preoccupations was guaranteeing satisfaction of their personal interests, at the expense of any collective consideration.[38] The reproduction of

environment by diversifying their assets, redefining and combining resources. It is an attempt to hold resources that can be justified or assessed by more than one standard or measure'.

[37] V. Kabaline, 'Privatization and Restructing of Enterprises: under "Insider" or "Outsider" Control', pp. 241–89, in S. Clarke (ed.), *Conflict and Change in the Russian Industrial Enterprise*, Aldershot: Edward Elgar, 1995; V. Kouznetzov, 'Un point de vue sur la privatisation en Russie', pp. 155–64, in R. Delorme (ed.) (note 8); R. Bim, 'Ownership and Control of Russian Enterprises and Strategies of Shareholders', *Communist Economies and Economic Transformation* 4, 1996, pp. 471–500; L. Cook and V. Gimpelson, 'Exit and Voice in Russian Managers' Privatisation Strategies', *Communist Economies and Economic Transformation* 4, 1995, pp. 465–84.

[38] I. Gurkov and G. Asselberg, 'Ownership and Control in Russian Privatised Companies:

paternalist forms of domination was strengthened by this, as well as the reproduction of community spirit in the enterprise; in other words, what happened was a reinforcement of traditional domination.[39] For these reasons, comparisons made with mafioso systems can be accepted.[40] The extreme aspect of the Russian experience, by comparison with the reality of Polish, Hungarian and Czech enterprises, probably lay in the absence of legal guarantees (in the form of independent institutions), the presence of a generalised barter system, and the massive prevalence of relations of loyalty or private subordination, within varied organisational forms: kinship, the corporation, the clan, the mafia, the criminal organisation.

The German example is radically different from this picture. For three reasons at least, the break with the old system was complete, which meant completely different strategies.[41] First, the resources accumulated under the old regime were massively wiped out by the monetary union on 1 July 1990. The conversion of the sums invoiced into deutsche marks ruined in one blow contracts signed within the framework of the former Comecon. The radical imposition of an economic regime dominated by demand automatically ruled out any reconversion of resources derived from a supply-dominated system. The transfer of regulations, technical standards and modes of representation of interests was wholesale, and this reduced the possibilities of local adjustments by enterprises. Meanwhile, because of the nature of the West German system of industrial relations the trade unions were thrust aside, outside the enterprise; while within enterprises, on the other hand, works councils had to be set up. Companies taking over enterprises were therefore forced to look for strategic support among the technical staff of the enterprise, and not from 'representative' organisations that were discredited and confined to very limited redistribution functions. Lastly, a considerable 'social net' peculiar to West German law limited the harsh social impact of the inevitable staff reductions in enterprises. It was possible to experiment with forms of compromise with professional actors and with government officials who had plentiful resources—especially financial, but also in terms of experience. Private costs were cut in this way, while public costs increased.

Evidence from a Survey', *Communist Economies and Economic Transformation* 4, 1995, pp. 195–211.

[39] M. Brie, 'Russland. Die versteckten Rationalitäten anomisch-spontaner Wandlungsprozesse', pp. 44–61, in H. Rudolph (ed.), 'Geplanter Wandel, Ungeplante Wirkungen', *Jahrbuch WZB*, 1996.

[40] F. Varese, 'Is Sicily the Future for Russia? Private Protection and the Rise of the Russian Mafia', *Archives Européennes de Sociologie* XXXV, 1996, pp. 224–58. See also G. Favarel-Garrigues' chapter in this volume.

[41] For bibliographical references on the special features of the East German industrial situation, see F. Bafoil, 'Les apprentissages de la transition est-allemande', *Sociologie du Travail* 2, 1996, pp. 163–78.

In contrast, it was possible in Poland to reduce the burden of 'harsh constraint' on a wide scale. No crushing psychological defeat happened. The trade unions remained important partners in some circumstances. Local authorities and regions showed a damaging lack of financial resources or competence, which among other consequences led actors to reshape some of the former compromises, undoubtedly to the detriment of full effectiveness of free market regulation—but also for the good of continued social peace.

3

SHENYANG, PRIVATISATION IN THE VANGUARD OF CHINESE SOCIALISM

Antoine Kernen

Since 1978 the Chinese reformers have embarked on gradual liberalisation of the economy. This process, already continuing for some time, remains a very special case because, especially, of the rate at which it is pursued. While China is joining in the privatisation trend, the economic reforms, carried out in stages, have had important consequences for the form that process has taken. Until the 15th Congress of the Chinese Communist Party, which met in September 1997, the rare formal sales of enterprises still had an experimental character. And even after that date, sales of state enterprises' assets were part of their transformation into shareholding enterprises, which makes it generally possible to avoid the term 'privatisation'. However, for over twenty years, while experiments were made with 'Socialism with Chinese characteristics' and then a 'Socialist market economy', covert privatisation has occurred. A gradual withdrawal of the state from direct management of the economy, not admitted for a long time, has occurred outside the private sector. Today, while that long phase of hidden privatisation is being completed, it appears that the emergence of a small private sector relatively independent of political authority has served as a bluff to mask other, more powerful logics of social recomposition. Privatisation has developed essentially within the administration and state enterprises.

The absence of a formal process of ownership transfer has had certain consequences. It has encouraged the—often illegal—appropriation of economic resources by the ruling elites of the country, thanks to continued vagueness surrounding definition of ownership. Since then China, which some had imagined to be on a disciplined march towards modernity, has appeared corrupt, inegalitarian and even mafia-like. Because of the increase in economic crime the image of an absentee state developed. Through a great variety of approaches and aspects, Sinologists have for about twenty years simultaneously depicted an all-powerful state and described its erosion under the impact of a multiplying social networks. This idea of an all-compassing but eroded state was useful, but it is time to go beyond it. Adopting some elements of the analysis set out above by Béatrice Hibou, we shall be suggesting the hypothesis that the Chinese state is not simply breaking up before our eyes. It continues to build itself up through the daily practices of actors.

The corruption cases that have recently shaken the city of Shenyang provide a useful example. Today the Chinese and international press describes the former mayor as a person who enriched himself by offering protection and respectability to a mafioso businessman of the city, controlling the drugs and cigarettes traffic and a good deal of the prostitution. And yet when Mu Suixin, a young mayor of under 40, took the reins of the municipal authority in 1997, he represented a break with the image of an ageing and corrupt 'conservative' leadership. By his attitude and his statements, he aimed to breathe new life, a life of openness and modern ideas, into a city caught up in the problems of conversion of its heavy industry. The dashing Mu Suixin was to be found everywhere on the local scene, but he also travelled the world in search of investors. In his public performances he was distinguished by his tone and his audacity, as when he proposed to sell about a hundred enterprises for one symbolic yuan. And that dynamism was not just a façade: he put his ideas into action by starting major infrastructure works, remodelling the city centre and increasing foreign investment.

This example shows that privatisation cannot be summed up as the autonomisation and the—real enough—criminalisation of a section of the bureaucracy. It is best to go beyond that first aspect, to realise that the moment of transition was that of installation of a new *gouvernementalité*. We shall set out this hypothesis by showing how privatisation in China, despite growing evidence of increasing delegation of management of enterprises, has had a highly state-oriented character. Thus the various levels of the Chinese state expend considerable energy on the creation of new large-scale industrial groups so as to retain a central role in the process of modernisation. In the area of management of urban poverty and unemployment, the government has also been able to respond with surprising rapidity to this new challenge. So the paradox of a state as actor in the transition needs to be taken into account, as well as the multiplying of networks and their criminalisation.

Yves Chevrier's work has already demonstrated lines of continuity persisting between the imperial era and the modern Chinese state.[1] The power of civil servants and the weakness of controls, today as yesterday, make the development of local compromises possible. Yet the strength of local factors, emphasised by a number of recent studies, does not challenge the unity of a symbolic order that is more proclaimed than institutionalised.[2] But beyond a state-control trajectory characterised by weak institutionalisation, leaving large spaces for informal and local arrangements, the evolution of the model needs to be understood. In the coming few pages analysis of daily life in the Shenyang municipality will illustrate how privatisation cannot simply be seen either as a mere retreat by the Maoist state, or as a return to the age-old trajectory of the Chinese empire. This new mode of government whose outlines we will be trying to trace is an original synthesis, very much influenced, in Shenyang, by the heritage of Socialism in that vanguard city.

A former bastion of socialism

Shenyang, like Shanghai and Wuhan, is one of the oldest industrial cities in China. Located in the heart of a mineral basin rich in iron and coal, the city has been a centre for development of the steel industry, a heavy consumer of energy. The origin of this early industrialisation goes back to the nineteenth century when the Japanese, Russians and Chinese were quarrelling over Manchuria. The change from exploitation of natural resources to the development of an industrial base took place gradually at first, through rival actions by those three states; then the Japanese colonial occupation (1931–45) developed a considerable industrial base in Shenyang. During this period it turned into an industrial centre of nearly two million inhabitants.[3] But it was with the establishment of Communist rule that the city assumed a first-rank role in the Chinese economy. In 1949, as the only important centre of heavy industry, it was promoted as the vanguard of Chinese Socialism and was the object of every attention from the new regime. Thus it benefited extensively from the Soviet big brother for the

---

[1] Y. Chévrier, 'L'Empire distendu: esquisses du politique en Chine des Qing à Deng Xiaoping', pp. 263–95, in J.-F. Bayart (ed.), *La greffe de l'Etat, les trajectoires du politique*, vol. 2, Paris: Karthala, 1996.

[2] M. Blecher and V. Shue, *Tethered Deer: Government Economy in a Chinese County*, Stanford University Press, 1996; J.-C. Oi, 'The Role of Local State in China's Transitional Economy', *The China Quarterly* 144, December 1995, pp. 1132–49.

[3] Kang Chao, *The Economic Development of Manchuria: The Rise of a Frontier Economy*, Ann Arbor, MI: University of Michigan Press, 1983, p. 6 (Michigan Papers in Chinese Studies, 43).

implementation of several major industrial projects. During the first years of the new regime, the tall chimneys of the metal industries proliferated, while their black smoke was the pride of the inhabitants. The modernisation of China, too long delayed, became a reality in Shenyang.

In this showcase of Chinese Socialist industrialisation, vanguard enterprises built houses and health facilities for their employees, organised their leisure activities and offered, in addition to wages, bonuses and gifts in kind.[4] Under this almost perfect arrangement of economic and social life the lives of the inhabitants, happy to be working for the advancement of Socialism, were organised in minute detail. So few workers of this city, a city richer than the Chinese average, doubted that they really were the new masters of China. Today that situation is a thing of the past, but it continues to influence the development of reforms in Shenyang, through the strength of worker reactions and, indirectly, the energy applied by the municipal authorities to softening the shock of transition. Shenyang's transition to the market economy is the privatisation of the vanguard of Chinese Socialism.

The economic record of the regime's first thirty years was not bad—far from it—in Shenyang. The city became the capital of the most industrialised and richest province in China, ranking first in heavy industry production and fifth in light industry production.[5] Today, when the province is feeling the need for aid from the central government, those who seek it like to recall that Liaoning contributed, through taxation, to the modernisation of the rest of China. Between 1952 and 1988, in fact, a sum of 122 billion yuan was paid, to which must be added gifts of industrial products and millions of tonnes of iron ore, coal, steel and oil. Besides being richer, Liaoning also has a better trained workforce; the various technical universities of Shenyang and Dalien are, or used to be, well respected. Many cadres, even at the national level, were trained there. In addition, until the reforms, Liaoning's contribution to the development of the country also included the despatch of 60,000 engineers to other regions of China.

During the first years of reforms, the city's industrial growth was still rapid. The consumer goods sector had a veritable boom. The city's bicycle plant, which has now gone bankrupt, at that time increased its production by 50 per cent. The *weijing* (potassium glutamate) factory, also bankrupt

---

[4] Chengshen Dan and Guohong Li, *Zhongguo zibenzhuyi gongshangye de shehuishuyi gaizao, Liaoning juan, Shenyang fence* (The Socialist transformation of industry and capitalist business, section on Shenyang in Liaoning province), Beijing: Zhonggong Dangshi Chubanshe, 1992, pp. 222–32.

[5] *Liaoning tongjiju ye zhongdang sheng xuanchuan, 1949–1884 Liaoning 35 nian: jingji he shehui fazhan chengjiu* (Department of Statistics and Department of Propaganda, 1949–1984, 35 years of history of Liaoning: exploits of economic and social development), Shenyang: Liaoning Renmin Chubanshe, 1992, pp. 35–50.

today, increased its output by 70 per cent. It was the same for other consumer goods produced in the city: watches, washing machines, sewing machines, beer and cigarettes.[6] Only in more recent times did Shenyang's industries encounter difficulties, because of increased competition, bad management, unwise investment, and the weight of social costs (especially retirement pensions). The engine of Socialist industrialisation had to face a change in the rules of the game of modernisation. Now raw materials, energy and labour are costs that handicap the profitability of an enterprise.

After twenty years of reforms, the city's industrial scene is badly damaged. Officially 60 per cent of the enterprises of the city's between industrial departments are running deficits.[7] The situation of the 224 major enterprises is even more critical, since almost 80 per cent of them are still considered to be in a difficult situation.[8] Some are just waiting for bankruptcy, no longer caring even to pay wages.[9] At the end of 1996, counting all types of enterprise, the city of Shenyang had 997 which had ceased production, employing 270,000 workers.[10] Over the province as a whole, the number of laid off workers (*xiagang*) is officially 1,650,000 or 16 per cent of the active urban workforce and 13.5 per cent of all employees laid off in China.[11] The record rates of unemployment in the city and the province as a whole show both the importance of the Liaoning industrial base and, of course, the seriousness of the crisis.

How quiet privatisation was carried out

Despite the gravity of the crisis hitting that part of China, the reforms offered opportunities to the urban elites. The upheavals in the state organisation allowed the people in senior executive positions in the city—military people, administrative employees and managers of enterprises—to take advantage of this change. It was at the heart of the state economy, always presented as a victim of transition, that strategies of readaptation of the old elites took place.

[6] Ibid., p. 104.

[7] *Shenyang Ribao* (Shenyang Daily), 23 August 1997.

[8] *Shenyang Ribao* (Shenyang Daily), 12 August 1998.

[9] A. Kernen, 'Out of Work in the State Sector' in Orville Schell and David Shambaugh (eds), *The China Reader: The Reform Era*, New York: Vintage Books, 1999, pp. 343–58.

[10] Among these enterprises, two-thirds were state enterprises and one-third collective enterprises. In Shenyang specialists distinguish new and older collective enterprises; the older ones, having developed the same type of operation as state enterprises, have to cope with fairly similar problems today.

[11] *Liaoning jingi shehui xingshi fenxi yu yuce, jungji yu shehui lanpishu 1997–98* (The economic and political situation in Liaoning: analyses and forecasts, economic and social Blue Book 1997–1998), Shenyang: Liaoning Renmin Chubanshe, p. 28.

A new type of entrepreneur first appeared in state enterprises as a result of various reforms that significantly increased their margin of manoeuvre. First the 'system of economic responsibility', and then management contracts (*shengbao*) changed the role of heads of enterprises. But while the heads of state enterprises became 'senior managers', the status of state employees remained largely unchanged. Hence the internal operations of those enterprises only changed a little, even if a new vitality was expressed in the development of affiliated enterprises. Officially, these new subsidiaries were supposed to contribute to solving the problem of overstaffing of state enterprises, but they rapidly turned out to be at the centre of the enrichment strategies of the city's elites. Indeed, because of a not very clear definition of the ownership status and the great variations in their relations with the mother enterprise, these subsidiaries rapidly succeeded in diverting the most profitable elements of the state enterprises in their direction.

To understand the haste of the 'new senior managers' to get around the wage constraints in state enterprises, it needs to be remembered that the payroll costs there were notoriously higher, because of the various social benefits, all paid for by the enterprise, enjoyed by permanent employees. In the view of some economists, provision of housing, schools and hospitals, as well as the payment of retirement pensions, increased payroll costs by nearly 40 per cent compared with other sorts of enterprise.[12] In an 'old industrial bastion' like Shenyang, some of these costs were particularly heavy. The cost of pensions was often nearly 40 per cent of the state enterprises' wage bill, because of the relatively low retirement age, increased life expectancy and the relatively old age of the enterprises. Besides their financial cost, the state workers had acquired over the thirty years of Socialism a rhythm of work and work habits that were all the more difficult to alter because they had for long retained their 'privileged status'. In the social organisation of state enterprises they were, until recently, protected from their superiors' production-oriented tendencies. The reason was that while the new senior managers had wide autonomy in the areas of accounting and creation of subsidiary enterprises, it was not so for employment and wages. In other words, they did not have the means to put their workers to work. In a short document extolling the advantages of turning state enterprises into shareholding enterprises, the head of one enterprise is quoted as saying, 'Before the reforms, even for someone who wanted to control production strictly it was impossible to stop losses, theft

---

[12] Geng Xiao, *Managerial Autonomy, Fringe Benefits, and Ownership Structure: a Comparative Study of Chinese State and Collective Enterprises*, Washington, DC: World Bank, 1991 (Socialist Economies Reform Unit, Country Economies Department, Research Paper Series, 20).

and absenteeism...'[13] These common practices among state workers often lay behind the development of supplementary activity. Highlighting these 'straddling strategies' allows us to cast doubt on the image of phlegmatic and apathetic state workers; in fact they were also actors in the transition.

In addition, the power of the 'new senior managers' was limited in time. In fact, as a general rule, they only held their posts for a few years before being transferred, incidentally without regard for the results achieved by the enterprise. In these conditions the development of additional activities was often preferred to a slow, difficult and hazardous reform of the mother enterprise. This system of rotating the personnel at the top—whose aim, paradoxically, was to prevent a gradual move towards autonomy—not only had the opposite effect, but also governed to a great extent the way in which the city's administrative elite appropriated economic wealth for themselves. So during the first twenty years of the reforms the state enterprises became above all the centre of a multitude of networks, at all levels of the enterprise, serving as the basis for a multitude of subsidiary activities. They maintained and developed new rents, easing the reconversion of part of urban society.

The development of new economic activities within state enterprises was only a part of the privatisation process. In fact the privilege of setting up affiliated businesses did not belong only to heads of enterprise and their hangers-on; all the state administrative bodies (*danwei*) were able to develop such activities. Schools and universities started numerous evening classes and set up consultancy offices; the city's heavy industries diversified into restaurants, massage parlours and karaoke bars; even the city police established businesses specialising in import-export trade with Russia or the sale of aphrodisiac products. These are fairly anecdotal examples, but they illustrate a really important state of affairs. Jiang's call to the army to give up its industrial and commercial activities in 1998 only confirms it. The development of additional activities in the state bodies as a whole followed the example of the industrial sector, among large sections of the population, but reproducing the existing hierarchies almost to perfection. So network privatisation certainly proved a very efficient means of carrying out reshaping of the elites.

The excesses of these new activities, encouraged by various legal means, were periodically condemned by the press or in the course of anti-corruption campaigns. Bad senior managers or civil servants using their power to

---

[13] *Jingji yanjiu bianjibu & Zhonggongzhongyang dangxiaojingji yanjiu zhongxin* (Publishing office for research on economic affairs and Centre for Economic Research of the Central Party College), *Guoyou zhongxiao qiye gaige tansuo* (Research on the reform of state medium and small enterprises in China), Beijing: Jingji Kexue Chubanshe, 1996, p. 170.

develop economic activities on their own account were publicly con-demned. Thus at the end of the 1980s Shenyang was struggling like all the big cities against the 'scourge' of bureaux (*gongsi*) which, playing on the dual price structure, bought at official planning prices to sell at market prices.[14] Some years later the provincial government sent 500 cadres into the most indebted enterprises to help them resolve problems in production and management.[15] This attempt by the administration to reassert control over state enterprises showing too little concern for their growing indebt-edness involved, in Shenyang, the despatch of two hundred cadres 'to reduce the debts while showing by concrete, real and practical steps that the administration has changed its attitude and is now at the service of the enterprises.'[16] And more recently official criticism of the state enter-prises has been aimed directly at misappropriation of state assets by senior managers. Following an inquiry ordered by the government, Wang Baoxi was the first—in an article entitled 'How is the capital of state enterprises disappearing?'—to estimate the annual losses at 50 billion yuan.[17] Once this first taboo had been broken, he and others described the ways in which some senior managers succeeded in appropriating the assets of their enterprises.[18]

The aim of all the manifold activities of senior managers was, through playing with accounts, to 'leave debts to the mother enterprise, which will declare bankruptcy.'[19] In addition it has been proved that the new, usually profitable activities sponsored by the state enterprises kept separate ac-counts and only rarely helped to balance the mother enterprises' books. So non-profitable activities remained in the state sector and profitable ones steadily gained autonomy. After initially backing the development of sub-sidiaries, today the senior managers use them to empty state enterprises of their most productive activities. This transferring of activity only worsens the structural difficulties of state enterprises which, in certain cases, are being gradually changed into shells empty of all content. The situation is summed up in the popular saying, 'The monk is rich but the monastery is falling into ruins' (*fu le heshang, quiong le miao*).

---

[14] Xianmin Shi, *Tizhi de tupo-Beijing shi Xichengqu getihu yanjiu* (Research on private enterprises in the Xicheng district of Beijing), Beijing: Beijing Shehui Kexueyuan Chubanshe, 1993, p. 80.

[15] Foreign Broadcast Information Service CHI-92–051/16 March 1992, p. 58.

[16] *Shenyang Ribao* (Shenyang Daily), 28 March 1992.

[17] Baoxi Wang, 'Guoyou zichan shi zemeyang liushi de?' (How is the capital of state enter-prises disappearing?), *Zhongguo gongye jingyi yanjiu* 5, 1995, pp. 22–4.

[18] Jin Pei, 'Guoyou qiye wenti: jiannan guoqi hequ hecong', in *Guanjian shike: Dangdai zhongguo jidai jiejue de 27 ge wenti* ('The question of state enterprises: how to get out of the serious difficulties', in *A crucial moment: 27 important questions to be resolved today*), Beijing: Jinri Zhongguo Chibanshi, 1997.

[19] *Shenyang Ribao* (Shenyang Daily), 5 April 1995.

This development makes it possible to understand why senior managers want their enterprises to be declared bankrupt. For some of them, in fact, the role of state enterprises in the transition has been completed; deprived of their most remunerative activities, they now represent nothing more than social costs and serious bank debts. Concerned for profitability, the new leaders are in a hurry to get rid of that burden. Bankruptcy can therefore be a way of closing a more or less lengthy phase of spontaneous privatisation. However, it has to be noted that in Shenyang, as in other parts of China, bankruptcies have remained few in number, essentially for political reasons. Without going into this theme here, it can simply be noted that it is through mergers or total or partial sell-offs that the rapid change of ownership has operated since 1997.[20]

The state and privatisation

This analysis centred on the growing autonomy of bureaucrats-turned-entrepreneurs pinpoints an important aspect of the transition—the 'selective recomposition of the former elites' through legal transfer or theft of state property.[21] But to focus exclusively on bad top-level management or unscrupulous bureaucrats means forgetting that privatisation, as well as the excesses it leads to, is an integral part of a new mode of governance. While the actors comprising the state have undoubtedly increased their margin of manoeuvre by gradually appropriating wealth, it should be noted that the state has to a great extent remained master of the process by fixing the rules of privatisation. The practices that appear to short-circuit the state also have a political dimension. This new mode of governance is not limited to a slow decay of the Maoist state, but is based on political management of the transition, establishing a new social order, in the absence of consensus. The proliferation of networks, which has facilitated the appropriation of state wealth by a 'new' class of entrepreneurs, is not the culmination of the economy's revenge over the state. Far from being based on a minimum state, or on reducing the state's action to ordinary dimensions, privatisation in Shenyang has been proceeding according to a very state-oriented mode. By controlling the rate of progress of the transition, and keeping a right of supervision over management of enterprises and foreign credits and investment, the state remains at the centre of the privatisation process.

[20] Antoine Kernen, *L'agonie de l'industrie lourde dans le Nord-Est Chinois* , Paris: Karthala, 2003.

[21] Y. Chevrier, 'Une société infirme: La société chinoise dans la transition "modernatrice"', pp. 229–315 in C. Aubert, Y. Chevrier, J.-L. Domenach *et al., La société chinoise après Mao entre autorité et modernité*, Paris: Fayard 1986 (Espace du Politique series).

In fact the Shenyang city authorities continue to arrange the reforms step by step, not hesitating to defer the application of some of their aspects. To ease social tension, for example, they deferred bankruptcies and redundancies until later. Officially, the senior managers no longer had to render accounts to anyone in that area, so they could rapidly get rid of the 30 to 60 per cent excess staff who were still with the enterprises. But things have not happened that way. The management of worker redundancies is still often outside the control of the enterprise management, if the municipal authorities think the stability of the city so requires. The authorities are still ordering banks to provide new 'stability loans' (*anding daikuan*) to allow payment of wages. And they do not stop at intervening when they consider their vital interests to be at stake—they intervene even in the running of industrial modernisation. Lastly, the appointment and dismissal of heads of enterprise remains the privilege of the administration. For example, one visit by Zhu Rongji to Liaoning was followed by a mini-purge among the management staff of state enterprises. By an administrative act more than three thousand management executives out of a total of 20,000 were replaced—15 per cent of the management staff of the province's 5,000 state enterprises.[22]

Insofar as the umbilical cord between the administration and its enterprises is not yet severed, the state continues to control their management, even if it is a more remote control. The political game in the transition is not revealed only in enrichment networks whose outlines and size we have revealed. The political order does not condition only the means of robbery of public wealth, it continues to act as a structure for the apparent disorder of the transition. The increase in autonomy of the senior management and bureaucrats cannot be summed up as an increase in disorder, but needs to be placed in a wider context, that of a new mode of governance. The state continues to impose its game in the privatisation process which is institutionalising a new management of inequality.

New management of the social side. In a concrete sense, privatisation in China, as in many countries of the world, has led to development of inequality within urban society. After an initial decade of reforms which skirted around the status of the workers, the 1990s were marked by abolition of the last privileges of state employment. In calculation of wages jobs for life gave way to temporary jobs, length of service to merit; the social advantages acquired over the previous decades have been steadily whittled away. Today, redundancies are multiplying, so much that the unemployed form 30–40 per cent of the active population of the city. However, the Shenyang city authorities have been proving particularly

---

[22] *South China Morning Post* (Hong Kong), 15 September 1997.

active in the social domain; the steady withdrawal of enterprises from that domain has been accompanied by increased activity of the administration in affairs of unemployment, health and retirement pensions. These gradual and partial reforms allow urban workers to retain certain privileges by comparison with their rural counterparts. Thus workers laid off (*xiagang*) have kept contact with their former enterprises, which have paid them a monthly allowance equivalent to 20–30 per cent of their former pay. This sets them apart from the urban unemployed whose allowances are more modest, and from migrant workers from the countryside who have no rights to any allowances. In addition, the enterprises have taken many measures aimed at taking some of their employees out of the labour market 'gently': there are many 'extended holidays', like maternity leave which extends over seven years, and there is early retirement at forty-two for women and fifty-two for men.[23] In general everything is done to take women out of the labour market. They therefore represent more than 60 per cent of the unemployed, and 95 per cent of them will probably never find a stable paid job again.[24]

But it would be wrong to think that the changes in the status of state-employed workers and the establishment of a new type of relations between employers and employees have occurred in a peaceful, harmonious step-by-step transition. The urban population reacted strongly to the loss of its social advantages. Demonstrations became so frequent as to be commonplace. Generally, the workers would take a petition to the authorities and ask to be received by the mayor or a high-up local official; in that way they sought to denounce to the higher authorities the injustices or embezzlements committed by the management of an enterprise, or else they simply asked for payment of their wages, pensions or unemployment benefits. During my stay in Shenyang in October 2001, demonstrations were staged more than once a day; one or sometimes two per day took place before the municipal offices. There were just as many before the seat of the provincial government, even if they took slightly different forms there—bringing together delegations of workers from other cities of the province, they were accordingly on a smaller scale. In all cases, workers' demonstrations remained limited in extent. Generally they consisted of some hundreds of workers or retired employees. When workers' protest movements became an everyday occurrence this did not open the way for expression of demands going beyond the bounds of an enterprise. As protest was divided into small segments, only exceptionally did the number of demonstrators

[23] *Shenyang Ribao* (Shenyang Daily), 18 January 1995.
[24] A. Kernen and J.-L. Rocca, 'The Social Responses to Unemployment and the "New Urban Poor"', *China Perspective*, no. 27, Jan./Feb. 2000, pp. 35–51.

go beyond two or three thousand. In fact the municipal authorities tolerated the laying of grievances before the city government, but firmly sup-
pressed any effort to organise a workers' movement. To be allowed to
proceed, the demonstrations had to retain a spontaneous character, to be
confined to one enterprise and not to disrupt business. Under such constraints, however frequent they were they could not give birth to a workers' movement on a national or even a regional scale. And only rarely did
workers' protests go beyond these established limits, to disturb urban order
temporarily.[25]

As for the official trade unions, one suspects that they did nothing to
advocate the cause of those they were supposed to represent. Certainly the
union sections in certain enterprises, on very rare occasions, backed
demands under workers' pressure, but they were quickly called to order.
The absence of reaction from the unions is also explained by their loss of
influence within enterprises since the beginning of the reforms. Increasingly top-level managers have worn two hats, as heads of enterprises and
senior officials of the Party.[26] The official attempts sometimes made to
strengthen the unions' power in the enterprises have been ineffective, like
the 1995 regulation which should have established checks on enterprise
managers' expenses claims.[27]

Since they could not pass through official channels, workers' protests
tried to get round them by setting up new autonomous trade union structures. In the first years of crisis in state enterprises these new organisations took the form of informal associations for workers' mutual aid. The
objectives announced were very minimalist, since these associations had
only one aim, to use their members' donations to assist the most deprived
families; but this was the first time that workers in state enterprises took
the initiative again after the events of 1989. In the psychosis caused by the
collapse of the USSR the municipal authorities reacted rapidly. Fearing
more than anything else the development of some degree of self-admin-
istration, they invested massively in management of the social side. To
avoid a situation like the Polish one developing, the trade unions set about
taking control of these self-governing associations, and taking over their
tasks themselves. That was how they began to change into official charitable organisations.

Workers' mobilisation had some effect on the organisation of the transition, but it was rapidly taken over by the authorities. Until today, faced

---

[25] I develop further this idea of a margin for manoeuvre or an 'opportunity space' in 'Les
ouvriers chinois réapprennent la "manif": vers l'invention d'une nouvelle gestion politique des conflits sociaux?', *Critique Internationale* 16, July 2002, pp. 14–23.

[26] *Shenyang Ribao* (Shenyang Daily), 8 November 1995.

[27] *Shenyang Ribao* (Shenyang Daily), 18 November 1995.

with the gravity of the situation, individuals have been embarking personally on charitable activity, like one teacher who set up a small mutual aid
network to help a young girl pupil whose father was in hospital and whose
mother was *xiagang*, or one entrepreneur who is funding a foundation for
action against poverty; but such cases are rare and do not result in creation
of NGO-type associations.[28] While in other countries the 'retreat of the
state' has left the field open for charitable associations of political or religious inspiration, in China individual initiatives are rapidly taken over
and run by organisations now in charge of management of social matters.
The Chinese state, through redefinition of the role of mass organisations,
aims to remain in sole charge. Since the beginning of the crisis, besides
the trade unions, women's associations and district committees have occupied this new space of urban poverty. Meanwhile the press, in an almost
euphoric mood, relates day after day 'successes' in this domain or visits
by officials bringing cheques, coal and tit-bits. There are also campaigns
of forced solidarity, in place of the former mass campaigns. The state, in
order not to allow a 'civil society' to emerge, is redeploying on the social
side on a massive scale. It is true that the reform of state enterprises has
been accompanied by a financial crisis unprecedented for the regime,
which explains why many unemployed people have simply not been getting pensions, wages or unemployment benefits. Urban poverty, which
the Communist regime had wiped out, has reappeared.

However, management of the social crisis by the city authorities is not
limited to that development of institutional charity. In order to occupy the
new space of poverty better, it has steadily established a minimal social
protection safety net to which every inhabitant of the city is entitled. In
addition, a considerable effort has been made to make re-employment easier. The aim of the municipal authorities, since 1994, has been to 'bring
back' state employees thrown onto the new labour market, but also to see
that the city's enterprises take on unemployed urban people rather than
immigrants. To help re-employment of the jobless, the authorities have
started numerous free training courses open to all the declared unemployed. The press has made a major information effort, publishing, for
example, a list of all the retraining courses available to the jobless.

Besides providing the most varied forms of training, the city authorities
want to 'change the mentality' of state employees, especially through short
courses which employees have to follow before their employment is termi-
nated. There everything is done to destroy their wage expectations and to
show the image of the modern employee, exploited and ill-paid, in the best
light. The press joins in gladly, spreading the idea that in the city very

---

[28] *Shenyang Ribao* (Shenyang Daily), 31 May 1998.

many jobs remain unfilled because of unemployed people's laziness. For example, it makes a big noise about an enterprise having problems in finding storekeepers or packers. It has to be admitted, certainly, that some unemployed people still prefer to hold on to the last advantages offered by their *xiagang* status by doing some petty trading, rather than accept a tiring job far from home and poorly paid. But as it is not simply a matter of 'mentality', the municipal authorities intervene to balance supply and demand on the labour market. They put pressure on enterprises to take on urban unemployed people, and more recently they have set up protectionist measures to make it more difficult to employ migrant workers. The enterprise leaders are responding to these demands with limited enthusiasm; they much prefer to employ migrant workers rather than city dwellers, considered as lazy and demanding.

All these measures, however, are still very inadequate for everyone in Shenyang to have a job. So for those who will probably never find a place in this new liberalised market, the municipal authorities have developed work programmes for the unemployed and a considerable number of workshops intended for women in particular. The central idea is that everyone must embark on some activity which can supplement unemployment benefit and, ideally, provide for his or her needs. With this aim the authorities are introducing numerous night-time markets and access to market trading (through reductions in fees and taxes). Trade unions or district associations supply the poorest, at lower cost, with products to sell on the markets. The income that the jobless get from these activities is not very great, but enables them to supplement the small benefits they receive from the state. The wide spread of petty trading of this sort is not, of course, enough to solve the employment crisis in the city. In addition, the emergence of these new sorts of trade increases competition and reduces the income of the smallest private traders. The result is that the number of non-subsidised private entrepreneurs is far from booming.

As the municipal authorities steadily take further charge of the social payments (unemployment benefit, sickness benefit, pensions) which the enterprises have stopped paying, it is clear that in parallel with privatisation a new form of management of the social side is taking shape—a minimalist one, certainly, but with a persistent social colouring. This model, despite its inadequacies, is inspired more by the welfare state than by the liberal minimum state.

New roles for states in modernisation? While the state is selling off small enterprises and disengaging from direct management of the bigger ones, it aims nonetheless to remain at the centre of the economic modernisation progress. To do this it is drawing on the examples of Japan and Korea, which have followed an alternative model of state intervention in the economy, through the creation of big industrial groups. These new bodies are supposed also to serve as engines for modernisation of the local economy, being given priority for state support in matters of credit and investment.[29] While the borrowing from those two historical precedents is explicit, the cloning of *chaebols* (the large industrial conglomerates of South Korea) in China remains a bit rough and ready. In many aspects the establishment of these new groups demonstrates continuity with the partial reforms or else expresses a new attempt at technological modernisation of the major industrial enterprises. The state, unable to take a decision to let the former showpieces of Socialist industrialisation go under, is making a final attempt at patching them up. It is true that the stakes are high symbolically, since the role of the state as an actor in development has been at the centre of China's path to modernisation for over a century. This source of legitimacy remains central to a Chinese context marked by economic liberalisation without political relaxation. Rightly or wrongly the Chinese government is very much afraid of the risks of instability that could arise from bankruptcy of these enormous industrial combines. This old fear of social movements that haunts the Chinese government has been further reinforced by the experiences of Poland and more recently of Indonesia.

Thus the creation of industrial groups is seen as the solution, to achieve 'cautious' modernisation of the 124 major industrial enterprises in Shenyang. There are about forty of these groups, called national interest groups, and about a hundred others of smaller size. Since they were sometimes created solely to prevent a bankruptcy, they do not always lead to changes in the operations of the merged enterprises. Hence the word 'group' does not have much specific meaning and has become equivalent to 'enterprise'. But while one may reasonably have doubts about the future of a number of them, it must be emphasised that the allocation of state aid is today selective. Henceforth the city authorities are basically concerned only with about twenty groups; these received, in the first six months of 1998, loans amounting to 1.3 billion yuan, about 52 per cent of the loans provided by the banks.

This policy of targeted aid is not new in itself, as about ten enterprises received 50 per cent of the 8 billion yuan invested in the city's industries from the early 1990s.[30] But now the municipal authorities' intervention goes beyond a mere credit policy. They organise restructuring and negotiate

---

[29] Wan Shaoling, 'Guanyu Liaoning jiejian rihan jingyan jiasu zujian zonghe shangshe de sikao' (Reflections on the acceleration in creation of multi-functional groups: borrowings from the Japanese and Korean experience), *Shehui kexue jikan* 3, 1995, pp. 24–8.

[30] *Shenyang Ribao* (Shenyang Daily), 30 August 1997.

with provincial and national authorities for administrative favours or debt relief. 'The various organs of the administration have created a chain of services to advise enterprises... These transactions have ended with visits by leaders of the various organs in charge of industrial modernisation in the city to each of the 18 groups. They fixed the direction of the reforms' objectives and laid down the stages for implementation.'[31] In concrete terms, where mergers and buy-ups are concerned, the city council is in the first rank among the negotiators. This was the case when the Changbei group took over a Fuxin enterprise, and with the industrial regrouping that took place around the Shenhua petrochemical group. Again, it was the city council that negotiated with the provincial and central state authorities the entry of the Changbei, Tongyong and Zhongkunang groups into the club of the '1,000 best enterprises', a distinction that gives preferential access to central government aid. Even so, the new role that the state authorities aim to adopt in technological modernisation remains in many ways a continuation of the partial reforms—so much so that one may wonder if the importance of these interventions is not more symbolic than real, allowing China to continue to think on the lines of a development state.

The recent corruption cases have done harm to the image of the city council's activism in the industrial and social domains. The mayor, Mu Suixin, and the deputy mayor, Ma Xiangdong, established the new social security system, set up numerous re-employment centres to help reduce unemployment, and facilitated foreign investment, but they used their positions of power at the same time to enrich themselves or favour their relatives, sometimes even by misappropriating funds allocated for social security. Faced with this situation, rather than taking offence at the double talk and cynicism of the leadership, it is advisable to understand the impossibility of tracing a boundary between the camps of Good and Evil. Officials of integrity do not exist; probably they never existed outside propaganda books. The clean sweep conducted within the municipality by the investigators sent from Beijing will no doubt soothe to some extent the feelings of the unemployed and pensioners who are not receiving their benefits, but it will in no way challenge the generalised practice of plunder by the elites in power. This voracious appropriation of resources controlled by the state is what constitutes the *gouvernementalité* of the transition, which is not fundamentally different from the similar processes taking place in Russia, for example. The development of networks, favoured by the

---

[31] *Shenyang Ribao* (Shenyang Daily), 25 July 1998.

steady and for long incomplete introduction of privatisation, has limited to the maximum the emergence of new actors, by operating a 'selective recomposition of the elites'.

Yet the packaging of privatisation remains very specific to the Chinese context. The reinvention of a new *gouvernementalité*, more indirect and less interventionist, has worked as in other countries to the benefit of a small group of privileged people, but it has also been characterised by a powerful security preoccupation. Having observed and drawn conclusions from the collapse of Communist regimes, the Chinese authorities are pre-occupied by the question of their own political survival. Hence, in Shen-yang, the municipal authorities are managing workers' demonstrations adroitly and seeking to retain their symbolically and managerially all-powerful position. The continuation of the social role of enterprises and still more of the city authorities, even if it is sometimes more virtual than real, is a reminder of the political limits that China has set to the disen-gagement of the state from the economic sphere.

Part II

PRIVATISATION OF
INTERNATIONAL INSERTION

In the ordering of international insertion, too, it is undeniable that non-state actors are now impossible to bypass. The management of international involvement is thus increasingly influenced by private actors, national and foreign. Does that mean that the state is under the yoke of these actors and transnational networks—that it has become just one more actor, and now a more ordinary one, in the negotiation and definition of norms of authority and legitimacy, and in the exercise of power, notably economic power?

The contributions that follow emphasise how states take these 'new' actors into account, sometimes being constrained by them, even though those actors also offer states unprecedented or revived economic opportunities. However, these chapters show above all how interpretations in terms of clear-cut alternatives (regulation by the state versus regulation by transnational networks and private actors; the state in control versus the state losing control; competition versus symbiosis) have little relevance for understanding real situations, as those are characterised by complex, ambivalent and fluctuating combinations rather than by clear-cut, univocal and stable alternatives. Thus multinational firms, 'international finance' and organised crime networks, as well as smugglers and highway robbers, deploy their strategies against states—or more precisely, against the regulatory pretentions of states—by deliberately subverting the law and exploiting national regulations and national borders. In other words, they try to use the rules and norms decreed by states as an instrument to their advantage. But, at the same time these actors strengthen state power, by providing it with new sources of wealth and new opportunities for accumulation and redistribution on the one hand, and on the other by defining their actions and strategies essentially in relation to that power. These 'new' international actors seek not so much to provide alternative referents for action and understanding as to play on those already in existence.

This point is fundamental: the various forces that influence international relations and the modalities by which states engage with the international economy derive from the same history and the same political economy. The nation-state remains the obligatory reference point for foreign relations, most notably because there can be no separation of the economic and political spheres, and because the resources obtained from relations with foreign countries are primarily political resources. In international relations, as in other spheres, the rise of non-state actors cannot be interpreted as a retreat of the state or as reduction of the state to an ordinary status, or the loss of its authority.

4

THE PRIVATISATION OF SOVEREIGNTY AND THE SURVIVAL OF WEAK STATES

William Reno

The connection between economic globalisation and the weakness of African states is widely noted. 'Where states were once the masters of markets,' Strange writes of stronger states elsewhere, 'now it is the markets which, in many crucial issues, are the masters over the governments of states.'[1] Nowhere does this seem to be more true than in Africa, where 47 of the continent's 53 states have implemented World Bank inspired reforms in which they have delegated to creditors significant power over their fiscal affairs. Markets exercise power in informal, often clandestine ways too. 'Some states,' writes Clapham, 'have been so thoroughly privatised as to differ little from territories controlled by warlords,' leading him to ask 'whether international relations can exist without states, and if so, what form such relations might take.'[2] African conditions would appear to provide the radical shifts in internal and external conditions that Spruyt and other critics of the neo-realist state-centric approaches would regard as a catalyst to create an alternative system.[3] Ruggie and others suggest

---

[1] Susan Strange, *The Retreat of the State: The Diffusion of Power in the World Economy*, New York: Cambridge University Press, 1996, p. 4.

[2] Christopher Clapham, *Africa and the International System: The Politics of State Survival*, New York: Cambridge University Press, 1996, pp. 273, 9.

[3] Hendrik Spruyt, *The Sovereign State and Its Competitors: An Analysis of Systems Change*, Princeton University Press, 1994, pp. 11–21. John Ruggie stresses that reordering a social

that the growing density of inter-unit transactions in fact overwhelms the capacity of even fairly capable states to manage local economies in their own interests.[4] These growing constraints on rulers of weak states in Africa, the proliferation of clandestine markets, and the seeming success of 'warlords' in conflict zones that survive to challenge and destabilise states suggest that the locus of decisive action has shifted away from states.

These developments show that that the nature of political authority in the weakest states has undergone dramatic transformation in post-Cold War Africa. The nature of these changes is examined below. But the argument here is that the apparent weakening of states in Africa does not translate into systemic change. Currently constituted states are not going to disappear anytime soon, even if the institutions of these states grow extremely feeble or even disappear altogether. This is because the global recognition of sovereignty remains a valuable political resource for rulers that possess it. This resource enables rulers to gain access to and manipulate external actors via longstanding devices such as global commercial norms and established diplomatic practices to extract resources from them. This strategy integrates external actors into informal political collations that rulers of very weak states use to compensate for their loss of control over commerce, the collapse of formal state institutions, and the rise of armed groups that challenge their hold on power.

The informal privatisation of external recognition of state sovereignty becomes a new basis for sustaining regimes and shapes their relations with local populations. In particular it encourages these regimes to exercise power more exclusively for the interests of individuals who make up these regimes and refrain from providing non-exclusive benefits such as order, security, or economic opportunity to populations. The former is a private exercise of power in its 'ideal' form since it represents the sum of the interests of members of the regime, while the latter is a public exercise of power in that the benefits it provides extend to all people in its realm, regardless of whether they pay the providers or not. Thus the argument here is that current norms of sovereignty with regard to very weak states enable rulers to alter the fundamental character of their internal authority in a manner that reinforces the external image of existing states. The implications of this argument are that external actors collaborate in this ruse because they benefit from the maintenance of an external status quo.

---

and material order is an opportunity for agents to reconceptualise this order: 'Territoriality and Beyond: Problematizing Modernity in International Relations', *International Organization*, 47:3 (winter 1993), pp. 139–74.

[4] John Ruggie, 'A Continuity and Transformation in the World Polity: Toward a Neorealist Synthesis', *World Politics*, 35:2 (January 1993), pp. 261–85. James Rosenau, *Turbulence in World Politics*, Princeton University Press, 1990.

Meanwhile, rulers of very weak states increasingly diverge from the global ideal of how states are organised internally, forcing outsiders to rely even more heavily on informal arrangements that bolster the external dimension of state sovereignty.

These changes are consistent with the growing internationalisation of both clandestine and informal economies. In much of Africa weak state governments advance an even broader economic integration than do corporations and creditors. But they also latch on to and manipulate the informal realm of economic integration in the clandestine and internationally regulated economies that warlord insurgents also favour. Thus openness to global liberalisation in most weak states is not the result of officials' conversion to a superior economic doctrine, nor is it a consequence of pressure on them from societal groups that benefit from this enterprise. Rather, these rulers of weak states use their prerogatives of sovereignty to manipulate the terms of international exchange in their favour. Positioned at the juncture between local and global economies, which sovereignty helps them maintain, these rulers control profitable global connections, profiting directly without the burden of actually having to provide services to their own populations.

This chapter elucidates the adaptability of rulers of very weak states and the importance of informal elements of state power—the role of personal relationships, state uses of ostensibly private business links to carry out tasks customarily assigned to states—in the new global economic environment that much of the literature on globalisation and on weak states has hitherto ignored.[5] Evidence from Africa's weakest states that have weathered the threats of insurgency indicates the important role that control over even very weak states plays in African actors' extension of their global commercial strategies. This applies to insurgents, perhaps would-be state-builders under other circumstances. For example, the Liberian warlord Charles Taylor maintained throughout the country's six-year civil war that his goal was to become the globally recognised President of the Republic of Liberia, which he did in July 1997 in an internationally

---

[5] Peter Evans, *Embedded Autonomy: States and Industrial Transformation*, Princeton University Press, 1995; Linda Weiss, *The Myth of the Powerless State: Governing the Economy in a Global Era*, New York: Cambridge University Press, 1998; Robert Wade, 'Globalization and Its Limits: Reports of the Death of the National Economy Are Greatly Exaggerated', in Suzanne Berger and Ronald Dore (eds), *National Diversity and Global Capitalism* (Ithaca, NY: Cornell University Press, 1996). Their analysis, however, is limited to the institutional apparatus of industrial states. Those that focus on the role of informal linkages in the context of weak states such as Martin van Creveld, *The Rise and Decline of the State* (New York: Cambridge University Press, 1999) portray these processes as decreasing the sustainability of weak states, in contrast to the view here that stresses the adaptation of elements of statehood, especially global recognition of sovereignty, to these other realms of power.

mediated election. Congolese rebel leader Laurent Kabila did not build a new empire with his international backers. Instead he hastened to distant Kinshasa to assume the mantle of ruler of an existing state. This assumption of global recognition of sovereignty did not mean that Kabila, Taylor or other rebel leaders had to give up their prior ways of doing business. All recognise and use the prerogatives of state sovereignty to expand and protect these informal, often clandestine business operations and to invite in new partners. This suggests that capacity to manage economic change derives at least as much from internal arrangements in weak states as from global processes.

This process of adaptation of states appears in what seem to be state-breaking tactics of officials like the destruction of local economies, withdrawal of any attempts to provide development in terms of creating community benefits, contracting out military tasks to private individuals and firms, the intentional destruction of bureaucracies, and alliances with a plethora of global, often clandestine commercial networks to accumulate resources. In fact, the pursuit of these strategies supports the survival of a state system in Africa, at least in its external guise. Each partner to the accommodation tries to capture the internal benefits of globally recognised sovereignty, which the holder manipulates to obtain private advantages in negotiating with the global actors. This also extends to governments outside Africa, which have interests in ensuring that existing borders remain intact and existing political entities continue to acknowledge certain obligations. Given this context, non-state armed groups are unlikely to form an alternative system. These insurgents will continue to seek power in the capitals of existing sovereign states.

Sovereignty and weak state bureaucracies

Limited internal bureaucratic capabilities have long defined Africa's weak states. Observing post-Second World War decolonisation, Bull and Watson wrote that 'much of the world is under the sway of states that are not states in the strictest sense... they do not possess authority, as distinct from mere power; they do not possess enduring legal and administrative structures... still less do they reflect respect for constitutions or acceptance of the rule of law.'[6]

Unable to carry out their own programmes of social or economic transformation, rulers of internally divided states feared organisations, including elements of the state bureaucracy, that might develop their own

[6] Hedley Bull and Adam Watson, *The Expansion of International Society*, New York: Oxford University Press, 1984, p. 430.

agendas.[7] Rulers in weak states pursued this strategy because they saw the growing threats from their own subordinates as coups overthrew rulers in other states. Between 1970 and 1989 in Africa, 72 per cent of the continent's leaders left office in violent circumstances. This fell to 43 per cent from the advent of multiparty elections at the end of the Cold War in 1990 to the start of 2003.[8] But even states holding elections are vulnerable to political violence. Elections played important roles in sparking violence in Congo-Brazzaville, Nigeria, Tanzania, Guinea-Bissau and Côte d'Ivoire. Between 2000 and 2002 protracted internal wars, measured in terms of 1,000 or more deaths, have occurred in fourteen of Africa's fifty-two countries.[9] Rulers facing these threats systematically undermined the cohesiveness of other collectivities, disrupting organisations of potential competitors for power before they arose. Thus the decline of state bureaucracies and public services that Zartman identifies as an indicator of state collapse appeared well before the 1990s[10] and, for a time at least, they were replaced with sustainable patronage networks based upon control of commerce as an alternative to failing state agencies.

Jackson argued that a postwar global institutional shift regularised external support for newly independent state rulers who battled their own societies. For example, the United Nations' 1960 Declaration on the Granting of Independence to Colonial Countries and Peoples provided diplomatic and material support for sovereignty within colonial borders, rather than backing alternative configurations of power that might have boasted stronger internal legitimacy and capabilities. He called these weakly institutionalised and under-resourced states 'quasi-states'.[11] Rulers of such states faced no urgency to boost the capacity of administration or mobilise populations to fend off external threats since the UN system stressed the legitimacy of sovereignty by right of succession to a colonial ruler, not by virtue of having fought to create a new state. Thus indigenous rulers of Congo obtained global recognition in 1960, despite domestic chaos and internal administrative feebleness. In contrast, the internally capable regime in Southern Rhodesia (later Zimbabwe) failed to gain global recognition of its unilateral declaration of independence by its minority white

---

[7] Joel Migdal, *Strong Societies and Weak States*, Princeton University Press, 1988, pp. 139–41.

[8] Author's calculation.

[9] Michael Eriksson, Margareta Sollenberg and Peter Wallenstein, 'Appendix A1: Patterns of Major Armed Conflicts, 1990–2001', *SIPRI Yearbook 2002: Armaments, Disarmament and International Security*, New York: Oxford University Press, 2002, pp. 55–64.

[10] I. William Zartman, 'Introduction: Posing the Problem of State Collapse', in I. William Zartman (ed.), *Collapsed States: The Disintegration and Restoration of Legitimate Authority*, Boulder, CO: Lynne Rienner, 1995, pp. 1–11.

[11] Robert Jackson, *Quasi-states: Sovereignty, International Relations and the Third World*, New York: Cambridge University Press, 1990, esp. pp. 76–7.

government in 1965. Regardless of its military strength, internal coercion and organisational capabilities, South Africa's government, by far the strongest in Sub-Saharan Africa, faced increasing marginalisation from global society until its 1994 transition to majority rule.

Rulers of sovereign states who lacked strong bureaucracies and the capacity to mobilise populations for big state-led projects found an alternative means to exercise authority through dominating the distribution of economic opportunities. At first this centred on manipulating economic regulations and distributing state assets to political allies, including ostensibly private individuals who could mobilise force—youth gangs and private security forces—on behalf of the regime. As political priorities overwhelmed interests in economic management, formal economies dwindled and state assets shrank. Politicians then extended their economic activities to the clandestine market. State power, even with few resources beyond armed force to back it up, remained valuable in this realm, since the capacity to declare activities illegal, then sell exemption from prosecution, still enabled political favourites to accumulate wealth while preserving means to punish opponents. Even growing impoverishment contributed to the stability of this system, since even critics of regimes had to consider whether they needed to make their peace with these political networks to secure exemption from insecurity and want. A striking feature of states like Congo, Sierra Leone, Liberia and Nigeria is the extent to which market control replaced state administration as means of dominating people. Rulers exchanged rent-seeking opportunities for political loyalty, resulting in the plundering of state assets that undermined rule-based bureaucratic behaviour. This gave individual clients considerable free rein to maximise their private benefits. Besides introducing a level of unpredictability and capriciousness in state bureaucratic behaviour that undermined any long-term productive investment, this behaviour left rulers heavily reliant on their foreign backers and business partners to find resources to pay off clients.

Nonetheless, global recognition of weak state sovereignty during the Cold War gave rulers capacity to translate sovereign prerogatives into diplomatic support for a superpower patron in exchange for military and economic aid.[12] French military assistance, for example, helped maintain favoured African rulers. In 1992, 600 French soldiers guarded Gabon's president. The French army intervened in Africa thirty times between 1963 and 1994, during which it deployed troops in six states and assigned

---

[12] Steven David, 'Explaining Third World Alignments', *World Politics*, 43:2 (January 1991), pp. 233–56; National Intelligence Council, 'The US-Soviet Competition for Influence in the Third World: How the LDCs Play It', NIC M-82–10005, April 1982.

military advisers in twenty.[13] Since 2002 French soldiers have guarded the regime of Laurent Gbagbo in Côte d'Ivoire from a rebellious faction of the army and other internal enemies. Such protection tilts the balance in favour of incumbent sovereign rulers in ways beyond military force alone, even if Gbagbo's supporters accuse the French force of aiding the rebels by preventing government attacks to retake captured territory. This is because if rebels are kept away from the capital they cannot convince outsiders to accept them as heads of an alternative state. It is rare to find a diplomat or foreign ruler willing to violate the status quo among UN member states. To recognise a rebel group as a sovereign authority would mean having to devise a mechanism to decertify the international standing of the failing state it replaces. This does not preclude foreign governments allying with rebel groups as proxies or supporting rebels as a replacement for a particular regime. But it is exceedingly rare, especially among other weak states, to support recognition of a breakaway or irredentist community, lest this set a precedent that would lead to challenges to other weak states.[14]

This continued status as globally recognised sovereigns also tilts the playing field in favour of established sovereigns for relations with established international firms. Foreign courts will grant standing to hear disputes between firms and recognised governments. They are exceedingly reluctant to grant standing to disputes with rebel groups. Thus an investor placing assets in rebel-held territory faces a high threat of expropriation, with no recourse in a mutually acceptable court. Underwriters will be reluctant to indemnify these operations if there is no court in which they and their client may seek redress. Likewise, investors, or at least savvy ones, will not risk their capital in such operations. This imbalance appears with enclave mining operations that are relatively immune from regime failures to control populations or effectively manage local economies. Such firms can often provide their own state-like functions within investment enclaves, providing their own security and utilities and managing private development projects for local people.[15] These may be risky ventures, but risk

---

[13] 'Spécial France-Afrique', *Marchés Tropicaux et Méditerranéens*, 18 December 1992, p. 3410; Guy Martin, 'Continuity and Change in Franco-African Relations', *Journal of Modern African Studies*, 33:1 (1995), pp. 12–15.

[14] Border shifts have been rare. Tanzania removed Uganda's Idi Amin from power in 1979 but made no claim to Ugandan territory. More aberrant was Morocco's conquest of the Spanish colony of Rio Oro and Somalia's attempted conquest of ethnic Somali Ogaden of Ethiopia. See Benyamin Neuberger, 'Irredentism and Politics in Africa' in Naomi Chazan (ed.), *Irredentism and International Politics*, Boulder, CO: Lynne Rienner, 1991, pp. 97–109. A more recent border change, in the appearance of an independent Eritrea in the 1990s, was dependent upon claims that this simply restored a colonial era border between an Italian colony and Ethiopia to its former status as an international boundary.

[15] For example, the British firm Lonrho used a private security force to guard its plantations and government installations. William Finnegan, *A Complicated War: The Harrowing of*

for regime and investor alike is offset by predictability of global commercial norms anchored in the stability of norms of sovereignty, rather than on internal stability that the weak state regime cannot provide.

This external regime of sovereignty by right also insulates weak states from the pressures of mobilising for war with foreign enemies. Scholars argue that this has been critical in allowing regimes to ignore performance pressures from among their own populations.[16] This gives incumbent regimes greater leeway to concentrate on accumulating resources among their own members, even if this is done at the expense of the welfare of local people. This configuration of power is not suitable for developing large internal markets. Thus the sorts of investors who will be interested in these states will be those that concentrate on extracting resources rather than selling things to large numbers of local customers.

The concrete result of this predatory dynamic of internal rule has been the scarcity of real bureaucracies in the Weberian sense of rule-governed behaviour in which officials define careers in terms of institutional goals. For example, civil servants in Congo (former Zaire) in 1990 received salaries worth only 6 per cent of values in 1960 at independence.[17] In Guinea, civil servant salaries on average in 1985 covered only 10 per cent of the recipient's subsistence needs.[18] The average monthly salaries of Zambian government workers in 1990 could feed a family of five for five days.[19] The shrinkage of state resources to support these vehicles for patronage meant that even low level officials started using their state offices to engage in local market activity, either selling exemptions to those willing to pay for it, or using the authority of their offices directly to engage in business. In the eyes of creditors and neo-classical economic doctrine, this activity is the consequence of rent-seeking officials who collaborate with

---

Mozambique, Berkeley: University of California Press, 1992, pp. 96–7. Firestone Tire and Rubber built Liberia's first highway, railway and telephone network and its bank was the government's primary private creditor. Amos Sawyer, *The Emergence of Autocracy in Liberia*, San Francisco: Institute for Contemporary Studies, 1992, pp. 248–50. In recent years, missionaries have run Chad's postal service and a French cotton company provided major roads. Robert Buijtenhuijs, 'Chad: The Narrow Escape of an African State' in Donal B. Cruise O'Brien, John Dunn and Richard Rathbone (eds), *Contemporary West African States*, New York: Cambridge University Press, 1989, pp. 52–3.

[16] Charles Tilly, *Coercion, Capital, and European States, AD 990–1992*, Cambridge, MA: Blackwell, 1992, pp. 192–227; Jeffrey Herbst, 'War and the State in Africa', *International Security*, 14:4 (spring 1990), pp. 117–39.

[17] Janet MacGaffey, 'Governance in Zaire' in Goran Hyden and Michael Bratton (eds), *Governance and Politics in Africa*, Boulder, CO: Lynne Rienner, 1992, p. 24.

[18] Alain Morice, 'Guinée 1985: État, corruption et trafics', *Les Temps Modernes*, 42:487 (1987), p. 125.

[19] Michael Barratt-Brown, *Africa's Choices*, Boulder, CO: Westview Press, 1996, p. 226.

societal groups to withhold revenue from the state.[20] It also represents a lower-level appropriation of prerogatives of sovereignty to turn state power into commercial advantage. Paradoxically, where creditors often see too much bureaucracy fostering rent-seeking behaviour, the problem facing rulers of weak states is too little real bureaucracy, leaving them incapable of carrying out an economic transformation independent of the interests of powerful strongmen and political clients.

The necessity of exercising control over these clients means that rulers tend to try to dominate clandestine markets too. This may make them rich, but regardless of their personal stake in this, it follows from the political need to make sure that no potential rival has free access to resources from which to launch their own bid to seize control over the state. For example, in 1980 four fifths of Ghana's cocoa crop was estimated to be smuggled out, much of it via the mediation of state officials.[21] Half of Angola's diamonds disappeared through clandestine channels in 1990, and these became a major venue for the struggle between rebels and government officials for control of this resource. Clandestine gold trade in former Zaire in 1992 was valued at $110 million, four times official exports. During that time, 4,600 tons of cobalt worth $118 million 'disappeared' from Zaire's state-run mines and clandestine diamond exports were estimated at $400 million.[22] Together, income from these trades in Zaire exceeded official state revenue and had become the major realm in which president Mobutu's regime exercised its authority.

This migration of weak state regimes into clandestine markets to control rivals is at variance with the classic neo-realist formulation that 'state behaviour varies more with differences of power than with differences in ideology, in internal structure of property relations, or in governmental form.'[23] If one takes into account the informal structures of authority, especially the commercially based elements that are dependent upon the stability of global norms concerning sovereignty, weak states are a fundamentally different type of political unit in the international system. They behave according to a distinct logic that derives from their different internal configuration of power. This particular organisation of property relations and internal structures of power explains why these state regimes behave as they do and is integral to explaining how they behave as they do,

[20] World Bank, *Adjustment in Africa*, New York: Oxford University Press, 1994, pp. 9–13.

[21] Jon Kraus, 'The Political Economy of Ghana', *Africa Report*, 25/2 (1980), p. 16.

[22] Kabuya Kalala, Tom de Herdt and Stefaan Marysse, *L'economie informelle au Zaire*, Paris: L'Harmattan, 1995, pp. 77–8.

[23] Kenneth Waltz, 'Reflections on Theory of International Politics', in Robert Keohane (ed.), *Neo-Realism and Its Critics*, New York: Columbia University Press, 1986, p. 329.

despite their exceedingly weak power, defined in terms of conventional state capabilities. It produces a bifurcated situation: polities that are exceptionally weak by most measures of power, yet surprisingly capable of invading and occupying social space in which people commonly organise to protest against or reform corrupt or illegitimate political systems, and adept at benefiting from coincident interests of a wide array of external actors. Here, behaviour is crucial for deriving power, and the power that weak state rulers exercise is found in the interstices of the norms and institutions of international society, especially *de jure* state sovereignty.

This is a strategy of rule that, like patronage at the expense of bureaucratic state institutions, is founded in crisis management. Changes in international convention have forced rulers and their rivals to rework old arrangements that were used to control politically valuable resources. Changes in the international system play a decisive role in moulding these innovations in internal politics. Post-Cold War development aid to Sub-Saharan Africa offers continuing incentives for weak state rulers to conform to at least the external elements of global conventions of statehood to generate resources needed to exercise domestic power.[24] Aid to Sub-Saharan Africa has remained steady from 1990 at about $18 billion annually. Disbursements over the past decade, however, show that donors penalise recalcitrant reformers. Aid to Somalia's Siad Barre dropped 70.4 per cent between 1985 and 1991 as his country lost its strategic value to the United States and attracted global condemnation for a dismal human rights record. Over the same period, Sudan's aid dropped 74.3 per cent, Liberia's dropped 30.5 per cent, and Chad's fell 38.6 per cent. On the other hand, reformers reaped rewards. Aid to Ghana rose 252 per cent, Uganda's rose 213 per cent, Benin's increased 159 per cent and Mozambique's registered 259 per cent growth.[25] The intention of this policy was to reward reform and promote the efficiency of internal state bureaucracies and their accountability to citizens.[26]

In some instances foreign aid has been an effective enticement for rulers to risk supporting more rule-based bureaucratic behaviour in places like Ghana and Uganda. But in these cases, rulers still find that small producers that are these states' main sources of taxable wealth could deny

---

[24] Nicolas van de Walle, *African Economies and the Politics of Permanent Crisis, 1979–1999*, New York: Cambridge University Press, 2001.

[25] African Development Bank, *African Development Report 2002*, New York: Oxford University Press, 2002.

[26] Donald Rothchild, 'The Impact of US Disengagement on African Intrastate Conflict Resolution', in John Harbeson and Donald Rothchild (eds), *Africa in World Politics*, 3rd ed., Boulder, CO: Westview Press, 2000, pp. 160–87.

rulers access to their products. Ghana's exports, for example, relied on cocoa for 59 per cent of their value in 1994. Coffee constituted 95 per cent of Uganda's export value during that year.[27] These commercial circuits are more difficult to control for distribution for political purposes, compared to more concentrated, portable resources. Their collection also requires delegation of authority to an extensive bureaucracy. As a World Bank researcher noted, even if rulers want to reform, they may baulk at the risks. 'The causation is circular. The threat of losing power can induce high officials to become even more corrupt...Corrupt leaders find the reform is risky if it releases opposition forces that undermine the current regime,' she writes, and ponders whether creditors are better off with an incumbent kleptocrat rather than a collection of predatory rebel groups fighting over the remnants of a collapsed regime.[28] What is a creditor to do? If creditors become too insistent on following agreements to the letter they risk losing their sovereign interlocutor. A country like Somalia that lacks a central government produces no officials who can acknowledge debts or pretend that creditors' policies will remedy that situation and produce eventual repayment.

In such cases rarely has reform been carried out in ways that have strengthened bureaucratic institutions or solidified reciprocal relations between producers of wealth and the state. On the contrary, Cameroon's president used privatisation of state enterprises to shift his patronage network from the collapsing state bureaucracy into a free-wheeling 'private' sector in which remaining state capacity to interfere in commerce is used to private advantage.[29] Likewise bank deregulation in Nigeria has been manipulated to open new opportunities for Nigeria's elite to control access to foreign exchange.[30] Thus rulers of weak states exploit the anxiety of outsiders to promote 'reform' in their realms. Pressure for reform gives these rulers new instruments in the form of 'privatised' enterprises that can be used to exploit additional, often clandestine, opportunities in the global economy.

---

[27] International Monetary Fund, *International Financial Statistics Yearbook*, Washington, DC: IMF, 1996.

[28] Susan Rose-Ackerman, *Corruption and Government: Causes, Consequences, and Reform*, New York: Cambridge University Press, 1999, pp. 199–200.

[29] Nicolas van de Walle, 'Neopatrimonialism and Democracy in Africa, with an Illustration from Cameroon', in Jennifer Widner (ed.), *Economic Change and Political Liberalization in Sub-Saharan Africa*, Baltimore: Johns Hopkins University Press, 1994, pp. 129–57.

[30] Peter Lewis, 'Shifting Fortunes: The Political Economy of Financial Liberalization in Nigeria', *World Development*, 25:1 (1997), pp. 5–22.

Post-Cold War sovereignty and state survival

Market 'reform' thus fits well into rulers' existing control over the accumulation of resources from markets that they can influence.[31] In Zaire, for example, more than half of the country's coffee crop in the early 1990s was smuggled across its borders. Much of this traffic flowed through links between private illicit trading networks and state officials.[32] Since the late 1970s, Sierra Leone's rulers have dominated partnerships with illicit diamond producers and smugglers. Providing 70 per cent of formal state revenues in the mid 1970s, diamonds' contribution to state revenues fell below ten per cent by 1988 as commerce was channelled into politicians' 'private' hands.[33] An estimated 90 per cent of Benin's foreign trade in the early 1980s, partly in the hands of officials, went unrecorded.[34] Guinea's president Sékou Touré (1958–84) presided over a bureaucracy that progressively integrated itself into the country's commercial life. Certain segments even held informal 'official' rights to smuggling, a practice that continued in the 1990s.[35]

Like Russia's oligarchy of the 1990s, the new entrepreneurs of the age of reform usually turn out to be those with good political connections to incumbent power structures, especially those who were most adept at working the informal networks and sinews of this system. These entrepreneurs could not seize these resources on their own. This transfer of assets is dependent upon collaboration with powerful state agents willing to exploit their sovereign prerogative to grant preferential access to their state's territory to select outsiders and to shield their transactions from prying eyes.

Underlining official collusion in this process, '*Débrouillez vous personnellement*' ('take care of yourself') was the motto of former Zaire's President Mobutu. 'Everything is for sale,' he said. 'Everything is bought in our country. And in this traffic, holding any slice of public power constitutes a veritable exchange instrument, convertible into illicit acquisition of

---

[31] Especially notable among African observers: John Frimpong-Ansah, *The Vampire State in Africa*, Trenton, NJ: Africa World Press, 1991; A. K. Koroma, *Sierra Leone: Agony of a Nation*, Freetown: Afro Media, 1996; Edward Lama Wonkeryor, *Liberia Military Dictatorship: A Fiasco 'Revolution'*, Chicago: Struggler's Community Press, 1985; Bala Takaya and Sonni Gwanle Tyoden (eds), *The Kaduna Mafia*, Jos University Press, 1987.

[32] Tom de Herdt and Stefaan Marysse, 'L'économie informelle au Zaïre' in Janet MacGaffey (ed.), *The Real Economy of Zaire*, Philadelphia: University of Pennsylvania Press, 1991.

[33] William Reno, *Corruption and State Politics in Sierra Leone*, New York: Cambridge University Press, 1995.

[34] Chris Allen *et al., Benin, the Congo, Burkina Faso*, London: Pinter, 1989, p. 134.

[35] Alain Morice, 'Guinée 1985: État, corruption et trafics', *Les Temps Modernes*, 487 (1987), pp. 97–135; Michel Gaud, 'Guinée 1994: au-delà de Conakry', *Afrique Contemporaine*, 173 (1995), pp. 3–13.

money or other goods.'[36] Even if foreign creditors and donors become dispirited—in former Zaire, for example, bilateral aid fell from $823 million in 1990 to $178 million in 1993—some regimes prove able to preserve some stability operating almost entirely in commercial channels. During this period, diamonds and gold worth an estimated half billion dollars left Zaire through clandestine channels.[37] Significant portions of this commerce flowed through presidential hands. Mobutu's personal control over the finances of the ostensibly state-run Gécamines mining conglomerate gave him access to resources, while other 'official' smuggling operations centred on associates' ventures, often in conjunction with foreign partners.[38] The president's security chief ran his own cobalt trading operations. Reaching beyond the frontiers of Zaire, he and other high government officials used prerogatives of their state positions to become intermediaries in clandestine diamond trade from Angolan rebels, a level of regime autonomy for which sovereignty served as a shield.[39]

Alongside the individual pursuit of market driven behaviour, one of the most striking features of the Zairean state was the extent to which officials abjured defining any programme of societal or economic transformation. The only semblance of bureaucratic state coherence was found in the state's (often confused) exercise of repressive capacity, which consumed an estimated 50 per cent of the official state budget in 1992.[40] By 1990, Mobutu's regime spent about four per cent of its official budget to support farming, which employed 80 per cent of the country's working people. Likewise, state expenditure for agriculture also fell to less than one per cent of official budgets in Gabon and Congo-Brazzaville in the 1980s.[41]

Externally imposed austerity programmes also can hasten a ruler's abandonment of bureaucracies. One third, or 20,000 of Sierra Leone's civil servants were laid off under a World Bank structural adjustment programme in the early 1990s, during a time when 75 per cent of the state

---

[36] Cited in René Lemarchand, 'The Politics of Penury in Rural Zaire', in Guy Gran (ed.), *Zaire: The Political Economy of Underdevelopment*, New York: Praeger, 1979, p. 248.

[37] 'Zaire', *Mining Journal*, 26 January 1996, p. 23.

[38] Michael Schatzberg, *The Dialectics of Oppression*, Bloomington: Indiana University Press, 1988, p. 53.

[39] 'Zaire: Dual Control', *Africa Confidential*, 16 April 1993; Filip de Boeck, 'Postcolonialism, Power and Identity: Local and Global Perspectives from Zaire' in Richard Werber and Terence Ranger (eds), *Postcolonial Identities in Africa*, London: Zed Books, 1996, pp. 76–80; François Missier and Olivier Vallée, *Les Gemmocraties: l'économie politique du diamant africain*, Paris: Desclée de Brouwer, 1997.

[40] This was the last year that Mobutu's regime published an official budget. Banque du Zaire, *Rapport Annuel*, Kinshasa: Banque du Zaïre, p. 9.

[41] Economist Intelligence Unit, *Zaire*, 1st quarter 1994, p. 11.

budget went to fighting a rebel insurgency,[42] highlighting the extent to which the regime had managed to detach itself from its state bureaucracy. In Zaire, World Bank reformers recommended trimming state employment from 600,000 to 50,000, a move that did not appear to trouble Mobutu or his associates.[43] Guinea's civil service rolls were cut in half in the decade from 1985 and 50,000, and one in thirty salaried workers in Ghana were laid off in the early 1990s.[44] Civil servants such as teachers, health care workers or agricultural extension agents are usually the first to go. These are people who make claims on resources but are of negligible value to rulers' political goals. In any case, large groups that eventually benefit from state services will be much slower to organise to support a reformer compared to the concerted opposition of strongmen whose payoffs are threatened. As the overall volume of resources falls, bureaucracies that do not generate politically useful resources become an expensive liability. Since the state had long ceased to perform as a mechanism to meet people's long-term survival needs, abolishing collapsing bureaucracies provokes little public protest.

Some argue that African precolonial history produced a politics in which discontented local leaders commonly escaped overbearing rulers by 'exit', migration to a frontier where they set up their own polity.[45] While the ease of withdrawal may account for the weak internal unity and the absence of compelling internal voices for reform, citizens also leave because the ruler kicks them out. Huge refugee flows, from Uganda and Equatorial Guinea in the 1970s to Zimbabwe, Burma and the former Yugoslavia—provoked by 'ethnic cleansing'—can become an easy way of ridding one's regime of troublesome subjects. Forced exit removes potential or actual rivals from resources that they can use to mobilise followers and renders critics unable to deprive the ruler of resources that he translates into political power. Likewise, the appearance of formal multiparty politics in states like Guinea, the Central African Republic, Chad and Equatorial Guinea, where formal state agencies exercise little real control over resources, permits dissatisfied citizens to complain in a non-threatening way and helps certify the weak state regime in the eyes of foreigners who control valuable resources.

[42] Ann Hudock, 'A Nation in Mourning', *West Africa*, 13–19 March 1996, p. 337.

[43] 'Zaire: World Bank's Guarded Optimism', *Africa Economic Digest*, 7 December 1994.

[44] On Guinea, Observatoire Géopolitique des Drogues, *The Geopolitics of Drugs*, Boston: Northeastern University Press, 1996, p. 195. On Ghana: Robert Armstrong, *Ghana Country Assistance Review*, Washington, DC: World Bank, 1996, p. 30.

[45] Igor Kopytoff, 'The Internal African Frontier: The Making of an African Political Culture', in I. Kopytoff (ed.), *The African Frontier*, Bloomington: Indiana University Press, 1987, pp. 3–84; Jean-François Bayart, *The State in Africa*, London and New York: Longman, 1993, pp. 34–5.

Since the ruler does not have to support an expensive bureaucracy, favoured entrepreneurs are unencumbered by demands for tax payments. The main constraints to expansion lie in the limits of sources of accumulation. Thus recruitment of new members to the ruler's alliance does not require the expensive expansion of bureaucracies. This minimisation of startup costs further increases the incentives to rulers to experiment with control over markets, rather than build effective bureaucracies to impose their authority. The social relationship in these transactions mirrors what later would be described as a 'looting model' of rebellion. This model explains the predations of contemporary rebels in Africa as due to the availability of natural resources.[46] This process of the appropriation of state sovereignty and commercial networks, however, suggests that this predation is rooted in the nature of rule that preceded wars and out of which 'warlord' armies developed. In Zaire, for example, President Mobutu signed a deal with the West German firm Orbital Transport and Raketen AG (OTRAG), giving it control over 150,000 square kilometres.[47] Sierra Leone's President Stevens used his partnership with a Lebanese businessman to take over state distribution of fuel and directly control diamond exports for their personal profit.[48] Much like contemporary predatory rebels, a Senegalese confidant of Benin's President Kerekou helped to organise a bank fraud and smuggling scheme for the benefit of himself and high government officials.[49]

This strategy of rule bears little resemblance to standard notions of the exercise of state sovereignty. For example, it detaches the exercise of political authority from control of a specific territory within globally recognised boundaries. Instead, political authority is connected to control of areas that contain natural resources or serve as transit trading centres. Rulers aim to deny these resources to rivals and exercise tight enough control for associates to benefit at the pleasure of the ruler. This leaves the ruler free to abandon populations who do not control resources that can be of benefit to the ruler's patronage network or who do not occupy commercially valuable territory. Bereft of state services and unable to withhold resources from predatory officials, the activities of these people become of little concern to the ruler. Collapsing infrastructure thus need not be a sign of collapsing authority. The former Belgian Congo, for example, had 90,000 miles of motorable roads at independence in 1960. By 1985 only

[46] Paul Collier and Anke Hoeffler, 'Loot-Seeking and Justice-Seeking in Civil War', Washington, DC: World Bank Development Research Group, 1999.

[47] Clapham (note 2), p. 252.

[48] 'Sierra Leone: Rape', *Africa Confidential*, 28 November 1984.

[49] Maurice Chabi, *Banqueroute: mode d'emploi un marabout dans les griffes de la maffia béninoise*, Porto Novo, Benin: Editions Gazette Livres, 1994.

12,000 miles were motorable.[50] Not registered in these statistics are the proliferation of private air cargo companies (rising from four in 1977 to 27 in 1995) that knit together enterprising strongmen, their president and foreign buyers of Congo's mineral resources.[51]

It is not the extent of corruption that distinguishes these polities, even if actual levels of appropriation are quite high in places like Indonesia and South Korea. Rather, it is the social relationships for which the appropriation of resources occurs. Thus one finds yet another aspect of how weak states are qualitatively different from conventional states in their internal organisation, a difference that sovereignty helps smooth over as weak state rulers organise their relations with outsiders.

Privatisation of state sovereignty

Rent-seeking activity in the state should create incentives for enterprising rivals to redeploy resources to the public realm, reap popular acclaim and use that to kick out corrupt rulers, or so some conventional wisdom goes.[52] In principle, private transnational firms should prefer this outcome as greater bureaucratic efficiency makes the local business environment more predictable. But as noted above, even a committed reformer in a weak state would face considerable short-term risks. Foreign firms, however, have other options for securing a stable business environment. A direct method is to employ a third party on behalf of their state partners to solve their mutual problem of instability. The use of mercenaries to protect foreign enclave investment has received much attention.[53] But third party partners providing stability encompass a wider range of organisations.

Chad's government, for example, has attracted a consortium of oil producers to open an oilfield there. The World Bank, stung by criticism that its projects have resulted in environmental degradation and official repression, appointed a board of outside experts to study the project. The World Bank also stipulated that 80 per cent of revenues had to be spent on domestic public services under supervision of a board that includes local NGOs. Despite these arrangements, Chad's president has wasted little

---

[50] John Ayoade, 'States Without Citizens', in Donald Rothchild and Naomi Chazan (eds), *The Precarious Balance: State and Society in Africa*, Boulder, CO: Westview Press, 1988, p. 196.

[51] 'Animateurs des Services', *Le Soft de Finance*, Kinshasa, 20 January 1996, p. 5.

[52] Jeffry Frieden and Ronald Rogowski, 'The Impact of the International Economy on National Policies', in Robert Keohane and Helen Milner (eds), *Internationalization and Domestic Politics*, New York: Cambridge University Press, 1996, pp. 25–47, World Bank, *Adjustment in Africa*, New York: Oxford University Press, 1994.

[53] Abdel-Fatau Musah and J. Kayode Fayemi (eds), *Mercenaries: An African Security Dilemma*, London: Pluto Press, 2000.

time diverting part of the oilfield revenues to buy arms to fight his internal rivals. Creditors threatened to delay the oil project but carried on when they received 'assurances' from the president that this would not happen again. Despite repeated violations of the agreement, creditors and oil companies remain committed to the project.[54] Creditors even added Chad to the role of the Highly Indebted Poor Countries initiative, promising substantial write-downs of the country's huge official foreign debt.[55] What are creditors to do? If the World Bank walked away from this project it would have to abandon immediate arrangements to write down Chad's uncollectable debt. It would have to confess that its efforts to become involved in the internal politics of a client state had failed. One could even imagine concern over whether a precipitous departure would destabilise the government's hold on power.

This latter concern would be serious in the case of Chad. Its president has recently faced resistance from the Mouvement pour la Démocratie et la Justice au Tchad (MDJT) and Mouvement de Renouveau National (MRN), both led by former government ministers. He and his predecessors in the past have faced challenges from (among others) the Armée Volcan, Conseil Démocratique Révolutionnaire, Forces Armées du Nord, Forces Armées Occidentales, Forces Armées Populaires, Frolinat Originel, Frolinat Fondamental, Front de Libération du Tchad, Front Populaire de Libération du Tchad and Front pour la Libération Nationale du Tchad (Siddick and Goukouni wings), and finally the Mouvement Populaire de Libération du Tchad. What are a president, banker and foreign firms to do? The most reasonable strategy is to stay with the president they have got, because he possesses sovereign authority. Various rebel groups may be stronger, more competent or nicer to local people. But none possess sovereignty (at least until one captures the capital), and thus none can validate contracts with foreign firms to the satisfaction of foreign courts, underwriters or investors, and multilateral creditors certainly cannot engage rebel groups. These partners will be especially inclined to stick with the president they have if they think the alternative might lead to protracted stalemates among multiple rebel groups. The president and foreign firms are the biggest winners because, once again, stability and resources come from outside the tumultuous weak state, in this case courtesy of creditors.

Insurgencies based upon controlling cross-border trade and natural resources, however, still pose a challenge. Behaving much like the rulers they challenge, insurgents abjure mobilising populations, except to pit

---

[54] 'Statement to the European Parliament's Development Committee, Chad Programme and Chad Cameroon Pipeline Project', 21 June 2001.

[55] IMF, 'Decision Point Document for the Enhanced Heavily Indebted Poor Countries (HIPC) Initiative', 4 May 2001.

farmers against moneylenders or organise gangs directly to exploit resources such as alluvial diamonds or timber. Like weak state rulers, they
lack their own programmes of economic or social transformation, and are
thus threatened by organisations, including state bureaucracies, that might
acquire one. This strategy characterised Mozambique's Renamo in the
1980s, but became more common in the 1990s as insurgents battled what
had become de-bureaucratised patronage networks of a corrupt state regime. Insurgencies such as Liberia's National Patriotic Front of Liberia,
Sierra Leone's Revolutionary Unity Front, Uganda's Lord's Resistance
Army and Nile West Bank Front and Congo's Alliance des Forces Démo-
cratiques pour la Libération all focused on capturing rent-seeking opportunities from their opponents. This mimicry extends to the strategic uses
of the devices and norms of states to exploit opportunities for private accumulation. It is typical that rebel organisations in weak states insist that
people under their control use a special currency. This creates economic
borders, the control of which personally benefits fighters.[56] Like their weak
state ruler brethren, rebels try to accentuate and exploit economic boundaries so that they can profit from their positions at the nexus of markets.

The crucial difference between rebels and weak state rulers is that the
latter possess globally recognised sovereignty, permitting them to manipulate prerogatives of sovereignty that are not available to insurgent leaders. Weak state rulers' international connections are far easier to manage,
compared to insurgents'. For the ruler, global recognition provides rulers
with an established position as a prerogative of sovereignty. The rebels
struggle to construct an alternative encompassing system that controls
exchanges on two sides of a border that they erect. This is nearly impossible to maintain, since insurgents also fear effective bureaucrats as potential rivals. They cannot provide a stable business environment on either side
of their internal boundary. Insurgents are thus reduced to skimming off
profits of trade between two or more chaotic areas through the imprecise
decentralised instrument of armed fighters who are more likely to help
themselves to profits than to share them with their superiors. In contrast,
rulers of states are positioned astride a 'real' border. Behind this they can
engage their business partners; the external side provides order and predictability in the relationship through the efforts of other agents described
above.

Weak state rulers use their power to permit legitimate access to a territory to attract private business partners. Rather than basing the appeal of
his state on the effectiveness or capabilities of his (moribund) state

---

[56] For Liberia, see Bayo Ogunleye, *Behind Rebel Line: Anatomy of Charles Taylor's Hos-
tage Camps*, Enugu, Nigeria: Delta Publications, 1995, pp. 134–46. For Somalia: 'Monopoly Money', *Indian Ocean Newsletter*, 14 June 1997.

bureaucracies, the ruler has a commercial appeal which lies in his willingness to share the benefits of this privatisation of prerogatives of sovereignty. He uses sovereignty to keep other business groups away from natural resources, provide protection from external scrutiny and equip his partners with official documents to certify (or help conceal) transactions. In Sierra Leone, for example, non-citizens were sold diplomatic passports, some of which were feared to have fallen into the hands of drug traffickers.[57] In Congo-Brazzaville, the prospect that former President Sassou-Nguesso could fight his way back to State House appears to have been crucial in his successful efforts to secure material and political support from the oil company, Elf Aquitaine, and the French government.[58] This was a risky strategy; had their client failed, the oil company would have been frozen out of this market with little recourse. It was the sovereign status, not the man that shaped Elf's decision. Earlier Elf helped arrange a loan for Sassou-Nguesso's opponent, President Pascal Lissouba, to purchase weapons before he was forced from office.

For foreign commercial partners, sovereignty remains an essential ingredient of any long-term business strategy. There is as yet no basis in commercial law, at least in Britain or the US, for indemnifying firms against expropriation by non-sovereign insurgents.[59] Nor have firms that have done business with insurgents (usually in hopes that they will replace incumbent regimes) been shielded from prosecution in courts of either headquarters or host states for violation of contractual agreements.[60] Global commercial jurisprudence does not yet extend benefits of its order to transactions with insurgents. Some firms may identify opportunities for quick profits in the extremely unregulated environments of places lacking authoritative bureaucracies, both in weak states and in insurgent-held territory. But they must do so with the understanding that business in the latter is isolated from the legal apparatus that provides predictable relations with firms' creditors, underwriters, and government regulators in other states where it does business.

---

[57] 'New Envoys', *West Africa*, 8–14 July 1996, p. 1052; K-Roy Stevens, 'Former Ecowas Scribe on Trial', *West Africa*, 12–18 August 1996, p. 1276. Passport fraud is a problem elsewhere too. For example, Mbye Saine, '3 Former Ministers Evicted', *The Point*, Banjul, The Gambia, 28 October 1996.

[58] Howard French, 'Brazzaville and Oil Port Are Taken by Rebels', *New York Times*, 16 October 1997; US Congress, House International Relations Committee, 'Situation in Central Africa', 5 November 1997.

[59] Marian Nash, 'Contemporary Practice of the United States Relating to International Law', *American Journal of International Law*, 90 (April 1996), pp. 263–5.

[60] Compare, for example, National Patriotic Reconstruction Assembly Government [NPFL-held Liberia], 'Memorandum of Understanding', and 'Firestone Restart Timetable', 16 January 1992; and Republic of Liberia, Ministry of Finance, 'Memorandum on Behaviour of Firestone During the Liberian Civil War', 6 May 1993.

These advantages help explain why African 'warlord' insurgents nearly always aim to capture State Houses, or at least force rulers to share power. For example, Charles Taylor's NPFL controlled the bulk of Liberia and some trade networks extending into neighbouing states from 1990 to 1993. Taylor had access to far greater amounts of money than did the internationally recognised government of Liberia, which occupied a tiny coastal enclave from mid 1990 to 1996 and, reports Clapham, generated a gross product of a mere $250,000 in 1993![61] Furthermore, he wielded enough power to deny others access to his realm and to conclude agreements with foreign firm partners. During this time, a few large firms like Firestone Tire & Rubber did business with him. But most established firms left by late 1992 as it became apparent that Taylor would not soon occupy the Executive Mansion in the capital. Firms that did business with Taylor did not expect to benefit from conventional state services such as utilities (Taylor and his associates demanded that firms supply these to them as well) or even security (which firms provided privately). Instead, firms bargained with Taylor in the expectation that he would become the president of the Republic of Liberia, no matter how internally weak that state may be, or even if he continued to behave as a warlord once in control of a sovereign state. This was an impression that he went to great lengths to cultivate overseas,[62] even as he spoke to people in areas he controlled in terms of a 'Greater Liberia' and other alternatives that would require changing international borders or establishing a new state. This limitation became evident when Taylor could not take command of the sovereign state after his failed October 1992 'Operation Octopus' military offensive, and his foreign commercial partners began to abandon him (*see Table*).

The prize of sovereignty for commercial benefit appears to forestall secessionist urges in other cases. In former Zaire, foreign firms did business with a seemingly successful insurgent, Laurent Kabila. Kabila was able to join his interest in replacing Mobutu with those of firms anxious to find a more suitable state ruler who could guarantee them access to minerals.[63] Kabila's 1996–7 offensive did not portend disintegration as some predicted. In fact, Kabila and his diverse, multinational array of partners needed recognition of sovereignty to satisfy their aims, not the least of

---

[61] Clapham (note 2) p. 230.

[62] National Patriotic Reconstruction Government of Liberia, *The Legal Status of the National Patriotic Reconstruction Government as the Defacto Government of the Republic of Liberia*, Gbarnga, Liberia, no date.

[63] For example, Gorham/Intertech Consulting, 'Cobalt 94: Opportunities, Problems and Survival Strategies', November 1994 conference, Vienna, VA, outlined the need for cobalt producers to back alternatives to then Zairean president Mobutu who would have more predictable control over associates, but stressed that such partners would have to become globally recognised rulers through taking control of the capital.

Table 4.1 CHARLES TAYLOR'S SOURCES OF ACCUMULATION, 1990–94
($ millions*)

	1990	1991	1992	1993	1994
Diamonds	100	100	150	50	50
Timber	15	21.3	30.3	25	15
Rubber	29	27	27	1.5	1
Iron ore	40	30	25	nil	nil
Total	184	178.3	232.3	76.5	67

* Round figures are approximate.

Sources: William Twaddell, US Assistant Secretary of State for African Affairs, 'Testimony Before the House International Relations Committee,' Washington, DC, 26 June 1996; 'Le Libéria: une économie de guerre profitable', *Marchés Tropicaux*, 28 July 1995; Ross Reeves and Michel Moulard, 'Postwar Strategy for Forestry Development and Environmental Management' for Ministry of Planning and Economic Affairs, Monrovia, 1993; Liner Bills of Lading, Greenville and Buchanan, 1991–2; Interim Government of National Unity [Liberia] Bureau of Concessions, 'GOL—Firestone Historical and Future Relationship—A Fiscal Policy Perspective', 31 March 1993; documents from National Patriotic Reconstruction Assembly Government [Charles Taylor's organisation] Forestry Development Authority and Economic Affairs Committee, 1990–3.

which was to carry through with private business deals while minimising the capacity of freelancing local elites to do the same.

Global recognition of a state's, and by extension a regime's sovereignty is the anchor for international commercial jurisprudence. The external constitution of sovereignty gives weak states independence from external threats (as Jackson stressed in his analysis of the quasi-state) that also extends to protection from scrutiny of internal commercial arrangements. But firms and global jurisprudence have as yet found no credible alternative to a global society of sovereign states to secure commercial interests.

Recognition of even the weakest states provides firms with stability, order and finality in relations with a single set of interlocutors, at least in global society beyond the weak state's recognised borders. This translates into a preference for the status quo in internal state politics and admonitions against sharing sovereign prerogatives with non-state authorities. Firms thus share interests with officials in strong states in maintaining Africa's state system, weak though its members may be, as authoritative interlocutors with outsiders.

Stronger states, legal custom, international organisations, and other firms (such as underwriters) supply stability and order, and reduce risk to firms for their dealings outside the boundaries of the weak state. Firms that are able to do business with weak state rulers who need firms to help control internal markets can then grab opportunities that collaborative privatisation of sovereignty can provide. Sovereignty remains as a veil over the domestic practice of governance, or over its lack. The non-institutional, often clandestine nature of these partnerships further shields them from external critics who tend to focus on institutional manifestations of supposed state collapse in Africa. This external provision of order—in which both weak states and their foreign partners behave as free riders—is critical to the generation of shared benefits of partnerships.

The dichotomous internal-external nature of these partnerships also determines the character of firms involved in weak states. Enclave mining firms are most adept at exploiting global protection for property and contract enforcement outside weak state boundaries. Internally, these firms can manage anarchy and provide their own security and infrastructure, often as part of a political arrangement with a ruler anxious to remove insurgents or potential rivals from mineral resources that he cannot control himself. In contrast, intellectual property depends on internal state regulation to prevent appropriation and unauthorised distribution of valuable material. Intellectual property is more likely to appear in very weak states in the hands of thieves who use the weak state's sovereignty, whether with the ruler's authorisation or not, to shield their operations from external scrutiny. The proliferation of pirated audio and video tapes, CDs, and computer software in places like Lagos and Abidjan attests to the vulnerability of property that cannot be easily matched with private security.

But for the enclave operation, the internal incapacities of weak state authority bestow a competitive advantage on firms able to manage internal anarchy. Smaller, less established firms appropriate high-risk niche markets that they can use in bargaining with their larger, more established competitors. A key component of this strategy includes partnerships with weak state rulers who use firms to deny resources to rivals, and filling in for essential state bureaucratic functions like conducting relations with outsiders and exercising coercion.

For example, some small mining firms have used mercenaries to protect mine sites. This removes presidential rivals from resources and generates revenues that are used to meet the state's financial obligations to creditors. This in turn releases more loans (sometimes directly from international financial institutions to firms, but guaranteed by host state governments) and foreign aid.[64] The presence of these firms creates opportunities for key politicians enjoying presidential favour to form joint ventures with foreign entrepreneurs. A number of operations of this type linked Executive Outcomes, a South African mercenary outfit, and a Canadian mining firm. In the mid-1990s such operations maintained mining operations in Sierra Leone, Uganda and Angola. In Sierra Leone, those operations

---

[64] Joint ventures can also spin off fake non-governmental organisations that style themselves as organisations such as 'women's movements' and such to gain access to money from bilateral aid programmes.

generated 35 per cent of the country's export earnings in 1996. In Sierra Leone and Uganda, they have helped to train local anti-insurgency units that have played key roles in not only containing rebel activities, but also cowing politically unreliable regular militaries.[65] Other firms pursue similar arrangements in the Democratic Republic of Congo, Mozambique, Angola, the Central African Republic and Congo-Brazzaville, defending mine sites in strategic locations near rebel concentrations from freelance strongmen.

This type of business operation requires a high degree of meddling in internal affairs on the part of firms. This is tolerable to weak state rulers who fear threats that indigenous rule-based bureaucracies would pose to their own authority. This level of involvement would unsettle stronger state rulers who would be less desperate or less commercially involved with their foreign partners. More established firms with more far-flung investments are thus more constrained in internal involvement and leave commerce in the weakest states to more flexible competitors. Flexible operators in turn take on tasks of protecting themselves and their presidential partners, and thus gain from a bargaining position they could not assume in states where officials can provide internal protection from risk and disorder. Smaller firms can thus derive some commercial benefit from their superior skills at claiming some of the resources that manipulation of sovereignty can provide. They can sell these to larger, more established partners through becoming agents or intermediaries. This is especially the case in the diamond market where large firms are anxious to maintain market share, yet would have a more difficult time becoming so integrally involved in internal political affairs of host governments, if for no other reason that other host governments may become suspicious of the firms' motives and reliability.

Interstate politics and Africa's shadow states

Rulers of weak states thus reconstruct their authority through manipulation of outsiders' norms concerning sovereignty. Their strategies not only solidify their weak states' relations with transnational actors, but also bolster their capacities in relations with other states. This offers officials in strong states new ways to manage relations through the private agents that constitute the external component of the weak state ruler's strategy. These foreign officials seek to disengage from Africa, largely for budgetary reasons now that politicians detect little strategic value in relations with what have become internally chaotic states. The alternative is influence on the

[65] William Reno, 'African Weak States and Commercial Alliances', *African Affairs* vol. 96 no. 383 (April 1997), pp. 165–86.

cheap, acquired through accommodations with transnational firms that do business with weak state rulers. The weak state-foreign firm partnership produces order and promotes accumulation, both useful to foreign officials anxious to reduce political pressures from constituents to address chaos and humanitarian emergencies in far-off places. The prospect of boosting weak state revenues also heartens creditor officials who are loath to dismiss debts as uncollectible, as noted above.

Officials from stronger states also find that they can integrate this partnership into privatised and decentralised aid and peace-keeping programmes. For example, firms spun off from the mercenary firm (and its associates) that have protected Angolan (since 1993) and Sierra Leonean mine sites (since 1995) have bid for United Nations Angolan Verification Mission contracts to remove mines, provide logistical support for aid programmes and build infrastructure. When these new ventures involve local politicians as partners, the broadened politician-foreign firm collaboration can tap into new, external sources of wealth.[66] Similar arrangements appear among individual foreign military trainers in Sierra Leone and local politicians who set up their own 'NGOs' to attract grants from bilateral aid agencies and foreign private donors.[67]

The use of private intermediaries also helps insulate officials in other states from political debates surrounding budget appropriations or political risk of foreign policy operations. An American company, Military Professionals Incorporated, helped train the Angolan military. This firm also advised and helped arm the Bosnian Muslim army in former Yugoslavia. In both cases, private agents pay for the foreign 'aid'. In Angola, the weak state's capacity to produce oil and mine other resources paid for MPRI's operation. The firm employed retired US military officers, giving weak state officials preferential access to US politicians and foreign investors. In the Bosnian example, Saudi and other 'philanthropists' financed Bosnian rearmament, preserving US officials from foreign policy debates in the US Congress and creating informal channels through which US officials could support Bosnian Muslims against the wishes of some of their NATO allies. It is thus likely that officials in weak states can extend their new private partnerships to include backers in other states, provided they remain interlocutors for a globally recognised state.

---

[66] Human Rights Watch Arms Project, *Angola: Between War and Peace*, Human Rights Watch, February 1996; interviews with officials from Canadian Forces, South African National Defence Force, July 1997 and November 1997.

[67] Interviews and observations, Sierra Leone, January 1996. One such group consisted of a Congolese businessman who had earlier won contracts to import and distribute food aid to Mozambique. In Sierra Leone he, a US mining entrepreneur, and a local politician called their organisation a Christian charity, soliciting cash donations and used medical equipment.

The international relations of weak states increasingly mix a style of nineteenth century precolonial European relations with chiefs on the African coast and middle power relations with African rulers during the Cold War, an 'imperialism by invitation'.[68] The difference from the nineteenth century, however, lies in the inviolability of currently existing sovereignties. There is as yet no widely accepted mechanism for decertifying failed states. Weak states therefore cannot decisively succumb to more cohesive and internally capable rivals, contrary to the analysis of Herbst.[69] Even those states lacking great power capabilities find that support for weak state rulers, particularly through commercial intermediaries, is a cheap way to assert power. Libyan, Iranian and Israeli officials have been more sensitive to the internal vulnerabilities of rulers, even during the Cold War, mainly because these states had fewer resources that they could distribute in return for diplomatic support. Officials in these states have a longer experience of addressing the internal political needs of weak state rulers and are thus likely to continue to do so where they can exploit their experience and existing contacts. This advantage extends to Russia and South Africa too, where Cold War security establishments that built ties with vulnerable African rulers are privatising themselves and converting security links into commercial partnerships.[70]

Echoing the main proposition in this chapter, two scholars wrote: 'Rather than proceeding from the assumption that all states are sovereign, we are interested in considering the variety of ways in which states are constantly negotiating their sovereignty.'[71] External support for a static vision of external domains of sovereignty remains surprisingly strong, however. Weak states exist within this interstice of the state system because they continue to define themselves as juridical equals to other states, even though they lack centralised systems of government and do not provide collective goods to citizens. This suggests that dichotomies between internal and external sovereignty in Africa are likely to continue, especially given the commercial and political advantages to outsiders.

---

[68] Michael Doyle, *Empires*, Ithaca NY: Cornell University Press, 1986.

[69] Jeffrey Herbst, 'Responding to State Failure in Africa', *International Security*, 21:3, winter 1996/97, pp. 120–44.

[70] From South Africa, private military firms like Executive Outcomes, Omega Support, Panasec and Combat Force boasted ties to apartheid era military networks to advertise their expertise. The appearance of Ukrainian air support services in Sierra Leone, Angola, Congo Republic and elsewhere (often with their own trading firms) highlights the commercialisation of former Soviet military networks. Almazy Sakha Rossiya, a large Siberian mining firm in Angola, also appears to benefit from previous close ties between Angolan and Soviet military authorities.

[71] Thomas Biersteker and Cynthia Weber, 'The Social Construction of State Sovereignty', in T. Biersteker and C. Weber (eds), *State Sovereignty as Social Construct*, New York: Cambridge University Press, 1996, p. 11.

5

POWER IS NOT SOVEREIGN:
THE PLURALISATION OF ECONOMIC
REGULATORY AUTHORITY IN THE CHAD BASIN

Janet Roitman

The frontiers of power are changing. Or at least this is what we are compelled to conclude when we see how transformations in local, inter- and transnational politico-economic relations have caused unprecedented relationships in the contemporary world. This is evident in instances of mass mediation, which have allowed community and place to become largely unhinged, and in the transnational realms created by new financial instruments and technologies, where time and place are uncoupled and hence jurisdiction unsettled. Under the somewhat vague rubric of 'globalisation', these complicated matters are problematised in terms of certain tropes: territory, place, and space are perhaps foremost among them.[1] Their predominance has significant consequences for how we confront the problem of transformations in the nature of power and authority in the world today.

This emphasis on space and place—on the changing geography of power—is, of course, warranted. A great part of what we are witnessing— the increasing mobility of capital and labour, the intensification of disciplinary mechanisms and regulatory authority associated with world financial institutions, the rupture of boundaries brought on by new technologies and media forms, and the extension of diasporas as distinct geo-political entities—results from, and contributes to, the destabilisation of the territorialising project of the nation-state.[2] Thus while inter- and transnational

---

[1] See, of course, David Harvey's fascinating interpretation of 'space-time compression' and the annihilation of space in *The Condition of Postmodernity*, Oxford: Basil Blackwell, 1989.

[2] This is most clearly demonstrated by Arjun Appadurai. See his 'Disjuncture and Difference in the Global Cultural Economy', *Public Culture*, 2/2, spring 1990, pp. 1–24; and

phenomena are by no means new aspects of nation-based geopolitics, the idea, for example, that 'the national economy' is a naturally occurring part of the nation-state—that 'economy' is naturalised as 'national'—is only now being interrogated.[3]

The concerns of this chapter follow this line of thought. In a very general sense, the problem of circumscribing the economy—or 'the economic'—is approached in terms of modalities of power, considering the exercise of power in trans- and sub-national regions (e.g. regional economies dependant on transnational markets in capital, goods, services or labour) and ambiguous territories (e.g. borders). While one cannot avoid the subject of space/place when reflecting on contemporary geographies of power, the great emphasis placed on 'locating' power—in its new forms and expansive networks, for example—tends to obstruct our understanding of historical practices of power. In other words, there is a tendency to seek out the supposed locations of power while slighting the matter of its modes of exercise. Although this is perhaps warranted as a first step in delineating unprecedented relationships and connections across national space, one wonders how power can be perceived outside of its mode of practice. How do we know that it is there unless its effects have been noted, its exigencies performed by its very subjects?[4]

This is the question taken up here in reference to the Chad Basin, where emergent sub- and transnational regimes of accumulation and authority have come to dominate the Nigerian, Cameroonian, Nigérien, Chadian and Centrafrican borders. Their effective authority over certain economic activities, regional or international resources, and local populations puts them in competition with the nation-state. I will argue that, while this situation seems 'oppositional', it does not necessarily imply the demise of the nation-state in the face of non-national forms of accumulation and power. In fact, one can argue that the relationships between the two realms are highly ambiguous: they are often reciprocal and complicitous as much as they are competitive and antagonistic. That is, while antagonisms are noted when it comes to the state's official regulatory authority over these regional economies, complicity is evident insofar as the state is dependent upon these regional economies for rents and the means of redistribution. Likewise, while these networks can be described as trans- or sub-national,

---

Modernity at Large: Cultural Dimensions of Globalization, Minneapolis: University of Minnesota Press, 1996.

[3] Benedict Anderson claims that the concept of the 'national economy' dates from '[a]s late at least as the founding of the League of Nations', being intrinsically linked to the very doctrine of self-determination. Cf. his 'Introduction' in G. Balakrishnan, *Mapping the Nation*, London: Verso, 1996, p. 7.

[4] M. Foucault, *The History of Sexuality. Volume I: An Introduction*, New York: Vintage Books, 1990.

they make important, or even essential, contributions to the national political economy. Moreover, while these regimes of power and wealth may be described as novel realms of thought and action, they are nonetheless inscribed in the same logical—or epistemological—order as that of the nation-state.

The Chad Basin can be described as a region of competing sources of wealth, regulatory authority and welfare. In order to clarify this situation, I will first briefly review the ways in which networks of wealth creation arise out of strategies for accumulation that are defined by, and take advantage of, opportunities and constraints produced by the imperatives of the global political economy, such as deregulation and privatisation. In the Chad Basin, these latter processes have resulted in a military-commercial nexus which has become the legitimate basis of livelihood for many people of the region. The continuity of this complex of relationships is partly ensured by the exercise of newly articulated claims to rights in wealth, which, while often working to undermine the integrity of the national political-economy at the point of regulation, are nonetheless deemed licit by participants and local observers.

What we see is the institutionalisation not only of relationships defining networks, but of particular definitions of licit wealth and manners of appropriating wealth. I suggest that this process is dependent on the frontier, both literally and conceptually. The transgression of national economies and political regimes is a border and bush phenomenon in the Chad Basin. And, as I explain below, the political frontier and the economy of the bush are defined by new concepts of wealth (e.g. spoils) and manners of appropriating such wealth (e.g. rights-in-seizure). But these are not marginal: these concepts and practices are assumed by those who work the bush and border, as well as those tending to the state bureaucracy and the national economy. While defined by their subversive relationships to official regulatory authority, these trans- and sub-regional activities are on the frontiers of wealth creation. They are among the few means of accessing hard currency, scarce luxury goods, and state-of-the-art technology, as well as markets in small arms, minerals, gems and drugs. More generally, they produce wealth in times of austerity and serve as essential mediations between the state and the global economy. As such, they are an important resource for representatives of the national economy, providing new rents for the management of internal conflict and the redistributive logics of national politics, and a means of insertion in the world economy. Therefore, although some practices associated with emergent regimes of accumulation and wealth may undermine forms of authority defined by the nation-state, they also contribute to its capacity to exercise power over wealth and people.

This conclusion runs contrary to some recent observations of the relationship between transnational networks and the state. Because regimes of wealth and power such as those described herein demonstrate effective authority over certain resources, activities and persons, they are often described as antagonistic to the nation-state. That is, beyond undermining a particular regime, they are said to be new sites of sovereignty and hence a threat to the absolute and unique status of the nation-state. Without necessarily ushering in the demise of the nation-state form, networks of power which seem to parallel or compete with the nation-state—financial markets, agglomerations of non-governmental organisations, transnational mafias—are said to constitute potential domains of sovereign power.[5]

In general, regimes of wealth and power compete with the nation-state in the Chad Basin only insofar as they undermine official regulatory authority. New manners of creating wealth, and articulating and exercising legitimate rights-in-wealth, have been normalised through the military-commercial alliance described herein. This has given rise to new figures of regulatory authority in the region. However, these arrangements are part and parcel of the political logics of the state: they contribute to the viability of state power through the production of rents and possibilities for redistribution. And, more importantly, the precepts underlying these apparently novel relationships, activities and modalities issue out of, or are consistent with, those practiced in the existing political economy or historical socio-juridical order. In reflecting on this point, I close by indicating how conclusions as to the emergence of novel forms of sovereignty in the contemporary global political economy are driven by the mutually-constituting problematics of locating power and conceptualising state power as sovereign.

The global context of the regional political economy

In many ways, the scenario I refer to in the Chad Basin illustrates the local effects of global processes. While commercial networks that span the borders of Cameroon, Nigeria and Chad have historical precedents in the trans-Saharan and east-west Sahelian economies, their resurgence in recent years is in part due to the effective incorporation and novel use of

---

[5] Cf. A. Ong, *Flexible Citizenship: the Cultural Logics of Transnationality*, Durham, NC: Duke University Press, 1999; R. Latham, 'Identifying the Contours of Transboundary Political Life' in T. Callaghy, R. Kassimir and R. Latham (eds), *Intervention and Transnationalism in Africa: Global-Local Networks of Power*, Cambridge University Press, 2001, pp. 240–83; C. Nordstrom, 'Out of the Shadows' in T. Callaghy, R. Kassimir and R. Latham (eds), *Intervention and Transnationalism in Africa: Global-Local Network of Power*, Cambridge University Press, 2001, pp. 216–39.

resources derived from international markets. As elsewhere on the continent, marginalisation from certain world markets (e.g. export crop commodities) and the proliferation of certain resources for accumulation (e.g. drugs, small arms) have resulted in a drive for new forms of economic integration.[6] These include sometimes risky and hence often lucrative ventures such as the trade in small arms flowing through Sudan, Libya, Chad, Cameroon, Nigeria and Niger, and Algeria; provisioning of ongoing conflict in Niger, Chad, the Central African Republic, and the Sudan which involves transiting petrol, hardware, electronics, grain, cement, detergent and (most often stolen) cars and four-wheel drive trucks; the ivory trade centred around Lake Chad and the Central African Republic; the transfer of drugs between the Pakistani crescent, Nigeria, and Western Europe; and large-scale, highly organised highway banditry.[7]

These types of commerce and the trading regimes they found are influenced by the global political economy in several ways. First, the deregulation of both world and local markets has exacerbated dependencies on certain international markets in the regional political-economy. This is the case for the international markets in small arms, mercenaries, private security forces and militias, which recently have gained prominence in the region. Today, one notes a proliferation on the continent of arms from Eastern Europe, the independent Republics of the former Soviet Union, China, South Africa and Angola, and the increased circulation of mercenaries from France, Belgium, South Africa, ex-Yugoslavia and Pakistan.[8] The formalisation of these once secretive flows is summarised by the

[6] Cf. J.-F. Bayart, S. Ellis and B. Hibou, *The Criminalization of the State in Africa*, London: International African Institute in association with James Currey (Oxford) and Indiana University Press (Bloomington and Indianapolis), 1999.

[7] On Kalashnikovs and the Chadian economy, cf. *Jeune Afrique*, 19 November 1992, pp. 28–30. On the continental drug economy, cf. Observatoire géopolitique des drogues, *Géopolitique des drogues 1995*, Paris: La Découverte, 1995. On highway banditry, cf. F. Soudan, 'La guerre secrète', *Jeune Afrique* no. 1871, 13 November 1996 and F. Dorce, 'Cameroun: cette guerre qui cache son nom', *Jeune Afrique Économie*, no. 229, 18 November 1996. More generally, cf. J.-F. Bayart, S. Ellis and B. Hibou (note 6) and K. Bennafla, 'Rapport sur les échanges transfrontaliers informels au Tchad', unpubl. ms., Université de Paris X-Nanterre, February 1996 and 'Entre Afrique noire et monde arabe. Nouvelles tendances des échanges "informels" tchadiens', *Revue Tiers Monde*, XXXVIII, 152, October–November 1997, pp. 879–96.

[8] These points are briefly reviewed in various parts of Bayart *et al.* (note 6) and in many issues of *L'Autre Afrique*. See also *La France Militaire et l'Afrique* , Brussels: Éditions Complexe-GRIP, 1997; 'Burundi: trafics d'armes et aides militaires', Human Rights Watch; M. Friedman, 'Kalachnikov: trente années de rafales', *Jeune Afrique* no. 1701–2, 12–25 August 1993, pp. 98–101; 'Afrique: le nouvel empire des mercenaires', *Le Figaro*, 15 January 1997; J. Harding, 'The Mercenary Business', *London Review of Books*, 1 August 1996, pp. 3–9; and R. Banégas, 'De la guerre au maintien de la paix: le nouveau business mercenaire', *Critique Internationale*, no. 1, autumn 1998, pp. 179–94.

comments of Captain Hoffman: 'I am a mercenary. I "rent" my services to foreign countries for money. Many of us prefer the term "technical consultant"...'[9] This increasingly explicit and normalised presence has led both private concerns and public power increasingly to employ private security forces (e.g. Wackenhut, Executive Outcomes) to defend oil fields, mines, airports, company headquarters, government buildings and residential neighbourhoods. High-placed government officials and military personnel are often implicated in the operations and revenues of this economic sector, such that the security business is now an important vocation in the regional political economy, helping to sustain the international traffic in arms and men.[10] This has been abetted by the fact that programmes for economic and political liberalisation put forth by the World Bank and the International Monetary Fund have resulted in the privatisation of state-run industries as well as internal security.

Indeed, the conditionalities of international financing are another contributing factor to transformations of the regional economy. This can be seen through the impact of structural adjustment programmes, which privatised industries and downsized armies, leading to swollen ranks of the unemployed, who seek opportunities for accumulation in the emergent markets of the region. No social category of the population has been spared. In Chad, for example, the military demobilisation programme started in 1992 has generally been eclipsed by soldiers' ability to recycle themselves through various regional rebel groups (e.g. the Mouvement pour le Développement around Lake Chad or the Forces Armées pour la République Fédérale in southern Chad); to enter into the small arms traffic, for which they have contacts and expertise; or to 'enter the bush', often working as road bandits with organised groups of Cameroonians, Nigerians, Nigériens, Centrafricans and Sudanese.[11] Likewise, the local

---

[9] *Jeune Afrique*, no. 1701–2, 12–25 August 1993, pp. 92–5.

[10] See the references in footnote 8, paying particular attention to B. Hibou, 'The "Social Capital" of the State as an Agent of Deception, or the Ruses of Economic Intelligence', in Bayart *et al.* (note 6), pp. 69–113. See also S. Ellis, 'Africa and International Corruption: the Strange Case of South Africa and Seychelles', *African Affairs*, vol. 95, no. 379, April 1996, pp. 165–96.

[11] Between 1992 and 1997, 27,000 Chadian military personnel were supposed to be demobilised and disarmed. Since Kalashnikovs had become a veritable currency as well as a means of accumulation in the region (circulating especially between Chad, Niger and Libya), upon collection of the 30,000 CFA francs promised in exchange for their military uniforms and arms, most Chadian soldiers reinvested in the arms market. See *Jeune Afrique*, 19 November 1992 (note 7); 'Armée: lumière sur la démobilisation et la réinsertion', *Le Progrès* (N'Djamena), 13 May 1997, pp. 10–11; 'Lorsque démobilisation rime avec développement', *N'Djamena Hebdo*, 281, 15 May 1997, pp. 6–7; M. B. Teiga, 'Une armée, certes, mais combien de divisions...', *L'Autre Afrique*, 17–23 December

urban-based merchant class, which produced its rents through debt-financing up until the late 1980s[12] was forced to reconfigure its economic activities with the contraction in bilateral and multilateral aid. Their past engagements as transporters and suppliers for public works projects have been reformulated in terms of the remaining or evolving possibilities for enrichment: their convoys have taken up the paths running through Nigeria, Cameroon, the Central African Republic, Chad, Libya and Sudan (e.g. smuggling petrol).

And since privatisation and the downsizing of public enterprises accompanying structural adjustment programmes have inflated the ranks of unemployed youth, growing hordes of young men have followed the paths of the merchants' convoys. Those who once found employment in local agro-industry, the health and education sectors, and development and public works projects now work as transporters, guards, guides and carriers along the Nigerian, Cameroonian and Chadian borders. One might argue, in fact, that the urban networks that have predominated over the countryside for several decades are becoming increasingly dependent upon economic strategies pursued by the unemployed and recently dispossessed. In many ways, the urban economy is now subservient to the 'economy of the bush'. As a recent report on the monetary situation in the Franc Zone notes, the 'urban exodus' of bank notes and coinage—notably smaller denominations, which are virtually impossible to procure in large towns and cities—is largely attributable to the vitality of the rural sector, and especially the border and bush economy.[13]

1997, pp. 14–15; and Bennafla, 1996 (note 7), who notes that, 'Many "deflated" soldiers rush to buy back a khaki uniform and an arm as soon as they are pensioned off' (p. 65, my translation). This was confirmed in interviews with military and civil administrators, as well as human rights activists in N'Djamena.

[12] J.-F. Bayart, *L'État en Afrique*, Paris: Fayard, 1989.

[13] 'Un billet de banque, ça peut couter cher...', *L'Autre Afrique*, 13–19 August 1997, pp. 66–8. F. de Boeck describes how young Zairean urbanites have migrated to rural areas along the Angolan border in order to partake in the diamond economy. This has lead to their inclusion in a 'dollarised' economy—the bush economy, as opposed to the city, becoming the very source of tokens of wealth and consumption. See his 'Domesticating Diamonds and Dollars: Identity, Expenditure and Sharing in Southwestern Zaire' in P. Geschiere and B. Meyer (eds), *Globalization and Identity*, Oxford: Basil Blackwell, 1999. This does not mean, as both de Boeck (ibid.) and K. Bennafla ('Mbaiboum: un marché au carrefour de frontières multiples' in J. Egg and J. Herrara (eds), 'Echanges transfrontaliers et intégration régionale en Afrique subsaharienne', *Autrepart*, no. 6, 1998, pp. 53–72) note, that investment practice has also been reoriented from the urban centres to the bush. Revenue procured through commercial and financial activities transpiring in the latter is often invested or consumed in cities and major towns.

Producing wealth on the frontier: the economy of the bush

In sum, the stimulation of economic activity in the bush is partly a result of the combined efforts of the economic refugees of structural adjustment programmes and decreased foreign aid, on the one hand, and the military refugees of downsized and under-financed armies, on the other. In the Chad Basin those recently discharged during the demobilisation campaign in Chad have joined up with unpaid soldiers from Cameroon, Nigeria, Niger and Sudan, as well as the guards and guides who have worked the bush trails trafficking contraband goods (especially petrol) for almost a decade now. Together, they raid border markets and highways.[14] Their activities have transformed border areas, which are speckled with settlements that serve as depots, hide-outs, and bulking and rediffusion points. Some 'are quietly flourishing...as local entrepôts specialized in precision goods such as radios, cassette-recorders, watches, etc. as well as petrol retailing and currency exchanges.'[15]

What is especially novel about this situation, and what makes it worth noting with respect to the dynamics of transregional political-economies and the nation-state, is that the dismissed, dispossessed and unemployed who have taken to the bush, highways and borders are making claims to rights to wealth. Many unemployed young men have some form of education, sometimes having finished high school, and yet they find themselves obliged to scavenge and traffic for money. They often talk about their situation as a state of 'war', where forced appropriation and seizure are the norm, being practiced by customs officials, police, gangs, armed bandits, and themselves.[16] And those who normally benefit from rights-in-seizure also complain about lack of compensation; regular soldiers protest (often through mutinies, as in the Central African Republic, and just recently Niger) against insufficient and irregular salaries, lack of basic infrastructure (e.g. sleeping quarters, food), and even essential equipment to carry out their duties (petrol, ammunition).[17] Likewise, demobilised soldiers

---

[14] Read K. Pideu, 'Une province abandonée aux coupeurs de route', *La Nouvelle Expression*, 243, 28–31 March 1995, p. 6; Soudan (note 7); Dorce (note 7); and 'L'Insécurité dans le nord Cameroun', *N'Djamena Hebdo*, January 1997.

[15] E. Achu Gwan, 'The Nigeria-Cameroon Boundary and Nigerians in Cameroon, Paper submitted to the Nigeria-Cameroon Trans-border Cooperation Workshop', Yola, Nigeria, 25–30 May 1992, p. 23.

[16] Commentary on visions of wealth, freedom, and violence by young illegal petrol sellers in northern Cameroon can be had in J. Roitman, 'Objects of the Economy and the Language of Politics in northern Cameroon', PhD dissertation, University of Pennsylvania, 1996; J. Roitman, 'The Garrison-Entrepôt', *Cahiers d'Etudes Africaines*, 150–152, XXXVIII-2–4, 1998, pp. 297–329; and J. Roitman, *Fiscal Disobedience: An Anthropology of Economic Regulation in the Chad Basin*, Princeton University Press, forthcoming.

[17] This has been reported in many places. See footnote 10 above as well as the descriptions of various national armies in 'Pauvres, inefficaces, incontrôlables...Que faire des armées

maintain that their indemnities are inadequate. For many this, combined with lack of training for occupations in the civil or private sectors, is what compels them to 'enter the bush', the implication being that, for those who join rebel groups, their rationale is *alimentaire*—or about food more than politics.[18] In that sense entering the bush is not just about 'shadow' economic and political activities. The economy of the bush may have its covert or even insurgent aspects, but it is equally a realm of well-known strategies of accumulation, legitimated patterns of establishing rights over wealth, and definitive organisational and financial connections to state power.

Like the urban merchant class, the economic wellbeing of the political class is in many ways dependant upon this pool of supposed surplus labour. While it is seemingly expendable—as the 'downsized'—the latter's positions on the frontiers of wealth creation has rendered it indispensable to the political logics of productivity and especially extraction.[19] This apparent contradiction arises from the logics of displacement and combinatory strategies pursued by those who have 'entered the bush': they are productive, thus being targeted as sources of wealth, and yet unstable, so confounding to manners of extraction based on traditional methods, such as taxation based on a census. Those working the bush and border roam from city to hinterland; make simultaneous use of the CFA franc, Nigerian naira, and American dollar; procure several national identity cards; exercise the vote in various national elections; and refer to heteroclite renderings of various Islams, Christian movements, Western ideals of democracy and human rights, and local practices of power and agency relating to self realisation and community.

To be sure, as nomads, migrants, refugees, the unemployed, the homeless, fugitives, brigands and even separatists, those who work the borders are often pegged as that which has erupted out of (or been expelled from) the non-correspondence between nationalised space and deterritorialised practice.[20] While their precarious situations are often rightly attributed to

---

africaines?', *L'Autre Afrique*, 17–23 December 1997, pp. 8–19, including the section (pp. 14–15) on Chad.

[18] Footnote 10 and ibid. While state resources for public spending have diminished as a consequence of structural adjustment programmes and embezzlement, presidential guards and private militias associated with executive power are well paid and in a timely manner, these outlays being mostly off-budget. Evidently, the right to redistribution is gauged according to certain representations of utility (be they well judged or not: witness Mobutu's Special Presidential Division).

[19] This ambivalence is a direct consequence of their status as targets of regulatory authority. Cf. Roitman, 'The Garrison-Entrepôt' (note 16). For a more extensive study of the unstable terms of regulatory authority in northern Cameroon, see Roitman, *Fiscal Disobedience* (note 16) in which tax, prices and the *population flottante* are all reviewed as an intrinsically related, and significantly unstable, ensemble of regulatory targets.

[20] By 'deterritorialised practice' I am limiting myself to situations where the ultimate refer-

the rise of novel transnational forms of accumulation and their associated markets, the peripatetic and those living in states of dispersion have always been problematic to territorialisation.[21] Without taking the time to comment upon that, suffice it to say that in the Chad Basin today, the domestication of nomads, street hawkers, the ambulatory, the clandestine, smugglers, and the 'informal economy' more generally depend fundamentally on whether or not these categories are represented as 'foreign' with respect to the nation, 'subversive' with respect to society, and 'irrational' with respect to the economy. Their claims to rights in wealth are judged accordingly; the state consistently refuses to address the question of the conditions of wealth creation for these populations. And yet their insistent exercise of those claims through seizure, contraband, banditry, highway robbery and smuggling is intrinsic to the perpetuation of certain aspects of state power.

Legitimating wealth creation: the contest of regulatory authority

Recourse to the bush, the intensification of economic activities along borders, strategies to evade official regulatory authority, and rebel movements seeking compensation through violence or retribution all seem to point to the demise of the nation-state in the Chad Basin. It is fair to say that those who control unregulated activity and armed factions are in competition with the nation-state for financial power derived from regional and international markets, as well as the authority to extract from local populations. But to speak of competition is not to say that the demise of the nation-state is impending or that the form of power defined by the nation-state is no longer assured. While the failings of state power on the African continent are noted daily in journalistic and academic writing, life on the continent is rife with occasions to experience the efficacy of state power: mobilisation of the opposition in Cameroon met with a crushing militarised response, as did the Ogoni movement in Nigeria.

Nevertheless, while certain strengths of African states are all too evident for their citizens, it is true that state regulatory authority is no longer assured in most countries of the continent. Grasping the extent to which

---

ent is the nation-state. In that sense, I am refraining from conclusions as to its significance as 'nomadology', an alternative mode of representation (or even non-representation) and power. On the latter, see G. Deleuze and F. Guattari, *A Thousand Plateaus*, Minneapolis: University of Minnesota Press, 1987. On the possibilities for non-representational forms of power and critique thereof, see C. Miller, 'The Postidentitarian Predicament in the Footnotes of A Thousand Plateaus: Nomadology, Anthropology, and Authority', *Diacritics* 23/3, fall 1993, pp. 6–35.

[21] This has been underscored in recent writing about diasporas, although much of that commentary celebrates the novelty of diasporic states.

state regulatory authority is being displaced by other agents of regulatory authority means ascertaining the extent to which the regimes of accumulation associated with the latter are institutionalised and legitimated. Of course, in the field of state power, alternative forms of power—and regulatory authority—always exist because no form of power is totalising. But the question remains: are appropriations which found viable regimes of accumulation legitimated in practice, giving rise to new figures of regulatory authority in the Chad Basin? And this, in spite of their being associated with often extreme violence.

As noted above, the commercial and financial activities that constitute regional networks of accumulation are among the few remaining opportunities for employment and enrichment in the Chad Basin. One of the main ways in which regional élites (prominent merchants, ex-military personnel) exercise regulatory authority is by controlling access to such possibilities for accumulation, thus determining the right to employment and enrichment. This takes place at the highest levels of business through commissions on deals, right-of-entry taxes, tribute and royalty payments to maintain political and commercial relationships, protection fees, and even payment for safe delivery of goods procured through customs fraud or for their 'legal' passage through customs. And it transpires at the everyday level of business through levies on local merchants; protection and entitlement fees paid by young men engaged as guards, guides, runners and wardens; entry taxes paid at unregulated border markets; and tolls on roads near these economically sensitive outposts.

No doubt many of these payments are made under coercion.[22] Yet many people are often quite willing to make payments for access to privileged commercial relationships, international markets, and the more lucrative local sites of accumulation, since these provide the means for socio-economic mobility in times of scarcity. Furthermore, payments made to ensure access to markets, essential commercial and financial relationships, and protection serve to formalise the various kinds of traffic involved, be it that of small arms across long distances or smuggled petrol through a mountain pass. This makes such activities less unpredictable in terms of both logistics and revenue. Moreover, contributions to those who regulate access to, and participation in, these commercial and financial activities

---

[22] Cf. Bennafla's description ('Mbaiboum: un marché au carrefour de frontières multiples' (note 13), p. 68) of payments made at barricades along the route to Mbaiboum, a flourishing, unregulated (until recently) market at the confluence of the Cameroonian-Chadian-Centrafrican borders. Even though the state administration attempted to regulate this intense centre of border traffic by implementing official *tickets de marché* and licensing fees paid by merchants, unofficial 'rights to entry and exit' are still also paid to regional henchmen at the market itself.

are not without services rendered. These include protection and a formal cadre, but they also involve the redistribution that takes place through the financing of schools, mosques, churches and medical clinics. In Chad and northern Cameroon, prominent merchants are famous for building mosques and Muslim schools in home villages; today, these have begun to pepper the no-man's-lands and new frontier towns along national borders. And in Mbaiboum, a mushroom 'town-market' on the Chadian-Cameroonian-Centrafrican border, Ibo merchants from Nigeria built a church in 1996.[23]

Those who find themselves outside the bounds of national welfare and security come to judge prestations associated with unofficial regulators as legitimate since they grant access to possibilities for accumulation, protection and services. In this sense, the relationships that local populations establish with those controlling regional networks of accumulation respond to their claims to rights to wealth. As the foot soldiers of the economy of the bush insist, the expanding trade in unregulated goods is quite often a source of economic empowerment and freedom. Both assert rights to engage in commerce regardless of means. Those who smuggle Nigerian petrol into Cameroon frequently described their activities as part of 'democratisation', since 'anyone can participate' and their supply keeps petrol prices low, thus aiding the impoverished consumer.[24]

State appropriations frequently take the form of seizure, especially in market places, where impoverished state officials chain merchants' stores shut and haul them in pick-up trucks to prison, and on roads or border crossings, where renegade customs officials and gendarmes skim off from trucks and travellers, usurping contraband. These (often violent) modalities of expropriation are increasingly perceived as 'fair game', or are taken up as an operative rationality.[25] For the local populace, the extractive power of non-state regulators is logical—or legitimate—according to certain paradigms of social order, equitable distribution and retribution. Thus while recourse to these networks of accumulation and acquiescence to their associated figures of authority may be inspired by a contraction in material wealth and access to such wealth (the 'marginalisation of African economies'), it also transpires from the extension of the discursive field in which wealth and value are figured. 'Spoils', for instance, are now an ambivalent sign in the regional lexicon of wealth: once associated with war and asocial forms of wealth creation, they now signify the disavowal

---

[23] Ibid., p. 69.

[24] On the relationship between their status as a fiscal subject and their perceptions of the free citizen, see Roitman, 'The Garrison-Entrepot' (note 16) and Roitman, *Fiscal Disobedience* (note 16).

[25] On this last point, refer to A. Mbembe and J. Roitman, 'Figures of the Subject in Times of Crisis', *Public Culture*, 7/2, winter 1995, pp. 323–52.

of particular social obligations, such as tax and debt. As with fraudulent commerce, what is seized cannot be taxed. And for those living in a web of international and local debt relations, seizure is a means of reversing the social order implied by such obligations. Furthermore, spoils now signify a new sociability of exchange insofar as they are a new means of redistribution.[26]

This is part of the normalisation of practices of wealth creation through seizure in the Chad Basin today. Regional entrepôts and border settlements—which are safe havens for refugees, smugglers, guards and guides—generate distinct, and often validated, regimes of violence. They are not always seen as lawless outposts; depending on one's vision of wealth, authority and freedom, they can also be sites of protective, sustaining power.[27] Most importantly for the local population, the forms of violence associated with their particular modes of appropriation are inherent to certain strategies for socio-economic mobility.[28] Since they are hubs for the redistribution of wealth, economic competition and welfare, social hierarchies generated in their midst endure to the extent that they are deemed to rectify or subvert either longstanding or recently created conditions of exclusion.

As has been noted, those who have managed to direct the financing, labour recruitment and material organisation required by such networks include leaders of factions or rebel groups (e.g. the Mouvement pour le Développement around Lake Chad) and the local merchant elite (e.g. the Shuwa Arab élite in Kousseri, Cameroon and in N'Djamena, capital of Chad). They also involve military officers who find rents on fraudulent commerce more attractive than their official salaries, leading to their denomination in Chad as '*les douaniers-combattants*'—literally, 'customs officials-soldiers' or, more prosaically, 'fighting customs officials'.[29] These

---

[26] This is reminiscent of practice during the nineteenth century *jihad*, when 'spoils' were articulated from within the discourse on legitimate property and wealth. Today, *jihad* is an important reference, but its import stems from its association with a world movement for political affirmation and redistribution.

[27] On this notion of power with respect to the *jihad* movement, see M. Last, 'The Power of Youth, Youth of Power: Notes on the Religions of the Young in Northern Nigeria' in H. d'Almeida-Topor *et al.* (eds), *Les Jeunes en Afrique*, vol. 2, Paris: L'Harmattan, 1992, pp. 375–99.

[28] This is not particularly African: cf. Weber, Braudel, Tilly. With respect to the African context, cf. J.-F. Bayart (especially on war as a historical mode of insertion into the world economy), 'L'invention paradoxale de la modernité économique' in J.-F. Bayart, *La réinvention du capitalisme*, Paris: Karthala, 1994, pp. 9–43.

[29] This was noted during my stay in northern Cameroon and Chad, and from interviews. Scant references include: on the guerrilla movement around Lake Chad, see G. Faes, 'Le dernier maquis', *L'Autre Afrique*, 1, 21–27 May 1997, pp. 64–9; on demobilised soldiers,

commercio-military alliances and their counterparts in the bush are emergent figures of regulatory authority in the Chad Basin. Their exactions and levies are often tolerated and even sanctioned by local populations—who achieve socio-economic mobility and gain needed security—as much as those exercised by the state. As regulators, they certainly compete with the nation-state in its capacities to extract.

And yet this scenario cannot be reduced to a matter of national—that is, Cameroonian or Chadian—involvement in these sub- and transnational networks of trade and accumulation. Commercio-military alliances involve renegade militias, demobilised soldiers, gendarmes, customs officials, well placed military officers, local political figures, members of the opposition, and government ministers. To say that this amalgam of personalities making up such alliances results merely from the involvement of national figures in corrupt practices perpetrated by regional traffickers would be an oversimplification since sub- and transnational regimes of accumulation, redistribution, and security are legitimated alongside the nation-state. In the early 1990s, goods stolen during a road hold-up in Cameroon were discovered later in a sub-prefect's office. In Chad, an administrator with the postal service refused to comment on the identity of road bandits who attacked her convoy because, as she said, 'they know me very well', implying that they were, like herself, members of the state bureaucracy. And when people from a Cameroonian village pursued a gang of brigands across the frontier into Chad, they were stopped by the Chadian village chief who handed them over to the very same gang. One report noted, 'These men proved to be dissident members of the Chadian military who obey a certain Commandant Kah.' Arms seized on the Cameroonian side of the border included a bazooka, something not in plentiful supply in the local village markets.

While it is true that transnational phenomena present notorious problems for state regulation,[30] the scenario of the Chad Basin, like that of other places, demonstrates how such networks become part and parcel of the political logics of the state, contributing to its ability to fulfil essential

---

see note 14 above; and on the military's rent-seeking activities, see A. Abba Kaka, 'Cette fraude qui tue!', *Le Temps* (N'Djamena), 69, 9–15 April 1997, p. 8 and S. Ngarngoune, 'Alerte au Sud', *N'Djamena Hebdo*, 280, 8 May 1997, p. 4. Although not specifically referred to herein, the region comprising southern Chad, the North province of Cameroon, and the Central African Republic presents an analogous situation, the main differences being the identity of the rebels (e.g. the Forces Armées pour la République Fédérale led by Laoukein Bardé) and the nature of wealth (diamonds from the CAR or gold dust in southern Chad).

[30] On the creation of new legal regimes, cf. S. Sassen, *Losing Control? Sovereignty in an Age of Globalization*, New York: Columbia University Press, 1995.

political imperatives such as extraction and redistribution.[31] This takes place, for one, through various manners of appropriation. For example, the Cameroonian administration has recently implicated itself in the recently established market-town of Mbaiboum. In 1987 Mbaiboum appeared on the Chadian-Cameroonian-Centrafrican borders as a hub of unregulated commerce in local industrial goods (salt, sugar, textiles) and consumer items (clothing, cassette players, hardware, cement), as well as gold, drugs, arms and diamonds. In the early 1990s, commercial activities in Mbaiboum intensified dramatically. In 1992 a Cameroonian customs station was established at Mbaiboum. Although the state has provided neither water nor electricity to this booming 'town', it now manages to take in 20 million francs CFA each year through the sale of *droits de marché* (market dues) and licences.[32]

And yet this formalisation of once unregulated activity does not imply the usurpation of power. Unofficial regulators of this commerce still exercise their 'rights' on local populations: they collect 'entry and exit' duties in the market (5,000–10,000 CFA per vehicle) and tolls on incoming roads (10,000–50,000 CFA for trucks), not to mention commissions and protection fees on the more lucrative trade in gold, arms and diamonds.[33] No measures are taken to quell these unofficial taxes and Cameroonian customs policy has been described as 'accommodating' or even 'encouraging', with very low levels of taxation on goods, and a minimum amount of surveillance of the national identities of population flows through borders.[34] Furthermore, military escorts have been established between Mbaiboum and certain outlying cities so as to protect merchants from the insistent pillaging and brutalities of road bandits. In Chad some claim that those who conduct such military escorts (the Garde Nationale et Nomade) are less concerned with protecting imperilled citizens than with securing fraud:

Unfortunately, in Chad, most of the laws governing the Customs service are put to ridicule. The simple resolution stating that 'a customs officer must not operate

---

[31] On this point, see B. Hibou, 'Retrait ou redéploiement de l'État?', *Critique Internationale*, 1, Autumn 1998, pp. 151–68. Some might argue that this is true for a regime or government, but not the state. That is, they understand the idea that the continuity of a regime may stem from appropriating the logics of wealth creation manifest in transnational networks, but insist that state sovereignty is at peril owing to the lack of authority exercised over such networks themselves. But if these networks contribute to the very viability of state functions (extraction, enabling productive economic sectors, redistribution), they perpetuate the viability of the state as a political institution as much as a particular regime.

[32] See K. Bennafla's detailed descriptions of Mbaiboum: 'Mbaiboum: un marché au carrefour de frontières multiples' (note 13), p. 54 and p. 68.

[33] On market and road taxes, see ibid., p. 68. Information on the trade in gold, arms and diamonds (and perhaps rhinoceros horns) is based on confidential interviews in Cameroon.

[34] Ibid., p. 66.

beyond the border' has not been respected. On the pretext of thwarting smugglers, the military and elements of the Garde Nationale et Nomade du Tchad—or alleged customs officials—ride at breakneck speed through the city crammed into their Toyotas [pick-ups], causing numerous accidents. The victims are most often peaceful citizens who have nothing to do with fraud. In reality, this chase between customs officers and smugglers is a pretence. It is, to some extent, a strategy that involves escorting the vehicle containing the smuggled goods all the way to the marketplace, for fear of being intercepted by other customs officials who amble along the roads. Without this tacit complicity, merchandise would not be imported from abroad.[35]

Indeed, the Chadian and Cameroonian states have every reason to facilitate border traffic, which provides remuneration for under- and unpaid military officials, who convert to customs officials, and fills state coffers through licensing.

But this does not necessarily mean rendering 'legal' unregulated traffic. The state can offer a legal structure for these activities without altering the fact that they are either formally illegal or based on fraud. This means producing administrative paperwork for transactions without taking into account certain quantitative or qualitative aspects of the commerce involved, thus producing a false legal status for merchants. This is typical practice along the borders of all states in the Chad Basin, and represents one way in which the state is sometimes at the heart of the proliferation of sub- and transnational networks of accumulation and power. Evidently, this false legalisation contributes to the economic well-being of under- and unpaid state administrators, who are reimbursed for such services. But it also contributes to the state's financial liquidity.

Traffic between the Chad Basin and the Sahara has proved one means of accessing hard currency in a context of the non-convertibility of local currencies. In Niger, for instance, the state is central to the organisation of the illegal trade in American cigarettes. As Emmanuel Grégoire notes: 'The Nigérien state has, in effect, set up a legislative framework which organises this traffic and obtains significant customs receipts, estimated at about 6 billion francs CFA in 1994 and 1995, or the equivalent of a month and a half of functionaries' salaries, which are six months past due (January 1998). Operators act in perfect legality in Niger, with fraud transpiring only at the cost of neighbouring states which prohibit imports of foreign cigarettes to protect its own industry (Nigeria) or tax them strongly for the same reason (Algeria and Libya).'[36] In this instance, state agents collude

---

[35] A. Abba Kaka, 'Cette fraude qui tue!', *Le Temps* (N'Djamena), 69, 9–15 April 1997, p. 8.
[36] E. Grégoire, 'Sahara nigérien: terre d'échanges' in J. Egg and J. Herrera (eds) (note 13), p. 100, my translation.

with, and are dependent upon, intermediaries (e.g. Tuareg)[37] who control
certain trade routes and are notorious for providing security in dangerous
zones (such as the south of Algeria and the Niger-Chad border) not only
for personal profit, but also to respond to the insolvency of the state and its
associated political risks (e.g. the demands of unpaid state bureaucrats,
including police and *gens d'armes*).

This scenario partially explains how insolvent states are somehow able to
expand their administrative corpus: in Cameroon, for example, 20,000 new
functionaries were added to the rolls from 1987 to about 1997, despite the
fact that there was no new recruitment during that time.[38] It also confirms
the point that commercial policy in Africa (and elsewhere, such as Russia)
is defined in terms of lucrative opportunities: 'International commercial
policy…is not designed primarily by the relevant (*competent*) administration (with its ensemble of rules on customs duties, quantitative restrictions, the standardisation of regional commercial agreements, etc.), but by
a certain number of influential actors, both public and private, who define
such policy in function of possibilities for fraud and contraband, so as to
ensure mastery of access to parallel markets and fraudulent practices.'[39]

The state thus benefits from profitable situations produced by competing regimes of power. It is sometimes also the instigator of proliferating
unregulated, under-regulated or falsely regulated activities, and even becomes dependent upon those wielding power (e.g. regulation of access)
and expertise (e.g. security) in sub- and transnational networks. While these
endeavours potentially undermine state regulatory authority and national
security, they also contribute to the viability of the state through the production of new rents and possibilities for redistribution among strategic
military, political and commercial personalities.[40] This is, of course, a
question of financing both political clients and strategies to prevent the

---

[37] Emmanuel Grégoire notes the special talents of the Tuareg of Hoggar as '*passeurs*'
between Algeria and Niger (ibid., p. 95). He also indicates that the Niger army often
offers protection for convoys running illegal deliveries between Niger and Libya (p. 101).

[38] Hibou, 'The "Social Capital" of the State as an Agent of Deception' (note 10).

[39] Hibou, 'Retrait ou redéploiement de l'État?' (note 31), p. 156, my translation.

[40] This is similar to the situation in Algeria, as described by L. Martinez, who demonstrates
how the civil war in Algeria has not led to the disintegration of the state. The Algerian
state found economic and political advantages through a specific manner of regulating
conflict and control of resources. Recourse to the army and private militias as a means of
ensuring exclusive control of certain resources (e.g. oil) is legitimated owing to the state
of war, thus permitting the the state to finance the reconstruction and consolidation of
essential alliances. Also, surveillance of the general population has been given over to
militias, who benefit from accumulation via violence and increase their power. See
L. Martinez, 'Les groupes islamistes entre guérilla et négoce. Vers une consolidation du
régime algérien?', *Les Études du CERI*, no. 3, August 1995; and L. Martinez, *The Algerian Civil War*, London: C. Hurst, 2000.

emergence of a counter-élite or counter-power.[41] It is a matter, then, of the very formation and maintenance of a dominant political class—or the stability of a regime. However, beyond political payouts and underwriting political stability, rents (or wealth) thus produced are essential to 'an extremely complex system of revenue transfers from formal and official circuits to parallel ones, from urban households to rural ones, from the richest to the most dispossessed (via allocations to families; social expenditures and diverse benefits such as school fees, health, funerals, participation in customary ceremonies…).'[42] These forms of redistribution are a primary mode of the exercise of state power.

Indeed, appropriating rents associated with sub- and transnational networks of accumulation—and thus collaborating with and managing their associated figures of financial power and regulatory authority—means creating wealth for off-budget activities (e.g. hiring private security companies as presidential guards or financing political parties) and state functions (e.g. paying administrative salaries or financing external conflicts). In this sense, the regional networks described herein are a resource which contributes to the political logics of predation that define the historical exercise of state power in Africa.[43] And yet this is not to reduce this situation to a historical-cultural necessity: similar situations can be found in Colombia, Peru, Algeria and Russia, where tributary relations between the state and sub- and transnational networks of wealth and power prevail. Moreover, while this form of intermediation between state power and emergent figures of power may be interpreted as in keeping with certain historical continuities (e.g. the role of intermediaries in the Atlantic slave trade or the imposition of colonial power), its specificity, today, arises out of certain ruptures in the global political economy.

As Béatrice Hibou argues, state consolidation on the continent is now increasingly taking place via indirect, or non-bureaucratic, means. This is in large part due to the emergence and deregulation of particular markets (e.g. in small arms, mercenaries, private security companies), as described

---

[41] In Cameroon, the Biya regime's tolerance—or even sanctioning—of high military official's involvement in the arms, drugs and counterfeiting sectors is well-known and generally interpreted as a means of redistribution.

[42] A. Mbembe, 'Épilogue: Crise de légitimité, restauration autoritaire et déliquescence de l'État', in P. Geschiere and P. Konings (eds), *Itinéraires d'accumulation au Cameroun*, Paris: ASC-Karthala, 1993, pp. 367–8.

[43] This is a longstanding thesis of J.-F. Bayart, articulated in many places. On the multiple manifestations of the predatory logics of state power, cf. *L'État en Afrique*, Paris: Fayard, 1989, and on the '*dédoublement de l'état*' in the form, for example, of '*conseils administratifs*', cf. 'The "Social Capital" of the Felonious State, or the Ruses of Political Intelligence' in Bayart, Ellis, and Hibou (note 6), pp. 32–48. On *dédoublement* as a mode of power, see A. Mbembe, 'Provisional Notes on the Postcolony', *Africa*, 62/1, 1992, pp. 3–37.

above. But is this manner of exercising power via indirect mediations a novel aspect of state power in Africa? Recourse to private, foreign agents, for example, is a longstanding manner of ensuring the effective exercise of state power; in Africa, this has involved the use of external alliances, such as the Cold War powers, or external resources, such as foreign aid, to manage internal conflicts and the demands of factions constituting the basis of state power.[44] In that sense the reconfiguration of power on the continent today is less a matter of entirely novel practices of the exercise of state power than of novel ways of negotiating the changing world economy, or managing extraversion. It is, as Achille Mbembe has argued in another context, an attempt to 'redeploy networks of reciprocity, allocations, and compensations that were once amalgamated in the heart of the single party [state].'[45] In the Chad Basin sub- and transnational regimes of accumulation are critical connections to today's external rents; they are another means of insertion in the world economy. Figures of regulation associated with these regimes are critical to the consolidation of state power even though they work to undermine state regulatory authority. And they represent, through the production of wealth on the frontier, one place where the tentacular effects of state power are redeployed in its quest for the means to redistribute.

Power is not sovereign

One question remains: are emergent figures of regulation in the Chad Basin alternative locations of political power? If the sub- and transnational networks described above can be defined as both national and non-national, they are 'new spaces' insofar as they belie the assumption that the preeminent locus of power is the nation-state form. But are they new forms of power arising out of the disjunctures between the local and global or the national and non-national? Or are we beginning to approach them from novel points of view, which tend to destabilise the national referent? This brings us to the conceptual question put forth at the beginning of this chapter: is power located at all?

Some might argue that the situation in the Chad Basin warrants reference to 'new spaces' since novel manners of conceptualising and arrogating wealth are being institutionalised in practice, giving rise to unprecedented power relationships. While these practices arise out of the historical templates of wealth, appropriation and violence in the region (e.g. seizure and

---

[44] This is what Bayart terms 'extraversion'. Cf. ibid. See also Hibou, 'Retrait ou redéploiement de l'État' (note 31).

[45] Mbembe, 'Epilogue' (note 42).

spoils in *jihad*), they are nonetheless driven by novel, transnational phenomena, like emerging markets.[46] The razzia has been given new *élan*
with the diffusion of Kalashnikovs in the Chad Basin. Nonetheless, to say
that power relations have been—or are being—transformed by transnational phenomena is to speak of a qualitative change involving not just
new spaces *per se*, but new forms, new techniques, new rationalities, and
new modes of self-government. This is important since emphasis on place
and space in much writing on the new locations of power slights the question of transformations (or not) in the exercise of power.

This failure to consider modalities for the exercise of power is intrinsically related to the problematisation of state power as sovereignty. I have
argued that the demise of certain metaphors and historical institutions that
once regulated communities (economic development, national progress,
social welfare) has rendered certain modes of appropriation (razzia, seizure, debt) and their associated figures of authority (militias, *douaniers-
combattants*, foreigners) potential alternative sources of regulatory authority.[47] But are these new sovereigns? Or new forms of sovereignty? More
specifically, if the constitution of state power is dependent upon the power
of non-state regulators, do these latter instances represent new forms of
sovereignty? Most typically, answers to these questions about sovereignty
are conceptualised according to the larger problematic of 'locating' new
forms of power.

Since sovereignty, as a definition practiced in classical political theory
and jurisprudence, is supposed to summate the founding properties of
'statehood', it is thought to be constitutive of the state itself and is thus
vested with powers of its own. As a foundational politico-legal concept,
sovereignty itself is assumed to be self-evident.[48] This is why most present-

[46] It is worth noting, however, that, beyond the specifics of the nature of contemporary geo-
political relationships, forms of technology and types of commodities, this situation
resembles that produced during the time of concessionary companies on the continent, as
well as the Atlantic slave trade. Reflection on the present refiguring of relationships
between wealth, appropriations and violence should take that into account.

[47] The demise of institutions and metaphors that once served as regulatory concepts does
not imply that there is no longer a structure of explanation for present conditions—the
disenchantment reading of contemporary African history. For an otherwise interesting
interpretation of that kind, see J. Ferguson, *Expectations of Modernity*, Berkeley: University of California Press, 1999, and see the debate over his book (R. Fardon, F. Nyamnjoh,
J. Roitman and J. Ferguson in *Politique Africaine* 81, 2001, pp. 177–95). For a similar situation to that described here, see Paul Richards, *Fighting for the Rain Forest: War, Youth,
and Resources in Sierra Leone*, Oxford: James Currey, 1996.

[48] '…the more sovereignty is thought to explain, the more it itself is withdrawn from explanation. The theoretical sovereignty of sovereignty leaves sovereignty itself essentially
unquestioned; the more constitutive sovereignty appears to be, the less unconstituted it
becomes.' Jens Bartelson, *A Genealogy of Sovereignty*, Stockholm Studies in Politics 48,

day commentary on transnational phenomena often confounds sovereignty and power. The state, as an abstract, unitary object of knowledge and a political subject in international political theory, *is* such because of sovereignty. And yet sovereignty is simply the unrestricted and determining power of the state as a political subject in the system of states.[49] Sovereignty is thus a given as the foundational concept and defining property of 'stateness' and the very presence of the state. The quest to define and, moreover, locate sovereignty stems from the presumption that sovereignty is the indivisible unit constituting the political system.[50]

From that conceptual point of departure, it is quite logical to apprehend the impact of transnational events and instances in terms of the potential displacement of the sovereign status of the state by emergent forms of power. These include financial markets or global capital markets and their associated legal regimes; agglomerations of non-governmental organisations or institutions of transnational civil society; and, more generally, extra-state politico-economic networks.[51] In spite of its foundational relationship to the politico-legal concept of the state, many observers allege that sovereignty is not necessarily a form of power limited to the infrastructures of the state, postulating that there are now sovereigns other than the state.[52]

University of Stockholm, 1993, p. 15. And see especially Chapter 2, which has greatly informed my own thoughts.

[49] On the circularity of sovereignty, see M. Foucault's writing on *gouvernementalité*. Here, he establishes distinct understandings of the finality of sovereignty as opposed to government. While 'to govern…means to govern things', and hence has a finality of its own, 'the end of sovereignty is the exercise of sovereignty'. He says: '…whereas the end of sovereignty is internal to itself and possesses its own intrinsic instruments in the shape of its laws, the finality of government resides in the things it manages and in the pursuit of the perfection and intensification of the processes which it directs; and the instruments of government, instead of being laws, now come to be a range of multiform tactics.' In 'Governmentality' in Burchell, C. Gordon and P. Miller (eds), *The Foucault Effect: Studies in Governmentality*, University of Chicago Press, 1991, pp. 94–5; and see also ibid., pp. 10–22.

[50] Cf. Bartelson (note 45), esp. p. 25. And read pp. 23–31 on the problematic of sovereignty and space, or how space becomes an object of political knowledge, with sovereignty being the metaphysical condition establishing the unity of the modern state.

[51] See J. Smith, C. Chatfield and R. Pagnucco (eds), *Transnational Social Movements and Global Politics: Solidarity Beyond the State*, Syracuse: Syracuse University Press, 1997; R. Price, 'Reversing the Gun Sites: Transnational Civil Society Targets Land Mines', *International Organization* 52, 1998, pp. 613–44; C. Cutler, 'Locating "Authority" in the Global Political Economy', *International Studies Quarterly* 43, 1999, pp. 59–83; C. Cutler, V. Haufler and T. Porter (eds), *Private Authority and International Affairs*, Albany: State University of New York Press, 1999; C. Nordstrom, 'Out of the Shadows' (note 5), pp. 216–39.

[52] S. Strange, *The Retreat of the State: The Diffusion of Power in the World Economy*, Cambridge University Press, 1996; J. Rosenau, *Along the Domestic-Foreign Frontier. Exploring*

This viewpoint is, of course, based on a particular assumption: that sovereignty is a form of power that we can define and locate in human sociopolitical and economic relationships. While sovereignty is less frequently taken to be a timeless essence of the state,[53] it is still referred to as a fixed reference; its ontological presence is assumed as constitutive of the modern political system. Hence, in keeping with its presumed constitutive conceptual and empirical power, sovereignty is treated as a timeless feature of political reality. Often, this form of power is defined as a structure of governance, as in the top-down approach associated with Susan Strange, or it is depicted in terms of situational power that is deployed across boundaries or sites of power capable of reshaping the character of states in the world today.[54] These structures, networks, domains or zones are said to be generative of sovereignty insofar as they are fields of social authority that produce codes, rules, norms and significations, thus structuring the practices and relations of those under its dominion. They are thought to be the predominant referents of the government of people and things, as well as value. According to this general description, my regulators may be describe as sovereigns.

In the Chad Basin relationships defining the military-commercial complex have been institutionalised over time, and this field of social authority structures practices and induces certain rationalities for those in its midst. But to say that such an emergent domain is a predominant referent for action, understanding and authority is to speak of the exercise of power and not necessarily sovereignty. These domains are said to be as powerful as or more powerful than the state in the government of people and things, but this does not clarify the extent to which they are part of the same logical space as the nation-state. If their codes, rules and norms are structuring

Governance in a Turbulent World, Cambridge University Press, 1997; R. B. J. Walker and S. H. Mendlovitz (eds), *Contending Sovereignties*, Boulder, CO: Lynne Rienner, 1990; S. Brown, *New Forces, Old Forces and the Future of World Politics*, New York: Harper Collins, 1995; D. Armstrong, 'Globalization and the Social State', *Review of International Studies* 24, 1998, pp. 461–78; M. Shaw, 'The Historical Sociology of the Future', *Review of International Political Economy* 5, 1998, pp. 321–36. For more subtle views, see S. Sassen, *Globalization and Its Discontents. Essays on the New Mobility of People and Money*, New York: The New Press, 1998; and D. Smith, D. Solinger and S. Topik (eds), *States and Sovereignty in the Global Economy*, London: Routledge, 1999.

[53] See, for example, A. Giddens, *The Nation-State and Violence*, Cambridge: Polity Press, 1985, esp. pp. 263–4; some of the contributions to C. Czempiel and J. Rosenau (eds), *Global Changes and Theoretical Challenges*, Lexington: Lexington Books, 1989; P. Evans, 'The Eclipse of the State? Reflections on Stateness in an Era of Globalization', *World Politics*, 50/1, October 1997, pp. 62–87.

[54] Strange (note 52); R. Latham, 'The Contours of Transboundary Political Life' and C. Nordstrom, Out of the Shadows', both in T. Callaghy, R. Kassimir and R. Latham (eds) (note 51), pp. 69–92 and 216–39 respectively.

in a determining way, or in a way that usurps or parallels state power, how has this become logically possible? That is, how have the claims to authoritative status and unqualified jurisdiction become normalised such that they are not contested as illegitimate (read illogical)? If we answer that question, there is no clear means to conclude that such power is sovereign.

Assertions that sovereignty exists in circumscribed domains where one is compelled to act or even think in a specific way, or where subjects are constituted in terms of particular (non-state based) political and economic rights, are in keeping with a particular conception of power. This takes power as productive; it is a situation which gives rise to subjects who are 'caught up in a power situation of which they themselves are the bearers'.[55] Attempts to grasp the exercise of power understood in this sense have inspired acute attention to the structuring power of relationships and institutions, as well as the disciplinary effects of codes, techniques and rationalities. However, the incorporation of much of this work into debates about globalisation has displaced this analytics of power into the realm of an analysis of sovereignty *in spite of* the fact that this analytics of power was inspired by the very critique of the ever-present subject of the juridical sovereign in analyses and representations of power.[56]

As Michel Foucault maintained, the abiding juridical representation of power is constructed out of the prohibitive thematics of repression and law; yet this manner of representation is 'utterly incongruous with the new methods of power whose operation is ensured not by right but by technique, not by law but by normalization, not by punishment but by control, methods that are employed on all levels and in forms that go beyond the state and its apparatus.'[57] And yet Foucault's critique is not based on the mere point that the juridical mode of representing power is 'outdated' or fails to account for new forms of power. His move towards an analytics, as opposed to a theory, of power involves the formulation of a 'definition of

---

[55] M. Foucault, *Discipline and Punish: the Birth of the Prison* (trans. A. Sheridan), New York: Vintage Books, 1977, p. 201.

[56] So much emphasis has been placed on Foucault's thoughts on power and knowledge and disciplinary techniques that his explicit preoccupation with the effects of the language of political philosophy on conceptualisations of power, the relational nature of power, and the seemingly unsurmountable problems of origins and history devoid of subjectivity have been slighted. Foucault spoke of 'the system of Law-and-Sovereign which has captivated political thought for such a long time. And if it is true that Machiavelli was among the few—and this no doubt was the scandal of his "cynicism"—who conceived the power of the Prince in terms of force relationships, perhaps we need to go one step further, do without the persona of the Prince, and decipher power relationships', *The History of Sexuality*, vol. 1 (trans. R. Hurley), New York: Random House, 1978, p. 97. See also 'Two Lectures' in C. Gordon (ed.), *Power/Knowledge: Selected Interviews and Other Writings 1972–1977*, London: Routledge, 1981, p. 102.

[57] *History of Sexuality* (note 56), p. 89.

the specific domain formed by relations of power' so as to comprehend historical practices of power.[58] For this agenda, an ultimate source of power and the possibility of its possession are irrelevant since power is productive of relationships and subjectivities and not repressive or a simple matter of interdiction.[59] Thus sovereignty (if it is anything) is not a condition of unqualified power or absolute authority since the omnipresence of power is not its totalising capacity or unqualified unity: '...power is not an institution, and not a structure; neither is it a certain strength we are endowed with; it is the name that one attributes to a complex strategic situation in a particular society.'[60] From this point of view, the networks and domains often described as new spaces of sovereignty or emergent sovereigns are new configurations of power, the question of their sovereign status being irrelevant.

In other words, if we accept that states of power are constantly engendered at the multiple points of its exercise, the question of sovereign status, understood as totalising in any particular domain or an instance of unqualified unity, is nonsensical since such situations simply do not obtain. Furthermore, this means that the infrastructures of the state, or the points of the exercise of state power, extend beyond the specific institutions of the state itself, or even the state as a unified and coherent entity. This is manifest in homes, schools, hospitals, factories, armies, and, I would add, world financial markets, international mafias, and non-governmental organisations. While the latter may be defined as non-state based, they are surely points of the exercise of state power—and hence not potentially sovereign as 'globalised' institutions.

In that sense, the precepts underlying apparently novel relationships, activities, and modalities issue out of, or are consistent with, those practiced in the existing political economy or socio-juridical order.[61] The endurance of sub- and transnational regimes of accumulation and power depends upon the normalisation and legitimation of new registers of value and the

---

[58] This is possible only if the 'juridical and negative representation of power' is finally disarmed ('cutting off the king's head'). Cf. ibid., p. 82 and pp. 86–91.

[59] Ibid., p. 94. For commentary, see 'Thematics of State and Power' in M. Dean, *Critical and Effective Histories*, London: Routledge, 1994, with special note of pp. 152–73. See also Foucault, *Discipline and Punish* (note 55), pp. 167–9.

[60] Foucault (note 56), p. 93.

[61] This point is inspired by Giorgio Agamben's reflections on how the state of exception is the very product of the extant regime of truth. He shows how the state of exception is normalised, and how such arrangements endure even though—or perhaps because—they are devoid of 'distinctions between outside and inside, exception and rule, licit and illicit.' Cf. his 'The Camp as the Nomos of the Modern' in H. de Vries and S. Weber (eds), *Violence, Identity, and Self-Determination*, Stanford University Press, 1997, pp. 106–18. I thank Luca D'Isanto for this reference.

articulation of rights to wealth that were heretofore deemed asocial or irrational (e.g. spoils, rights in wealth through seizure). However, these may be perfectly consistent with those exercised by the nation-state. That is, new ways of valuing and governing may emerge in the peripheries of the infrastructures of state power, all the while confirming the right and logic of extant modes of thinking and enacting power.

Thus new figures of power may emerge on the horizons—as in the case of agents of regulatory authority in the Chad Basin—which do not destabilise our manner of thinking and exercising power. Instead of wondering about whether or not new types of sovereignty are in our midst, we should pay attention to the precursory matter of whether or not the intelligibility of the very idea of sovereignty has been destabilised with recent changes in the global political economy. Debates about globalisation have spurred the problem of the intelligibility of sovereignty insofar as they raise the issue of the status of the nation-state in the international and transnational contexts. But this is not a new problem; it is one of the founding debates of classical political science. The real question is whether we can discern changes in the organisation of knowledge, or the production of valid statements about what the state is or is not. Of course, this partly arises out of interpretive struggles. But do new claims to sovereignty (e.g. indigenous peoples) come out of, or contribute to, the reorganisation of knowledge? Or are they simply part of the history of 'self-determination', and thus part of the extant template of knowledge?

To say that something has changed in a particular way does not address the question of *how* such change has become logically possible. For instance, certain figures of regulatory authority may be qualified as emergent in the Chad Basin simply because they were not there previously. But this in itself is dependent on qualitative changes in various domains, such as the international economy, leading to the definition of new realms of logical thought and action, like the military-commercial nexus. This gives rise to unprecedented possibilities for the organisation of economic and political life, as in the 'bush economy' described herein. The ultimate question is whether such changes across domains are the result of transformations in the organisation of knowledge, or in the prevailing manner of producing valid statements: 'this is (legitimate) regulatory authority' or 'this is a (legitimate) sovereign'.

What is important here is not the actual emergence of regimes of regulation or even structures of power that supposedly counter or undermine state sovereignty, but the extent to which these emergent figures of power produce or partake of new forms of knowledge that work to destabilise the concept itself. As Jens Bartelson has shown in his genealogy of sovereignty,

'...sovereignty does not merely mean different things during different periods.'[62] It is transformed with transformations in epistemic arrangements: '...to write the political history of sovereignty is to write a political history of the knowledges that makes sovereignty intelligible...a history of this referent and its formation in time.'[63] This is neither a history of the evolution of the concept of sovereignty—conceptual history—nor a matter of ascribing stable definitions of sovereignty over time. Rather, it is a history of ruptures, or a reading of the discursive practice of sovereignty, which has mutated dramatically in consonance with changes in the organisation of knowledge as well as its articulation with various knowledges.[64]

For instance—and to oversimplify greatly—mutations in the discursive practice of sovereignty have accompanied changes in conceptions of time and history (e.g. modern time as linear, which grants the possibility of change in the future) as well as modes of organising and validating human knowledge. For instance, from the Classical Age to the Renaissance and then to Modernity radical changes have taken place in ways of apprehending causality, which led to the figuration of power as a measurable property, as opposed to a disposition or relation.[65] Likewise, the classical table ordered states in

a continuous series according to their interests, and were well able [theoretically and practically] to entertain relations with one another; but these relations were never themselves representable within the table. With modernity, this set of relations becomes an organized reality, a system of relations analogous to, interdependent with and yet qualitatively different from those relations which together constitute the modern state as a coherent and functional totality.[66]

In setting these transformations forth, Bartelson's point is not that new definitions or types of sovereignty emerged with changes in the epistemic order, but that the intelligibility of sovereignty has been disrupted in keeping with clashes and contradictions within and between knowledges. He shows how the idea of the state as an abstract entity became a logical (and even ontological) possibility through a particular practice of the definition of sovereignty. While we cannot discern radical transformations in our own epistemological grounding or interpretations of being—and hence draw conclusions as to whether or not sovereignty is once again in crisis as far as its intelligibility is concerned—we can identify which political subjectivities

---

[62] J. Bartelson (note 45), p. 224.

[63] Ibid., p. 46.

[64] Read ibid., pp. 39–78.

[65] Ibid., pp. 147–8.

[66] Ibid., p. 171. This is, of course, the constitution of the sovereign state and international system as logically and historically interdependent, and the point at which we know what the state 'is' and is not.

are sustained or have emerged within extant and reconfigured logical spaces of political thought and action.

In the Chad Basin regulatory authority is clearly in crisis. While not necessarily undermining state power, regulators, acting on the basis of the military-commercial complex, and the regulated, who often assume their tactics of wealth creation and rights to extraction, are political subjectivities that arise out of novel configurations of power and wealth while remaining consistent with the epistemological foundations of state power and modalities of exercising power, more generally. In other words, dominion over persons and things may be surfacing out of ambiguous interdependencies (state/non-state) while remaining consistent with the exigencies of the exercise of state power.

6

A PRETENCE OF PRIVATISATION: TAIWAN'S EXTERNAL RELATIONS

Françoise Mengin

With the exclusion of the Republic of China from the inter-state community in the 1970s, almost all the world's chancelleries broke off all relations with Taipei, while in parallel private actors—especially big businesses—expanded relations with this new industrial country. The development of Taiwan's external relations has thus been based on a principled separation of the political and the economic. But these relations have involved the state even so. The Japanese and American governments lost no time in ensuring a minimum institutional framework for commercial dealings with Taiwan, by privatising the essential part of diplomatic and consular functions—sovereign functions par excellence. In contrast the involvement of European states has been more reactive, following various private initiatives, forcing Washington at a later stage to revise some of its initial positions.

For about fifteen years—between the late 1970s and the early 1990s—Taiwan's foreign relations therefore developed in a spontaneous way following custom, independently of international law. By analysing those relations, then, one can understand the challenging of the state's economic sovereignty and hence the emergence of new forms of government.

Relations confined to the private sphere

Taiwan's diplomatic weakness is real: fewer than thirty states recognise the Republic of China which, since the admission of the People's Republic of China to the UN in 1971, belongs only to ten or so inter-governmental organisations, none of them linked to the UN system.[1] But at the same

[1] While partly excluded from the inter-state community, Israel and apartheid South Africa never experienced isolation like Taiwan's. Those two countries never ceased to be repre-

time Taiwan has become a 'newly industrialised country' (NIC), fully integrated into international trade.[2] Indeed political isolation does not mean autarky, and Beijing has never been against its diplomatic partners expanding economic, cultural and scientific relations with the island, on condition that this does not call the principle of Chinese unity into question—any relations that can be taken as suggesting even simple *de facto* recognition by a state, or any dealings implicitly blocking the way to forcible reunification (such as arms sales), are implicitly forbidden.[3]

In fact only the Japanese and American governments were confronted, at the time when they recognised the People's Republic of China, with the question of the form of their future bilateral relations with Taiwan, in 1972 and 1979 respectively. No other state, notably none of the Western European states, had developed substantial trade with Taiwan before the late 1970s,[4] even though some of them had continued diplomatic relations with the Republic of China after the withdrawal of the Nationalist government to the island. Japan's official disengagement from Taiwan was complete and immediate; following a non-governmental agreement signed on 26 December 1972, management of bilateral relations was taken over by two private associations created for that purpose.[5] In addition, any indication of making the relations official was carefully avoided: interviews between the staff of one of the associations and members of the partner country's government were on no account to take place on the association's premises; similarly, senior Taiwanese officials accompanying a trade delegation to Japan had to present themselves as simple experts and travel on ordinary passports.[6]

In 1979 the United States also relegated the whole range of its dealings with Taiwan to the private sphere, but without disengagement on the part of the American state authorities. The Taiwan Relations Act, adopted on

---

sented at the United Nations (even though South Africa was deprived of its rights there), and they maintained diplomatic relations with almost all the world's chancelleries.

[2] During the 1980s Taiwan became the eleventh trading power in the world and the twentieth economic power, and with Japan alternately the first or the second holder of gold and foreign currency reserves.

[3] This limiting framework has never been defined as such, but derives on the one hand from the undertaking given by almost all Beijing's diplomatic partners to recognise the People's Republic's sovereignty over Taiwan, and on the other from the repeated pressure of the Chinese government to avoid any 'officialising' of Taiwan's foreign relations.

[4] In 1974 more than a third of Taiwan's exports were directed to the United States, and almost a third of its imports came from Japan, while trade with Europe accounted for less than 15 per cent of the island's foreign trade.

[5] The Interchange Association on the Japanese side, the East Asia Relations Association on the Taiwanese.

[6] Source: interviews, 1992.

10 April 1979, entrusted the management of bilateral trade to private bodies whose remit embraced those of diplomatic and consular institutions, except for the symbolic function of representing the state.[7] However, the American Congress guarded against a legal vacuum by laying down expressly that national and international legislation in force would be maintained, except for the Mutual Defence Treaty of 1954, abrogated in 1979. Above all, these *ad hoc* relations were integrated into the normal process of framing and control of US foreign policy; the operations of the American Institute in Taiwan and of all the agreements it might conclude were placed under the tight control of Congress. European governments, although they did not have to deal with a significant amount of trade, also sought to prevent any possibility of relations with Taiwan becoming official—banning any meetings at ministerial level, or even at the high administrative level, such bans being often based on explicit provisions.[8]

It was in fact political isolation, more than diplomatic isolation that was imposed on Taiwan. The impact of disengagement by governments generally—whether Japanese, American or European—can be measured on the one hand by the legal significance of the breaking of diplomatic relations, and on the other by the issues that have been openly closed off by various administrative authorities. In fact the breaking of diplomatic relations does not mean *ipso facto* that dealings are limited to the private sector;[9] it does not have any legal effects, but it does have practical ones due to the

---

[7] These were the American Institute in Taiwan and the Coordination Council for North American Affairs. Employees of the American Institute in Taiwan have to be placed on secondment if they are civil servants (Section 11 of the Taiwan Relations Act).

[8] Thus a circular from the West German Foreign Ministry on 19 November 1984 (341–321.00 CHT) recommended that there should be no meetings between representatives of the German government and the Taiwanese government. Similarly, a circular of 14 October 1986 signed by the Belgian Prime Minister Wilfried Martens (Circular 14/055/002 on Belgium's Relations with Countries with which it has no Diplomatic Relations: Taiwan) laid down that Belgian officials should avoid all contact with representatives of Taiwan, should not give them any audiences and should not attend official ceremonies. Source: interviews, 1991.

[9] In fact a break in diplomatic relations does not imply withdrawal of recognition, unless there is an explicit provision in that sense; see especially Lucien Sfez, 'La rupture des relations diplomatiques', *Revue Générale de Droit International Public*, XXXVII (2), April–June 1966, p. 390. Although the establishment of diplomatic relations brings with it mutual recognition, that recognition is not withdrawn by a break in relations. In reality this argument seems pointless in the case of Taiwan, insofar as the Nationalist government, until the early 1980s, demanded to be recognised as the government of the whole of China, and not only as the government of Taiwan. And a government can only be recognised within the limits of its own claims (D. P. O'Connell, 'The Status of Formosa and the Chinese Recognition Problem', *American Journal of International Law*, 1956, p. 415). However, recalling the principle gives a useful indication of the legal implications of a break in diplomatic relations.

absence of a permanent mission protected by appropriate immunity;[10] in addition, development of commercial dealings can take place in a legal framework, bilateral or multilateral.[11] In other words, inter-state relations can be established in the absence of diplomatic relations.

To manage these dealings the consular institution seems most suited, as it is closely linked to the development of international trade and is independent of all mutual recognition or establishment of diplomatic relations.[12] International practice has in fact many relevant examples, especially in cases of divided nations.[13] The Nationalist Chinese consulate in Papeete was maintained after relations between Paris and Taipei were broken off in

[10] As the Vienna Convention of 1961 on diplomatic relations rejected the formula of a 'right of legation' considered as an attribute of the state, the establishment of diplomatic relations is interpreted as an agreement concluded between states providing for the exchange of diplomatic missions whose agents, for the efficient accomplishment of their tasks, enjoy appropriate immunities. See, among others, Claude-Albert Colliard, 'La Convention de Vienne sur les relations diplomatiques', *Annuaire Français de Droit International*, vol. VII, 1961, p. 9.

[11] Not only does the breaking of diplomatic relations not have the effect of abrogating treaties, except when there is an express provision to that effect; it leaves the possibility open for two states to negotiate and sign new treaties.

[12] Article 2, para. 3 of the 1963 Vienna Convention on Consular Relations. Consular functions are in fact sufficiently broad to cover all commercial interests. Beyond specialised functions—registration of births, deaths and marriages, legal and quasi-legal assistance for nationals, etc.—consular posts have general competence which leads them, on the one hand, to encourage the development of bilateral economic, cultural and scientific relations and, on the other, to carry out an information mission on the development of the economic, cultural and scientific situation in the state where the consul resides. This competence can prove crucial for states that have broken off their diplomatic relations. In the exercise of their functions, consular agents also enjoy a system of immunities, certainly less extensive than those of diplomatic agents, but making it easier to carry out their tasks.

   The possibility of continuing official relations in the form of consular relations with the Republic of China was considered by General de Gaulle in 1964, as is shown by his instructions to Jacques de Beaumarchais (then *chef de cabinet* of the Foreign Minister, entrusted with the conduct of secret talks with representatives of the Chinese government in Berne): 'All that we can say is that we hope to keep at least a consulate in Formosa for the defence of our interests' (Charles de Gaulle, *Lettres, Notes et Carnets*, January 1964–June 1966, Paris: Plon, 1986, p. 31).

[13] For example, at a time when the Hallstein Doctrine had not been abandoned by Bonn, the opening of consulates of the German Democratic Republic in Phnom Penh and Baghdad did not lead the Federal Republic of Germany to break relations with Cambodia or Iraq. Bonn also agreed to maintain its relations with the United Arab Republic despite the presence of an East German commercial mission and consulate in Cairo, on condition that there was no express recognition of East Germany by the UAR (Charles Rousseau, 'Chronique des faits internationaux', *Revue Générale de Droit International Public* XXXII (3), July–September 1961, p. 576). Similarly, the breaking of relations between France and Vietnam was not followed by a break in consular relations between the two countries (*Le Monde*, 26 June 1965).

1964. Its closure the following year, at the request of the French government, was not motivated by Taiwan's lack of status, but by a determination to exclude any foreign presence from French Polynesia at the time
when it was being made a nuclear experiment area. Similarly, the British
consulate at Tamsui was only closed in 1972, while Britain had recognised the People's Republic of China in 1950. However, Beijing's refusal
to raise Sino-British diplomatic relations to ambassador level while London maintained a consulate in Taiwan was a good proof of the Chinese
side's determination to oppose any turning of the island's foreign relations into official ones.

Beyond the institutional setting, the development of commercial dealings with Taiwan also experienced occasional blockages of a political
nature. In particular, what were called sensitive areas (such as the sale of
nuclear material or the granting of landing rights) effectively demanded
cooperation from government bodies which presumably had little inclination to intervene in relations with Taiwan. Thus Taiwan, although it signed
and ratified the Nuclear Non-Proliferation Treaty, is no longer a member
of the International Atomic Energy Agency based in Vienna. Therefore it
can no longer make trilateral agreements with the IAEA and a supplying
country to subject its installations and materials used to a multilateral system of controls and guarantees.

With France the question arose in 1983, at the time that two contracts
were signed for the delivery by COGEMA of enriched uranium to Taiwan.[14] The solution adopted then was to include those French exports in
the inventory of the trilateral agreement signed in 1971 between the
Republic of China, the United States and the Agency. That agreement,
which had remained in force after 1979, ensured international control and
peaceful use of the material delivered to Taiwan.[15] But while that solution
allowed governments to avoid any formal commitment in commercial
dealings with Taiwan, it exposed those deliveries to the risk of suspension
of the agreement or of possible ill-will on the part of the US authorities,
who could always seek to place obstacles in the way of competition liable
to harm the USA's own nuclear industry.[16]

---

[14] The first was signed with the Taiwan Power Company for the supply of 100 per cent of
the enriched uranium needs of the island's fourth nuclear power station. Following a
delay in the building of that power station, in 1986 there was an amendment to the contract which authorised spreading of the supplies over all the four power stations (CO-
GEMA's share was therefore raised from 25 to 30 per cent). The second contract was for
the supply of enriched uranium to the Institute of Nuclear Energy Research.

[15] Agreement of 6 December 1971 (published on 14 March 1972).

[16] It was in fact always possible for the American authorities to refuse the inclusion of non-
American nuclear fuel to Taiwan among the material covered by the trilateral agreement
signed by Washington.

The question of granting landing rights for a Taiwanese airline is another indication of how far governments have disengaged on principle from all relations with Taiwan. Landing rights have a political connotation, less because of the flag shown on the fuselage of national airlines' aircraft[17] than because of the rules governing air traffic law, whose inspiration differs greatly from that of maritime law.[18] An agreement between two states is in fact necessary to exchange access to air space and to determine the conditions for air services to operate between the two countries concerned. More generally, a close link has been established between state sovereignty and commercial aviation.[19] However, traffic rights can also be obtained through unilateral administrative authorisation delivered by the competent air traffic authorities to operators applying for them.[20] Thus China Airlines negotiated in its own name with its foreign counterparts for agreements on establishment and operation of regular air services. But even in these conditions many politico-administrative obstacles have interfered with the maintenance or opening of air links with Taiwan.

Pressure from the People's Republic of China on Japan was sufficiently strong, soon after the break in relations between Taipei and Tokyo in 1972, for the intergovernmental Japan-Taiwan agreement to be replaced by an agreement signed between private bodies, and for Japanese flights to Taiwan to be operated by a subsidiary of Japan Airlines—Japan Asia Airways—established for the purpose, while the Taiwanese airline's aircraft were never to be alongside those of People's China on Japanese soil.[21] Above all, those pressures led the Japanese foreign minister, Masayoshi Ohira, to declare on 20 April 1974 that his government did not recognise the flag displayed on Taiwanese aircraft as a national flag, or China Airlines as a national airline.[22]

---

[17] The fact that a state's flag is run up in the territory of another state never implies mutual recognition between those two states.

[18] In fact maritime law, inspired by custom, assigns considerable importance to principles of courtesy that inspire the Law of Nations. On this specific question, a state cannot close its ports to foreign private ships (cf. Martine Rémond-Gouilloud, *Droit maritime*, Paris: Pédone, 1988, pp. 78, 79); only considerations of public order can justify refusal of access by a ship.

[19] On this question, see especially Michel G. Folliot, 'La négociation aéronautique', in Philippe Breton and Michel G. Folliot, *Négociations internationales*, Paris: Pédone, 1984, pp. 73, 74.

[20] Jacques Naveau, *Droit du transport aérien international*, Brussels: Emile Bruylant, 1980, p. 56.

[21] Initially, in Tokyo, an interval of six hours was maintained between flights by the Chinese and Taiwanese airlines; then, when the new Narita airport was opened in 1978, China Airlines aircraft continued to land at Haneda airport, the flights to Osaka having meanwhile been discontinued.

[22] In the face of a strong reaction by the Taipei government—which ordered the immediate suspension of all flights between Taiwan and Japan—his successor, Kiichi Miyazawa,

In Europe, only the Netherlands established rapidly—in 1983, at the time of the expansion of bilateral trade—a direct air link with Taipei, even agreeing to its being operated by the national airlines. In doing so, however, The Hague was taking advantage of a temporary freeze in its relations with Beijing, following the sale of two submarines to Taiwan. In the case of France the question of landing rights for China Airlines arose also in the early 1980s, and has been periodically highlighted as trade between the countries has expanded. But ten years had to pass before all the politico-administrative obstacles were lifted: in 1993 an agreement was reached for the air link to be operated by Air Charter, subsidiary of Air France, and Eva Air, a private Taiwanese airline. But this solution was accepted at the very moment when the context of French-Taiwanese relations, a context of ever increasing competition, had considerably reduced the advantages that the French side could expect from a Paris-Taipei air link. Agreements of the same sort were reached, though the negotiations were less difficult, by other European countries: Austria in 1991, Britain and Germany in 1993.

Despite the determination that the European governments always showed to avoid getting involved in development of relations with Taiwan, and the constant vigilance of Beijing in this matter, a process of 'officialising' of bilateral relations became unavoidable even so, through the initiative of various private actors.

State authorities solicited by business lobbies

When Taiwan joined the ranks of the NICs in the 1970s, some businessmen tried, in most countries of Western Europe, to establish a minimal institutional framework that could promote their countries' commercial dealings with Taiwan. Their initiatives had a purely economic motive—there was no question of anything that could be called a pro-Taiwan or pro-China stance.[23] These lobbies, at first limited to a few people, included a growing number of industrialists, including those in the armaments

---

was obliged to declare on 1 July 1975 that for countries having diplomatic relations with the Republic of China, the 'sun in a blue sky' was truly the flag of a state. On this affair see Ralph N. Clough, *Island China*, Cambridge, MA: Harvard University Press, 1978, pp. 195–7.

[23] A contrary example in this respect was that of the Dutch firm of Philips, which in the early 1980s was the biggest foreign investor in Taiwan. In fact Philips' establishment in Taiwan was one of the rare economic operations in which the Nationalist-Communist division worked in Taiwan's favour. Mr Philips, who was very anti-Communist, was a personal friend of Chiang Kai-shek and, while he was head of his firm, forbade all relations with the USSR or the People's Republic of China (source: interview, 1991). Even so, Mr Philips did not promise to promote the interests of other Dutch enterprises in Taiwan.

industry, as well as parliamentarians.[24] At the same time, these lobbies took on institutional form themselves, notably with the formation of *ad hoc* committees within employers' organisations or parliamentary friendship associations. After some leading figures had agreed to set up private associations in most European countries—in France, associations governed by the law of 1901—to serve as antennae for various Taiwanese ministries, European offices were opened in Taiwan,[25] separate from the German and French cultural centres which had an exclusively cultural purpose.[26] As a result, the institutionalising efforts of private actors led immediately to a division according to nation-states, so that the competence of each Taiwanese office in Europe was limited to the territory of

---

[24] With the prospect of arms sales to Taiwan, the 'Taiwanese' lobby in France did not recruit support only among the armaments industry, but also among parliamentarians whose constituencies included a number of companies interested in arms sales to Taiwan, or even the homes of engineers working in those enterprises. Among the constituencies represented on the National Assembly Defence Commission, some did not include any defence industries; but the engineers often chose to live in those more residential zones, and so their deputies were also interested in the survival of that industry.

[25] The first unofficial Taiwanese representative offices in Europe:

   1972 *Paris* Association pour la Promotion des Échanges Culturels et Touristiques
           Vienna Institute of Chinese Culture
   1973 *Zurich* Far East Trade Service
           Madrid Centro Sun Yat-sen
   1974 *London* Free China Centre
           Bonn Fernost Information
   1975 *Luxembourg* Centre Dr Sun Yat-sen
   1976 *Brussels* Chambre de Commerce Sino-Belge
           Paris Centre Asiatique de Promotion Economique et Commerciale
   1979 *The Hague* Far East Trade Office
           Lausanne Centre Sun Yat-sen
   1980 *Frankfurt* Free China Association
           Oslo Taipei Trade Centre
   1981 *Stockholm* Taipei Trade, Tourism and Information Office

[26] The first European representative offices in Taipei:

   1974 Spanish Chamber of Commerce
   1976 Anglo-Taiwan Trade Committee
   1978 Association Française pour le Développement du Commerce avec l'Asie
   1979 Hellenic Organisation for the Promotion of Exports in Taiwan
           Belgian Trade Association
   1981 The Netherlands Council for Trade Promotion
           The Austrian Trade Delegation
           German Trade Office
   1982 Trade Office of Swiss Industry
           Swedish Industries' Trade Representative Office
   1983 Danish Trade Organisations' Taipei Office
   1989 Institute for Trade and Investment, Ireland
           Italian Trade and Economic Center

one state and, similarly, each European office in Taiwan advertised one nationality only.[27] In addition, while the Taiwanese representatives were from the beginning offshoots of various ministries, and thus only fictitiously private, their European counterparts in Taipei only had to defend their private interests—with the notable exception of the French offices.

In most cases it was employers' groups that got together to establish a representative office in Taipei.[28] A frequently chosen formula was that of a chamber of commerce,[29] while for the promotion of Dutch, Italian and Swedish interests, a procedure in between direct intervention by state authority and by one or more professional organisations was employed.[30] In contrast, to represent French economic interests a Trade Office of the Direction des Relations Economiques Extérieures (DREE) of the Economic Affairs Ministry was reconstituted in 1978, but in the form of an association under the law of 1901, the Association Française pour le Développement du Commerce avec l'Asie. That association's sole office overseas—the one in Taipei—was funded by the DREE, was headed by officials temporarily seconded from that government body, and reported on its activities at least as much to its 'responsible ministry' as to the chairman of the association. But the association was set up on the initiative of some leading figures in the business lobby. Similarly, the Cultural Affairs department of the Foreign Ministry in its turn opened an unofficial

---

[27] Advertised it literally—although exclusively private, several of these offshoots of business groups displayed a flag in their Taipei offices.

[28] The British, Swiss and Finnish offices were financed by private business, the Belgian association was dependent on the metal construction industries' federation Fabrimetal, and the Danish office was established by the joint action of four bodies covering a wide range of Danish economic activity (the Federation of Danish Industries, the Danish Chamber of Commerce, the Danish Agriculture Council and the Federation of Crafts and Small Industries). Source: interviews, 1991.

[29] Even if their names do not suggest it, some European bodies in Taipei are in fact offshoots of national chambers of commerce. This is the case not only with the Spanish Chamber of Commerce—established by the High Council of Chambers of Commerce, Industry and Navigation—but also with the German office, dependent on the Association of German Chambers of Commerce, and the Austrian Trade Delegation which was dependent on the Austrian Chamber of Commerce. Source: interviews, 1991.

[30] Thus the Dutch office came under a professional body specialising in the promotion of foreign trade, the Netherlands Council for Trade Promotion, a private foundation depending for 70 per cent of its funds on the Netherlands ministry of Economic Affairs and for the rest on ministries likely to be interested in projects in Taiwan. Similarly, the Swedish office depended on the Swedish Trade Council, funded in equal portions by private business groups and by the Foreign Ministry—foreign trade having been attached to that ministry in Sweden in 1982. As for the promotion of Italian exports, it was in the hands of the Institute of Foreign Trade which had about 85 offices around the world and was jointly financed by the ministry of Foreign Trade and by contributions from businesses using its services. Source: interviews, 1991.

office in Taiwan—the Association Française pour le Développement Culturel et Scientifique en Asie—under pressure from private actors.

These experiences can however be assessed in different ways. While the French offices were indeed offshoots of ministries, the privatisation of their status showed clearly the French authorities' intention not to proceed to normalisation of bilateral relations. Generally speaking, beyond the differing legal solutions adopted, the procedure that was adopted in all countries showed a determination to keep bilateral relations with Taiwan out of the official sphere. In contrast to the public debate aroused in the United States by the adoption of the Taiwan Relations Act, the establishment of European institutions in Taipei was surrounded by the greatest secrecy. Even so, a start was made to normalisation of bilateral relations; in particular, the status of every one of the offices established for dealing with the Taiwanese authorities was made practically identical with that of diplomatic missions, since they enjoyed immediately most of the privileges and immunities of such missions.

This process of normalisation continued with the establishment of procedures for issuing visas. That question was quickly raised by the various lobbies, since Taiwanese businessmen, senior officials and government members, travelling for professional purposes but as private citizens, were obliged to apply for their visas through a third country when they travelled to Europe;[31] the ponderous process involved could only increase the advantage of the United States or Japan in the island's external trade. The first initiative came from the government of Belgium: at the Belgian Trade Association's office in Taipei, Taiwanese nationals were given copies of authorisations from the Ministry of Justice, with which they could obtain visas on their arrival in Brussels. The French Foreign Ministry took a further step when it agreed in 1985 that one of its officials on contract would be responsible for issuing visas in Taipei itself, within the DREE's unofficial agency. This procedure, inspired by the American example, did not however lead to restoration of consular relations between Paris and Taipei, since the visas were issued under the seal of the Consulate General in Hong Kong. Subsequently almost all the other European governments followed this practice.

---

[31] This question did not arise for the United States because the American Institute in Taiwan, which took over American interests in Taiwan after the break in diplomatic relations, provided a visa issuing service. This was not equivalent to consular relations because the visas were issued under the seal of the consulate in Hong Kong; but it enabled Taiwanese to apply for and receive their visas directly on the island, within a period comparable to that prevailing in countries where there were American consulates. With Japan, a comparable system was established, but without the visa appearing in the passports of Taiwanese nationals.

With the establishment of this procedure, the organisational chart of the semi-official French presence in Taipei became particularly complicated: a Trade Office re-established under the cover of a private association, exclusively dependent on the DREE and headed by an official temporarily seconded from that government body; a 'visa service' established in the offices of the Trade Office, but headed by a contract official of the Foreign Ministry, responsible for issuing visas under the seal of the French Consulate General in Hong Kong and working in close collaboration with that diplomatic mission; an office of the Cultural Relations department of the Foreign Ministry, also re-established in the form of a private association, and under the responsibility of a contract official from that department. The institutionalising process followed the path of rationalising the French presence, and thus of 'officialising' Franco-Taiwanese relations. But nearly eight years had to pass before these adjustments were completed. There was no hierarchical authority common to the three bodies before 1993, despite the appointment in 1986 of a retired ambassador to head the 'cultural' office, despite the new name given to that office—the French Institute in Taipei—in 1989, and despite the appointment of a minister plenipotentiary, who had retired early, to head it in 1990. But in 1993 a serving diplomat, temporarily placed on secondment, was appointed to head the Institute, and all the semi-official services, which had meanwhile been given additional resources and staff, were regrouped within the Institute.

Leaving aside the many administrative vicissitudes—and slip-ups and lost opportunities resulting from them[32]—the various stages of the institutional remodelling of France's semi-official presence in Taiwan corresponded to a normalisation of bilateral relations. Since 1993 the French Institute in Taipei has hardly differed, even though it is on a smaller scale, from its American counterpart, the American Institute in Taiwan, since it operates, in a formally private framework, along the lines of an embassy.

Most of the other representative structures have developed in the same direction. The Belgian Trade Association opened in Taipei in 1979 by a trade federation (Fabrimetal) was made responsible in 1985, under a convention signed for five years with the government, for managing all Belgian interests in Taiwan and then, in 1988, for issuing visas, under the seal of the consulate in Hong Kong. The case of Sweden is even more significant: headed for ten years by a private businessman, the Swedish Trade Council office was in 1992 placed under the responsibility of two career diplomats. Similarly, the Anglo-Taiwan Trade Committee was entirely

---

[32] On this point see Françoise Mengin, 'Les relations entre la France et Taiwan de 1964 à 1994, Contribution à une étude des relations extérieures d'un non-État', Political Science doctoral thesis, Institut d'Etudes Politiques de Paris, 1994, pp. 633–8.

financed by the private sector and managed between 1976 and 1992 by businessmen, and then similarly placed under a career diplomat.

In parallel with the reshaping of institutions, the growth of trade raised the question of some minimum codifying of relations. So, in order to remove French supplies of nuclear fuels from dependence on American goodwill, a new solution was found to replace the arrangement including them under the trilateral IAEA-US-Taiwan agreement; in 1990, the Institut de Protection et de Sûreté Nucléaire (IPSN) of the Commissariat à l'Energie Atomique on the French side, and the Atomic Energy Council on the Taiwanese side, signed two documents to that end. While there was certainly no question of international agreements signed between states—which would, notably, have needed to be ratified—those texts were evidence of relations going beyond the strictly private sphere, since they involved public bodies and provided for the possibility of multilateral checks and guarantees (those of the IAEA) and, in case these proved impossible, bilateral ones (those of the IPSN).

The attempts to regulate access by Taiwanese fishermen to the economic zones of the French South Pacific Territory similarly illustrate the ambiguity of all negotiations bringing in state authority. To measure fully the nature of the bilateral relations, what matters here is not so much the technical disagreements that caused the talks opened in 1991 to fail and the conditions that paved the way for them. The Quai d'Orsay's demands at that time related to three points:[33] the officials making up the French delegation[34] must be presented as mere experts; the agreement must be private, and hence concluded between private associations;[35] and, lastly, the talks must take place, in Taipei, in a private setting. The following year, fishing talks held by the Taiwanese authorities with Russia were held under similar conditions.[36]

At the same time, however, various governments agreed, following the French example, to liberalise contacts at ministerial level. Since the end of the 1980s serving Taiwanese ministers had succeeded in being received by their European counterparts, exclusively in a private capacity[37] and

---

[33] Source: interviews, 1991.

[34] It comprised representatives of the three territories as well as officials of the Foreign Ministry and the Overseas Departments and Territories.

[35] On the French side there were two associations governed by the law of 1901, one for French Polynesia and the other for New Caledonia and Wallis and Futuna; on the Taiwanese side, the Taiwan Deep-Sea Tuna Boatowners and Exporters Association.

[36] Source: interviews, 1992.

[37] Among the first to be received in this way should be mentioned the Communications minister Kuo Nan-hung, received in February 1989 by Jean-Marie Rausch and Michel Delebarre, then minister of Foreign Trade and minister of Transport and the Sea respectively; the meetings took place in the offices of the Regional Councils of Lorraine and

generally through the intervention of business lobbies. Strict secrecy could however be maintained around these visits, which frequently did not take place on ministry premises. The initiative taken by France in 1991 had very different implications. When it was agreed to send a serving minis-ter[38] to Taipei, no subterfuge—not, in particular, the fact that the visit was called a private one—could conceal the establishment of government-to-government relations between France and Taiwan. In addition, the minis-ter was accompanied by a delegation comprising not only businessmen but also the Prime Minister's special envoy to Asia, Jean de Lipkowski; the deputy chairman of the National Assembly Defence Commission, Jean-Yves Le Drian, who was also deputy mayor of Lorient;[39] and ten senior officials of various government departments including the Foreign Minis-try. In addition, two normal practices for ministerial visits were followed on this journey: the holding of a press conference and the signing of a working document, in the form of a memorandum.[40] In these circum-stances the 'private' character of bilateral relations no longer had any rela-tion to reality, but was entirely in the realm of words.

Most important, this visit was followed, a year later, by a visit by the then French Secretary of State for Foreign Trade, Jean-Noël Jeanneney, also in a private capacity. The arrival in Taipei, within the space of a year, of two French serving ministers tended to prove that the development of trade was now inseparable from contacts at government level. The other Euro-pean countries followed the French example; in 1991 and 1992, twenty-four members of European governments made the journey. This intensify-ing of relations eventually led the United States to lift its formal ban on such visits.[41] For the time being, only the Japanese authorities maintained the embargo on all ministerial visits to Taiwan and, in addition, remained

---

Nord-Pas-de-Calais. In August 1989 the Taiwanese minister of Economic Affairs, Chen Li-an, was received by Roger Fauroux and Hubert Curien—respectively minister of Industry and Regional Planning and minister of Research and Technology—in the lounge of the Hotel George V in Paris. Two years later, it was apparently on the premises of the Ministry of Capital Works and the Secretariat of State for Foreign Trade in France that Eugene Chien, Taiwan's minister of Transport and Communications, was received by Paul Quilès and Jean-Noël Jeanneney. Source: interviews, 1992.

[38] This was Roger Fauroux, then minister of Industry and Regional Affairs.

[39] Lorient was where the La Fayette frigates whose sale to Taiwan was then under discus-sion were built.

[40] The memorandum, signed on 9 January 1991 by the French minister of Industry and Regional Planning and the Taiwanese minister of Economic Affairs, dealt with the cre-ation of a working group to study ways to strengthen bilateral cooperation through joint ventures and transfer of technology.

[41] In December 1992 the US Secretary for Commerce went to Taipei; so, the following March, did the Assistant Secretary for Commerce in the new Clinton Administration.

very reticent about Taiwanese ministers passing through Tokyo being received by their Japanese counterparts.

Finally, French arms deliveries to Taiwan represented a major step in going beyond the limits laid down by Beijing on ties with Taiwan. The sale of La Fayette frigates was envisaged in the late 1980s, and in December 1989 France's inter-ministerial commission for the study of exports of armaments (CIEEMG) authorised the directorate of naval shipyards to submit a bid in response to Taiwan's invitation to tender. But the French Prime Minister, in giving his decision, laid down that the frigates must not be delivered armed; the contract must be only for hulls equipped with means of propulsion and a system of electronic equipment. While the government went back on its initial decision a few days later,[42] the sale was nonetheless authorised in September 1991 and the contract signed by the Thomson-CSF Group and Taiwan's naval dockyards.[43] The Quai d'Orsay communiqué however took pains to reduce the contract to a 'purely' commercial affair, to the extent that the sale was of unarmed hulls only and did not involve establishment of official relations between France and Taiwan, while the French government upheld the principle of the unity of China on this occasion.[44]

As with the ministerial visits, this contract became all the more important because it was quickly followed by a second. While George Bush, on 2 September 1992, asked Congress to authorise the sale of F-16s to Taiwan, the French government approved the sale of Mirages a few days later. The Taiwanese authorities opted for both American and French aircraft.[45] In this area too, there was an instant copycat effect: encouraged by the French sales, business lobbies in the Netherlands and Germany multiplied pressure on their respective governments for authorisation of the sale of

---

[42] On the reasons for this about-turn, see Françoise Mengin, 'Rethinking the Europe-Taiwan Relationship', *The Pacific Review*, 4/1, p. 33; and F. Mengin, 'Les relations entre la France et Taiwan' (note 32), pp. 438–40.

[43] The contract was for 16 La Fayette class frigates, for a sum of $4.8 billion (*Le Monde*, 5 September 1991).

[44] The French Foreign Ministry issued this statement on 27 September 1991: 'The French government has decided to authorise French businessmen to start negotiations with Taiwan on the sale of unarmed hulls of frigates. This is a purely commercial affair which does not imply any official relations with the Taiwan authorities. In taking this decision the French government has taken account of China's preoccupation concerning its security and the integrity of Chinese territory. France reaffirms the joint Franco-Chinese declaration of January 1964 according to which the government of the People's Republic of China is the sole legal government of China. France will continue to work for the development of friendly relations with the government of the People's Republic of China in all domains.' (Source: AFP)

[45] 150 F-16s for $5.8 billion (*Le Monde*, 15–16 November 1992) and sixty Mirage 2000–5s for $3.5 billion (*Le Monde*, 19 November 1992).

Dutch and German submarines to Taiwan, which seemed to be imminent during the winter of 1992–3.[46] It seems to have been only the sanctions decreed by Beijing against France, soon after the sale of the Mirages, that put an end, for the moment at least, to the German and Dutch plans. While the American government, to justify its decision regarding China, stressed that the United States had promised to maintain a certain superiority in quality for Taiwan (though accompanied by a reduction in volume), the French government, in contrast, emphasised again the commercial nature of a sale of arms, in this case combat aircraft, to Taiwan.[47]

The limits to political-economic separation: a twofold reactive process

The growing, though disguised 'officialisation' of bilateral relations can be interpreted in two ways. It may be thought that the private sphere has borrowed institutional procedures and patterns from normalised relations in order to facilitate commercial relations, with state authority carrying out ever wider delegation of competence. But the process can also be interpreted as a steady 'normalisation' of bilateral relations; all the institutions and procedures developed by private actors are, according to this view, gradually encroached upon, 'taken over' by the organs of foreign policy, to handle everything except representation of the 'accredited' state. This would mean that the privatisation of diplomatic activity was now only a fiction.

In fact the development of trade with Taiwan brings out both these logics, in two successive sequences. In so far as the involvement of private actors has occurred one step at a time, the business sector has simply tried to make up for the absence of diplomatic and consular relations by securing prerogatives of state authority. The issuing of visas can thus be

---

[46] See, among other sources, *Far Eastern Economic Review*, 21 January and 4 February 1993, and Ingrid d'Hooghe, 'The 1991/1992 Dutch Debate on the Sale of Submarines to Taiwan', *China Information* (Leiden) VI (4), spring 1992, pp. 40–54.

   In particular, the Taiwanese lobby in the Netherlands emphasised that if Paris persisted in authorising arms deliveries to Taiwan, The Hague should follow the same route so that Dutch businessmen were not disfavoured within the EEC (ibid., pp. 44, 48; Michel Korzec and Georg Hintzen, 'Het eeuwige schip' (The eternal ship), *Financieel Economisch Magazine*, 12 December 1992, p. 31).

[47] Roland Dumas declared on 10 January 1993 over the RTL radio station that the export of combat aircraft was 'a decision of a commercial nature' which 'should not compromise good relations with Beijing. France has only one policy towards China, the one and only China, the People's Republic of China': 'Grand Jury RTL-Le Monde' broadcast (*Le Monde*, 12 January 1993).

analysed as a functional delegation by the public to the private sphere.[48] Similarly, the various advantages enjoyed by unofficial representative institutions[49] can be seen simply as privileges, exceptional under common law, that are granted to private persons, because they were granted in a partial, *ad hoc* manner, on the basis not of an international agreement,[50] but of mere administrative regulations.[51] Thus they were granted on a provisional basis, and, notably, there was not always strict reciprocity. Similarly, again, ministerial visits can be analysed in terms of inter-state relations—relations between a business sector and the administration responsible for it—even though the Taiwanese authorities were determined to bring out the inter-governmental aspect of those visits and that way of exploiting the visits, in turn, could have been a motive for the backing given by the minister to the private sector.

But in this way there was normalisation of bilateral relations, insofar as institutions and procedures copied from those of diplomatic and consular relations were reproduced almost identically, and the initiative for their development came more and more from the state authorities, no longer from private bodies which were now relegated to the role of 'sub-contractors'. There thus arose what can be called relations of substitution, with different layers of normalised relations being invaded by the organs of foreign policy.

The establishment of these relations of substitution was closely linked to the prospects for key contracts, which led in the early 1980s to a two-fold reactive process: the political implications of commercial dealings grew, and what amounted to competitive bidding among governments led them to take many initiatives. From the moment when Taiwan was seen as a promising market for key contracts—for projects for a fourth nuclear power station, nuclear fuel reprocessing, a high-speed rail link, underground railways, a deep water port, motorways, etc.—trade with Taiwan could not be based in a sustainable way on autonomy of the economic sphere in relation to the political, whatever the official rhetoric might go on saying.

---

[48] France was a borderline case since the person concerned was a civil servant on contract to the Foreign Ministry. But for other European countries, it was definitely offshoots of the business sector that were responsible for issuing visas in Taipei.

[49] Diplomatic privileges and immunities, or communications facilities (sending of telegrams with ciphered messages, installation and use of a radio transmitter, diplomatic bags).

[50] The Vienna Convention of 1961 on diplomatic relations or that of 1963 on consular relations.

[51] A law, however, in the case of the United States (Section 10 (c) of the Taiwan Relations Act).

There is no definition of 'key contracts', but in its generally accepted sense the term refers implicitly to the amount of money involved and the importance of the contract in terms of the balance of trade and jobs. Key contracts thus inevitably involve senior officials, even members of the government, as the projects are closely followed by some government departments, those responsible for foreign trade and industry in particular. Correspondingly, it is difficult for the private actor to avoid turning to the government actor, because of the overlapping of technical and political considerations.

While the politico-administrative dimension is never absent from the logic of a key contract, it has a particular importance in the case of Taiwan, since it can be used to start a process of 'officialising' of bilateral relations. Such a linkage has rarely been made explicitly by the Taiwanese authorities.[52] But the mere fact that it has often been mentioned, at least by businessmen,[53] inevitably reinforced the pressure from the various lobbies. The fact remains that the Taiwanese authorities have generally tried to develop, within the framework of these projects, high-level contacts or codifying and cooperation efforts.

However, the Taiwanese market's potential for key contracts was explicitly described when the Taipei government launched the so-called Six-Year Plan at the beginning of 1991. Besides setting out a number of macro-economic targets, that plan provided for investment, before 1996, of $303 million[54] without recourse to external financing, to prepare Taiwan for the transition from an industrial economy to a telecommunications and services society. In fact it was more a 'white paper' than a plan in the strict sense, since the targets were not matched by precise financial commitments and the plan put forward few new projects. But those new projects were included together in a single document, and their mobilising effect among Taiwanese and foreign investors was thereby increased. In fact that Six-Year Plan became one of the central themes of the budding bilateral dialogue between Taiwan and each of its non-diplomatic partners,[55] and a competitive bidding process took place among foreign governments, which were encouraged to multiply goodwill gestures towards Taipei to get contracts awarded to their businesses.[56]

---

[52] F. Mengin, 'Les relations entre la France et Taiwan' (note 32), pp. 416–20.

[53] Sources: interviews, 1989, 1990, 1991, 1992.

[54] This—people were fond of stressing at the time—was three times the cost of the Kuwait reconstruction plan.

[55] On the diplomatic objectives of the Six-Year Plan, see *Minsheng Bao* (Taipei), 8 August 1991.

[56] This, however, involved forgetting that democratisation of the Taiwanese regime was already far advanced by this date. Hence the process of decision making was no longer

If France played a leading role in this domain in the late 1980s and early 1990s, it was probably because key contracts then accounted for an important part of its commercial dealings with Taiwan. Between 1986 and 1989 their value rose from 427 million to 2 billion francs, reaching 3.1 billion in 1988. Comparison between Italy and France is revealing in this respect. The two countries had comparable volumes of trade with Taiwan at the end of the 1980s.[57] But only France was engaged at that time in a process of 'officialising' its relations with Taiwan; it was not until September 1989 that the Italian business sector set up a representative office in Taipei, the Italian Trade and Economic Center, and in the early 1990s no visa issuing procedure had yet been set up. While these two countries' volumes of trade with the island were comparable, key contracts accounted for a much greater proportion in France's dealings with Taiwan.

It has to be recognised, then, that at the very moment when the economic role of nation-states was considered increasingly obsolete, private actors did not seek to break free from the state framework. Quite the contrary—the involvement of businessmen was organised within a strictly nation-state framework on the one hand, and with the aim of reproducing the forms and procedures of inter-governmental relations on the other. If the development of trade required a minimum institutional framework, the island's lack of status could have suggested that private actors invented ways to get round the state. But in fact it was only after the process of reconstitution of inter-state relations had been started on a considerable scale that businessmen were tempted to mobilise at a transnational level, notably in 1988 with the creation of a European Chamber of Commerce in Taipei.[58]

Lastly, some will surely suggest that there has indeed been a challenging of the state, because the limitations imposed on trade with Taiwan by the Chinese government have frequently been exceeded under pressure from business lobbies; but in so far as their involvement has always been devoid of any 'political' stance—that is, of any desire to open the Taiwan

---

restricted to government bodies, but now depended on a legislative Yuan whose area of competence is wider than that of Western parliaments. A number of projects, and their financing in particular, were to come up against a powerful environmental lobby in the Yuan—this happened with the fourth nuclear power station, for example—and the divergent interests of a number of provincial parliamentarians (in the case of the high-speed train project).

[57] In 1988, trade between Italy and Taiwan was worth $1.4 billion and trade between France and Taiwan $1.5 billion; in 1990, the figures were respectively $1.8 billion and $2.2 billion (source: Euro-Asia Trade Organization, Taipei).

[58] The aim of this initiative was to allow European enterprises to face American competition in Taiwan in better conditions. It was independent of all European Community institutions.

question—their action has, on the contrary, led to preservation of the status quo in the Formosa Straits.

A dilatory system

On their side chancelleries have been unable to prevent establishment of inter-state relations with the Taiwan entity, even if dealings have been confined in theory to the private sphere. In fact, since 1949 the division of China has constantly been managed through recourse to legal fictions. As a technique for resolving antinomies, legal fictions are not absent from international law.[59] In each case it is not so much the objective situation that is ignored, as the legal consequences attached to the reality. At the outset of the Cold War determination to oppose Communism led the majority of governments[60] not only to back a widely discredited regime, but also to recognise it as the sole government of the whole of China, of which it in fact controlled only one island two hundred times smaller in size than the mainland. With the beginning of détente, on the initiative of the United States, the inter-state community adopted, with a few exceptions, the principle of effective rule, recognising the government that controls the vast majority of the country's territory. But in doing so it substituted one fiction for another, since it promised to recognise the unity of the nation and the sovereignty of the newly recognised government over an island which was still outside its control; the original fiction turned out to be reversible. The culmination of the illusion came when, as in the case of France, such promises—which had never been explicitly made—none the less became the guiding principle in relations with the two Chinas.[61]

Beyond the question of state recognition, development of relations with Taiwan brought about new legal paradoxes which were, in turn, resolved by recourse to fictions. The same device was applied to acts that went against the fiction of the Beijing government being the government of the whole of China; secondary fictions were grafted onto the main one. In their case it is the objective reality, not the legal consequences of that reality, that is denied: para-diplomatic representative offices are considered as mere private associations; visas are issued under the seal of another

---

[59] Indeed, recognition is a discretionary act left to the appraisal of each sovereign state. Hence each state is able 'to refuse to recognise reality, considering it to be impossible to oppose, or to recognise the unreal, considering it to exist': Jean J. A. Salmon, 'Le procédé de la fiction en droit international public' in C. Perelman and P. Foriers (eds), *Les présomptions et les fictions en droit*, Brussels: Emile Bruylant, 1974, p. 126.

[60] Except for the majority of Asian states—apart from Japan—and some European states, like the United Kingdom in 1950 and France in 1964.

[61] See F. Mengin, 'Les relations entre la France et Taiwan' (note 32), pp. 621–7.

consulate; serving ministers do not travel in that capacity; arms supplies are presented as simple contracts between two civil enterprises although the procedure for sale of military material involving government bodies—even a decision by the head of state—has in fact been applied; bilateral negotiations are conducted by senior officials, presented as mere experts, with aim of signing an agreement concerning two governments but in fact linking two private enterprises. A logic of pretence has been established.

Far from leading to effective normalisation, systematic recourse to legal fictions has had the aim of hiding the existence of a state, not abolishing it or changing it—which could, over time, have raised the question of its recognition. So the development of Taiwan's foreign relations has occurred tangentially, since each additional 'arrangement' has aimed to keep Taiwan out of the community of nations. In contrast the relations—embryonic ones, certainly—that some chancelleries have maintained with so-called national liberation movements suggest a process of state recognition that may or may not come about.[62] But relations with Taiwan have led to unofficial or substitutive normalisation, establishing inter-state relations without state recognition.

This case is *sui generis*; relations followed an entirely classical pattern, though in fictional space. To deal with an exceptional situation there was, in this case, no change in the machinery for regulation of inter-state society; no original arrangements were devised, except for recourse to a dilatory system making it possible to hide the state dimension while preserving its dynamics. While this new arrangement is based on a process of fiction, and its motives are exclusively economic, it all relates to the national interest as most realistically understood.[63]

Hence the institutionalising process, being included within the nation-state dimension, could only lead to inter-state competition among the various European partners—a development that was skilfully kept going by the Taiwanese government. From the moment when the community of states agreed on rejecting any reconsideration of the status quo in the Formosa Straits, international mobilisation—including unofficial relations—could have made it possible to avoid this process of rivalry, which led to competitive bidding and also, for each country involved, to tension with Beijing and, finally, to lost opportunities on both the Chinese and the Taiwanese markets. As far as France was concerned, for example, that

---

[62] One thinks particularly of Western states' relations with the PLO; on this point see F. Mengin, ibid., p. 566.

[63] As understood in the so-called classical or realist theory of international relations, the idea of the national interest refers not only to the security of a state or its rank, but also to the economic or social well-being of its population considered as a whole.

competitive bidding provoked periodic protests from the People's Republic of China, and notably led to an overt crisis with Beijing following the sale of the Mirages; it was resolved in a way costly to the French side, both politically and economically.[64]

The official relations established between the European Community and mainland China meant that Brussels could not establish ties with Taipei. But the institutional framework of commercial dealings, and the procedures set up—delivery of visas and regulation of arms sales, for example—could have been devised at that level. In fact, while the European Union is not absent from Taiwan, its involvement is a function of that of European governments.[65] There is no question of looking at the matter in normative terms here—only of suggesting, on the contrary, the power of attraction that the nation-state setting still has in international relations.

While Taiwan's foreign relations cannot be placed into any category, the exception can none the less have some use as an indication. In this unprecedented situation the state has remained an obligatory point of reference, even where all conditions seemed to be present for a lasting separation of the economic and the political to occur. The development of commercial dealings with Taiwan has not led to relegation of the political sphere to the sidelines; quite the contrary—it has enhanced the nation-state aspect of business competition. Hence the Taiwan case is as revealing about private actors' strategy as it is rich in methodological lessons. While growing internationalisation of major enterprises certainly forces the state to come to terms with private actors, the latter in reality seek not so much to break free from the nation-state framework as to use it for their profit. Rather than proposing a debate in terms of alternatives—the transnational level versus the governmental level—analysis should therefore concentrate above all on the connections between private and public logics, and on interaction between the economic and political spheres and the national and international spheres. In this way it definitely becomes pointless to adopt a holistic approach concerning the state, or to assume in advance a marked differentiation between the public and private spheres.

---

[64] See F. Mengin, 'Les relations entre la France et Taiwan' (note 32), pp. 659–71. See also F. Mengin, 'La politique chinoise de la France. Du mythe de la relation privilégiée au syndrome de la normalisation', *Critique Internationale*, no. 12, July 2001, pp. 92–4, 97, 98.

[65] Since the beginning of the 1980s, members of the Commission have travelled to Taipei. An unofficial representative office of the Commission was to be opened in Taipei in the spring of 2003. On some recent developments concerning relations between Taiwan and Europe, see F. Mengin, 'A Functional Relationship: Political Extensions to Europe-Taiwan Economic Ties', *The China Quarterly*, no. 169, March 2002, pp. 148, 149, 151–3.

Part III

POLITICAL TRANSITION AND THE PRIVATISATION OF THE STATE

According to the implicit rhetoric of aid donors, the process of economic liberalisation—and with it, the rise of the private sector, a diversification and multiplication of actors accompanying growth of more open economies, etc.—favours political transition, notably through the virtues of competition and transparency and the end of political and partisan interference in the economy. The extension of principles of liberalisation and the privatisation of the economy to the sovereign functions of the state is hence supposed to be part and parcel of this movement towards greater political openness and consideration of the expectations and demands of society. This is what is sometimes called 'free market democracy'.

The following chapters, however, suggest that relations between economic liberalisation and political transition, between 'privatisation' of the state (or its 'societalisation', as it can also be called using Hannah Arendt's analysis) and the reconfiguration of power relations, are complex. Concretely, they show how present changes are influenced by previous historical configurations. The worldwide extension of the 'privatisation' of the state can never be interpreted as a process of political homogenisation and increasing affinities among transition experiences. Still less is there any question of a uniform process towards democratisation or a hypothetical Western model of being in the political. On the contrary, the analysis of concrete situations shows that economic liberalisation can fit into any political arrangement, but also that it then has very different social and political significance in each case. Present-day modes of government, far from constituting a radical break with the previous order, are most often derived from the same conception of power as that which prevailed before. Obviously, this does not mean that nothing changes and that the political and social order is immutable. But the present-day changes, and especially the—at least apparent—dominance of economic aims and preoccupations, or the pluralisation of actors and modes of exercise of power, assume forms that are necessarily derived from history, the particular history of each country. Hence the spread of liberalisation and privatisation is not in itself synonymous with either more open politics or continuity in politics.

7

IS CHINA BECOMING AN ORDINARY STATE?

Jean-Louis Rocca

The platitudes about the 'bankruptcy' of the state have not spared China, and certainly the change from a state thought to be all-powerful in the early 1980s to a state liberalising the economy and steadily less able to perform sovereign functions (public order, taxation, etc.) was bound to lead to overestimates of that state's decay. But the dangers in such overestimates rapidly became apparent when the gap between a society considered to be atomised and a state supposed to be in decay was filled by emphasis on the 'market' or the 'people', or by prophesies of chaos. Some saw the absence of a strong state as sealing the short-term victory of the market economy and democracy;[1] others thought that China was destined to go through a period of mafias and the law of the jungle.[2]

Those two *a priori* theoretical positions do not contribute much to understanding of the changes in the Chinese state. How can the image of bankruptcy of the state, corruption and increasing powers in the hands of local actors on the margin of the economic and the political be connected with another image, equally present in analyses, of China as a country under an authoritarian, indeed totalitarian regime? Should it be considered that the state may be concentrating on the most repressive of its tasks— maintenance of public order—and giving up the rest? But in that case, how to explain that, for all the tax extortions organised by local authorities, taxes end up by being paid at least partly into the treasury? That despite the massive redundancies decided in the name of economic efficiency, city dwellers reduced to unemployment do not all fall into real destitution? That despite the constant deficiencies in management of water supply, major water works are undertaken? That in spite of the protective power of bureaucratic networks, officials are disciplined or transferred for incompetence or dishonesty? That the economy is being transformed and is growing at a steady rate? How to explain that the wielders of power remain the *deus ex machina* of economic dealings and accumulation and that, since the events of 1989, democratic contestation is definitely marking

---

[1] The majority of American Sinologists remain devoted to this thesis.
[2] See Jacques Andrieu, 'Chine, une économie communautarisée, un Etat décomposé', *Revue Tiers-Monde* XXXXVII (147), July–September 1996, pp. 669–87.

time?[3] All these questions impel the consideration that beyond the 'chaos or market forces' dilemma there is an institutional power in action.

Replies that can be contributed to the questions posed by Béatrice Hibou in the Introduction allow us to define the nature and place of that institutional power in China. We shall observe that if China is not experiencing either privatisation of the economy or privatisation of the state, while the state is still far from corresponding to the ideal Weberian type, it is quite simply because the way in which the concepts of 'private' and 'public' are generally used does not allow us to grasp the reality of China. In addition, in re-reading some of the works classed under the heading of critiques of modernity, one may wonder whether the basic distinction between private and public can be a basis for examining political modernity at all. Those concepts relate to the analyses by Jürgen Habermas, who sees the appearance of a 'bourgeois public sphere' as the quintessence of political modernity: 'The bourgeois public sphere may be conceived above all as the sphere of private people come together as a public; they soon claimed the public sphere regulated from above against the public authorities themselves, to engage them in a debate over the general rules governing relations in the basically privatized but publicly relevant sphere of commodity exchange and social labour. The medium of this political confrontation was peculiar and without historical precedent: people's public use of their reason (*Öffentliches Räsonnement*).'[4]

It is generally considered—in a startlingly sweeping glance back at history—that since the seventeenth and eighteenth centuries, the political systems of Western societies have been dominated by the reciprocal creation of those two spheres. Such a view overlooks even the latter part of Habermas' book, in which he makes two points clear: first, that the sphere under discussion is not something universal, since it is limited to the bourgeois public domain, and secondly, that it has declined since the nineteenth century, to decay altogether in the twentieth. The 'liquidation' of the political sphere in Arendt's sense[5] is carried out through two processes:

Only this dialectic of a progressive 'societalization' of the state simultaneously with an increasing 'stateification' of society gradually destroyed the basis of the bourgeois public sphere—the separation of state and society.[6]

---

[3] This does not mean—quite the contrary—that the population has been absent from the scene. Since the early 1990s protest movements have been multiplying, but only exceptionally are they aimed at the regime itself.

[4] Jürgen Habermas, *The Structural Transformation of the Public Sphere: An Inquiry into a Category of Bourgeois Society*, Cambridge, MA: MIT Press, 1989, p. 27.

[5] In Hannah Arendt's view the political domain is opposed to the private and social domains in the sense that it is the place where common decisions are taken, abstracted from special interests: Hannah Arendt, *The Human Condition*, University of Chicago Press, 1958.

[6] Ibid., p. 142.

Through this twofold process, the political sphere ceases to be an autonomous area for determining the rules of life in community, and is invaded by social and especially economic considerations. The state tends to control more and more aspects of life, but political decisions are taken directly for and by society, through the conflict among social interest blocs (trade unions, political parties, eminent persons, various associations, lobbies, etc.) which are connected or seek to be connected with the sources of power in a direct and institutional way; this contributes to manipulation, and soon the elimination, of publicisation of debate.

If political modernity destroys the bourgeois public sphere, it also liquidates the private sphere. Everything that depended on the private domain (work, the rearing of children, protection against the uncertainties of life, inheritance, etc.) is now a matter for society, more directly for the socialised state. As Hannah Arendt put it, 'the contradiction between private and public, typical of the initial stages of the modern age, has been a temporary phenomenon which introduced the utter distinction of the very difference between the social and public realms, the submersion of both in the sphere of the social.'[7]

Is this model not applicable to China today? Does it not enable better understanding of the blurring of distinctions, the straddling between the public and private spheres emphasised by increasing numbers of works? Several factors tend to justify this theory and demonstrate that there is a process of becoming more 'ordinary' going on in China. The Chinese transition, far from corresponding to the mythology of the entrepreneur class and the victory of private activity, seems to fit the pattern of a capitalism of great financial powers, quite close to what is seen in developed countries. So there is not so much privatisation of the economy as an assertion of powerful political-business interests appropriating financial resources. Similarly, Chinese society is marked not so much by an assertion of private life as by an expansion of the areas of life subjected to socio-political constraint. To give just one example, state control over births and the constraints of modern life (emphasis on standard of living, and urbanisation) join together to impose a standardised image of the urban family: one couple, one child. Another aspect of modernity in China is the state's abandonment of any desire for political change. Yesterday it was the arm of political ambition, but today the state is gradually placing itself at the service of society: economic preoccupations (growth, investment, profitability) and social ones (standards of living, social services) form the essential part of state ambitions. The culmination of this 'societal-

[7] Ibid., p. 69.

isation' of the state is the delegation of some its public tasks—*de facto* in rural areas, *de jure* in the cities—to structures emerging from the social or para-social sphere. Of course this process is only beginning, and is encountering many obstacles, but it is a manifestation of a change in the state which subjects the categories of 'private' and 'public' to the constraints of the social sphere.

Socialisation of property

In Hannah Arendt's view, the coming of the modern world has been paradoxically marked by a retreat on the part of private property, which 'lost its private use value which was determined by its location and acquired an exclusively social value determined through its ever-changing exchangeability.'[8] The Chinese situation is close to this analysis, with the difference that it was not necessary to challenge private property, only to prevent it from getting established.

The role of private business in the Chinese economy remains marginal. Some stress the fact that many public or collective enterprises are managed like private enterprises, but that is to confuse management with capital. The big financial groups controlled by the provincial or municipal governments are no less 'capitalist' in their mode of management than big foreign groups. It is precisely the decisive role of collective economic interests—moral persons, in other words politico-economic power centres—prevailing over individual interests, that makes China like other countries. Firms have become essential actors in the economy and the individual entrepreneur, when he exists, is obliged to lean on some financial power or other to grow and develop. Whereas in the developed countries the 1990s saw a massive reorganisation of assets within giant capitalist firms,[9] in China the government—contrary to all orthodox theory on transitions—backed the growth of powerful, autonomous groups capable of competing with world giants.[10] The holding company has become the dominant mode of organisation of Chinese capitalism.[11]

What is specific to China is not so much the basis and direction of the economic restructuring as its form, which is almost entirely devoid of any legal element. Those collective entities—political-cum-family clans, local

[8] Ibid., p. 69.
[9] Peter Nolan and Wang Xiaoqiang, 'Reorganising amidst Turbulence', *Economic and Political Weekly*, 28 March 1998, pp. 707–16, quotation on p. 708.
[10] Ibid., p. 711.
[11] Charles de Trenck *et al., Red Chips and the Globalisation of China's Enterprises*, Hong Kong: Asia 2000, 1998.

administrative authorities, wielders of military and police power, etc.—impose their will with extreme brutality and generally without any legal appearances. In the countryside land remains under public ownership and only rights of use for a limited period are recognised. Certainly those rights change hands without too much difficulty, but they do so in a legally hazy context which is hardly conducive to protection of ownership. The authorities can, at any moment, sell land to foreign operators or confiscate it to develop it on their own account. One cause of the numerous protest movements that break out every year in China is in fact the way in which land is confiscated, and the small amounts paid in compensation to the peasants. As for rural enterprises, their status is particularly complicated. In some cases the enterprise is managed by an 'owner' and has all the appearances of a private capital enterprise, while in fact it 'belongs' to an administrative authority. In others the capital is collective, that is, it comes from a state institution, while the real 'owner' (the one who manages the business and pockets the profits) is an individual (often an official personality himself) or a family.[12] Economic activity is dominated by what Jean Oi calls 'basic state corporatism', a sort of transformation of local bureaucracy into a unified entrepreneurial class.[13]

There is an identical situation in urban areas. Private entrepreneurs can only remain private if they agree to cooperate with the wielders of power. Restaurant owners and traders must pay their dues to the local petty bureaucracy. The industrialist must get the most influential officials financially interested.[14] At a higher level, the big industrial and financial groups are not owned by independent individuals or even groups of individuals, but by regional-bureaucratic cliques that are neither mafias nor simple offshoots of the state administration. Patronage and use of 'contacts'—family, local, friendly and other contacts—form the structure for the battlefield for control of wealth creation.[15]

---

[12] Christopher Findlay, Andrew Watson and Harry X. Wu (eds), *Rural Enterprises in China*, New York: St Martin's Press, 1994; Samuel P. S. Ho, *Rural China in Transition. Non-agricultural Development in Rural Jiangsu, 1978–1990*, Oxford: Clarendon Press, 1994; Ole Odgaard, *Private Enterprise in Rural China. Impact on Agriculture and Social Stratification*, Aldershot: Avebury, 1992.

[13] Jean C. Oi, 'The Role of the Local State in China's Transitional Economy', *The China Quarterly* 144, December 1995, pp. 1132–49; Jean C. Oi, 'Fiscal Reform and the Economic Foundations of Local State Corporatism in China', *World Politics* 45, October 1902, pp. 99–126.

[14] Jean-Louis Rocca, 'L'Etat entre chiens et loups. Résistance anti-taxes et racket fiscal en Chine populaire', *Études Chinoises* XI (2), 1992, pp. 77–140.

[15] On this question see Margaret M. Phearson, *China's New Business Elite. The Political Consequences of Economic Reform*, Berkeley: University of California Press, 1997. This book's *problématique* and conclusions are different from my own, but the author illustrates

At a more individual level, private property is equally little respected. Since the beginning of the reforms, hundreds of thousands of people have been driven out of their houses in city centres to make way for property development. At the same time, because of the large scale of property speculation, it is very difficult to know to whom that land belongs. Not only can parcels of land change hands with the waving of a magic wand, few people know who is hidden behind the property promotion companies.

The increasing finance-orientation of the Chinese economy is another element making for uncertainty about private property.[16] From now on the property that 'counts' is to be that represented by non-material assets. Those assets, coming from former state enterprises, or from the profits of earlier property investment or investment in the various economic zones, come and go as opportunities change. There is nothing stable in all this, and the isolated or ill-protected individual has every chance of finding himself ruined after reaching the top. Foreign operators of Chinese origin know something about this; most of them have no real legal guarantee over their investments, and some have ended up in prison because of their uncompromising attitude to the local bureaucracy.

In short, what is decisive today in the Chinese economy is not the action of entrepreneurs developing their businesses through respect for private property, but the competition among collective interests for the control of assets with fluctuating forms: collective interests that count on their political power alone to protect those assets and make them profitable. Control over wealth thus seems more important than control over property.

What is striking here is how rapid the process of socialisation of capital has been. By avoiding the bourgeois capital phase of the seventeenth and eighteenth centuries, which respected Reason and Law as reference points, China—to use Habermas' analysis—seems to have done without several centuries of capitalist integration. Now China is witnessing the reign of massive economic power centres, though with one essential difference from foreign groups: it is not the power of their enterprises that gives power to the economic entities, but the power of collective entities that determines the power of enterprises in continual transformation and redeployment.

Building of the social state

The Chinese state has abandoned its mission of economic development and social transformation in favour of a role of simple accompaniment of

---

well the conservatism and the eminently political aspect of the process of creation of the new business elite.

[16] It is equally surprising to see how fast Chinese enterprises have passed from subsidies to debt, then from debt to the bypassing of intermediaries to finance their development.

dynamic forces in society, 'management' of growth and social treatment of problems accompanying that growth. Not only did the command economy system disappear, but more fundamentally, criteria of economic efficiency and social stability became the standards of reference for state action. Henceforth, at all levels of the administrative hierarchy, officials were to be judged by those criteria.[17] Certainly an inefficient or dishonest official may remain in his position if he has good protection, but the reprieve is always temporary, if only because protection has a mounting cost that implies a certain amount of economic success and the population no longer hesitates to rise up against bad officials. This radical change in the state's mission leads obviously to a socialisation of its operations, but in different ways depending on whether cities or rural areas are concerned. On that point a contrast can be made between urban zones in crisis, where what can be called 'bureaucratised socialisation' is taking hold, and the countryside where a much more radical socialisation is being operated.

In the big cities of the centre and north of the country, as the Socialist employment paradigm has been challenged in the name of 'rationalisation' of the labour market (redundancies, and reappraisal of the social protection system and social benefits), the state has had to make the 'social' side the centre of its mission, and to delegate a part of it to 'society' itself.[18] These terms have to be put in quotation marks, for in the minds of the state authorities society is the aggregate of organisations that form the framework of society. These include mass movements (trade unions, the Women's Federation, the Communist Youth League), 'organs of the people's self-government' (residents' committees), enterprises, even street offices that are the lowest level of the administrative chain. So it is not society that is in charge of social work so much as its traditional representatives. Before it was the state that created jobs and distributed labour; today job creation is directly taken over by the para-public sector, the state authorities being content to fix the targets, take some general measures and provide funds. It is trade unions or local organs of the Women's Federation who start vocational training courses for the unemployed and provide the initial funding to launch an individual enterprise. It is district committees and street offices that create markets where only the unemployed can obtain trade licences.

---

[17] See Jean-Louis Rocca, 'L'entreprise, l'entrepreneur et le cadre. Une approche de l'économie chinoise', *Les Etudes du CERI 14*, April 1996.

[18] Antoine Kernen and Jean-Louis Rocca, 'La réforme des entreprises publiques en Chine et sa gestion sociale. Le cas de Shenyang et du Liaoning', *Les Etudes du CERI 37*, January 1998. The hypotheses of this study, based on a mission in July 1997, have been confirmed by another mission carried out in September–October 1998. See also Antoine Kernen's chapter in this volume.

Similarly the emergence of a charitable sector has helped strengthen this 'bureaucratised social sphere'. In Socialist China poverty was 're-served' to rural zones or to a fringe of enemies of the regime; but for some years now, the liquidation of state jobs and the considerable reduction in 'welfare funds' (*fuli*) have led to the emergence of a 'new urban poverty'. Here again, it is 'representatives of society' who promote, organise and control the creation of aid funds for the poor. Private charity certainly exists, but it remains linked to the circle of family and friends and does not lead to the emergence of a charitable sector in the form of associations.

The emergence of this 'bureaucratic socialisation' is scarcely surpris-ing in view of urban society's lack of autonomy in relation to the regime. Since 1949 urban zones have had to pay in this way both for their 'bad class origin'—as the seat of capitalism and vice—and for their strategic importance for the regime, as centres of industrialisation and the Chinese proletariat. Urban society has no autonomous field for interaction in rela-tion to the regimentation imposed by the bureaucracy (enterprises and districts). Seen from this point of view, employees of state enterprises rep-resent an extreme case. They are by definition dependent on the bureau-cracy. But for the same reasons the city is also the place of privilege—a space that must be watched, certainly, but must also be satisfied in the dis-tribution of social advantages for the sake of patronage.

The reforms have not entirely destroyed these organic links, and real urban destitution is still reserved today for the migrants from rural areas who, being 'strangers', cannot take advantage of the socialised state.[19] The financial aid for the 'new urban poor', though modest, gives them a privileged position in the crisis.[20] Certainly these ambiguous relations have not stopped protest movements; quite the contrary, for some years the big industrial cities have been the scene of a considerable number of demonstrations, petitions, strikes, sit-ins, even urban riots in protest at massive redundancies and non-payment of pensions and wages. What characterises urban society is not so much the absence of expressions of discontent as the lack of a true structuring and autonomous development of that discontent in relation to the official political programme, the absence of a social logic confronting the state. Most of the movements fol-low a logic of blackmail: the idea is to use the threat of a major challenge to social stability to put pressure on the local authorities for them to help people in difficulty.[21]

---

[19] Most of the urban beggars are peasants.

[20] The prospects for the future are however definitely less brilliant. The arrival of succes-sive waves of young people in search of jobs will probably lead the bureaucratised social arena into a very serious crisis.

[21] See my paper delivered to the annual meeting of the Association for Asian Studies (Chi-cago, 13–17 March 1997), 'Local Bureaucracy and Popular Protest in Contemporary China'.

Hence the assumption of responsibility for social work by para-state bodies is a sign of adaptation of the city to the constraints of socialisation of the state. Even so, it is a real change. From now on political tasks, and tasks of repression and propaganda, give way to questions of daily life in the preoccupations of mass movements and district administrative bodies. Hence those in charge have to swallow their pride to deal with the mechanics of society, and have to show greater sensitivity to the preoccupations and material demands of the people over whom they have responsibility. Now their work has to respond to criteria that the people can keep under close check, thanks to the proximity of the government and its increasingly ordinary character. The labour crisis endured by city dwellers further increases the difficulty of such a change, since it is essentially the para-state bodies that have to undertake the 'management' of the crisis.

The specific aspects of the urban situation appear clearly when the characteristics of 'societalisation' of the state in the cities and in the rural areas are examined. The first striking point in the countryside is the assertion of clearly non-state patterns of thought: in the wake of de-collectivisation and the liberalisation of economic activity, old lineages, the family, and territorial units like villages and cantons have become points of reference on wide scale. But there is not so much a return to a traditional outlook as a re-investment in pre-Socialist social relationships which are fitted into—and not opposed to—those created by the Socialist era. So there is not a revival but a re-invention of a form of social life on the basis of a 'stock' still present in memories[22]—social life that serves as a back-up for development of economic activity.

The various solidarity groups (lineages, sub-lineages, lineage segments, families, villages) are true autonomous spaces with their own social norms, increasingly often taking over responsibility for state tasks. This 'social domain' does not, even so, constitute a 'traditional' sphere in opposition to the development of the market economy.

Besides the maintenance of order, a task to which rural society has for long been made to contribute, today there are also education and some infrastructure and public works and installations of local importance, among the domains from which the state has withdrawn. In rural industry, it is true, the structure of the labour market is very closely linked to 'community' points of reference; the best paid jobs are reserved for sons of the soil. But economic transactions are not governed by the principles of moral economy alone. References to cold calculations of profitability and economic efficiency are not at all absent from economic actors'

---

[22] The book by Hua Linshan and Isabelle Thireau, *Enquête sociologique sur la Chine 1911–1949* (Paris: PUF, 1996) gives an idea of the richness and complexity of that stock.

preoccupations.[23] Similarly individuals' social capital does not consist only of 'natural' relations (family or proximity ties), but can also be the product of an individual's personal history. For example, friendships developed during military service or stays in the city are added to the social capital today.

In a parallel process the official policy of deconcentration of power to a very low level in the administrative hierarchy has been accompanied by a more informal encroachment on central government powers by local authorities. In this way the funding of state expenditure is to a wide extent ensured through direct levies on the income of peasants and rural enterprises. National taxes have been subjected to a policy of general relief, while local taxes, on the contrary, are collected very strictly. Meanwhile, as local authorities have the possibility of levying 'taxes' (*fei*), abundant extra-budgetary funds are available for use at the discretion of the bureaucracy—which does not fail to cause many abuses.

The dual aspect of 'societalisation' of the state in rural areas—society taking responsibility for certain state tasks, and the local bureaucracy gaining autonomy vis-à-vis both the central authorities and political constraint—complicates relations between rural society and the state on the one hand, and between that same rural society and the local political authorities on the other. Rural particularist feeling is expressed through a hierarchy of points of references in ever widening concentric circles, all of which exclude the state, seen as a predatory power. However, opposition to the state in principle does not stop state norms penetrating rural society. Legal norms are in fact sometimes used by the peasants, when it comes to catching local officials in the wrong—that is, when the law corresponds with their interests. In some protest movements petitioners quote the texts of laws limiting tax levies or requiring the holding of elections.[24] The attitude of rural dwellers is in reality highly ambiguous. What they are against is not the state as such, an abstract power, so much as the local

---

[23] On these themes, see the works of Jean C. Oi, 'The Fate of the Collective after the Commune', pp. 15–26, in Deborah Davis and Ezra Vogel (eds), *Chinese Society on the Eve of Tiananmen: The Impact of Reform*, Cambridge, MA: Harvard University Press, 1990; 'Fiscal Reform and the Economic Foundations of Local State Corporatism in China' (note 13); *Cadre Networks Information: Diffusion and Market Production in Coastal China*, Washington DC: World Bank, December 1995 (Occasional Paper no. 20); *Rural China Takes Off: Incentives for Industrialization*, Berkeley: University of California Press, 1996.

[24] On this theme see Kevin J. O'Brien and Li Lianjiang, 'The Politics of Lodging Complaints in Rural China', *The China Quarterly* 143, September 1995, pp. 756–83; Kevin J. O'Brien and Li Lianjiang, 'Villagers and Popular Resistance in Contemporary China', *Modern China* 22/1), January 1996, pp. 28–61; Kevin O'Brien, 'Rightful Resistance', *World Politics* 49/1, October 1996, pp. 31–55.

wielders of power whose margin of autonomy has increased considerably since the start of the reforms.

Regarding those local officials, the 'societalisation' of the state has not been accompanied by major political changes. In most cases, those holding power have remained the same. However, with the strengthening of the domain of non-institutional social interaction and the legitimising of social objectives, they have had to re-focus their actions on the economic growth of the region for which they are responsible, and put aside political tasks.[25] The good official is now the one who ensures the prosperity of the region. The interests of non-state groups and those of the state representatives thus converge to some extent, in a common attachment to what is called 'localism'—an ideology according to which everything must be done, by the political authorities and by the social side alike, to preserve local prosperity,[26] to favour the interests of local groups. To some extent only, however—local power also means imposition of taxes, predatory or otherwise, which continues to be poorly received by the population.

Unfinished 'societalisation' of the state

'Societalisation' of the state does not mean withdrawal by the state. Quite the contrary, as Habermas notes, 'societalisation' of the state and 'stateification' of society go together. It should not indeed be supposed that the state spends its time taking back from society what it has handed over: 'Interventionism had its origin in the transfer onto a political level of such conflicts of interest as could no longer be settled within the private sphere alone';[27] and 'Competition between organized private interests invaded the public sphere'.[28] Thus the state becomes a place of arbitration, but— this is the essential point—not one representing the public interest. On the contrary, the public sphere becomes a space for struggle among social interests, the general interest appearing as the product of assertion of the most important, most powerful social interests. In face of the complexity of this continual transmutation of numerous professional, private and geographical interests into the general interest, a process of bureaucratisation, of routinisation of processes of interlinking is gradually established, through the proliferation of channels of communication created between

[25] Paper given to the annual meeting of the Association for Asian Studies (note 21).

[26] The courts and police systematically favour locally-based enterprises; customs barriers are set up on the borders between different administrative units to stop 'foreign' products competing with local products; people refuse to sell raw materials to neighbours and possible competitors; etc.

[27] Habermas, op. cit., p. 142.

[28] Ibid., p. 179.

the state and organisations standing for social interests (trade unions, professional organisations, lobbies).

For China this integration of society into the machinery of state is problematic. First it raises problems of combining of social interests. Professional interests, which are horizontal by nature, and which in developed countries make it possible to unify the social space and give a universal dimension to interests, are either non-existent in China (among peasants and workers) or very weak (like associations of private businessmen). For reasons of social stability the state limits the possibilities of interests combining together. The various professional bodies that have flourished for some years have to accept a form of control; they have to serve state objectives. As for lobbies (associations, NGOs, etc.), while they are beginning to appear—there are charitable and environmental organisations—they are set up under the patronage of influential leaders.[29] For the moment, the interests at work are of a geographical sort, or within the state arena. The narrow focus of particular ways of thinking (from village and lineages to the province, via districts in rural zones and quarters in urban zones) is a considerable handicap for the creation of true social interlinks and more universal visions of matters to be resolved. However, social interests are beginning to become part of the new reality of the socialised state. It is striking to note that the protest movements in the countryside attack the local wielders of institutional power but seek the backing and mediation of higher levels. In a sense the state authorities are called to witness the danger represented by the anti-economic attitude of some officials. How, people ask in substance, can one overtax the rural economy when one needs all the financial resources that it produces to sustain growth and continue to improve the standard of living?[30]

At the same time the presence of social interests at the very heart of the state is another essential problem. For example, state employees have had until today the possibility of negotiating directly with the state without forming an interest group; and obviously, as the state takes on a more social dimension—that is, gives priority to economic targets and social interests—this negotiation seems more difficult, as is shown by the massive redundancies of recent years. But even so, the conditions of these redundancies show that there is still an organic link between the state and the working class.

The straddling of major economic interests and political positions also contributes to limiting the expression of real competition among social interests. If there is a tendency towards increased autonomy for the political-business elites, it is autonomy gained not at the expense of the state—

---

[29] For example, Zhu Rongji for the environmental movement.
[30] See the works of Kevin O'Brien and my paper to the AAS (notes 24, 25).

they are in the state—but at the expense of society. The public sphere is, so to speak, under direct, internal influence, without any institutional mediation. The process of routinisation, through formal or informal processes, is only beginning.[31] Plenty of work remains to be done to make this bureaucracy efficient, and notably to eliminate centrifugal and arbitrary tendencies within it and make it a force at the service of the social state, through respect for legitimate interests, administrative procedures and political decisions.

The ideas of 'societalisation' of the state and 'stateification' of society seem to back up Yves Chevrier's arguments about the 'Over-Stretched Empire'. It may be recalled that in his view the historical trajectory of the Chinese state passes through phases during which the state power concedes a certain amount of autonomy to society, but without any real institutionalising of the social domain.[32] However, it may be wondered whether China is not in the process of getting away from this historical pattern, because of the takeover of the political sphere by the demands of the social arena and, especially, those of the economy. The state has given up all strictly political aims, that is, any intention of transforming China in the name of a model of social organisation. To return to Hannah Arendt's statement of the issues at stake, today political questions centre around the concerns of shopkeepers or family heads: how to increase wealth, how to distribute it, how to repay debts, how to satisfy members of the family while respecting the hierarchy. Having given up any sort of 'transcendence', the state cannot continue to stay in the middle of the ford, even if the ford is wide and difficult to cross. What matters now is arranging, through 'societalisation' of the state and 'stateification' of society, pacts for arbitration and interlinkage between established social interests.

Paradoxically, this new Chinese state is more efficient than before. Since it no longer speaks of a place outside society, its decisions encounter less opposition than in the Maoist era. By giving legitimacy to non-state dynamics and ways of thinking and social demands, it can count on a certain amount of support from the social side against the local bureaucracy, so long as it changes sides and backs the latter against the former

---

[31] The role of 'echoing chamber' now played by the People's National Assembly should be particularly stressed. During its annual sessions a multitude of interests (above all geographically-based ones, but others also) find expression; this is not without influence on the management of state affairs.

[32] Yves Chevrier, 'L'Empire distendu: esquisse du politique en Chine des Qing à Deng Xiaoping', pp. 263–395, in J.-F. Bayart (ed.), *La greffe de l'Etat*, Paris: Karthala, 1996. See also the Postface by Chevrier in this volume.

when social stability so requires. Today the Chinese state is less powerful than in the past, but it is more central, better placed to intervene in struggles among social interests. Sometimes it even seems more indispensable than ever, when 'public' arbitration is called for in conflicts among administrative units and movements in defence of local interests,[33] or when China's place in the world is at issue. Then the state becomes the ultimate incarnation of the public interest, but in a context in which particular interests no longer oppose each other or cannot do so.[34]

However, if China seems to be getting away from its historical trajectory, it is doing so both in its own way (in its own time) and within a space and time that are outside its control. On the first point, the severe impact of the changes must be emphasised. China has passed from a situation where political objectives were everything and society nothing to one where the social must command the political. So what is happening is a contraction of time. Capital has become social (controlled by socio-political groups) even before the question of private ownership has been really posed. Previous social arrangements have been challenged almost overnight, while the 'societalisation' of the state deprives the latter of any power to build a 'new' social domain. The state is satisfied with ensuring overall reproduction of society.

As for the 'global time' in which China is now living, it inevitably escapes the control of the over-stretched state. To give just one example, the labour crisis is not only a Chinese crisis. The state cannot respond effectively to this crisis that is coming to destabilise society a bit more, except by renouncing its process of 'societalisation' and putting on its development-state and ordering-of-society boots once again, and thus bringing the political sphere back in authoritarian fashion. The dilemma is simple: how can the dual tendency of 'societalisation' of the state and 'stateification' of society be continued, when the question of simple survival is posed again, in acute form, for hundreds of millions of Chinese?

[33] For example, a protest movement developed against Shanghai in less favoured provinces. The metropolis is accused of draining the essential part of value added towards itself by controlling the final stage of production of many industrial products. The state had to intervene to limit the effects of this discontent.

[34] The importance of this role of intermediary with the outside world needs to be stressed; it is shown by the stakes involved in the negotiations for admission to the WTO, and the difficult trade relations with the United States.

8

PRIVATISATION AND POLITICAL CHANGE IN SOVIET AND POST-SOVIET RUSSIA*

Gilles Favarel-Garrigues

'Semi-criminal state capitalism', 'crony capitalism', 'liberal-bureaucratic corporatism', 'great criminal revolution', 'racket economy', 'mafioso state', 'predatory oligarchy'—the diversity, originality and vagueness of the labels attached to Russia since the early 1990s perfectly illustrate observers' perplexity at the emergence of an unknown regime.[1] Most of these expressions underline first the difficulty of separating political from economic change, in a context in which the elites interpenetrate with each other symbiotically and the privatisation process is presented as a crucial reform, guaranteeing the irreversible rejection of Communism and the transition to democracy and the market economy.[2] In addition they give an overriding importance to the 'criminal phenomenon' in the process of change,[3] thus giving post-Communist Russia a negative and worrying image.

In any social context, crime is defined in relation to prevailing norms, and the post-Communist transformation can probably be rightly understood as a period of coexistence of competing rules and values. What is

---

* This paper was written before the financial crisis of August 1998.

[1] On these labels, see Myriam Désert and Gilles Favarel-Garrigues, 'Les capitalistes russes', *Problèmes politiques et sociaux* 798, 22 August 1997, p. 3.

[2] The instigators of the privatisation process have often repeated that the creation of a class of small property owners would act as a leaven for democracy.

[3] Here I consider that I am following on from the reflections by David Stark and Laszlo Bruszt, who criticise two perceptions that, in their view, dominate analysis of change in the countries of the former Soviet bloc: transition as imitation and transition as involution. They prefer to speak of transformation rather than transition: 'In contrast to the transition problematics that is common to both, we see social change not as transition from one order to another but as transformation—rearrangements, reconfigurations, and recombinations that yield new interweavings of the multiple social logics that are a modern society': David Stark and Laszlo Bruszt, *Postsocialist Pathways: Transforming Politics and Property in East Central Europe*, Cambridge University Press, 1998, p. 7.

crime in such conditions? I would like to suggest elements of an answer to that question, exposing the modalities and stages of privatisation of the Russian economy since the mid-1980s, and then studying the links between entrepreneurial practices, penal policy and protection of property rights. But privatisation needs to be perceived in a broad sense: by reforming property rights, it brings about redistribution of control over the means of production, and that has consequences for the distribution of power in society.[4] Hence it is important to examine the links between privatisation and changes in the rules of the political game in Russia.

The stages of privatisation of the Russian economy

In the USSR the relaxation of state control over the economy began before the official launching of the privatisation process in 1991. A particularly fruitful phase for accumulation of capital was observed between 1987 and 1991. The stages of privatisation of the economy often correspond to the stages of enrichment of Russian capitalists.

Cooperatives. The process began about 1987–8 with decrees and then a law on cooperatives:[5] this reform, very liberal for that time, enabled profits to be made that were huge in the Soviet context, and the police forces did not have to ask for an account of the origin of capital invested.[6] Disagreements in the highest ranks of the party-state between 'conservatives' and 'reformers' led rapidly to contradictory measures that blocked development of the cooperative sector: much heavier taxation, revised and corrected legislation, increased bureaucratic interference.[7] However, these new constraints did not scare the newcomers,[8] and they strengthened the

---

[4] S. Malle, 'La privatisation en Russie: spécificité, objectifs et agents' in M. Lavigne (ed.), *Capitalismes à l'Est: un accouchement difficile*, Paris: Economica, 1994, p. 109.

[5] The law on individual work activity (November 1986) was the first text relating to privatisation of economic activity in the Soviet Union. The context of the time weakened it: during the summer of 1986 the campaign against illicit income was at its height. Few individuals took advantage of this reform to start up in business as nothing at that time guaranteed that the reform would be lasting.

[6] The ministry of the Interior issued in 1987 a confidential circular instructing agents of the services engaged in action against economic crime not to show zeal in that area. Source: reading of the circular during an interview conducted in that department at Yekaterinburg in June 1997.

[7] On this question see A. Jones and W. Moskoff, *Ko-ops. The Rebirth of Entrepreneurship in the Soviet Union*, Bloomington: Indiana University Press, 1991 (chapter 4).

[8] As proof of this it is sufficient to examine the picture drawn by Janos Kornai of 'the growth of the so-called cooperative sector in the Soviet Union'. The number of cooperative members rose from 15,000 in January 1987 to more than three million in July 1990: Janos Kornai, *Le système socialiste. L'économie politique du communisme*, Presses Universitaires de Grenoble, 1996, p. 521.

organic link between cooperatives and illegal activity: there was conceal-ment of income and tax evasion, besides the active corruption of the offi-cials responsible for registration of cooperatives. The links had certainly existed from the outset; the world of organised crime and the underground economy very quickly noted the opportunities offered by the cooperatives. Other cooperators—engineers, often young, presenting themselves as hon-est men, moved by an adventurous 'market romanticism'[9]—were quickly led to make contact with the illegal side, at various levels: corruption (among the administration and the police), tax evasion, contracts with criminal organisations for protection or for obtaining credit at a time when the banking sector was making its first steps.

Spontaneous privatisation. From 1988 onwards a number of commercial structures developed within enterprises, ministries and Communist Party organisations. These structures, varying in form (associations, *Konzerns*, scientific and technical centres) represented equally varied expressions of the collusion of private and public interests. They were generally founded by members of the Nomenklatura, for they had at their disposal the re-sources indispensable for economic initiative. As Natalia Lapina recalls, 'The men in power began to conquer the market, thanks to the "capital" provided by their personal contacts, their financial resources and the levers of command in their hands. Enterprises launched by Nomenklatura members formally had the status of private companies, but in reality they enjoyed solid support from the state...'[10] The structures of the Communist Youth Organisation (Komsomol), in particular, made it possible to develop commercial or banking activity from the late 1980s without any external constraint:[11]

Between 1988 and 1993, ministries were replaced by *Konzerns*, state banks by com-mercial banks, supply committees and contract allocations by stock exchanges,

---

[9] Some of these actors have published their memoirs, e.g. Mark Masarski, *Put naverkh Rosiiskogo* (The rise of a Russian biznesmena), Moscow: Mezhdunarodnye otno-shenriya, 1994. Other memories have been recorded in posthumous collections: Vladi-mir Tikhonov, *Kooperatsii: za I protiv* (Cooperatives: for and against), Moscow: Pik, 1991. The language used in these writings confirms these people as pioneers of the free market and adventurers of reform. Mark Masarski, one of Boris Yeltsin's economic advisers dur-ing the 1996 presidential campaign, is currently considered as one of the richest men in Russia ('I manage capital of tens of billions'). Of his beginnings he has said, 'When I founded my new cooperative, I lived in my mother's house, I fed myself from the produce of my kitchen garden, I received no wages. I and my 150 men, we tightened our belts to the last hole; we were all convinced that work is the father of wealth.' Interview in *Kommercheskii Vestnik* 3–4, 1994.

[10] Natalia Lapina, 'Le secteur privé en URSS de 1986 à 1991: structure et acteurs du marché', *Le Courrier des Pays de l'Est* 400, June 1995, p. 15.

[11] Some of the most influential banks in the mid-1990s, such as Menatep and Inkombank, were founded in the same way.

joint ventures and large central buying agencies. This is how that phase of rampant privatisation took shape: (1) the ministry was abolished; (2) over its remains (in the same building, with the same furniture and the same staff) a *Konzern* was set up in the form of a joint stock company; (3) the minister was pensioned off; (4) a controlling stake was passed to the state and the remaining shares were distributed among the top staff of the ministry. Generally, the *Konzern* was headed by the second or third person in the abolished ministry. That was how the famous Gazprom was created.[12]

There were several methods of privatisation available to the state enterprises. Within those enterprises, from 1988 onwards, commercial companies were frequently created around the most profitable assets, the most competitive units of production.[13] Meanwhile, a number of leasing contracts were signed in the same period. The enterprise signed a lease agreement with the supervising ministry; it had the right, after a certain lapse of time, to buy the leased assets. It then turned itself into a joint stock company; privatisation was complete. This procedure was followed for small units, stores, workshops. It was very advantageous, because the purchase price was fixed at the start of the lease, without taking account of inflation. In the end, real big deals were made in this way. Patronage, even nepotism rapidly worked their way into these opportunities. In the Urals, we noticed that this happened particularly within numerous small cities built around a factory; the manager and the head of the local administration often had full power to distribute those resources among their entourage.[14]

Privileges. The economist Anders Aslund, former adviser in Gaidar's team, believes that in Russia

in the overwhelming majority of cases, the wealth comes from three principal sources: credit on advantageous terms, export licenses (oil and gas, raw materials and metals), allocations of rights to import. These methods of enrichment, which emerged in 1988 in response to the partial deregulation of the Socialist-type

---

[12] Olga Kryshtanovskaya, 'Finansovaya oligarkhiya v Rossii' (The financial oligarchy in Russia), *Izvestiya*, 10 January 1996. The author is head of the department for elite studies at the Institute of Sociology of the Russian Academy of Sciences.

[13] Natalia Lapina gives an example: 'The big Dynamo electric engine factory in Moscow is an example of this establishment of the market: the first cooperatives were founded there in 1988. They began by using equipment and installations placed at their disposal by the enterprise, then they gradually turned themselves into joint stock companies after adoption of the relevant decree. In the next stage those companies joined together to form 12 companies whose shares were bought up by the management. That was what happened with Dynamo, which is formed from the regrouping of 12 companies.' Lapina (note 10), p. 16.

[14] Gilles Favarel-Garrigues, 'Le processus de privatisation à Ekaterinbourg et dans sa région', DEA dissertation, Institut d'Etudes Politiques de Paris, 1994, p. 51.

economy, took on an extraordinary dimension in 1991, when the Soviet economy collapsed completely.[15]

Credit was given to the industrial sector at derisory rates of interest (10–25 per cent) in a context of galloping inflation (2,500 per cent in 1992). Industrialists and bankers took advantage of the windfall. Export licenses enabled senior officials or other entrepreneurs to buy raw materials according to prices then prevailing on the Russian market and sell them on the world market at world prices. Allocations of rights to import were supposed to encourage imports of foodstuffs at a time of serious shortage; for that purpose traders bought foreign exchange from the state at a derisory rate, but resold the products at a high price. They were thus the sole beneficiaries of the operation.

Anders Aslund's thesis seems to us questionable and polemical. First, it underestimates illicit forms of enrichment (smuggling, extortion, embezzlement for example). Secondly, it seeks to absolve the instigators of the privatisation process of responsibility for the spectacular enrichment of a small number.[16] In fact the reform is very often legitimised by an argument emphasising that it confers a general regulatory framework on the transfer of ownership, whereas until then the operation was carried out in a discreet, 'spontaneous' and derogatory fashion, according to the resources and networks available. According to this argument, the privatisation process in fact reflects the state authorities' determination to put an end to iniquitous practices.[17]

This said, Anders Aslund's thesis has the merit of giving the full importance due to an essential resource for profiting from the economic reforms: the existence of solid contacts in the Soviet and then the Russian administration. During the period of privatisation of economic activity, no enterprise, no bank could exist without good contacts with the administration. Three sorts of entrepreneur could thus be envisaged: agents of the state themselves, with direct access to the country's economic resources; businessmen, criminal or not, with established contacts (kinship or friendship contacts, for example) with key agents of the administration; and businessmen prepared to purchase that missing resource and accept the

---

[15] Anders Aslund, 'Novykh russkikh obogatili tri osnovnykh istochnika' (The wealth of new Russians comes from three main sources), *Izvestiya*, 20 June 1996.

[16] Anders Aslund was, with Jeffrey Sachs, one of the principal Western advisers recruited by the Yegor Gaidar government to implement the shock therapy of 1992. His role is described in A. Aslund, *How Russia became a Market Economy*, Washington, DC: Brookings Institution Press, 1995, pp. 16–21.

[17] This opinion is relayed, for example, by D. Vasiliev, 'Rossiiskaya programma privatizatsii i perspektivy ee realizatsii' (The privatisation programme in Russia and its prospects of achievement), *Voprosy Ekonomiki* 9, 1992, p. 14.

rules of corruption. Some senior officials, with a perfect knowledge of the 'most modern financial techniques', had considerable influence.[18] State employees accumulated the rent provided by the situation.[19] The privatisation process, contrary to the way its instigators talked, perpetuated this phenomenon.

The privatisation process. It was only in 1991–2 that the privatisation process was officially launched.[20] The first phase is often called 'mass privatisation' (1992–4). An anonymous voucher worth 10,000 roubles was sent to every citizen of Russia, including minors, as a property right. This voucher could be exchanged for a share in an enterprise or a store, entrusted to an investment fund supposed to make it produce profits, or resold according to price fluctuations. The voucher was supposed to symbolise people's capitalism, the leaven of democracy: 'We do not need a handful of millionaires but millions of shareholders', said a slogan of Boris Yeltsin's. 'For each one of us, the voucher is an entry ticket to a free economy.'[21]

Despite some observers' optimism,[22] this phase of privatisation brought a number of problems. Certainly a strictly quantitative assessment brings out progress in terms of reducing state property. Overcoming such obstacles as the political instability at the time of the reform, and the unprecedented size of the task to be accomplished, may be considered a success for the government. However, the negative effects of the reform are clearly identifiable.

---

[18] This was the case with A. Vavilov, former First Deputy Finance Minister in the Chernomyrdin and Gaidar governments, member of the board of Gazprom and Norilsk Nickel. See Myriam Désert and Gilles Favarel-Garrigues (note 1), pp. 43–5.

[19] *Izvestiya* has revealed that the manager of the Property Fund of the Vologda region earned a salary equivalent to about £10,000 per month, 'almost as much as the president of the United States': *Izvestiya*, 6 November 1997.

[20] The two basic texts were the privatisation law of July 1991 and the privatisation programme for 1992, adopted by the Supreme Soviet in June 1992. It has to be recalled that the Supreme Soviet was then opposed to President Yeltsin, hence the mounting delay. That conflict was to end in bloodshed in October 1993.

[21] Statement of the President to the citizens, *Rossiiskaya Gazeta*, 20 August 1992.

[22] Some economists consider the operation a success. The most instructive work in this respect (the title is eloquent in itself) is probably M. Boycko, A. Shleifer and R. Vishny, *Privatizing Russia*, Cambridge, MA: MIT, 1995. It should be noted that one of the authors (Boycko) headed the Russian body responsible for launching privatisation, and then became minister for Management of State Property until November 1997. He was smeared by the scandal of Chubais' book (see *Nezavisimaya Gazeta*, 15 November 1997). Anders Aslund also pronounced a positive judgment on the outcome of the reform (*How Russia Became a Market Economy* (note 16), pp. 265–71). This approach is criticised by Jacques Sapir who shows, in particular, how the privatisation process created new opportunities for corruption: Jacques Sapir, *Le chaos russe*, Paris: La Découverte, 1996, p. 284.

As Viktor Kuznetsov rightly noted, 'Comparison of the results obtained in mid-1994 with the objectives defined by the law is meaningless.'[23] However, those objectives should be recalled to understand how the reform was legitimised. They were to encourage the creation of a class of shareholders who could be expected to join in the establishment of a market economy with social orientation; to improve the productivity of enterprises; to establish social protection financed by the proceeds of privatisation; to work towards financial stabilisation; to create a competitive sector and de-monopolise the economy; to attract foreign investment; and to prepare for later forms of privatisation, once the phase of exchanging vouchers for shares had been completed.[24]

In practice, the expected economic effects did not come about, and the reform worsened the loss of credibility of the reformers and their reforms, notably because there was a perception of a plot by the political, economic and criminal elites to 'rob' the country;[25] in addition, the social consequences were often tragic, including hunger strikes in some factories in the Urals. In most cases the vouchers did not give real access to share ownership; they were resold to the highest bidder, sometimes pocketed by the investment funds, and they only conferred weight in decision making within the enterprise if the employees formed a homogeneous group.

Privatisation benefited a small minority that had, from the outset, necessary resources at its disposal to make profits: money, contacts, and possible use of violence. This was particularly the case in 'small-scale privatisation' (stores, restaurants, workshops, small enterprises); in the region of Sverdlovsk, according to the economic crime police unit, 60 per cent of privatised assets were in the hands of the criminal underworld in 1995.[26] Pressure on competitors, during contests and auctions to determine owner-

---

[23] Viktor Kuznetsov, 'La privatisation en Russie 1992–1995', *Le Courrier des Pays de l'Est*, 400, June 1995, p. 23.

[24] These objectives were formulated in the 'Programme for privatisation of municipal and state enterprises for 1992' adopted by the Supreme Soviet of the Russian Federation on 11 July 1992.

[25] Stanislas Govorukhin's recent work is one of the emblematic illustrations of this perception, notably his films *We Cannot Live like This* (1990), *The Russia We have Lost* (1992), *The Great Criminal Revolution* (1994). The scenarios of those three films were partially reproduced in a work translated into French and published as *La grande révolution criminelle*, Lausanne: L'Age d'Homme, 1995.

[26] This figure is estimated on the basis of observation of the proceedings of auctions and competitions. In truth it is of little interest, because the intrusion of criminal circles into smallscale privatisation takes varying forms (loans, credits, management, controls) and, in addition, has no consequences for the population as long as the local bakery is not turned into a gambling den! The only interest of this estimate, often repeated in the regional press and during interviews, lies in the fact that the police acknowledge relations between reforms and crime.

ship, was almost systematic.[27] Arrangements with the administration, notably with the local and regional representatives of the State Committee for the Management of State Property (Goskomimushchestvo, GKI),[28] responsible for organising and implementing transfer of ownership, were notorious. They commonly took the form of supply of and demand for services, such as keeping the place and date of coming auctions out of the local press, so as to keep potential competitors away. The contract murder of the director of the St Petersburg office of the GKI during the summer of 1997, six years after the launching of the privatisation process, showed clearly that high stakes were still associated with such official functions.

To sum up, the Russian example confirms the observation by Béatrice Hibou that transfer of ownership does not necessarily lead—far from it— to 'a new manner of managing enterprises', primacy for 'criteria of efficiency and profitability', achievement of a true 'market economy', 'changes in relations between employers and employees', 'injection of fresh financing'.[29] In fact, to grasp the meaning of the Russian privatisation process, the political benefits for its originators need to be considered. This reform, likely to be unpopular, was carried out in a highly delicate situation in 1992. Price liberalisation, implemented in January by Yegor Gaidar as part of—in fact incomplete—shock therapy, hit the ordinary people who saw their purchasing power fall. The Communist opposition in the Supreme Soviet worked to block the process. Opinion polls did not fail to reveal the negative attitude of the population to the reform. Even so, the team in power managed to get the reform carried out; no mass protest movement emerged. How can this be explained? It seems in fact that the ways chosen by the instigators of the reform to give it legitimacy were well chosen. The privatisation process was presented from the outset, in continuation of the Soviet economic reforms,[30] as a measure making it possible to attain two objectives: economic efficiency and social justice. The distribution of vouchers to the whole population, the proclaimed determination to end irregular practices and spontaneous privatisation,

---

[27] Observation of this process at Yekaterinburg, September–October 1993.

[28] Gosudarstvennyi Komitet po Upravleniyu Gosudarstvennym Imushchestvom (State Committee for the Management of State Property). This body exists at the central level (A. Chubais was its director), and at the regional level and sometimes the municipal (in big cities only). It is attached to the corresponding administrative authority. While it was initially provided that the framework for reform should consist at all levels of two bodies, one reporting to the administration (GKI) and one to the Soviet (the Property Fund), the dissolution of the Soviets after the events of September–October 1993 led to concentration of tasks within the services of the GKI.

[29] Cf. Béatrice Hibou's chapter in the present work, p. 41.

[30] A. Hewett, *Reforming the Soviet Economy. Equality versus Efficiency*, Washington: The Brookings Institution, 1988.

gave the reform legitimacy in the eyes of the people, at least initially. As that confidence risked being eroded away, the rulers of Russia had to carry out the privatisation process as rapidly as possible, to guarantee that it would be irreversible.

Since 1993 the Russian trajectory of capitalism has been characterised by two phenomena. On the one hand, capitalism has been consolidated through the formation of huge empires, industrial and financial groups.[31] The new phase of the privatisation process, called 'cash privatisation', was launched in 1994; its aim was to give enterprises efficient owners, ones who could inject capital for investment. This phase was particularly characterised by increased involvement of the banks in the country's big enterprises and factories. Banks already had portfolios of shares and therefore privileged customers. With the plan called 'loans for shares', started by a presidential decree of 31 August 1995, the banks refloated factories in difficulty, and in doing so became their owners. The auctions organised were often a pretence; much ink has been spilled on the conditions in which the Norilsk nickel, copper and platinum giant, or the Russian communications monopoly Sviazinvest, were acquired.[32] On the other hand, capitalists maintained complex and renewed relations with the political arena. Businessmen entered politics, in the State Duma or the regional Dumas. Officials managed relations with commercial banks. The pressure exerted by the collective representatives of industrial and financial interests on political decisions became professional and diversified.[33]

Before turning to the relations between capital and politics, and their influence on modes of government, attention must be paid to the nature of relations between privatisation and criminal activity. In Russia as in the West, the two terms came to be confused in a strictly moral judgment. The appearance in the press of the term *prikhvatizatsia*, short for the noun *privatizatsia* and the verb *prikhvatit* (to seize), is significant in this respect. Without falling into other-worldliness, we would like here to give some elements of an explanation of this attitude, and to show what can be said or not, from the viewpoint of existing sources, about the criminalisation of the economy in such an exceptional situation.

---

[31] On these groups, see I. Starodubrovskaya, 'Finansovo-promyshlennye gruppy: illyuzii i realnost' (Industrial and financial groups: illusions and reality), *Voprosy Ekonomiki* 5, 1995, pp. 135–47; Lev Freinkman, 'Ekonomika i organizatsiya promyshlennogo proizvodstva' (The economy and the organisation of industrial production), EKO 10, 1994, pp. 2–19, translated into English as 'Finance Capital and the Formation of the New Industrial Structure in Russia', *Problems of Economic Transition*, August 1995, vol. 38 no. 4, pp. 77–91. These papers are partly reproduced in Désert and Favarel-Garrigues (note 1), pp. 25–32.

[32] Désert and Favarel-Garrigues (note 1), pp. 48–9.

[33] Ibid. pp. 36–45.

Privatisation and criminalisation

Between 1986 and 1996 the rules of the economic game were turned upside down, and this led to a change in the dimensions and nature of economic crime as defined by Soviet and then Russian legislation.

Is there discernible growth of economic crime? Statistics of recorded economic offences must be used with caution. First, as with all crime statistics, the conditions in which they are gathered and their significance must be borne in mind. They say more about the activity of law enforcement agencies than about the level of crime; they do not take account of the commonly latent nature of economic offences.[34] Secondly, the specific factors in a country and the specific period examined have to be noted. Until the mid-1980s the most common forms of economic crime were offences against socialist property, *pripiski* (falsification of productivity indicators in enterprises and of their conformity with the Plan) and speculation. Ten years later, none of these forms of offence appeared in the penal code. *Pripiski* had been linked to central planning, while speculation and offences against socialist property no longer had any place as offences in the context of privatisation and liberalisation of trade and prices. It should be added that before 1988, crime statistics were secret; examination of them was thus, at least initially, a novelty, a highly publicised social event, a symbol of *glasnost*, and this influenced perception of the phenomenon. So it is a very delicate task, methodologically, to compare levels of crime before and after the reforms. Hence we will give few figures, the essential point being to recall the general trends of the movements over the past ten years.

The recorded figures of general crime, as of economic crime, increased from 1988 onwards, after falling slightly during the very first years of *perestroika*. A period of sudden growth in recorded crime came between 1989 and 1993. Whereas in 1988 1,220,000 offences, including 215,000 offences against socialist property, were recorded, the figures reached 2,800,000 and 642,000 respectively five years later.[35] The share of economic offences as a proportion of recorded general crime has been expanding greatly over ten years. These figures reflect a trend towards more

---

[34] See Philippe Robert *et al., Les comptes du crime. Les délinquances en France et leurs mesures*, Paris: L'Harmattan, 1994 (2nd edn), pp. 13–51.
[35] *Izmeneniya prestupnosti v Rossii. Kriminologicheskii kommentarii statistiki prestupnosti* (Changes in crime in Russia: critical commentary on crime statistics), Moscow: Kriminologicheskaya Assotsiatsiya, 1994, pp. 16, 124. The collection of statistics with commentary covers the 1986–93 period. For raw data, the annual statistics are now published jointly by the ministry of Internal Affairs, the ministry of Justice and the Inter-State Statistical Committee of the Commonwealth of Independent States.

active struggle against economic crime. As indicators they have motivated the action of the Russian state and official language on the subject,
as well, to some extent, as perception of the crime problem. Figures for
the proportion of national product accounted for by the criminal economy, or for capital flight, are also difficult to handle, as they depend so
much on varying definitions of the object pursued. Without access to the
sources, it is difficult for us to join this debate.[36]

Changes in economic crime: frenzy and chaos. As for the nature of economic crime, it has been characterised by fundamental change. A study of
amendments to the penal code[37] reveals dozens of operations between 1989
and 1994: additions, repeals, substitutions. These operations have concerned either criminalisation and decriminalisation or the introduction of
lighter or heavier penalties. Criminal law policy from 1988 onwards was
in fact increasingly erratic, torn between the political and economic
imperatives of a Soviet state at the end of its run. The borders between
rules and offences, between the licit and illicit, went through a period of
severe disturbance.

The nature of Soviet criminal law, in which there were typically broad
and vague categories, to some extent explains these chaotic developments.
It has been noted that corruption (active or passive) could be punished
under different articles of the Soviet penal code.[38] In reaction to orders
issued by the hierarchy, the local police services were tempted to inflate
certain indicators at the expense of others. If a campaign was launched
against 'dilapidation of socialist property', the police forces had to prove,
at the local level, that they had heard the message. Their only way of proving it was in statistical summaries (quarterly, half-yearly or, most usually,
annual) of their activity in that area.[39] On the other hand some offences,
while important in practice and clearly designated by an article of the
penal code, were not well accounted for, as in private enterpreneurship for
example. There were many articles in the Soviet press about the *tsekho-
viki*, entrepreneurs who manufactured everyday consumer goods (usually

---

[36] On the proportion of proceeds of crime in national product, see the special feature in the
weekly *Kommersant*, 13 June 1995. On capital flight and varied estimates of the amounts
involved, see Vladimir Tikhomirov, 'Capital Flight from Post-Soviet Russia', *Europe-
Asia Studies* 49/4, 1997, pp. 591–615 (table on p. 603 shows variations in estimates).

[37] This Code, adopted in 1990, lasted until 1996.

[38] A study of corruption analyses this phenomenon: W. A. Clark, *Crime and Punishment in
Soviet Officialdom. Combatting Corruption in the Political Elite (1965–1990)*, Armonk,
NY: M. E. Sharpe, 1991, pp. 73–6.

[39] Gilles Favarel-Garrigues, 'La politique soviétique de lutte contre les infractions
économiques à travers les archives du Comité du Parti de la région de Sverdlovsk (1965–
1982)', *Revue d'Études Comparatives Est-Ouest* 2, June 1997, pp. 155–206.

clothing) in illegal workshops; but, because of their role, they were never the object of a specific struggle campaign even if they were most often punished for misuse of socialist property, since the means of production belonged to the state.

Many changes to the penal code in fact consisted of new incriminations: 'Incriminating means defining a crime, in the broadest sense of criminal offence; hence, defining and dividing: defining a situation or a form of behaviour sometimes unknown until then; dividing the social space into licit and illicit activity, and, more precisely, restricting the space of freedom by a new prohibition.'[40] Without going into details, several waves of incrimination can be observed, especially in the early 1990s. They were supposed to fix the new rules of the economic game: regulation of competition, taxation, price fixing, commercial activity, foreign currency transactions, customs operations.

Is it true, as a result, that privatisation of the Russian economy was characterised by its criminalisation? This question, which is usually slanted by moral judgment, raises the question of the pace of transition. The economic reform agenda corresponded only partially to that of the legal and judicial reforms.[41] Police and justice professionals complained of never being consulted before the major economic reforms. They also deplored contradictions at work in the crime policy of the Party leadership. The example of cooperatives is particularly eloquent. Several months after the law—and many cooperatives had been founded before the law— the penal code was modified. The article punishing extortion (*vymogatel'stvo*) was now made applicable to the cooperative sector, no longer to the state or public sector alone. In the intervening period extortion had remained unpunished. Economic behaviour and the rules prevailing in the economy developed much faster than the legislative framework defining economic crimes.

The survival instinct impels the businessman to calculate, to weigh things up: how to pay less in taxes, which financial plan to adopt, which sector of activity to develop and where? When we founded 'Interkvadro', there were no laws governing joint ventures. When we turned it into a limited company, no official had any idea what that meant. To be ahead of one's time, that is the meaning of enterprise.[42]

---

[40] Mireille Delmas-Marty, *Les grands systèmes de politique criminelle*, Paris: PUF, 1992, p. 306.

[41] In this sense Russia is far from satisfying one of the essential conditions for democratisation: the building not of a market, but of an economic society, a concept including a clear regulatory system. See J. Linz and A. Stepan, *Problems of Democratic Transition and Consolidation*, Baltimore and London: Johns Hopkins University Press, 1996, p. 14.

[42] Interview with businessman Lev Veinberg in *Kapital*, 1 November 1995. This influential manager was arrested and suspected of active corruption in 1994.

The economic reforms were devised and implemented without any reflection on social, economic and political practices affected by their application. The privatisation process, for example, amounted to a transfer of resources to government officials. It was clear a *priori* that the risks of corruption, collusion and illicit arrangements were enormous.[43] But no safeguards—in terms of control over application of directives—were provided for. Within the GKI the hierarchy asked only for formal accounts: only quantitative indicators of the activity of regional and local branches (the number of enterprises privatised per month) were checked. In these conditions corruption and overlapping of public and private interests tended to become the norm in the privatisation process. Similarly, the impassable barrier between the 'economic reform' and 'legal reform' fields led entrepreneurs to fix their own boundaries between the licit and illicit.

The entrepreneur, by definition, is someone who takes an initiative. He is a creator, an innovator. He does not break the law, he gets around it, he finds loopholes in it. That is his nature...Several times a day, people suggest that I should undertake three or four businesses capable of making me rich fast...I remain deaf to that advice. Not because I am afraid of going against some directive or some ordinance—generally there are none!—The moral frontiers are established by themselves in my mind. An inner voice acts and says: No. There is a frontier that distinguishes what is criminal from what is not. It is not a question of law here, but of morality.[44]

The necessary collusion between economic enterprises, the bureaucracy and the criminal underworld was blatant, but difficult to interpret in terms of crime, as the penal code which defines crimes was characterised by very great instability between 1988 and 1996.[45] However much determination the political leaders might show, regulation of the economy 'from the top' did not succeed in asserting itself, and from 1988 entered into dialectical relations with entrepreneurial practices.

The action of law enforcement agencies and its consequences for criminalisation of the economy. This competition of rules had multiple consequences. Not only did it reopen the question of the notion of criminal offence, it disrupted and confused the action of the police. In 1986, when

---

[43] Cf. Daniel Kaufmann and Paul Siegelbaum, 'Privatization and Corruption in Transition Economies', *Journal of International Affairs* 50/2, winter 1996, p. 423.

[44] Interview with Lev Veinberg (note 42).

[45] The coming into force of the new Russian penal code in January 1997 should have settled this problem, even if many amendments could have been foreseen in the short term. Certainly the text gave priority to defence of individual rights and could have aimed at regulation of commercial relations. On the new penal code see Léonid Golovko, 'Le nouveau code pénal de la Russie', *Revue de Science Criminelle et de Droit Pénal Comparé* 3, July–September 1997, pp. 561–77.

the law on individual work activity was adopted and a campaign of struggle against 'unearned income' was decreed almost simultaneously, a cartoon in the satirical weekly *Krokodil* summed up the situation by showing two policemen on duty in a *kolkhoz* market asking each other: 'What about that grandfather selling hand-made baskets? Shall we encourage him for his "individual work activity" or shall we punish him for "unearned income"?'[46]

The orders from the hierarchy were often contradictory. The 1986 campaign against unearned income, which faithfully reproduced—probably for the last time—the traditional Soviet campaigns of struggle against crime, aroused a particular feeling of injustice. In the press, when *glasnost* began, the perception of the reform was summed up in the observation that 'it is the small people who catch it, while the bigshots line their pockets'. Similarly, orders regarding the struggle against offences in the cooperative sector oscillated between a will to crack down on criminals and *laissez-faire*.[47]

The police lost the means to act. Their capacity for adaptation to ongoing changes in the economy was weak for ideological and technical reasons. As Soviet criminology was rigid, the officers in charge of repression of economic crime were used to dealing with embezzlement of public assets and funds, commercial fraud and speculation. When the cooperative sector was created, legal and economic consultancy cooperatives were founded very quickly. Management techniques, the possibilities offered by the new legislation and the loopholes to exploit, were learned informally. The police were unable to keep up—officers were ill trained in new management techniques. At the same time they were kept out of affairs concerning the activities of Communist Party organisations (more specifically those of the Communist Youth Organisation), which were zealously applying the reforms (founding cooperatives, banks etc.). Salaries declined in real terms. The police lost a part of their authority; because of *glasnost*, corruption, inefficiency and impotence among officers were increasingly denounced. In a documentary by Stanislas Govorukhin filmed in 1989, *We Cannot Live Like This*, the Soviet police officer is shown in a particularly harsh light: without a weapon, in a uniform of uncertain age conferring no prestige, impotent in the face of what is happening before his eyes, without authority. The following picture shows an impressive, over-armed New York policeman, proud of himself and his job.

In this situation there occurred from 1988 onwards, as in other professions, a sort of brawn and brain drain towards the private sector. *Glasnost*

---

[46] *Krokodil*, 23 August 1987.
[47] Marie-Agnès Crosnier, 'Le mouvement coopératif mis au pas', *Le Courrier des Pays de l'Est* 336, January 1989, pp. 66–9.

was slow to reach the internal functioning of the police forces: voicing internal problems was not easy. Among the rank and file, some chose loyalty or negligence while others opted to leave.

The hardships of the times were creating a renewed exodus from the force, with no corresponding desire to join a service seen as short on resources and low on morale, while the economic disincentive to join or remain within the militia was magnified by the way increased public concern over crime, as well as the greater wealth of some individuals, led to proliferation of private security firms and investigation agencies, offering substanitially higher salaries. Between January and May 1989 vacant posts within the police increased by 10,000, and by August 1990 the MVD was 60,000 understrength and the *druzhina*[48] had shrunk from 14,000,000 to 9,000,000.[49]

The police, like the other security forces (the army and the KGB), provided force for the protection of private interests and brains for strategic planning. The head of the security service of the Menatep bank, for example, was a former director of the Department for Struggle against Economic Crime in Moscow.[50] Legal experts and economists were also attracted by the dynamic and remunerative private sector. In the context of Russia in the late 1980s and in this specific milieu, voluntary or obligatory meetings with professional criminals were not uncommon. The perception of virtuous officers passing over to 'the dark side of the force' was characteristic of the period under study. 'We then saw some of our brothers joining the ranks of the enemy', confided an official of the regional prosecutor's office in Yekaterinburg.[51]

Privatisation of the economy, by producing enrichment and competition, effectively created new needs, and was accompanied by privatisation of property protection. From available information, it seems that the criminal underworld rapidly invested in the late 1980s in the sports sector, to ensure provision of protection services and arouse increasing demand. In view of the tense relations which developed between the police and the private sector, and the often bloodstained struggle for allocation of resources, strong-arm networks had to be created, able to defend private interests and sometimes to attack those of competitors or customers. Privatisation of the sports sector, or at least of those branches of the sector best able to train professional property protection staff, was a logical consequence of privatisation of the economy.

---

[48] People's militias entrusted with watching over public order.
[49] Mark Galeotti, 'Perestroika, Perestrelka, Pereborka: Policing Russia in a Time of Change', *Europe-Asia Studies* 45/5, 1993, p. 773.
[50] Nadine Marie Schwartzenberg, *La Russie du crime*, Paris: PUF, 1997, pp. 38–9.
[51] Interview in June 1997.

In Moscow Otar Kvantrishvili was murdered in the middle of the street as he was leaving the Krasnaya Presnia baths in April 1994. He was considered an 'authority'[52] in the criminal underworld. But officially Otar Kvantrishvili worked as director of the 'Lev Yashin' charity fund for defence of the social interests of sportspeople, and of numerous sports clubs. According to *Ivzestiya*, this former wrestling coach at the Dinamo sports centre 'was known for his compassion. At the same time, among the forces of order, he was considered one of the leaders of organised crime in Moscow.' At his funeral many sportspeople emphasised the role played by Otar Kvantrishvili in the promotion of sport among young people, and the relevance of his work on the ground.[53]

In Yekaterinburg Konstantin Tsyganov, one of the city 'authorities', based in the Uralmash factory district (this being one of the showpiece factories of the Soviet Union, in its size, production and siting), took over the running of sports clubs and youth centres sited on his territory at the beginning of the 1990s. He did not stop there; he organised the sale of sports goods and invested in the Uralmash football team.[54] Meanwhile,

at the end of 1991, the sudden cut in budgetary allocations from the ministries in Moscow led Uralmash, as well as many other factories of its size, into serious financial difficulties. According to correspondents in the district, the Uralmash organised crime group came to the rescue and penetrated the interior of the factory premises. The gangsters founded agencies for the purpose of buying the factory's products directly from the assembly workshops.[55]

The 'Togliatti experience' illustrates the trend towards public security escaping from the state domain. The city is particularly famous because it includes the gigantic VAZ car factory. The recrudescence of crime, especially theft, at Togliatti led the factory management to spend six and a half million roubles in 1990 (plus each year three and a half million roubles and 200 cars) to establish a municipal police force:

The UVD[56] retains all the key 'higher-function' departments such as criminal investigation, economic crime, and juvenile delinquency, and these will continue to be

---

[52] The term 'authority' in Russian denotes one of the highest echelons in the criminal hierarchy.

[53] *Izvestiya*, 7 April 1994.

[54] Besides oral sources, Tsyganov's personality is described in V. B. Zhitenev, *Mafiya v Yekaterinburge. Obshchestvennoe mnenie i pressa ob organizovannoi prestupnosti* (the mafia in Yekaterinburg: public opinion and the press on organised crime), Yekaterinburg, 1993. Despite its sensational title, this book is based on credible sources.

[55] V. B. Zhitenev (note 54), p. 26. This information comes from the press and is not verifiable, but it is plausible since the criminal organisation was undoubtedly eager to establish itself in its district. Tsyganov always strove to give himself the image of a benefactor. While the information may have to be used with caution, on the other hand there is no reason to doubt the principle.

[56] Upravlenie Vnutrennikh Del (Ministry of Internal Affairs).

funded through the usual channels. Within its precinct, though, the new force will take over patrol and basic investigation duties and will have its own police stations. Personnel will be provided with housing in their own areas, and there will even be 'district officers' whose apartments double as police offices.[57]

Insofar as the performance of state law enforcement agencies declined, as the use of violence became structured and expanded, and as rivalry among the rules of the economic game eventually reached a paroxysm, the early 1990s were characterised by partial loss of state control over economic regulation. At that time protection of economic interests very often involved secret organisations. As the criminal underworld became implanted in a given territory, its aim was to guarantee the working conditions of the economic agents that it protected. At Yekaterinburg one businessman, Andrei Panpurin, was in the headlines during the spring of 1993. He publicly announced his decision to work with the 'authority' Konstantin Tsyganov, at that time facing a homicide charge (he was gaoled in June 1993). Interviewed by the regional press about the new company he kept, he did not evade the questions and considered that Tsyganov, through his settling of conflicts, was a stabilising factor:

Konstantin Tsyganov is the guarantor not only of social peace, but also of the free development of private enterprise in the district. Working with him means being protected against extortion and crime and benefiting from better relations with the local administration, which increases the efficiency of the enterprise.[58]

So the new economic rules, competing with those characteristic of the Soviet economic system, could be defined and guaranteed by private economic agents, not by the political authorities. Those agents could come from the Soviet criminal underworld. In that sense, privatisation of the economy was sometimes confused with criminalisation of the economy. Two commonly accepted ideas must however be dismissed: this phenomenon must not necessarily be seen as a factor for destabilisation and disorganisation, and not every private sector economic actor must be identified with the criminal underworld. For example, in the early 1990s banks very often refused to provide credit to individuals. If an entrepreneur needed money to carry out his plan, he had a choice between two solutions: either his contacts in the world of banking made it possible for him to get credit, or he resorted to other sorts of lender.[59] If one puts aside moral judgments, there is nothing to indicate that private agents, linked to criminal organisations or not, have been a *priori* incompetent in the way they run their

---

[57] Mark Galeotti, 'From Gorky to Tol'yatti: new Models for the Police', *Radio Liberty Report on the USSR*, 2 (35), 31 August 1990, p. 5.

[58] Interviewed in the regional daily *Na smenu*, 28 May 1993.

[59] Interviews with a number of young Yekaterinburg businessmen in October 1993.

businesses or carry out economic functions. On the contrary, administration officials and police forces expressed surprise at the ability of reputedly criminal organisations to manage their enterprises in a rational and innovative way.[60]

This said, those phenomena of privatisation offended people's thinking. Private enrichment went against the official rules of the Soviet economy, the favourable view given in the media of what had been taboo in the Soviet system (crime, social distinctions) shocked a great number of the population thanks to *glasnost*, and the impotence of the police encouraged general disorientation. Entrepreneurs, at first contemptuously called 'Nepmen' in reference to Lenin's New Economic Policy, displayed their enrichment and, visibly or otherwise, defended their interests. A heightened feeling of injustice developed rapidly. Collusion between politicians, businessmen and the criminal underworld was then often interpreted as proof of a plot hatched by a secret alliance against the people; Russia, it was said, was being robbed without scruple and struck by a 'great criminal revolution'.[61] The idea of a predatory and mafioso state reflected the disorientation and confusion among a large section of the population, which did not succeed in telling the difference between capitalism, privileges and organised crime. This feeling was far from being irrationally based:[62] as the capitalists in fact needed to defend their interests in such an unstable situation, they had either to build up or to rethink their integration into the political field. However, the various actors involved in this necessary collusion were not necessarily pursuing the same aims.

Political consequences of privatisation

We do not claim to have made an exhaustive study of the political effects of state withdrawal from the economy. In particular, we have left out the consequences of privatisation on the definition of economic policies and state policies in general. Our intention is rather to find some routes to

[60] Interviews with officials of the Regional Directorate of the Struggle against Economic Crime and the Regional Committee for State Property, Yekaterinburg, October 1993 and June 1997.

[61] Stanislas Govorukhin, *La grande révolution criminelle* (note 25). This instructive work, written between 1989 and 1993 by a film maker turned deputy, is probably one of the best accounts of the chaos and delusions aroused by the end of the Soviet system and the upsetting of the rules of the economic game. We have commented on it in *Revue d'Études Comparatives Est-Ouest*, 27/3, 1996, pp. 183–91.

[62] Recently Ivan Gladyshev, vice-chairman of the State Duma Committee for the Struggle against Organised Crime, was charged with murder. A firearm and false papers were found in his possession. *Le Monde*, 26 November 1997.

follow in reflection on the implications in terms of legitimacy, hierarchy and ways of exercising power.

The new economic rules, partly invented and applied by private actors, led to redistribution of capital and resources in the broad sense (money, influence, contacts), by comparison with the rules in force during the Brezhnev era. Certainly there were already in that era illicit entrepreneurs coming from the underground economy, who were differentiated from the rest of the population. But now private entrepreneurs developed in complete freedom; in doing so they altered some rules of the Soviet political game, challenging hierarchies and modes of legitimisation in particular.

The emergence of entrepreneur deputies. Why did businessmen decide, from the early 1990s onwards, to go into politics? There is no obvious answer to this question. We think that differing strategies behind these decisions must be distinguished. Some people were elected as deputies to defend corporate interests, others aspired to a political career after doing business, others again were not uninterested in obtaining parliamentary immunity. Anne Le Huérou considered that 'besides parliamentary immunity, [serving as a deputy] meant advancing one's interests in dealings with the administration, and possibly entering into conflict with it from a position of some legitimacy.'[63] Even though such legitimacy was not indispensable—there were other ways of advancing one's individual or collective interests in dealing with the administration through much more informal relations—this was indeed the nature of the problem.

The sources of legitimacy changed, for money was now part of the resources capable of giving access to a deputy's seat. Personal enrichment, which aroused great hostility in the later 1980s, a few years later aroused a mixture of admiration and suspicion about the origin of the wealth. At the local level many deputies used their financial resources to start patronage networks. Candidates began to resort to 'patronage machines' at the time of parliamentary elections, like the deputy Yevgeniy Zyablitsev, who offered food and services during the December 1995 campaign.[64] Money also created inequality in political communications in pre-election periods. As political competition was subject only to feeble regulation, no holds were barred. For example, one of the two candidates for the post of Mayor of Yekaterinburg, during the 1995 electoral campaign, published a pseudo-sociological investigation, distributed in all the city's letter

---

[63] Anne Le Huérou, 'Pouvoirs locaux et pouvoirs régionaux à Omsk' in Marie Mendras (ed.), 'Russie. Le gouvernement des provinces', *Nouveaux Mondes* 7, winter 1997, p. 141.

[64] S. Sen, 'Sverdlovskaya oblast': protsess politicheskogo strukturirovaniya' (The Sverdlovsk region: the political reconstruction process), *Ural: Politika, Ekonomika, Pravo* 1/22, January–February 1997, p. 37.

boxes, showing that his rival was 'objectively' an incompetent and irresponsible mayor.

We have already observed, in connection with the Uralmash plant and the 'Togliatti Experience', that some social actors fulfilled, at the local level, functions that were presented as responses to the deficiencies of the state. Such a role was also claimed by some entrepreneurs when they entered politics. During the regional elections in 1994 at Omsk, Anne Le Huérou notes that

the most original initiative probably remains the one taken by a candidate who set up an ambitious programme in his constituency to 'guarantee to all physical, material and moral security', oscillating between open confrontation with the administrative authorities when he intruded on the prerogatives of the state (setting up private security guards in front of schools) and offering of services out of desire for cooperation (as when he proposed to provide part of the cost of a police station, etc.).[65]

To some extent hierarchies were overturned. In the Soviet Union positions of power had been held by people who had followed two sorts of career: within the administrative apparatus (*apparatchiki*) or within the productive sector and economic institutions (*khoziaistvenniki*).[66] The traditional elites still belonged to the dominant circles, but now they had to come to terms with people who had followed entirely different trajectories—authentic self-made men who had influence over economic decisions. Malik Gaisin, for example, had no higher education; in the 1980s he progressed in the unofficial economy, working in illicit production workshops. He founded his first cooperative in Sverdlovsk (the Soviet name for Yekaterinburg) at the end of the 1980s, and then a limited company which, through the privatisation progress, specialised in massive buying of vouchers, the privatisation cheques distributed to the population in 1992. Thus he acquired holdings in the industrial sector in the region.[67] He currently claims—and nobody says it is untrue—to own 10 per cent of industry in the Urals, with share packages in more than a hundred enterprises. His four bodyguards never leave him, his four daughters are educated at home by tutors.[68] Malik Gaisin is today a deputy in the state Duma, elected in 1995 in one of the Sverdlovsk region constituencies. This example illustrates a trend towards diversification of the channels for social advancement.

[65] Anne Le Huérou (note 62), p. 141.
[66] James Hughes, 'Sub-National Elites and Post-Communist Transformation in Russia: a Reply to Kryshtanovskaya and White', *Europe-Asia Studies* 49/6, September 1997, p. 1031.
[67] The Sverdlovsk region is dominated by the industrial sector.
[68] This information was published by the national daily *Kommersant*, 22 June 1995. That daily has a reputation for strict accuracy, especially in the economic domain.

Capital and politics. The collusion between capital and politics is evident, and quite obviously goes beyond elections. Indeed, becoming a deputy is a marginal expression of entrepreneurs' determination to participate in political decision making. Lobbying assumes different shapes according to whether it addresses executive (administration) or legislative (Duma) bodies.[69] For an entrepreneur it is not necessary to become a deputy himself; financing the campaign of a candidate ready to defend certain types of interest is just as good. However, putting pressure on the administration remains the most fruitful way, since 'having institutional access to the organs of the executive allows access to the places where decisions are made. Success is not guaranteed even so, for the status and the political weight of the body concerned make an enormous difference.'[70]

The relations between capital and politics, more precisely between banking and political power, raise questions about the problem of management of public funds. In Russia, only half the state funds pass through the Treasury department in the Ministry of Finance (created in 1994); the other half fills accounts in registered commercial banks: 'All the sensitive ministries manage their budgets in this way. In theory, the Finance Ministry only keeps its funds in the Central Bank of Russia…in reality, the Ministry's budgetary accounts are partially opened in so-called "authorised" banks, which deal in a certain fashion with the treasury of state bodies.'[71] The initially high number of these establishments, and the lack of transparency in operations, led to losses for the state: 'A report drawn up by the Russian Audit Office in 1996 mentioned that the list of registered banks was established by a commission including representatives of those establishments.'[72] In January 1997 the government fixed more selective criteria for approval, and selected thirteen commercial banks. The appointed managers' influence weighed on some political decisions, for example— as we have seen—concerning privatisation of industrial giants through the 'loans for shares' plan. The registered banks[73] also intervened in the choice

---

[69] A. A. Neshchadin, 'Lobbizm v Rossii: etapy bolshogo puti' (Lobbying in Russia: stages on a long road), *Sotsiologicheskie Issledovaniya*, 3 and 4, 1996; the contemporary period is covered in issue no. 4 of 1996, pp. 3–10. A. Yu. Zudin, 'Rossiya: biznes i politika' (Russia: business and politics), *Mirovaya Ekonomika i Mezhdunarodnye Ostnosheniya*, 3, 4 and 5, 1996; issue no. 3 concerns forms of organisation of the business world, numbers 4 and 5 look at relations between the government and business circles. Extracts from numbers 4 and 5 are reproduced in Désert and Favarel-Garrigues (note 1), pp. 36–43.

[70] Ibid., p. 38.

[71] Alexandre Huet, 'Banque et finance en Russie', *Le Courrier des Pays de l'Est* 420, July 1997, p. 16.

[72] Ibid.

[73] We prefer to translate *'upolnomochennye banki'* as 'registered banks' rather than 'authorised banks'.

of economic agents that the state decided to back, as the allocation of credit on advantageous terms to enterprises or companies by the state authorities aroused the interest not only of corporations in particular sectors, but also of banks, since the sums allocated passed through their accounts.[74] Private management of public money was therefore at work in Russia, even though the disadvantages of such a situation seemed to be increasingly realised.

In these conditions, the number of connections between the political elite and the world of business should cause no surprise. The financing of political campaigns is one of the most obvious forms of this. The collusion between the two sectors does not fear the light of day; it can take the most direct form of appointments. Thus Boris Berezovsky, chairman of Logovaz (the leader of the Russian motor industry sector), was appointed Assistant Secretary to the Russian Federation Security Council in October 1996; Vladimir Potanin, chairman of the Oneximbank, became First Deputy Prime Minister in August 1996.[75] These appointments should not be seen as indicating genuine and natural support from bankers for Yeltsin's cause—only support for those actually in power. The 'Manifesto of the 13', published in most of the big national dailies on the eve of the 1996 presidential election and signed by thirteen eminent representatives of the business world, is revealing in this regard.[76] It called on the leaders of the 'democratic' and 'Communist' camps, Boris Yeltsin and Gennady Zyuganov, to 'seek a political compromise capable of sparing Russia serious conflicts that would threaten its fundamental interests.' This tactical manoeuvre, in a climate of uncertainty hanging over the result of the vote, showed that the financial decision makers were ready to come to terms with a possible Communist team in power, even if they preferred to continue working with the existing team.

Privatisation and decentralisation. Russian political life seems to have been dominated, in the 1990s, by deals and bargains. This was not characteristic only of the relations between politics and finance; it related more generally to the struggle for resource allocation, in a context where it was important to influence the making of rules for the political game. That struggle, for example, pitted the centre against the regions, or rather the

---

[74] A. A. Neshchadin, 'Lobbizm v Rossii: etapy bol'shogo puti' (Lobbying in Russia: stages on a long road), *Sotsiologicheskie Issledovaniya*, 4, 1996, p. 9.

[75] On the appointments that aroused most interest, see Désert and Favarel-Garrigues (note 1), p. 53.

[76] This manifesto, published in the Russian dailies on 27 April 1996, has been partially translated in 'Russie 1993–1996: une fragile démocratisation' (edited by Roberte Berton-Hogge), *Problèmes Politiques et Sociaux* 772, 13 September 1996, pp. 18–19. It was signed by Boris Berezovsky and Vladimir Potanin among others, as well as by other chairmen of registered banks.

protagonists who presented themselves as defenders of territorial interests.[77] It is not surprising that centre-region relations are currently so personalised. Power is concentrated in the governors, at the head of regional executives: 'Despite the increasing heterogeneity of regional economic situations, the emergence of new inequalities and new cleavages in society, the outlines of one common mode of government appear: the executives regain the upper hand and the representative assemblies are relegated to walking-on parts; the links between political power and the economic and financial structures are as obvious as they are impenetrable.'[78] Rich regions have challenged the centre's control over economic resources located on their territory. The degree of personalisation of centre-region relations has meant that the share-out of resources is not only a matter for internal debate in the public sector. Collusion noted at the central level is found again at the regional level.[79] The example of the Bryansk region is typical: in 1993, the director of the regional Committee for State Property (the body in charge of implementing privatisation) was appointed governor, that is, head of the administration. Until 1995 his position made it possible for him to run the sale of state property as he wished. This period, during which the pace of the sell-off got faster, was said to have witnessed peaks of patronage, corruption and embezzlement.[80]

In Russia today it is important to look into the withdrawal of the state from one of its sovereign functions, raising of taxes. Here the logics of privatisation and decentralisation overlap. The opaque nature of budgetary operations and relations between administrative heads and the banking sector—which reproduce at the regional level the collusion noted at the centre—suggests that private interests are involved. Between Moscow and the rich Sverdlovsk region (rich in industry and natural resources), areas of disagreement invariably have an economic origin: sharing of assets, taxation, free disposal of natural resources.[81] James Hughes notes

---

[77] On the building of Russian federalism, see Marie Mendras (ed.), 'Russie: le gouvernement des provinces', *Nouveaux Mondes* 7, winter 1997; Anne Gazier, 'Fédéralisme et auto-administration locale en Russie: un cadre juridique flou et ambigu', in 'Russie: qui gouverne les régions?' (edited by Jean-Robert Raviot), *Problèmes Politiques et Sociaux* 783, 18 April 1997, pp. 11–19.

[78] Ibid., p. 4.

[79] James Hughes shows that at the regional level, the distinction between the political elite and the economic elite is artificial. James Hughes, 'Sub-national Elites and Post-Communist Transformation in Russia: a Reply to Kryshtanovskaya and White' (note 66), pp. 1017–36.

[80] Jean-Charles Lallemand, 'Le gouvernement régional à Briansk et Smolensk', paper delivered at round table on 'Etat et province en Russie. Dynamique de la régionalisation et enjeux du pouvoir', CERI, Paris, 1 December 1997.

[81] Gilles Favarel-Garrigues, 'La région de Sverdlovsk et le pouvoir du gouverneur' in Marie Mendras (ed.) (note 77), pp. 161–91. In the same work, on the economic dimension of

that the regional elites seek to maintain their influence through the privatisation process.[82] On budgetary questions there is rivalry between central and regional political and economic elites, since administrative authorities and banks are involved. The governor of the Sverdlovsk region insists that it is unacceptable for money collected in the region to profit the Moscow financial groups exclusively and not their regional counterparts. The struggle for allocation of resources, aroused by privatisation of the Russian economy, leads to strategies of instrumentalisation of centre-region relations.

In some regions specific taxes have appeared. Jean-Charles Lallemand notes that in Smolensk an illegal tax, called the 'environmental tax', was introduced by a decision of Governor Glushenkov, to be paid by every vehicle passing through the region. This tax was illegal because the decision was taken without the central and regional legislative organs being involved. The money was collected by the GAI (the highway police) and transferred into an obscure 'American-Russian Assistance Fund' to which members of the regional administration were linked. This tax was not a strictly regional issue, because the motorway from Moscow to Warsaw passed through the Smolensk region. The use of the money thus collected was not transparent: the press spoke sometimes of gifts made by the 'American-Russian Assistance Fund' to retired people, but did not get down to investigations.[83]

The limits of change. Among the component parts of the political field touched by privatisation of the economy, then, were hierarchies, modes of legitimisation and the partial assumption by private actors of responsibility for certain areas of state authorities' intervention (public security, taxation, the budget, regulation of the economy, social services). It is too soon to determine how long these phenomena will last and to identify the outlines of possible 're-sectorisation'. Will the state authorities seek to move back into the sectors in which private actors are competing with them, or will they rather seek to stabilise this situation? We shall take care not to interpret this phenomenon as an expression of 'the retreat of the state', to use Susan Strange's phrase, as this problem includes so many complex factors and so resembles a minefield. We prefer to confine ourselves to

---

centre-region relations see Marie Mendras, 'Le réveil politique des provinces', pp. 27–46; Jacques Sapir, 'Les Russies économiques', pp. 47–82; James Hughes, 'Régionalisme économique en Sibérie', pp. 105–26. James Hughes confirms that the three economic issues which we have noted are indeed the principal causes of tension between the centre and the Siberian regions (pp. 111–19).

[82] Hughes (note 81), p. 113. See also Darrel Slider, 'Privatization in Russia's Regions', *Post-Soviet Affairs* 10/4, 1994, p. 387.

[83] Jean-Charles Lallemand (note 80).

two questions so as to moderate the vision of political change in Russia. Does privatisation of the economy lead to challenging of the state's position as the basic organisational structure of society? And does it involve at the same time a break, in terms of modes of government, with what prevailed in the Brezhnev era?

The answer to the first question appears to us to be clearly negative. The Russian example confirms what has been said much more generally about historical capitalism:

Politics is about changing power relations in a direction more favourable to one's interests and thereby redirecting social processes. Its successful pursuit requires finding levers of change that permit the most advantage for the least input. The structure of historical capitalism has been such that the most effective levers of political adjustment were the state-structures, whose very construction was itself, as we have seen, one of the central institutional achievements of historical capitalism. It is thus no accident that the control of state power, the conquest of state power if necessary, has been the central strategic objective of all the major actors in the political arena throughout the history of modern capitalism.[84]

In the Russian case, it is difficult, as James Hughes has shown, to distinguish between the economic elites and the political ones. As sources of enrichment are most often dependent on serving officials, it is absolutely unthinkable in Russia to contemplate self-enrichment without passing through contacts with agents of the state. Moreover, it is essential either to maintain or to create one's own political networks. Sovereignty of the state, far from being challenged, is in fact permanently legitimised by struggles for influence seeking to place men of confidence in strategic positions.

Can the attitude and language of regional elites concerning federal relations be interpreted as a challenge to the state, that is, to the mode of organisation of political power (territorial centralisation, differentiation, institutionalisation through a specialised administration)? Demands for autonomy and conflicts produced by the struggle for allocation of resources marked relations between subjects of the Russian Federation and the federal centre in the early 1990s. Except for the case of Chechnya, which we have skirted for lack of sources, those demands did not spring from real separatist feeling, but were rather declarations or threats used in negotiations with Moscow on the economic issues at stake in the federalism under construction. Some republics established on an ethnic base, like Tatarstan, certainly succeeded in negotiating their status with Moscow on advantageous terms.[85] Other regions had a more or less reduced margin of

---

[84] Immanuel Wallerstein, *Historical Capitalism*, London: Verso, 1996 (8th edition), p. 48.
[85] Jean-Robert Raviot, 'Le Tatarstan: une spécificité républicaine?' pp. 193–220, in Marie Mendras (ed.) (note 77).

manoeuvre, varying according to their economic importance in particular. In most cases, they did not have sufficient resources to back up their demands before embarking on conflict with the federal centre.[86]

Regarding the second question, a fundamental point needs to be noted: the Soviet modes of government have not been completely abandoned. Certainly the structures of the Party no longer duplicate those of the administration; nonetheless, the administration encounters rivalry of interests at the local level, whether private or collective (networks). Thus the head of the body responsible for privatisation in the Sverdlovsk region confided that important decisions were taken after consultation with influential associations of factory managers or bankers.[87] The opaque nature of administrative operations remains blatant; an organisational chart does not tell much about the real functioning of an organisation. Where an official has a resource at his disposal in a monopolistic fashion (goods or services—an official stamp, information, etc.), this creates an opportunity for corruption, in the Soviet and Russian cases as elsewhere.[88] This opportunity is reinforced by the standard of living of civil servants and the level of risk incurred (with defective control by the hierarchy and individualisation of decision making).

Legislative structures are certainly not neglected altogether. It can be advantageous for a businessman to become a deputy. In a more or less long-term strategy a lobby needs to influence the legislative process— the fixing of the rules of the game—in its efforts to defend its interests. But for the time being lobbying remains particularly well established in administrative departments. It is essential here to note the similarities with the rules prevailing during the Brezhnev period. These practices, indeed, did not come out of the blue. They should be understood as a continuation of methods for defence of sector interests in the Soviet system:[89]

---

[86] Thus the political elite of the Sverdlovsk region attempted a forcible takeover by proclaiming the Urals Republic in 1993. That tactic, against a background of economic concerns, came up against the intransigence of the federal government. Cf. Gilles Favarel-Garrigues, 'La région de Sverdlovsk at le pouvoir du gouverneur', pp. 61–191, in Marie Mendras (ed.) (note 77).

[87] Interview at Yekaterinburg, June 1997.

[88] Susan Rose-Ackerman, 'The Political Economy of Corruption', in Kimberly Ann Elliott (ed.), *Corruption and the Global Economy*, Washington: Institute for International Economics, 1997, p. 34.

[89] Janos Kornai has observed that 'the classic Socialist system is not immunised against the phenomenon known to Americans as…lobbying. Representatives of interests of various branches or sectors of industry, professions, trade unions and geographical regions strive to exert pressure on central bodies (on the subject of allocation of resources or appointments, for example)', Janos Kornai (note 8), p. 66. The basic work on pressure groups in the Soviet political system is H. Gordon Skilling and F. Griffiths (eds), *Interest Groups in Soviet Politics*, Princeton University Press, 1971.

The methods and working style of lobbies dealing with the administration of the President and the government have been slightly modified, but…have not been radically transformed. Corridor lobbying, already widespread during the period of stagnation, remains the most usual form…In this perspective what matters most is to have and to support 'one's own' agents in key positions. But in the hierarchy of the apparatus, official positions and a real degree of influence over decisions do not always coincide. That is precisely why participants in the lobbying process attentively observe the distribution of forces in key positions and the degree of influence over the leadership, including people who do not even appear on the official organisational chart.[90]

On the other hand, later these practices had different aims. To the extent that personal enrichment was ideologically approved, the dividing line between the defence of collective and of private interests naturally became thinner. Demands very often related to departures from the rules, to highly lucrative transactions:

The fundamental interests of pressure groups are concentrated around preferential customs duties, authorisation for privatisation of enterprises according to special procedures, awarding of state credit on advantageous terms and profits from state investments.[91]

The elements of continuity with the 'old regime' must obviously be taken into account in approaching today's Russia. Marie Mendras notes, on the subject of corruption, that three 'path dependency' factors must necessarily figure in analysis of the contemporary situation: 'the outsize and uncontrolled power of officials', 'the importance of the unofficial economy, the shadow economy', and 'the close interconnection between political or state elites and economic elites'.[92] An important addition, in our view, is the way in which the Soviet, then the Russian bureaucracy has operated; the work of local administrative bodies is assessed exclusively according to quantitative results. The privatisation process has been directed like a plan: the number of enterprises privatised determines its success. The concrete procedures for transfer of ownership are much less considered than the quantitative measure.[93] To understand this continued phenomenon, probably it is best to look again at the problem of relations between government and legitimacy in the Soviet Union. T. H. Rigby,

---

[90] A. A. Neshchadin (ed.) (note 74), pp. 8–9.

[91] Ibid., p. 9. Further on it is noted that agreements on direct state investment are not so attractive as before for enterprises.

[92] Marie Mendras, 'L'Etat, l'argent, la clientèle', *La Revue Tocqueville/The Tocqueville Review*, 19/1, 1998, pp. 40–1.

[93] The number of enterprises whose owners have changed is always underlined in order to demonstrate how successful the reform is. See for example Boycko, Shleifer and Vishny (note 22).

taking up Max Weber's analysis of modes of legitimisation, suggested that in Soviet society, which he called 'mono-organisational', domination was not based on the same sorts of legitimacy as in Western societies. The administrative structures of the party-state were oriented more towards goal achievement than towards respect for rules. Hence the legitimacy of agents of the administration was expressed more in conformity of their actions with the targets assigned—goal rationality—than in application of legal rules.[94] It seems that those modes of government—implementation of commands from the hierarchy, control over that implementation— were maintained in post-Soviet Russia. The change in economic policy was not accompanied by reflection on modes of intervention by the state authorities and application of decisions.

The phenomena of privatisation observed have occurred in a particular context of relations—dialectical and at the same time conflictual— between rival modes of regulation. Janos Kornai wrote that 'in such circumstances post-Socialist society will still remain for a long period a dual system, *sui generis*. It is a "mixed" system in which several elements of Socialism and capitalism live in cohabitation.'[95] What poses a problem is that this mixed system is not stabilised. Contrasting scenarios are entirely conceivable in a situation like this—increasing predation by an oligarchy reigning without sharing power and subjection of the people, simple retention of gains, re-dealing of cards, encouragement of personal enrichment. But for the moment, personal enrichment remains closely linked to access to administrative resources, in other words, contacts with public officials who have the ability to solve the problems entrepreneurs face. Widespread personal use of public office—even by the police—related to the development of the post-Communist economy represents the most obvious aspect of privatisation of the state in Russia.

[94] T. H. Rigby, 'Political Legitimacy, Weber and Communist Mono-Organisational Systems' in T. H. Rigby and F. Feher, *Political Legitimation in Communist States*, New York: St. Martin's Press, 1982, p. 10.

[95] Janos Kornai (note 8), p. 685.

9

'ASAL BAPAK SENANG' (AS LONG AS IT PLEASES THE MASTER): THE PASTORAL GOVERNMENT IDEA AND PRIVATISATION OF THE STATE IN INDONESIA

Romain Bertrand

'Who knows, maybe there is no "state" at all? The government offices are closed. Official vehicles gravitate around the beach and the cinemas. Maybe what is taking place during twilight periods like now does not derive only from laziness and corruption, but is equivalent to a display...of a more elaborate form of "civic privatism". The state, in fact, is getting fatter with new functions. It has penetrated in an unprecedented way into the heart of [ever expanding] areas of human life. But...this state looks less and less like a state, because it is less and less the focal point of our loyalty and devotion.' (Goenawan Mohamad, 'Twilight in Jakarta', 10 April 1982)[1]

'Maybe there is no state at all?': this disillusioned question deserves consideration, because in fact it expresses more than ordinary anguish over the inability of administrative institutions to respond to social expectations.[2] Goenawan Mohamad, a leading figure in independent journalism in Indonesia, was not out to echo the laments of those who consider the absence of the state—an unpardonable crime in exotic societies—as explaining and prolonging situations of chaos and social disorder. His purpose was different, and definitely more pertinent: to pose the problems surrounding the links between state intrusions into private space on the one hand and private takeover of sovereign functions of the state on the

---

[1] Goenawan Mohamad, 'Senja di Jakarta', *Tempo*, 10 April 1982, reproduced in G. Mohamad, *Catatan Pinggir*, vol. II, Jakarta: Pustaka Utama Grafiti, 1996, pp. 246–7.

[2] Goenawan Mohamad, born in 1941 in central Java, founded the weekly *Tempo* in 1971 and remained its main leader writer until the magazine was banned by presidential decree in June 1994.

other. The recent history of Indonesia, that of the New Order (1965–98) but also of the *Reformasi* which began after Suharto's resignation in May 1998, gives food for thought on this correlation.

At the same time as defiance of state power was spreading, and private use of the public domain proliferating, the intervention of the administration and the army at the heart of the most secret places of social existence was being strengthened. Imposition of a hierarchical model of the family unit and birth control, transformation of schools into places of indoctrination, creation of leisure camps for adolescents—these phenomena, products of a gigantic state offensive against the bastions of intimate life, contributed to the abolition of the lines of demarcation between the public and private spaces. This effort to place individuals' productive and reproductive behaviour under supervision claimed, in addition, a powerful array of justifications. It claimed to be based on a theory of the state able to overcome demands made in terms of public freedom. It constantly asserted the transcendent unity of the person and the state.

What lay behind such an assertion? The issue was not only imposition of prison-like restrictions on social life, but much more the legitimising of a system of domination centred on private takeover of state expenditure and revenue. Declaring the perfect congruity of the state and the body of society permitted holders of administrative offices to use their powers without restraint. At the level of social relations, this justification operation took the form of a well-known saying: *asal bapak senang,* 'as long as it pleases the master'. The writer and essayist Mochtar Lubis summed up the 'ABS mentality' (from the acronym of *asal bapak senang*) in these terms: 'keeping those who are in power happy while saving your own skin'.[3] The word *bapak* means any holder of a position of authority able to intercede with the state or other institutions, disregarding the law, in favour of a subordinate considered as his 'beloved child' (*anak buah*), that is, his 'protégé'. Originally reserved for people whose advanced age called for respect from the young, the word *bapak* evolved bit by bit to become an expression of deference towards any holder of power. Every social subordinate was now obliged to 'give *Pak*' to his superior in the hierarchy, if he wanted one day to enjoy the superior's bounty and wisdom:

Visit any shiny new glass-and-steel high-rise building in Jakarta, open the door and enter an office, you will find secretaries and clerks in homely worn sandals enjoying lax sleepy afternoon chats. President, ministers, directors, managers, army officers, in fact anyone becomes *bapak* the moment they are addressed by '*Pak!*' by their subordinates with respect, affection, and expectation. They are

---

[3] Mochtar Lubis, *Manusia Indonesia*, Jakarta: Idayu Press, 1977, p. 32.

morally bound then to strive to protect their men and women and take care of their interests even if this means circumventing laws, regulations and dues.[4]

The term *bapak* differs from the more neutral term *tuhan* (sir) or the now outmoded (except in aristocratic circles) term *gusti* (master, lord). It implies that the power relationship is perceived on the lines of the bonds between parents and children. In other words, it does not consist only of a power relationship (which can be reversed politically), but is also an area of expression of family feeling that forbids or regulates transgression.[5] The language of kinship, by making a relationship of domination something natural, was fully exploited as a cultural alibi for the process of 'privatising' of the state in Indonesia.[6] It justified private hands dipping into the public revenue by relating all exercise of authority to the model of the 'national family' (*keluarga bangsa*). The pastoral concept of power, as Michel Foucault noted,[7] leads to a system of domination in which authority relationships are described in the language of a lecture to one's family. President Suharto, who proclaimed himself the 'father of national development' (*bapak pembangunan nasional*), excelled in this respect. He was to be seen rebuking and mocking undisciplined students who jeered at him, and severely reprimanding, from his Bogor ranch and over national television, a handful of Sino-Indonesian entrepreneurs who were sacrificed to the xenophobic instincts of the common people. Admonishing in these cases was a strategy to wear away dissidence. Any move towards protest was instantly described as parricide and, of course, punished as such. Hence the extraordinary tone of trials where the accused seemed to be giving evidence not before a court facing a judge, but rather on a couch facing a psychoanalyst.

The end of the New Order regime in May 1998 hardly changed this situation. Using the metaphor of the extended family (*keluarga besar*) in the naming of political groups even became systematic when new parties

---

[4] Saya Shiraishi, *Young Heroes. The Indonesian Family in Politics*, Ithaca, NY: Cornell University Press, 1997, p. 95.

[5] See for example J.-F. Bayart, *The State in Africa: the Politics of the Belly*, London and New York: Longman, 1993, and *The Fictions of Cultural Identity*, London: Hurst, forthcoming.

[6] See B. Hibou, 'The "Social Capital" of the State as an Agent of Deception, or the Ruses of Economic Intelligence', pp. 69–113, in J.-F. Bayart, S. Ellis and B. Hibou, *The Criminalization of the State in Africa*, London: International African Institute in association with James Currey (Oxford) and Indiana University Press (Bloomington and Indianapolis), 1999; and J.-F. Bayart, 'L'Etat', pp. 213–30, in C. Coulon and D. Martin (eds), *Les Afriques politiques*, Paris: La Découverte, 1991. See also the Introduction to the present volume, by Béatrice Hibou.

[7] Michel Foucault, '*Omnes et Singulatim*: vers une critique de la raison politique', pp. 134–62 in *Dits et écrits*, vol. 4, Paris: Gallimard, 1994 (no. 291).

were created during the summer of 1998. People spoke of the 'great family of the National Awakening Party' of Abdurrahman Wahid (*keluarga besar PKB*) or the 'great family of the National Mandate Party' of Amien Rais (*keluarga besar PAN*). Politics remained a family affair. This was particularly visible in the litany of honorific titles reserved for the candidates contesting for power: *Ibu* (mother) Megawati, *Om* (uncle) Amien Rais, *Gus* Dur (*Gus* more or less means the eldest, the ideal big brother: *Gus* Dur is the nickname conferred on Abdurrahman Wahid).

So what should be explored above all is the origin of the arguments that, during more than three decades of the New Order, excused a complex game of unlawful practices spread all over the edifice of state power. A brief excursion into the modern and contemporary history of corruption in Indonesia will then show that embezzlement and bribery, in a paradoxical way, ensured 'socialisation' of the state, that is, its acceptance by the social elites.[8]

Intrusion of the state into private space: the legacy of the colonial government

The hypothesis that a 'pastoral idea' of power prevails in the organisation of authority relations in Indonesia may cause surprise. According to Michel Foucault pastoral power is 'a form of power that cannot be exercised without knowing what is going on in people's heads, without exploring their very souls...coextensive with life...and linked to production of truth: the truth of the individual himself.'[9] This form of power is derived from the 'Christian technology of the flesh'. In other words, it is linked to the practice of penitential confession which became standardised and regular in Western Europe in the sixteenth and seventeenth centuries, in the wake of the Catholic Counter-Reformation.[10] It is known that the Church's idea of guardianship of conscience very quickly spread into the arguments justifying the monarchical state. Robert Muchembled has shown that in the absolute monarchy system, the image of the sovereign was reinforced with the image of a father of a family, and vice versa. Church and State together contributed to the definition and spread of a paternalist *imaginaire* of

---

[8] For an example showing that privatisation and criminalisation of the administration can strengthen state centralisation rather than undermining it, refer to K. Barkey, *Bandits and Bureaucrats. The Ottoman Route to State Centralization*, Ithaca, NY: Cornell University Press, 1994.

[9] Michel Foucault, *Dits et écrits* (note 7), vol. 4, p. 229 (no. 306). Refer also to M. Foucault, *La Volonté de savoir. Histoire de la sexualité*, vol. I, Paris: Gallimard, 1976, pp. 177–206.

[10] Jean Delumeau and Monique Cottret, *Le catholicisme entre Luther et Voltaire*, Paris: Presses Universitaires de France, 1971, pp. 365–88.

authority relations. Pastoral power, a fruit of the simultaneous invention of the *subject* and the *faithful* in the West, thus belonged to a particular historically and geographically located trend in the political sphere, which cannot be identified with a general pattern of development of doctrines of kingship.

But how is it, then, that modern Indonesia, a stranger to feudalism as to Christianity,[11] has experienced that form of power? The 'colonial encounter'[12] may well have been one of the points of contact between Christian traditions of pastoral government and the creation of ideological preferences among the Indonesian political elite. Not through the Church and the missions, but through the state, permeated by religious ideas and practices. The origin of the authoritarian 'family-state' model, however, corresponds closely with an endogenous process. It appears as the product of reappropriation by the Javanese administrative elite of a theme derived from the Dutch colonial government's efforts to legitimise its domination.

At the end of the nineteenth century the Netherlands East Indies[13] went through profound change, linked with the transition from a regime of monopoly state capitalism to a free enterprise system. Dismantling of the state monopolies of production and marketing of horticultural surpluses began in 1862. This marked the end of the Obligatory Cultivation System (*Cultuurstelsel*) that Governor-General van den Bosch had instituted in the early 1830s. The vast tea, coffee and sugar plantations of the interior of Java, and especially the mountainous estates of the Preanger region and the *Oosthoek* Regencies, were broken up amid competition among private entrepreneurs. From then on the character of the indigenous labour force

---

[11] The pre-colonial political order in the East Indies differed from the European feudal model in that power was not calculated in terms of territory conquered, but in terms of capacity for control over the labour force (rights over men, not over land). On this point see Clifford Geertz, *Negara. The Theatre State in Nineteenth Century Bali*, Princeton University Press, 1979, pp. 129 and 134–5. The penetration of Christianity was held in check by the colonial government's enduring distrust of missionary activity. Throughout the colonial period, the number of conversions in Java remained infinitesimal in relation to the total population. On this point see Claude Guillot, *L'affaire Sadrach. Un essai de christianisation à Java au XIXe siècle*, Paris: Archipel/Maison des Sciences de l'Homme, 1981, pp. 34–53.

[12] Ann Kumar, *Java and Modern Europe. Ambiguous Encounters*, Richmond: Curzon Press, 1997. For a detailed introduction to the postcolonial studies which have developed theories of the bilateral implications of the colonial encounter, see Ania Loomba, *Colonialism/Postcolonialism*, London: Routledge, 1998, pp. 104–123.

[13] The Crown of the Netherlands retook possession of the Netherlands Indies in 1816, on the collapse of the Napoleonic empire. In 1848 the States General (parliament) secured a right of supervision over 'colonial affairs'. But it was only during the 1850s, on the initiative of the Liberals, that the 'overseas possessions' were subjected to effective parliamentary control.

had to be adapted to this new style of production. There was no longer any question of packing tens of thousands of *koelies*, snatched from their native lands, into insanitary hutments. On the contrary, mobility of energy and talent needed to be encouraged so as to improve the skills of the workforce and thus keep up with technical innovation.[14] So the state had to take more systematic and effective responsibility for questions of collective public health, education and 'moral improvement' of the indigenous population.

The primary aim of the colonial government became—to quote Michel Foucault's *Les mots et les choses* again—'care of the people', that is, methodical management of their energies and their movements. It was in the course of this redeployment of administrative tasks that there emerged a concern by the state to 'know everything' about the state of the indigenous people's minds.[15] An alert observer of life in the Netherlands East Indies, the Frenchman Joseph Chailley-Bert, a publicist for the colonial movement in the Third French Republic, noted:

At this moment [in the 1860s] [the Dutch] resigned themselves to abandoning, with the State Cultivation, their function as agents for cultivation, but not their position as government officials; they looked around them to find how to make themselves useful, after their first use had disappeared. It was at that moment that there began to arise in people's minds the outlines of a system of protection for the Javanese, especially the lowliest of them, those who were commonly called the small people (*de Kleine Man*)...But this new departure had unexpected consequences for them. The Dutch became passionate about their work and let themselves be carried away beyond what they had foreseen. It was certainly a different matter from managing cultivation...For entering men's lives, finding out about their needs and desires, watching over their interests and securing respect for their rights, the difficulty increased with the number...[The Dutch] wanted to see everything, know everything and do everything. They substituted themselves for the native chief, seeing him as suspect, and for the native himself, seeing him as incapable, and they assumed the whole burden...*public affairs and even private affairs*. The result was what one might expect. This huge task required extra staff, swelled government departments, imposed expenditure, burdened the budget.[16]

---

[14] Robert E. Elson, 'Sugar Factory Workers and the Emergence of "Free Labour" in Nineteenth Century Java', *Modern Asian Studies*, vol. XX, no. 1, pp. 139–74; V. J. H. Hooben, 'Labour Conditions on Western Firms in Colonial Indonesia: Outline of an Approach', *Jahrbuch für Wirtschaftsgeschichte*, Berlin Academy, vol. 1, 1995, pp. 93–109.

[15] The staff of the colonial administration—which numbered scarcely more than a hundred officials in 1860—expanded as new bureaucratic departments were created (such as the Topographic Department and the Statistics Department in charge of censuses). H. W. Van Den Doel, *De Stille Macht. Het Europese binnenlands bestuur op Java en Madoera: 1808–1942*, Amsterdam: Bert Bakker, 1994.

[16] Joseph Chailley-Bert, *Java et ses habitants*, Paris: Armand Colin, 1900, pp. 209–212.

'Entering men's lives, finding out about their needs and desires, watching over their interests'—that was the colonial government's new plan, after the privatisation of the plantation economy had deprived it of the mission which had been its justification for police intervention in society. This structural change in the imperatives and methods of surveillance of the indigenous people called for a corresponding reformulation of the 'imperial project'.[17] The old language of conquest, indifferent to the productive aspects of indigenous life as to its 'cultural' aspects, was no longer sufficient to explain and legitimise the colonial order. A 'civilising' argument had to be added, which meant taking care to listen to what the indigenous people were saying—to urge them to speak, note what they said, and question them with a new sort of fervour and concern. As Chailley-Bert shrewdly observed, the colonial state 'assumed the whole burden...public affairs and even private affairs'. It insinuated itself ever further forward into the daily workings of indigenous life. Multiple regulations interfering with the private lives of the colonial subjects—with their ritual calendars, their methods of cultivation, even their sexuality—led to a gradual blurring of the dividing line between the public domain and private interests.

The reformulation of the imperial project was based on two connected lines of thinking: colonial anthropology and the missionary pastoral approach.[18] It is important to describe these briefly, because it was within them that the arguments still used by the Indonesian state power today, to maintain a system of domination conducive to predation of public resources, were developed. Colonial anthropology was one of the many 'investigative procedures'[19] through which the colonial state at the end of the

---

[17] The concept of an 'imperial project' was put forward by N. Dirks in 'Colonialism and Culture' in Nicholas Dirks (ed.), *Colonialism and Culture*, Ann Arbor: University of Michigan Press, 1992. It designates the whole range of ideas, schemes of thought, images and preconceived notions that interacted in the production and spread of debate around the colonial activity of a state power. An 'imperial project' is the fruit of a long process of moral and ideological negotiation at the end of which some actors impose a space of problem formulation informing decision-making in colonial policy matters.

[18] The reflection that follows owes much to reading of Jean-François Bayart, 'Fait missionnaire et politique du ventre: une lecture foucauldienne', *Le Fait Missionnaire* (Lausanne), Cahier no. 6, September 1998, pp. 9–19, and Didier Péclard, 'Ethos missionnaire et esprit du capitalisme. La Mission Philafricaine en Angola', *Le Fait Missionnaire*, Cahier no. 1, May 1995.

[19] Bernard Cohn, *Colonialism and its Forms of Knowledge. The British in India*, Princeton University Press, 1996, p. 13. See also Arjun Appadurai, 'Number in the Colonial Imagination' in *Modernity at Large: Cultural Dimensions of Globalization*, Minneapolis: University of Minnesota Press, 1997, p. 117; and Bernard Cohn, 'The Census, Social Structure and Objectification in South Asia', pp. 224–54 in *An Anthropologist among the Historians and Other Essays*, Delhi: Oxford University Press, 1987.

nineteenth century sought, with an obsession never equalled before, to penetrate to the innermost depths of the 'native mystery'.[20] For the Dutch Orientalists at the beginning of the twentieth century, fully integrated into colonial decision-making circles,[21] anthropology had to be turned into a therapeutic means of acculturation. If the 'mentality of the natives' needed to be better known, said the director of the Anthropology Section of the Royal Colonial Institute in Amsterdam, J. C. van Eerde, it was to minimise the perverse effects of their entry into the modern capitalist order. Better to know 'them', so as better to assess their potential for attaining the norms and rules of Western civilisation; better to decipher the movements of their consciousness and culture, to stifle their inclinations towards resistance as quickly as possible; better to translate their thinking and decode their myths, to be able to conform better to their own criteria of legitimacy. That, according to van Eerde, was the ultimate aim of Orientalist knowledge. Thus anthropology had to become a 'pedagogy of the natives' if it hoped to contribute to the success of the colonisation enterprise:

If pedagogy is a policy for children, we may call colonial policy pedagogy for the natives: its aim is to adapt to their civilisation what is useful and desirable for them in our civilisation…In the Tropics, we can envy the native his dark skin, but to put a fur coat over his shoulders to assuage this resentment would be to lead him to his downfall; similarly, he would not endure the superfluous burden of the European's intellectual baggage…So it is up to anthropology to indicate what the native's psychological state makes it possible for him to endure…Does the scientific and well-balanced way of thinking that Western Europe has acquired after so many centuries really fit the mystic sphere of thought of the East? Does the inflammatory slogan of freedom not lead to license in a society that has hardly emerged from despotism? Are egoism and presumptuousness not levers used for undermining native society, the family, the tribe, the village and the region with all the mutual aid systems attached to them?… To take account of the general lack of spontaneity in the human mind, a long period of incubation is needed to get a new civilisation accepted.[22]

It would however be highly unjust to believe that the sole aim of all the anthropological writing of the years from 1900 to 1930 was to serve the

---

[20] Thommy Svensson, *State Bureaucracy and Capitalism in Rural West Java, Local Gentry versus Peasant Entrepreneurs in Priangan in the XIXth and XXth Centuries*, Copenhagen: Nordic Institute of Asian Studies, 1986 (Report Series no. 1).

[21] On this point, see Cornelius Fasseur, 'Leiden and Empire: University and Colonial Office 1825–1925' in W. Otterspeer (ed.), *Leiden Oriental Connections 1850–1940*, Leiden: E. J. Brill, 1989.

[22] J. C. van Eerde, *L'Ethnologie coloniale. L'indigène et l'Européen*, Paris: Editions du Monde Nouveau, 1927, pp. 24, 36, 45. J. C. van Eerde was one of the most influential anthropologists of the Netherlands.

brutal advances of the colonial power. Quite the contrary: the corporatist concern to preserve one's subject of study—'primitive cultures'—often led anthropology to denounce the modernising aims of the imperial state. Thus it opposed the too rapid opening up of a territory, or became indignant about the outlawing of customary practices. But what needs to be remembered about the premises of anthropological research is its obsession with uncovering the 'mystery of the natives', its persistent effort to make the intimate knowledge of the colonised people a shadowy zone of government. Even if it often condemned the intrusion of the colonial state into ever extended domains of the indigenous people's private lives, anthropological study instilled in the heart of the imperial project a desire to know, a frenzy for uncovering which profoundly influenced the way that state codified and tried to exercise its power. In that sense this type of knowledge served as a wellspring of the state's 'documentation programme', and hence as backing for a pastoral form of government.[23] By making the indigenous person an object of questioning, something unstated and calling for comment, colonial anthropology also made him an area for state intervention. By that very process it encouraged the tendency of the state power, first colonial and then independent, to establish thousands of disciplinary provisions aiming to bring the individual to confession. Thus colonial anthropology formed part of the origin of 'pastoral power'—that is, the mode of government which forces the individual not only to obey but also to admit, before institutions playing a perpetual game of truth, his love and obedience.[24]

So it is no accident that, in the history of the colonial system, the missionary pastor and the amateur anthropologist, the preacher and the scholar, were so often one and the same person.[25] Behind the will for knowledge immanent in the aim of controlling souls there was, invariably, a desire for confessions. Confessing was a sign of the congruence of the imperial aims and the missionary enterprise. Just as true conversion had value only through expiatory confession of the pagan faults that preceded it, genuine inclusion in the order of colonial subjection required repudiation of para-

---

[23] Bernard Cohn, *Colonialism and its Forms of Knowledge* (note 19), pp. 1–15.

[24] Extracting a confession is the distinctive sign of 'pastoral power' as defined by Michel Foucault: 'How is it that, in Western Christian culture, government of men asks of those who are governed, in addition to acts of obedience and submission, "acts of truth" which have a particular trait: that the subject is not only required to tell the truth, but to tell the truth about himself, his faults, his desires, the state of his soul…? How was this type of government of men formed in which one is not called on simply to obey, but to display, by proclaiming it, what one is…?': 'Du gouvernement des vivants', *Annuaire du Collège de France*, 1980, in *Dits et écrits* (note 7), vol. 4, p. 125.

[25] Jean and John Comaroff, *Of Revelation and Revolution: Christianity, Colonialism and Consciousness in South Africa*, vol. 1, University of Chicago Press, 1991.

sitical loyalties. The colonial state, even though it sometimes strengthened the guardianship role of clans and lineages so as to make better use of them, excluded in principle any object of loyalty apart from itself.

In the modern colonial history of Indonesia, this congruence of language and practice between colonialism and the missions reached its paroxysm when, after fiercely disputed general elections, a Christian government coalition acceded to power in the Netherlands. This coalition adopted the aim of giving the Dutch monarchy a colonial policy fitting the religious exaltation of the middle classes, which were then engaged in a cycle of collective introspection following a large-scale Puritan revival. The leader of the Anti-Revolutionary Party,[26] Abraham Kuyper, who saw in the state apparatus 'the arm of God', became the head of this government. Queen Wilhelmina then mentioned, in her Speech from the Throne in September 1901, the '*ethical duty* that the Netherlands, as a Christian nation, has to improve the living conditions of native Christians, to provide missionary activities with the funds that they needed, and to inform the [colonial] administration as a whole that Holland has a moral obligation to fulfil towards the people [of the Netherlands East Indies].'[27]

The Ethical Colonial Policy implemented from 1901 onwards, under the impulse of Queen Wilhelmina and Kuyper, aimed at the 'development' (*opvoeding*) of the Javanese. The 'improvement of native wellbeing', the watchword of the 'Ethicis' (supporters of the Ethical Policy), had a social aspect (fighting against serious poverty) and a moral one (conversion of the indigenous people to modernity, Christian and capitalist). The Ethical Colonial Policy, fruit of the conjunction of Christian doctrine and the doctrine of scientism, rooted itself in the idea that there was an 'exact science' of colonial government, for which new statistical knowledge was the instrument, and the transformation of the 'Native' into the Individual was the ultimate aim. It is true that the Ethical Policy never attained the ambitious objectives it had set itself, certainly not in terms of raising the standard of living of the popular masses. But it altered from top to bottom the perception of government action.

The theory of state action among the scribes of the Javanese Mataram Empire in the eighteenth century had been that government must keep the 'world's business' going while not interfering with invisible checks and balances. The sovereign, by propitiatory inaction proclaimed as ascetic prowess, ensured harmony between the divine macrocosm (*buwana agung*) and the social microcosm (*buwana alit*). Javanese royalty found signifi-

---

[26] Christophe De Voogd, *Histoire des Pays-Bas*, Paris: Hatier, 1992, pp. 181–6.

[27] Robert van Niel, *The Emergence of the Modern Indonesian Elite*, The Hague: Van Hoeve, 1970, p. 32, and Deliar Noer, *The Modernist Muslim Movement in Indonesia, 1900–1942*, Singapore: Oxford University Press, 1973, p. 165.

cance through rituals of silence and privation. Authority and austerity blended, since abstinence (*tapa*) and meditation (*samadi*) were evidence of the legitimacy of claims to the right to rule. The legitimate ruler acted in the invisible world (*dunia kang samar*) to which he had access on the strength of his self-denial exercises. Conversely, the Ethicis of Batavia had an ultra-voluntarist concept of political action, linked to an evolutionist view of indigenous societies. The idea that society could be *transformed* by decrees and regulations then progressed among the Javanese administrative elite.

The emphasis on seeking the love and gratitude of the Javanese,[28] which was an important theme of Dutch colonialist literature at the beginning of the twentieth century, reveals a real upheaval in the imperial domination strategy. It was no longer a matter of obtaining obedience by repression, but of winning confidence by persuasion. In other words, the colonial state embarked, at the beginning of the twentieth century, on a search for legitimacy. In that way it strove to consolidate its ideological base at a time when rivalry of imperial appetites and anticolonialism were getting stronger on the international scene. That was why use of the vocabulary of kinship to describe relations between colonised and colonisers became over-emphasised.

The historian Akira Nagazumi observes: 'The use of this metaphor of parent and child to describe the relationship between the government and native people is a recurring theme throughout the Ethical Period.'[29] The analogous images of teacher, guardian (*voogd*) and guide (*gids*) gained acceptance on a massive scale in textbooks of anthropology, digests of colonial law and the colonialist periodicals of the time. Since the 1860s members of the European branch of the imperial administration had in fact been urged by the Governor General[30] to call their Javanese counterparts 'younger brothers'.

This model of the 'just' colonial relationship was also found at the lower levels of administrative contact. Heather Sutherland has shown for example that 'The *priyayi*'s [the Javanese service nobility, integrated into the imperial administrative system] relationship with the people was authoritarian and paternalistic; they were expected to take care of the peasants as if they were their children while ruling them with a rod of iron.'[31]

---

[28] The nationalist uprising was thus to be seen as evidence of the indigenous people's 'ingratitude'.

[29] Akira Nagazumi, *The Dawn of Indonesian Nationalism: The Early Years of the Budi Utomo: 1908–1918*, Tokyo: Institute of Developing Economies, 1972, p. 43.

[30] Cornelius Fasseur, *The Politics of Colonial Exploitation: Java, the Dutch and the Cultivation System*, Ithaca, NY: Cornell University Press, 1992 (Cornell Studies on Southeast Asia).

[31] Heather Sutherland, *The Making of a Bureaucratic Elite: The Colonial Transformation of the Javanese Priyayi*, Singapore: Heinemann, 1979, p. 30.

The Orientalists contributed in this way to the freezing, through a legally regulated form of etiquette, of a code of behaviour that had hitherto been extremely fluid in expression. In the pre-colonial period, precedence protocols were constantly modified by court intrigues, while the Orientalists gave them an unchangeable character. Directives on the 'code of honour' (*hormat*), claiming to 'restore a tradition', reinvented it according to the functional demands of the colonial situation.[32] The most famous of those directives, made public in 1913, obliged senior officials of the Pangreh Praja—the indigenous branch of the colonial administration—to act towards *any* European in the same way as towards a member of one of the two great dynasties of Solo and Jogja (with bowing on one's knees, prostration, keeping the head bowed during conversation).[33] Worshipping a European sub-chief like a sacred monarch was a terrible humiliation for the Javanese aristocracy. The practice of 'friendly pressure' (*perintah alus*) exerted by district chiefs on village chiefs reluctant to implement government decisions was also intensified in the years from 1900 to 1920. This new method of persuasion gradually replaced the insults and physical violence that had characterised relations between village chiefs and European officials in 1830–60.

In September 1902 the reform-minded A. Idenburg, who declared that 'the aim of colonial rule was not to expand possessions but to encourage the advancement of indigenous people',[34] was appointed Minister of the Colonies. A wind of reform then blew through the colonial administrative edifice. An official of the Binnenlandsch Bestuur—the European branch of the colonial administration—described in laudatory terms, in his memoirs, the great transformation in the administrative staff of the Netherlands East Indies at the beginning of the twentieth century:

Never, perhaps, has any Government set itself so wholeheartedly and with such zeal and comprehensive thoroughness to building up the welfare of its subjects as the Government of Netherlands India in the beginning of the present century. Most of the officials at that time had fallen under the spell of Multatuli[35] during their studies at Leiden, and came to India as enthusiastic idealists, filled with ardour to take part in the great civilizing mission of the Netherlands. On their arrival they found a welfare programme as the official policy of Government; zeal for the well-being of the people was a condition of promotion, as *any who were reluctant*

---

[32] Robert van Niel, *The Emergence…* (note 27), pp. 31–2.

[33] Ibid., p. 92.

[34] Quoted in Eduard J. M. Schmutzer, *Dutch Colonial Policy and the Search for Identity in Indonesia, 1920–1931*, Leiden: E. J. Brill, 1977, p. 16.

[35] Pseudonym of Eduard Douwes Dekker, a former colonial official, author of a famous work (*Max Havelaar*) violently criticising the system of exploitation of the small peasants in the Netherlands East Indies.

to interfere with native life were likely to be regarded with disfavour as 'weak and recalcitrant administrators'.[36]

When the Ethicis finally came to power in Batavia,[37] they reoriented the imperial administrative apparatus towards collecting information on indigenous life. In the significant expression of De Kat Angelino, adviser on Native Affairs to the Governor General in the 1920s, 'The government did its utmost to get first hand information relating to the intimate nature of Indonesian society.'[38] The idea that there was an 'intimate nature' of the subjected society, an indigenous shadowy silence that needed to be brought to light, was the guiding principle of the redeployment of the state. Mapping of the territories, balancing of resources and population, recension of specific religious features, collection of Javanese manuscripts, were all responses to the supposed enigma of the indigenous people, which Orientalist studies had constructed while constructing themselves.[39]

Spread of the language of kinship

At the end of the nineteenth and the beginning of the twentieth centuries, then, the Netherlands East Indies, direct ancestors of modern Indonesia, were structured by a dense network of power relations expressed through the language of kinship. The colonial government was the 'father' of the colonised people, indigenous officials were the 'younger brothers' of their European colleagues, peasants were the 'devoted sons' of the service aristocracy responsible for keeping them docile. The idea behind this language offensive could be explained in a corresponding way: the problems of the colonial situation were, after all, just simple 'family affairs'. The kinship

---

[36] Resident G. L. Gonggrip quoted in J. S. Furnivall, *Netherlands India*, Cambridge at the University Press, 1939, pp. 382–3 (my italics).

[37] Batavia (modern Jakarta) was the administrative and political capital of the Dutch East Indies.

[38] De Kat Angelino, *Le problème colonial* (trans. E. P. van den Berghe), The Hague: Martinus Nijhoff, 1932, 2 vols., Vol. II, p. 86. This idea of an alternative indigenous world, incomprehensible and inhabited by occult forces, appears clearly in two of the most popular European novels of the time: Paul A. Daum's (1850–98) novel *Goena-Goena*, published in 1889 and dealing with Javanese witchcraft, and *De Stille Kracht*, published in 1900 by Louis Couperus (1863–1923). Those two works outlined the possibility of revenge by indigenous society against the European colonisers through harmful 'charms'. It was at that time that the figure of the Javanese 'sorcerer', the village healer (*dukun*), took on a negative connotation by analogy with the dominant discourse of European demonology.

[39] John Pemberton, *On the Subject of 'Java'*, Ithaca, NY: Cornell University Press, 1994, p. 104, for a summary of the process of literary construction of 'Java' in the language of Dutch Javanology.

vocabulary rebuilt from scratch an illusion of proximity between rulers and ruled, colonised and colonisers. It symbolically bridged the gap of contradiction of interests between colonial power and colonial subjects. It aroused among the colonial elites the reassuring feeling of being able to understand, and hence domesticate, the indigenous world at any time. However, this language of kinship should not be seen as exclusively the arm of the colonial government. In fact the leaders of the nationalist movement readily adopted it, because it enabled them to marry revolutionary zeal with social hierarchy. Since a family is ordered around the uncontested power of a father whose word is law, the national family must obey the orders of an unchallenged chief. Nationalist 'unanimism', that frenzied desire for communion between the People and its Guide, thus flowed into the *imaginaire* of the political elite to nip any social revolution in the bud. A radical overturning of the structures of authority would inevitably have endangered the privileged status of the elites of the nationalist movement, who sprang from the merchant bourgeoisie or the service nobility of Java.

Ki Hadjar Dewantara, a prince of Yogyakarta who became in the early 1910s a revered figure of resistance to the colonial oppressor, established in the early 1920s a network of alternative schools, Gardens of Knowledge (*Taman Siswa*). The aim of these schools was to turn Javanese youth away from the seductions of the West, described as decadent. In those schools, true nurseries of the nationalist movement,[40] absolute obedience was due to the teachers, whom the pupils called *Bapak*. Ki Hadjar in turn reigned as unchallenged master over his teachers, who called him 'Father'. The kinship analogy also made it possible to give meaning to the nationalist struggle. The struggle against the coloniser was always presented as the accomplishment of 'family fullness':

Borne up by the principle of the 'fullness and holiness of life', we can do no other than give primacy to the complete and holy Family, with its Father and Mother, who in every good family, stand side by side, have the same rights but different tasks, have a unity of interests, a unity of strengths, and a unity of soul.[41]

The image of the national family thus soothed the consciences of members of the *priyayi* caste, who refused to consider the end of colonialism as involving a passage to egalitarianism.[42] Ki Hadjar Dewantara's work was

---

[40] Kenji Tsuchiya, *Democracy and Leadership. The Rise of the Taman Siswa Movement in Indonesia*, Honolulu: University of Hawaii Press, 1990.

[41] Ki Hadjar Dewantara, *Karja Ki Hadjar Dewantara: Bagian IIA: Kebudajaan*, 1931 (?), Yogyakarta, 1967, quoted in David Reeve, *Golkar of Indonesia: An Alternative to the Party System*, Singapore: Oxford University Press, 1985, p. 10.

[42] Another reference text by Ki Hadjar Dewantara, which explains his idea of a structurally non-egalitarian political community, is 'Democratie dan Leiderschap', reproduced in

to have profound influence on Sukarno, who borrowed from him the concept of 'guided democracy' and declared him 'his friend and master in everything'.[43] This idea of the state as a living being, consisting of interdependent but not equally dispensable organs, is also found in the writings of *Raden* Soepomo, an influential figure in the Investigating Committee for the Preparation of Independence which met from 1943 onwards with the approval of the Japanese occupation authorities. Soepomo influenced the rejection of a proposal to mention individual rights in the text of the 1945 Constitution. An occasional admirer of Mussolini and follower of the theories of Social Darwinism, he conceived what he called the 'integral state' a whole, not differentiated from the body of society:

If we want to establish an Indonesian state in accordance with the characteristic features of Indonesian society, it must be based on an integralist state philosophy, on the idea of a state which is united with all its people, which transcends all groups in every field... The state is nothing but the entire society...According to the integralist view of the state as a nation in its ordered aspect, as a united people in its structured aspect, there is basically no dualism of state and the individual, no conflict between the state organization on the one hand and the legal order of individuals on the other... There is no need to guarantee the fundamental rights and liberties of the individual against the state, because the individual is an organic part of the state, with his own position and an obligation to help realize the state's greatness...[44]

Raden Soepomo's language shows how the kinship analogy, when allied with nationalist 'unanimism', slips towards a totalitarian conception of the state. This conception exalts harmony and the national community while reifying differences of status between rulers and ruled. The former—warriors (*ksatria*) and ascetics (*pandita*)—must govern; the latter—the common people (*wong cilik*)—must obey. If everyone fulfils the role assigned to him by the cosmic order, the political community will know prosperity. But if anyone departs from his essential duty (*darma*), chaos will befall the kingdom. This fatalistic vision of the social order was already present in the pre-colonial kingdoms, strongly marked by Hindu

H. A. Notosoetarjo (ed.), *Proses kembali kepada Djiwa Proklamasi 1945*, Jakarta: Lembaga Penggali dan Penghimpun Sejarah Revolusi Indonesia, 1959. An introduction to Ki Hadjar's work is to be found in Savitri Scherer, 'Harmony and Dissonance. Early Nationalist Thought in Java', MA thesis, Cornell University, Ithaca, NY, 1975.

[43] Ahmed Sukarno, *Sukarno: An Autobiography as Told to Cindy Adams*, Indianapolis, Kansas City and New York: Bobbs-Merrill Co., 1965. Sukarno liked to use the metaphor of the 'great family of the nation'.

[44] *Raden* Soepomo, speech delivered on 31 May 1945 before the Investigating Committee for the Preparation of Independence, reproduced in English in Herbert Feith and Lance Castle (eds), *Indonesian Political Thinking: 1945–1965*, Ithaca, NY: Cornell University Press, 1970, pp. 188–92.

influence. It was revived and amended in a 'fascist' sense by the theorists of the Javanese nationalist movement, who claimed Hindu descent. The later, nationalist history of the language of kinship, initially used by the colonial state to cover up the original injustice of its domination, suggests that its use was continuous, through the interruption caused by the Japanese occupation and the independence struggle.

Since colonial *gouvernementalité* operated through successive hegemonic steps forward and not only by bloodstained gestures of conquest, and wrapped the traumatic experience of subjection[45] in terms of family feeling, as well as institutionalising a 'plunder economy'[46] in which holding of state responsibilities was equivalent to a passport to illicit enrichment, it bequeathed to independent Indonesia—through intellectuals accustomed to those tricks of legitimisation—a principle for the political sphere clean contrary to the classical Western model of separation between the public space and private ambitions. The common culturalist approach[47] can easily attribute the extent of criminal behaviour by the Indonesian administrative elites to the enigmatic survival of a supposed 'Javanese patrimonialism'. But there it falls into the error of considering the language of kinship as a univocal *cultural effect*. In fact a careful examination of the colonial foundations of contemporary power relations shows that the art of predation, even if it wraps itself in the finery of tradition that has become folklore, appears as a *structural effect*. Predation amounts to a functioning principle of a system of domination centred on countless relations of subjection. In other words, there is no 'cultural predisposition' of Indonesians to robbery.[48]

---

[45] For an interpretation of modern colonialism as a system of domination producing 'neurotic structures' of personality, see the works of Frantz Fanon and especially *Black Skin, White Masks*, London: Pluto Press, 1986 (original publication in French 1952). Fanon's works are of direct interest to an archaeology of paternalist power. In *Black Skin, White Masks* he wrote, 'Militarization and the centralization of authority in a country automatically entail a resurgance of the authority of the father' (pp. 141–2).

[46] This expression, used by Béatrice Hibou for sub-Saharan Africa, is borrowed from W. G. Hoskins, *The Age of Plunder: The England of Henry VIII*, Harlow: Longman, 1988.

[47] A good example of this common approach is found in P. M. Laksono, *Tradition in Javanese Social Structure. Kingdom and Countryside. Changes in the Javanese Conceptual Model*, Yogyakarta: Gadjah Mada University Press, 1990.

[48] On the other hand this does not of course exclude the existence of a 'Javanese science' of banditry; nor does it exclude highway bandits and village gangsters (the famous *jago*, associated with martial arts brotherhoods and reputed to have powers making them invulnerable) very often playing a front-rank political role—particularly during the uncertain years of the consolidation of republican power. On these two points see Sartono Kartodjirdjo, 'Banditry and Political Change in Java', pp. 3–30 in S. Kartodjirdjo (ed.), *Modern Indonesia. Tradition and Transformation*, Yogyakarta: Gadjah Mada University Press, 1991; George Quinn, 'The Javanese Science of Burglary', *Review of Indonesian*

The language of justification of corruption and nepotism, in addition, can be used in many contradictory ways. The overthrow of despots, as well as applause of them, can be coded in the language of kinship. An illegitimate father can be repudiated, just as an 'uncle' removed from power can be honoured. Some supporters of Amien Rais, leader of the *Partai Amanat Nasional* and one of the two or three credible candidates for the presidency of Indonesia in 1999, called him *Om* Rais ('uncle Rais', a term often used by a disciple for a spiritual guide).[49]

The inheritance of modern colonial *gouvernementalité*, in Indonesia, is thus found at two levels. First, this mode of *gouvernementalité* favoured abolition of the lines of demarcation between the public and private spaces in the name of a pastoral idea of power. Secondly, it made systematic the description of power relations in terms of kinship. Two points need to be made clear here. First, it is certainly correct to say, as the culturalist school does, that these phenomena existed at the time of the great precolonial empires. The term *priyayi*, referring to the Javanese service nobility (entrusted with the administrative tasks in conquered territory) is derived, according to the historian Soemarsaid Moertono, from the expression *para yayi* (literally 'the junior brothers of the prince'); so, in the seventeenth century, court circles were using kinship metaphors to signify allegiance or seal an alliance. But to argue from this that the excesses of patrimonialism of the Indonesian state have their roots in the theories of pre-colonial Javanese kingship would be to underestimate dangerously the particular legacy of the colonial period. The colonial state, on the advice of the Orientalists, indeed emphasised certain aristocratic codes, and shamelessly introduced new ones, to satisfy the requirements of its daily operations. The period of Dutch imperial domination, in the history of modern Indonesia, is therefore like a moment of rewriting, hence reinvention of '*the* Javanese culture'.

And then, speaking of 'heritage' does not mean adopting determinism. The procedures of control and systems of justification perfected by the colonial state did not compel Indonesian political actors to adopt this or that sort of language or behaviour. But while they did not dispose Indonesians' conduct, they were at their disposal—that is, those actors could use those procedures and systems to claim the precious backing of Tradition. So those technologies and narratives of domination, which could be put to almost any number of strategic uses, were only one material among many others in the process of building forms of legitimacy.

---

and Malaysian Affairs, vol. IX, no. 1, March 1975, pp. 33–54; and Suhartono, *Bandit-Bandit Pedesaan di Jawa. Studi Historis 1850–1942*, Yogyakarta: Universitas Gadjah Mada/Aditya Media, 1995.

[49] See the readers' letters in the journal *Ummat*, the press organ of the Muhammadiyah.

The bapak *figure: a prop and a weak point in the*
Suharto regime

Indeed, the reason why the analogy of the 'national family' was emphasised as strongly as it was by the ideologists of the New Order was that
it enabled the people in power to reject the opposing theories of the political responsibility of rulers. The moral responsibility of the 'father of a
family' in fact ruled out any need to resort to any sanction, electoral or
parliamentary, against ministers and the President. Why on earth should a
'father' (a president, a minister) conform to the opinion of his 'children'
(the people)? Does he not know better than they what is good for them? Is
it not his duty to make up for their immaturity by assuming on his own the
heroic responsibility for watching over their interests? Lastly, is he not
obliged to chastise them severely to rear them better, if by chance they
commit the folly of contradicting or repudiating him?[50]

This paternalist side of the authoritarian coin was embodied, in Indonesia, in an iconography devoted to the uncritical apologia of the Father of
National Development and his benevolent tenderness towards his child-
people. Smiling, bending down to the emotional objects of his affection,
President Suharto was in the 1980s often represented as an affable and
understanding patriarch. When he inaugurated model farms, financed by
his charitable foundations, before a barrage of cameras, or paid live hom-
age on television to the victims of an epidemic or a disaster, *Pak Presiden*
always showed the compassionate smile of a sympathetic grandfather. This
propaganda strategy was based on a principle with serious consequences:
ties of blood, real or symbolic, take precedence over the laws of the country. In other words, a father must do everything to protect his children,
even if it means breaking the penal code.

One example will suffice to make this point clear. In July and August
1998 an unprecedented scandal provoked a major stir in the ranks of the
Indonesian army. Several human rights defence NGOs openly accused
General Prabowo Subianto, son-in-law of ex-President Suharto and then
director of the Bandung Military Academy, of having been responsible, as
commander-in-chief of the Special Operations Commandos (KOPA-
SSUS[51]), for the kidnapping, illegal detention and torture of 17 trade union

---

[50] On the contradiction between this paternalist theory of the power of the state and classi-
cal doctrines of political responsibility, see Y. B. Mangunwijaya, 'The Indonesia Raya
Dream and its Impact on the Concept of Democracy', pp. 79–88 in David Bourchier and
John Legge (eds), *Democracy in Indonesia 1950s and 1990s*, Clayton: CSEAS, Monash
University, 1994, and Adnan Buyung Nasution, *The Aspiration for Constitutional Gov-
ernment in Indonesia. A Socio-Legal Study of the Indonesian Konstituante 1956–1959*,
Jakarta: Pustaka Sinar Harapan, 1992, pp. 90–103 and 410–13.

[51] The Kopassus (short for Kommando Pasukan Khusus) are an elite corps of the army
(TNI-AD), 7,000 strong, used in 'special operations' for maintenance of order and

activists and student militants. Some of those militants who escaped from their hellish Odyssey testified to the tortures which they had endured in their detention, such as Pius Lustrilanang.[52] Summoned by a military tribunal to explain the reasons that had impelled him to 'tolerate' and 'cover up' such behaviour—obviously contrary to the Military Code[53]—General Prabowo Subianto replied with conviction,[54] 'Because I had an obligation to take care of my men (*melindungi anak-anak buahku*)'.[55] Thus one of the highest officers of the army admitted having gone knowingly against the code of honour which he had initially sworn to respect, for the sole purpose of sheltering his 'protégés' against any disciplinary bother, and all in the name of a higher moral rule: family spirit.[56] The metaphor of kinship thus served as an alibi for systematic bypassing of the law. Prabowo Subianto was behaving like a perfect *bapak*.

The *bapak*, the emblematic figure of the Suharto years, meant in popular parlance the class of the affluent in the ranks of state power who had, through their contacts and their far-gone opportunism, asserted themselves over ministerial offices and state enterprises. The *bapak*, recognisable by his expensive attire—luxury batik shirt, a gleaming gold watch, rings studded with precious stones—and his brand new car, his haughty air and the servile retinue around him, frequented the buildings of Jakarta and the resorts of Bali. Political cartoonists did not fail to make fun of his arrogance and his conspicuous consumption.[57] But beyond the ethnographic satire, that social type calls for some comments.

The *bapak* was both the most solid prop of the system of domination established by the New Order and its weak point. It certainly seems possible to apply to the Indonesia of the New Order the formula set out by the historian Robert Muchembled at the conclusion of his study of the 'new mechanisms of power' that helped to establish and maintain absolute monarchy in France from the fifteenth century to the eighteenth: 'From the King to the fathers of families was spread, in successive cascades, that

---

political security. Heirs of the first special commando of the Siliwangi Division, created in 1952 to intervene in western Java, the KOPASSUS are organised in five groups. See Robert Lowry, *The Armed Forces of Indonesia*, Sydney: Allen & Unwin 1996, pp. 86–9.

[52] On this affair see *Jakarta Post*, 11 August 1998, 'DKP Points Finger at Prabowo'; *Dë Tak*, 18–24 August 1998, 'Bukan Pangab dan Pangti, lalu siapa?' pp. 4–5; and *The Bali Post*, 11 August 1998, 'Prabowo Ditanya, Mengapa Menculik', pp. 1–2.

[53] Every career military person, in Indonesia, has to swear to respect the Soldier's Code of Honour (*Sapta Darma*).

[54] 'Itu Analisis Prabowo', *Kompas*, 11 August 1998; *Kompas*, 25 August 1998.

[55] In the expression *anak buah, anak* means 'child'.

[56] An expression which could be replaced in this case by 'esprit de corps'.

[57] See for example the last album by Benny Rachmadi and Muhammad Misrad, *Krisis... oh...Krisis*, Jakarta: Kepustaan Populer Gramedia, August 1998.

model of a powerful and terrible father.'[58] In the case that concerns us, this could be paraphrased as: 'From the *Pak Presiden* to the *Bapak Menteri* and down to the *Bapak Asisten* was spread, in successive cascades, the model of a father both sympathetic and fearsome.' In retrospect Indonesia under General Suharto looks like a gigantic pyramid of subordination. Or rather, like a vast network of local power relations, circumscribing mutually overlapping spaces of obedience. To obey one's *Bapak Direktor*, who obeyed his *Bapak Menteri*, and so on, was to back up the endogamous logic of state power and prepare the way for one's rise in the hierarchy. In the Suharto system, centred around the preservation of clique and caste interests,[59] the value of the law of the family was both practical in the literal sense—in the form of opportunities for enrichment linked to closeness of ties of blood with the President and those near to him—and as a general principle justifying nepotism, that is, a legal doctrine of transmission and patriarchal delegation of power. Mochtar Lubis, who became aware early on of the freedom-destroying implications of the family-state theory,[60] refused from the 1970s to go along with the '*bapak*isation' of social relations and called, in contrast, for a return to the austere egalitarianism of the revolutionary epic:

I propose that we stop using the word *bapak* for all officials and administrators and that we address each other as *saudara*. Isn't it more pleasant and accurate to say *saudara* Minister, *saudara* President, *saudara* General, *saudara* Director General, *saudara* University President?[61]

The phrase 'Brother President', in the ideological context of the establishment of General Suharto's power system, amounted to a criminal affront to authoritarianism.[62] Mochtar Lubis' irreverent words also expressed

---

[58] Robert Muchembled, *Culture populaire et culture des élites dans la France moderne (XVe–XVIIe siècle)*, Paris: Flammarion, 1978, p. 285. See also, by the same author, *Le temps des supplices. De l'obéissance sous les rois absolus, XVe–XVIIIe siècle*, Paris: Armand Colin, 1992, pp. 220–33.

[59] It is not possible here to count all the scandals affecting the 'Suharto family' during the 1990s. It can simply be recalled that the President's children and people close to him— like the industrialist Bob Hasan and his opposite number Liem Sioe Liong—had vast investment holdings whose financial profitability was directly linked to illicit favours granted by a docile administration.

[60] For a glimpse at the system of delegation of authority, refer to Hans Antlöv (ed.), *Exemplary Centre, Administrative Periphery. Rural Leadership and the New Order in Java*, Richmond, England: Curzon Press, 1994.

[61] Mochtar Lubis, *The Indonesian Dilemma*, tr. F. Lamoureux, Singapore: Graham Brash, 1991 (original edition 1977), p. 68.

[62] David Jenkins, *Suharto and his Generals: Indonesian Military Politics 1975–1983*, Ithaca, NY: Cornell University Press, 1984 (Cornell Modern Indonesia Project. Monograph Series no. 64), and Hamish McDonald, *Suharto's Indonesia*, Blackburn: Fontana Books,

realisation of the totally artificial character of the 'patriarchal tradition' invoked by General Suharto. Not only did the intrinsic ethnic diversity of the Indonesian archipelago make it impossible to turn the principle of patriarchate and patrilineal descent into a national cultural heritage (the Minangkabau society in western Sumatra is of a matrilineal type), but in addition the years of the Revolution (1945–9) confirmed the patriotic legitimacy of the use of the term *saudara*, which remains linked in the popular *imaginaire* with the figure of Sukarno, hero of the nationalist movement and first President of the Republic.[63]

The ordinary forms of privatisation of the state, and their condemnation in the Reformasi

This summary history of the language of kinship shows, basically, that all the efforts of the Suharto regime were concentrated on one precise objective: laying down that too strict separation between the public domain and private interests was harmful to preservation of national cohesion and an obstacle to the pursuit of prosperity. All evils were attributed accordingly to the Western parliamentary system, but especially that of leading to division in the national community. The principle of political responsibility of rulers of the state was reduced to a suitable size by acceptance of the President by acclamation. For according to the theorists and propagandists of the New Order, a precondition for successful integration into international capitalism—that is, smooth entry into the era of two-digit growth—was the rejection of ideological divisions that could erode 'national discipline'. In other words, only a populist type of power, in which the supreme leader communicates with his people bypassing the verdict of polling booths and the arithmetic of coalitions, was conducive to productive success. The President was the sole judge of the common good, since he was immanent in the will of the masses. He *was* the Nation, literally. Hence the Nation was his natural domain, which he used at will just as a prudent father manages his children's savings. As this invitation to predation was approved and blessed at the top level of the regime, it could not fail to arouse emulation among the lower strata of officials of the state.

This official language granted absolution to corruption, understood as diversion to private purposes of revenue and material advantages linked to the exercise of public responsibility. Besides, corruption was widely

---

1980. Mochtar Lubis' pro-American stance led, at the same time, to his ostracism from the intellectual scene.

[63] Benedict Anderson, *Java in a Time of Revolution*, Ithaca, NY: Cornell University Press, 1972.

tolerated in practice, and took sometimes surprising forms. With the revived freedom of expression in the Indonesian media following President Suharto's resignation, it is possible to get an idea of the variety of criminal practices in the civil service.[64] In July 1998 eight rectors of state secondary schools in Jakarta were removed from their posts following an internal investigation showing that they had all diverted into their own pockets a considerable portion of the school fees demanded from parents of future pupils.[65] In August *Bupati*[66] Maros was accused of embezzling 1.4 billion rupiahs from the Gowa Makasar Tourism and Development Corporation (GMTDC) of which he was in charge.[67] The *Bupati*s of Pekalongan (eastern Java) and Kalimantan Selatan (southern Kalimantan) were at the same period suspected of the same offence—the sum involved in the latter case, relating to the Adaro Industri company, reaching 70 billion rupiahs.[68] Many village chiefs (*lurah*), especially in eastern Java, were driven away from their posts by crowds of villagers accusing them of wrongfully appropriating communal land or else granting contracts for public works to private firms at uncompetitive prices, in return for payment. In this way a delegation of 500 villagers went to the Jatiawung district chief's (*camat*) office to demand that the *lurah* of Pasir Jaya, Syamsudin, be put on trial. The delegation accused him notably of 'selling' 2.8 kilometres of communal road to the PT Gajah Tunggal tyre manufacturer for 80 million rupiahs in 1994.[69] Handing over exclusive use of a part of the public highway to a private user, in return for money, was a significant example of 'privatisation of the state' in the crudest material sense.

It should also be recalled that law enforcement agencies in Indonesia practice privatisation of public revenue on a grand scale, since there is never any receipt for payment of a 'fine'. As another illustration of private encroachment on the public domain, some national historical monuments, such as the temples and steles around Malang in eastern Java, are entrusted

---

[64] For analyses highlighting the fact that power at the local level depended, from the late 1970s, on privileged relations with holders of state power—that is, intimate access to a source of power external to the confined village sphere—see Hans Antlöv and Sven Cederroth (eds), *Leadership on Java: Gentle Hints, Authoritarian Rule*, Richmond, England: Curzon Press, 1994; and Kenneth Young, 'Middle Bureaucrats, Middle Peasants, Middle Class? The Extra-Urban Dimension', pp. 147–66 in Kenneth Young and Richard Tanter (eds), *The Politics of Middle-Class Indonesia*, Clayton: Monash University, 1991.

[65] *Jakarta Post*, 30 July 1998, p. 3.

[66] The *Bupati*s are the officials responsible for supervision of a *kabupaten*, that is an administrative subdivision of a province (*propinsi*). Indonesia had 27 provinces until the secession of East Timor in September 1999.

[67] *Fakta*, no. 357, 15 August 1998, p. 21.

[68] Ibid., pp. 23 and 31.

[69] 'Village head urged to quit', *Jakarta Post*, 28 July 1998, p. 3.

to the management of families which draw means of subsistence from them without ever accounting for their activities to any administrative department. The Antiquities Office also expressed concern during the 1990s over cases of resale of valuable archaeological objects by employees of national museums.[70] Sections of road, rights to education, treasures in museums, rights over common property (teak forests, arable land, etc.): strategies of private enrichment can be directed at every part of the public domain, every bit of public revenue. Even the forces of the state can be used for private purposes—for example when rich traders at Menteng, on the day after riots, paid a squadron of police of the Polda Jaya or soldiers of the Kopassus (Special Forces of the army) to ensure protection of their homes or their shops.[71]

Rectors, policemen, governors, prefects, museum workers are all ready to play with the laws and regulations to make up for the slenderness of their lawful incomes. Recently the spokesman for the army admitted publicly that 70 per cent of the income of military personnel came from 'unofficial' sources. The salary of a two- or three-star general does not exceed 4 million rupiahs a month, and that of a five-star general (equivalent to a Chief of Defence Staff) is no more than 6 million rupiahs, including entertainment expenses. But when Admiral Widodo Adisucipto, the former commander in chief of the Indonesian armed forces (TNI) married his son Dony Murdono to the daughter of a Thai admiral on 1 February 2002 at Balai Sudirman, the ceremony (attended by nearly 2,000 people) cost him, so guests said, more than $700,000. The reception offered by Major General Sudi Silalahi (former commander of the powerful Brawijaya Division of Surabaya) for the wedding of his daughter Linda with the son of Brigadier Zulfahmi Rizal the next day was also *potlach* on a grand scale. Luxury cars, houses covering several hundred square metres at Bogor or Menteng or Kebayoran Baru (the wealthy districts of Jakarta), staying in luxury hotels in Bali costing $800 a night, dining in the grandest restaurants, sending children abroad for study: the lifestyle of the senior ranks of the Indonesian army definitely has no relation to official salary levels.

There is a still more worrying phenomenon: the rise in power of paramilitary militias which are substituting themselves bit by bit for the armed forces of the state. This is not something unprecedented. The Civil Security System (*Siskamling*), established in the mid-1980s, allows the police and the army to train civilian auxiliaries, like the *Satpam* and *Hansip*, who

---

[70] Personal communication from a warden at the National Museum in Jakarta, July 1998.

[71] For a panoramic view of corruption at the beginning of the 1980s, see B. Supryanto, 'Korupsi di Indonesia', *Kompas*, 23 December 1984, and Silalahi B. N. B. 'Korupsi, manifestasi penyakit jiwa atau produksi sistem yang kurang baik', *Jurnal Ekuin*, 14 December 1981.

after accelerated training become security guards in the private sector but act as informers and agents of the police. The 'people's security' corps (*Kamra*, from *keamanan rakyat*) were used by the army in 1999 to 'secure' Jakarta at the approach of the June elections, and then during the first session of parliament in July-August. These *Kamra*s, hastily recruited by the army, came to a great extent from the sleazy fringes of society in Jakarta, Surabaya and Medan; they had often begun service as *jago*s (hooligans) working for crime bosses in the 'red districts' (Tanah Abang in Jakarta, Dolly in Surabaya) and were linked to powerful protection racket gangs. Their recruitment into a corps of civilian auxiliaries of the state armed forces, while in theory it enabled the police to keep better watch on them, worsened the criminalisation of the state.

The boundaries between the underworld and the police have always been vague. The Pemuda Pancasila, the 'youth movement' set up by Sukarno in the late 1950s and then revived by Suharto to do dirty work for the regime (especially during the Golkar's election campaigns), were also part of that 'floating world' of professionals of violence, halfway between the state and big organised crime. But today the phenomenon of '*preman*isation' (from the word *preman*, meaning 'delinquent' or 'crime boss') on the margins of the state apparatus has reached alarming proportions: several million *Kamra*s, *Satpam*s and other *Hansip*s are at the disposal of those who want to engage the services of a *tukang bunuh* (hired killer) or hire a strong-arm team to break a strike. The new militias of the neo-fundamentalists, like the Front of the Defenders of Islam (Front Pembela Islam or FPI) and the Laskar Jihad, sometimes have real police missions delegated to them. Thus militants of the FPI have gone on the beat jointly with the police at Bogor, and the Laskar Jihad in 1999 obtained a free hand from some military authorities in eastern Java for their anti-Christian operations in the Molucca Islands.

With all these groups, the main problem is managing them once the period of their political usefulness has passed. For men who are one day granted prerogatives of violence and equipped and trained for murder do not lay down their arms easily at the end of their 'contract'. Besides tending to get stuck in the criminal economy of their places of deployment (as in Ambon), they follow the logic of mercenary activity, which in turn produces the logistics of organised crime. In addition, there is a deregulation of illicit markets, which leads experts at extortion—whether hooligans or policemen—to engage increasingly often in violent rivalry among themselves. Attacks on military barracks by police commandos (and vice versa) tend to show that the separation between the police and the army decreed in 2000 (and considered then as a step towards democratisation) has had perverse results when the question of control of illicit resources comes in. The special corps of various services—the green berets of the Kostrad, the red berets of the Kopassus, the Marines or Marinir, the Mobile Brigades of the police or Brimob—were very often involved in criminal affairs in the 'frontier zones' where they were despatched (in Aceh, Kalimantan or Papua Barat). The greater visibility of their brutalities can be explained by the shorter duration of their stay in a theatre of operations—since the limited time available for predation necessitates greater intensity in the exercise of violence.

From the most insignificant fiddle to the biggest financial scandals,[72] there have been billions of rupiahs that never reached the state treasury, or escaped its grasp. The economic crisis seems to have worsened the social impact of this criminal activity. In August 1998 BAPPENAS, the ministerial agency responsible for management of development projects, published a document detailing the allocation of funds for financing of programmes for sanitary repairs in the poor districts of Jakarta, as well as help for petty trade. These funds, coming essentially from World Bank grants, amounted to 17 billion rupiahs. But the BAPPENAS document spoke of budgetary allocations that in no way reflected the initial direction of the project accepted by the World Bank. For example, while the 'Social Welfare' element, aimed at 'improving social services for the poor, orphans and other abandoned persons [*sic*]', obtained 124 million rupiahs, 'support for Islamic law students in difficulty', managed by the ministry of Religious Affairs, was given 229 million! Similarly, the 'repairs to the road network' section mentioned a grant of more than 1.4 billion rupiahs, while 'development of small and medium-scale artisanal enterprises' was allocated only 65 million; and so on.[73] In short, the system of allocations flagrantly contradicted the outline agreement under which funds had been made available to BAPPENAS. Still more worrying, the portion of the funds provided for the poor communities of Jakarta was, from the beginning of 1999 (the date when the Social Safety Net Programmes came into operation), the object of a series of embezzlements at every point in the fairly complex system for transfer of funds. An NGO for legal defence of the underprivileged inhabitants of the capital, the Konsortium Kemiskinan Kota (Consortium against Urban Poverty), has shown, with proofs to back it, that many district chiefs concealed from the people under their authority the amounts to which they were legitimately entitled.[74]

---

[72] Like the speculation in the private debt of Pertamina (the National Oil and Gas Company) in the 1970s, or, more recently, the accounting concealment of 'bad debts' of state banks.

[73] *Social Safety Net Programs and Funds Allocations*, BAPPENAS, Jakarta August 1998.

[74] Konsortium Kemiskinan Kota, *JPS justru meminggirkan rakyat kota yang paling miskin dan terpuruk. Materi Konferensi Pers UPC*, March 1999: communiqué on an inquiry

Corruption in this case is no longer a matter of possible alternative redistribution of wealth, it involves strengthening of structures of social injustice. In addition, the distribution of considerable sums of money in the ministries in Jakarta on the eve of elections that could challenge the government party's monopoly was a perfect example of the 'money politics' that characterises Indonesia today.[75] Dirty money (*uang haram*) strengthens the aggregation of allegiances as well as the maintenance of social barriers.[76]

Since the fall of Suharto, however, public denunciation of corruption has taken new forms, spectacular ones that are politically effective at the local level. During the summer of 1998, especially after the production of an internal note of the World Bank stating that 20 to 30 per cent of development funds for projects allocated to Indonesia had been embezzled by the ministries responsible for managing them, several agencies and 'anti-KKN' study groups were set up. The acronym KKN stands for 'Corruption, Collusion and Nepotism' (*Korupsi, Kolusi dan Nepotisme*). The demand for 'moral improvement' of the state even found a party-political expression: several small parties, such as the Gerakan Keadilan dan Persatuan Bangsa (Movement for National Justice and Unity) created on 15 August 1998 on the initiative of former ministers and ex-governor Ali Sadikin of Jakarta, made the struggle against corruption one of their propaganda themes.[77] The strictly political effectiveness of some of those anti-KKN agencies is beyond doubt. In fact the Gowa anti-corruption association played a key role in exposing the embezzlement of public funds that eventually cost Abdurrahman Wahid the presidency. Alip Suwondo, Wahid's masseur, had raided the funds of foundations of the Bulog, the state agency for control of cereal exports. Unable to refute an accusation by parliamentary commissions of inquiry, Abdurrahman Wahid was deposed by an overwhelming majority on 23 July 2001, and replaced by Vice President Megawati Sukarnoputri.

But anathemas alone are not enough to deal fully with the problem posed by state banditry in terms of plunder of public resources. It is undeniable, certainly, that administrative performance deteriorates through constant bypassing of the law. But the degree of tolerability of state

---

conducted in February 1999 in 10 villages in the Jakarta Special District (*Kelurahan DKI*).

[75] 'Maraknya sindikat Uang Palsu', *Tajuk* no. 2, Th. II, 17–31 March 1999.

[76] 'Ayo, Pulangkan Uang haram', *Forum Keadilan* no. 25, th. VII, 22 March 1999, p. 75.

[77] See *Jakarta Post*, 15 August 1998: 'Big names form group for justice'. It should be noted that since the mid-1970s a number of anti-corruption legislative bills and proposals for regulation have been put forward and sometimes adopted. For a historical view of these legal initiatives see S. E. Juniadi Soewartojo, *Korupsi. Pola kegiatan dan penindakannya serta Peran Pengawasan dalam penanggulangannya*, Jakarta: Restu Agung, 1995.

intrusion into private space, and hence its social legitimacy, increase in proportion to the scraps of tax revenue or state property which, through the generosity of the corrupt, reach underprivileged people. Paradoxically, the redistributive effects of corruption compensate to some extent for the erosion of administrative services.

In Indonesia everyone, or almost everyone, hates 'the police' or 'the administration'; but everyone, or almost everyone, has a son-in-law who is a postmaster, a cousin who works at the town hall, or a friend who is a policeman. And everyone, or almost everyone, benefits in one way or another from that sort of contact: by getting a fraudulent building permit, by profiting from the generosity of a *Bapak* passing through, by evading a trial, by 'placing' a son with an influential acquaintance. The act of corruption often becomes intolerable only when its area of redistribution is reduced to the culprit alone. If a village chief takes advantage of his position to pocket a commission on a contract award, but takes the precaution of redistributing the profit widely among his fellow citizens, he will be less likely to face prompt removal than if he commits fraud for his sole profit. Of course this is not to minimise the seriousness of corruption, but simply to indicate what conditions can make it acceptable, and to try to understand how, far from undermining the state steadily more, corruption also ensures the socialisation of the state—that is, its striking of roots among social groups which would fight against it openly if they did not take advantage of its expansion at some level or another.

Rather than talking of a 'culture of corruption', then, it is better to talk of political corruption—that is, criminal practices arising from a type of *gouvernementalité* centred on the state's occupation of private life. The game of predation, in this sense, is not derived from a trait of the collective unconscious, nor from some psycho-pathological disposition, but from the demands of preservation of a style of control over society. Pastoral power, in this respect, amounts to etiology of corruption. This reopens the question of the very concept of 'privatisation' of the state. For if that concept designates solely the procedures and tactics of illicit appropriation of public revenue, it merely confirms analyses of corrupt practices. But if it describes a particular historical mode of socialisation of the state, included in the functional economy of pastoral power, it covers to some extent the process of social formation of the state. Every state apparatus, in fact, arises from an often ephemeral concordance between hegemonic aims and class or caste interests. Modern monarchical bureaucracy, says Emmanuel Le Roy Ladurie,[78] was rooted in the bourgeoisie's ambition to raise within its ranks a *noblesse de robe* able to rival the hated—but also

---

[78] Emmanuel Le Roy Ladurie, *L'Etat royal: 1460–1610*, Paris: Hachette, 1987.

envied—aristocracy. Similarly, in Java, collaboration of the service nobility with the imperial administrative project was derived in part from the old antagonism between the dynastic aristocracy and the big commoner families in the service of the sovereign.

So it was often rivalry of caste interests and ambitions that led to institutionalising of responsibilities, which was the inaugural stage for entry into state modernity. In other words, the state as a system of domination is also based on private allegiances and rationalities. Consequently, predatory levies are payment for the investment of hegemonic groups in a security arrangement guaranteeing their interests. Through embezzlement of public funds and suborning of officials, the state becomes, literally, an investment fund. When the historian Onghokam writes in the *Jakarta Post*, 'Corruption: the old name was tribute',[79] the exact significance of his words needs to be understood. The word 'tribute' comes from the Latin verb *tribuere*, 'to divide among the tribes'. Corruption, like any criminal act affecting public revenue, divides among the hegemonic tribes (the industrial bourgeoisie, the army, etc.) the dividends of their joint investment in the most profitable of limited companies: the state. From this perspective the cession of sovereign prerogatives to private enterprises represents a logical development—though certainly not a morally well founded one—of the process of social formation of the state.

What lessons can be drawn from these few reflections on Indonesia? First, it is best to abandon any effort to measure in a binary and mechanical way—in terms of weakening or strengthening—the state's capacity to maintain the monopolies that make up its classical definition (monopoly of the means of legitimate violence, monopoly of the means of managing a territory, monopoly of diplomatic relations).[80] On the contrary, it is clearly necessary to take account of the contribution made by mechanisms of socialisation of the state to the long-term renewal of the hegemony pact that lies at the origin of the state.

Secondly, these developments show us that corruption is not a simple process of extraction, but has its roots in modes of government. And this has implications once action against corruption starts being included in the political conditionality linked to disbursement of international financial aid. Today, 'anti-KKN' agencies are proliferating in Indonesia. But plans for action against corruption can only achieve their objectives if it is

---

[79] Onghokam, 'Corruption: The old name was tribute', *Jakarta Post*, 23 June 1983.

[80] Monopoly of means of violence, issuing of currency, diplomatic initiatives... On this point, see Bertrand Badie and Pierre Birnbaum, *Sociologie de l'Etat*, Paris: Grasset, 1982.

accepted that eradicating the process of 'privatisation' of the state implies radical rejection of pastoral power—that is, a transition to a different mode of *gouvernementalité*. In this sense, all the spectacular operations to hunt down the corrupt that are launched by a state still considering itself as the shepherd of the people are, however sincere their intentions may be, doomed to failure. For by their style of implementation they actually give credit to what they aim to destroy: the concern for ever greater meddling in the obscure recesses of fraud and smuggling. Public extortion of confessions by officials recognised as guilty of corruption is a sign of a worrying paradox. The more the power of the state seeks to undo the perverse effects of its mode of social formation—that is, the more it dislocates the criminal coalitions that structure its area of intervention—the deeper its imperial domination over individuals penetrates; and, accordingly, the more the expansion of its repressive system requires delegation of its prerogatives to external, private agencies of control.

It is for that reason that the most virulent denunciations of corruption, if they are not based in the last resort on criticism of pastoral power, lead to scandal, certainly, but not to change. In Indonesia those denunciations are old, and numerous. Short stories exposing the moral ravages of dishonest enrichment,[81] popular songs mocking the gluttony of 'office rats' (like Iwan Fals' *Tikus-Tikus Kantor* and Doel Sumbang's *Tarian Nepotisme*[82]), incendiary articles denouncing betrayal of the ideals of the state:[83] since the 1970s, sometimes in the strictest secrecy and sometimes in broad daylight in the national media,[84] a considerable mass of critical discourse has exposed the machinery of predation acting as a gangrene on the state. In contrast, rarely is heard any challenge to pastoral power, to that mad ambition of the state to want—as Joseph Chailley-Bert put it as far back as 1900—to 'see everything and know everything'.

Such challenges are indeed rare, but they do exist. For example, the historical criticism conducted skilfully by Onghokam can in fact serve as a formidable weapon in the struggle against pastoral *gouvernementalité*,

[81] See for example the portrait of the Bupati Ramli in Chairul Harun, 'Telepon', *Horison* XI (10–1), October–November 1976, pp. 332–5, or the portrait of Marno the Corrupted Incorruptible in Moeis Loindong, 'Di Balik Matahari', *Horison* 12, 1992, pp. 423–7.

[82] Iwan Fals, 'Tikus-Tikus Kantor' in *Salam Reformasi*, PT Musica's Studios, 1998, and Doel Sumbang in *Kaum Reformasi*, 'Tarian Nepotisme', 1998. The metaphor of 'rats' is commonly used for corrupt officials. See the short story 'Kucing Gubernuran' by A. A. Navis, published in *Horison* XXI (7), 1986, pp. 239–41, which recounts the rebuffs faced by a governor trying to get rid of 'rats' haunting the building where he works. The governor decides to adopt a horde of cats to get rid of the rats; but the cats cause him similar problems.

[83] See for example the article by Taufik Abdullah, 'KKN dan Ancaman Disintegrasi', *Tajuk* 12, 1–6 August 1998, pp. 74–5.

[84] Particularly in the national daily *Kompas*.

whose colonial roots are uncovered as well as its totalitarian tendencies. Appealing to the Law against the rule of the Norm, so long as it does not turn into uncritical defence of the rule of the 'true bureaucracy' over the body of society, can similarly turn out to be a powerful agent for dissolving the theories of the family-state. Goenawan Mohamad illustrates this option, present in the Indonesian ideological landscape in the 1950s:

In this giving of symbols, we call our country a family. At the head is the 'father' (*bapak*), usually the king or the head of state. It is as though we are able in this way to replace something that we lost when we 'separate' [this means the process towards individuation] and become our own selves. However, the difficulty is that the symbol comes to be no longer seen as a symbol, even though a country is never a family, and the head of state can never be like a real father to the citizens. And how is it possible to operate an economy in a 'family-like' way, when the state itself needs something that cannot be based on kinship—namely the law, and in particular law that protects the individual's right of ownership?[85] Doesn't the state, after all, definitely require a mechanism that is impersonal, namely bureaucracy?[86]

Goenawan Mohamad's courageous questioning remains ambiguous. In its renewed confidence in the regulatory power of the 'bureaucracy', it adheres to one of the guiding principles of pastoral government: administrative occupation of the intimate sphere. But at the same time, his plea for individual rights shows that he is conscious of the need to set bounds to the control of the state—even a 'healthy' state—over people's private lives. Perhaps that reasoning marked the ultimate limit of an unequal struggle. For pastoral power, punishing all the more severely because it claims to love, rearing all the more strictly because it aims to free the individual from his sins, inevitably succeeds in making itself desired by the very people that it grasps in the claws of its finicky affection. Therefore revolt against paternalist authoritarianism rarely leads to a routine of democracy; it leads much more surely to providentialist worship and frenzy, to the triumph of the herald of the masses. That, when all is said and done, is an individualised version of the shepherd state. That is probably the real cunning and the final victory of 'pastoral power': it always presents itself as its own alternative.

---

[85] According to Daniel S. Lev, who considers that the idea of a 'state based on law' (Negara Hukum) emerges among professional legal associations in reaction to constitutional negligence of individual rights: *Legal Aid in Indonesia*, Clayton: Monash University, 1987.

[86] Goenawan Mohamad, 'Keluarga', *Tempo*, 3 August 1991, reproduced in English in G. Mohamad, *Sidelines. Thought Pieces from Tempo Magazine*, Jakarta: Lontar, 1994, pp. 10–11.

10

POSTFACE

PRIVATISATION AND THE HISTORICAL PATHS
OF THE POLITICAL

Yves Chevrier

'Privatisation' is a global concept, circulating among the various socio-
cultural entities that interact in the globalised world of today. In these
various contexts it is generally associated with the notion that economic
relations are superseding political ones. However, if we argue that the
globalised world, far from being a homogeneous set of interconnected and
interacting markets, is a global scene where various historical trajectories
are brought together and interact without losing their individual momen-
tum and characteristics, we are faced with local contexts in which market
forces interact with local power not according to the universal laws of the
market economy, but according to the historical paths determined by the
long-term history of relations between public power and society. Thus it
would seem that, in order to understand fully the various phenomena
called 'privatisation', we need to emphasise the political setting, and,
more precisely, to look into the historical construction of the political in
these various contexts.

What is 'the Political'?

Throughout this essay the word 'political' is used as a noun ('the political'), in a way that may not be familiar to English-speaking readers. It
refers to but does not mean 'politics' or 'policies', that is, actions, social
actors, programmes and strategies of action aimed at the realm of public
affairs. The political is more than the public agenda and public institutions. But it is not 'the body politic', nor the polity, nor the 'political sphere'
as opposed to the state, the government. 'Governance' would come nearer

241

to the mark if it were not thought of as a technique, the province of experts and social engineers. Even though some, today, would argue that markets, or the legal system, ethical values or the social efficacy of the individual will suffice, the question of governance is primarily a political one. We could thus define the political as characterising relations of a special kind between public power (in the state, but not necessarily so, as the state is not a universal form) and the nexus of actions, discourses, norms and symbols (involving powerholders but also social elements, depending on historical conditions) related to the meaning and to the organisation of the community as a legitimate social entity: a legitimacy whose ultimate claims to existence do not lie in the powers that be, nor in religious or moral claims, but in those very relations.

The political is not the realm of ideas, or of norms and values as opposed to politics, power etc., more than it is a science or technique, and it is not an 'object', hidden or visible in social life. Like the social class according to Thompson's view, it is a set of social and normative relations, some of which make it very specific in the range of social actions because they are power relations encompassing the whole social body and meant to address the collective needs of the whole community. It appears as a social construction. And because it is socially constructed, the political is historically determined. It has a history of its own—the history of its constructions. As we see in this Postface, the political constructions we encounter in the course of history, even when they claim to be universal and above history, are narrowly related to the societies where they happen to take shape. However, since the political does not refer to 'society' in its usual sociological sense—because the political field, while it is a social field among others, has the distinctive feature that it articulates norms and actions which the social actors in other fields recognise as having a general value—the social history of the political should address this feature, which appears as its most general characteristic, both historically and geographically: namely, that it has been contextualised, if not always contested, as a specific realm of social activity. Since it has been socially constructed in the course of history, and since its social construction has entailed a hierarchy not only of power but also in the modes of social action and values, the processes, forms and norms of social hierarchisation may be claimed as a legitimate object of investigation for a comparative sociohistorical analysis of the political. This Postface speaks of a 'house', meaning not so much a political community—a common 'house' with the modern democratic citizenry as tenants—as the form related to social hierarchisation taken by the political at a given time in a historical collectivity.

The purpose of this chapter is not to achieve a complete analysis, but to explore some significant forms taken by the political in connection with the present emphasis on 'privatisation'. It is hoped that a critical review of the connections usually established in the current discourse and in the social sciences between the social and political phenomena conducive to 'privatisation', a primarily economic and worldwide phenomenon, will shed light and open vistas on the political dimension of history, leading, if only in a sketchy way, to a history of the political on the global scale. This will show that the current trends of de-politicisation associated with privatisation and globalisation, far from meaning that the political has come to an end or has achieved worldwide unification, lead to re-formed norms and to new forms of social action that are political in different ways—that is, to new episodes in the various histories of the political—while at the same time the political enters the history of its worldwide formation on the global stage.

Beyond the political? Questioning post-Mao China

Let us start our analytical and historical journey with a brief deconstruction of the academic and public notion of 'privatisation'. Throughout the 1980s the crises and reforms in the Communist systems were considered under the eminently political heading of progress of the free market and democracy. In the following decade, no less fascinated by the market but affected by a serious collapse of the political, the dominant theme was the return in force of the private sphere, which was supposed—starting with the economic arena, and all over the world—to reduce the surfeit of ideology from which the world was supposed to be suffering. The notion of privatisation was marked by that context but not really conceived through it; like the notions of liberalisation and democratisation earlier, it wore outsize trappings of universality and pragmatic evidence, but these trappings were worn away from the outset by a sort of conceptual depression. That grey area had an impressive power of seduction and fashionable impact, but it was simply going again over well known ground in a sterile way. This recalls T. S. Eliot's lines in *Gerontion*: '*Tenants of the house/ Thoughts of a dry brain in a dry season*'.

Let us take the example of China. Twenty years after Mao the Western media belatedly discovered a vast state enterprise sector when the 15th Congress of the Communist Party set out in October 1997 a programme for its overall restructuring, which those media instantly saw as privatisation. Leaving to specialists the task of examining the delay in these operations and their specific modalities, those Western commentators at one stroke erased the unique itinerary of the Chinese reforms—just as they had forgotten its specific features in the 1980s, reducing it to the then dominant paradigm of the impossibility of reforming Communism in the face of the progress of the free market and democracy, considered to be inseparable, irresistible and overwhelming. The Asian crisis was not enough to cast doubt on this supposed entry of China into the paradise of privatisation.

New facts were noted, certainly. Capital was less available, social risks were more pressing, ironic reversals of situations occurred: had the Chinese state not become, directly or indirectly, the owner of a substantial portion of the stock market capitalisation in Hong Kong? Beijing's stated determination to spare at least the social character of Socialist industrial ownership, if not its state character, was acknowledged. But most observers and actors, even so, have considered that despite the demands—those due to the prevailing situation, and political ones—of the post-Deng Xiaoping era, the criteria for public ownership are being aligned with those of private ownership; whatever the fluctuations, hesitations and legal complications on the borders separating the two sectors, the system of which they form part is destined to change in kind—that, *lato sensu*, is the meaning of privatisation in the Chinese context, since the idea seems still inadequate from the legal viewpoint, as T. Pairault explains.[1] Although banished from paradise, the elusive privatisation still remains the paradigm of our time.

The Chinese case shows how far this paradigm confuses two realities: the withdrawal of the state and/or its immersion in the economic sphere. The first development is that put forward by the prevailing discourse: it is based on a clear differentiation between the state sphere and the economic, or seeks to establish such a difference. Besides economic uncertainties, political resistance and social turbulence, the failures and delays in the process can be imputed to corruption and cultural factors—transitory or secondary phenomena that do not challenge the universality or the efficacy of the process. In this process the state, because its agents recognise the superiority of an independent realm of economic laws and economic realities, becomes the instrument of its own reshaping, and this leads to the rise of an autonomous economic sphere in which, thanks to the new logic of privatisation, the processes of state formation find new ingredients. But far from giving way before this idealised situation, Chinese reality imposes a different picture. The process has not created a privatising state, that is, a state institutionalising a privatised society both closer to the preoccupations of society as it is and more external to it. Rather, the reforms have produced a *privatised state*. While formal privatisations ('formal' in the sense of publicly instituted) marked time—whereas the reforms extracted an economic sphere from the political 'whole'

---

[1] On the legal aspect see Thierry Pairault, 'Droit de propriété et réforme du secteur d'Etat', *Etudes Chinoises*, vol. XX no. 1–2, spring-autumn 2001, pp. 7–40.

established by Mao—the state that was not formally carrying out privat-isation in fact privatised itself informally, through various processes straddling the new economic sphere and the political sphere. This devel-opment has been criticised and analysed in China itself.

In the West this unexpected trajectory forced specialists to modify their interpretations. Whereas in the 1980s the majority of them saw opposition between the state and society (with society progressing from the eco-nomic to the political arena, in opposition to the state), now the state was seen as ubiquitous, accompanying and promoting economic and social changes instead of opposing them or contradicting their 'ideal' logic. According to this view, the state was not following another ideal logic, any more than it was supposed to be immersed in pure market forces. It was in fact immanent in a different reality. While the 1980s had been seen as a period of political differentiation of society, the dominant trend in the fol-lowing decade was to relate everything to an atomised social domain, including the state. The state was no longer perceived in its constructed aspect. It was seen through its deconstructed features, appearing as an eroded, corrupted, fragmented state, traversed by networks that were under-mining its state character. It was disappearing in a community-oriented universe fragmented by invading networks, whose economic and cultural dynamics aggravated the collapse of the political by blocking the con-struction of a politically organised civil society. At the same time conflicts within the state, described in terms of a retreat of ideological issues to give way to patronage interests linked together in the form of networks, were an additional indication of the retreat of the political in the face of a strongly culturalised social sphere.

Paradoxically, then, the return to the state, which was the theme of media and academic discourse on the Chinese reforms in the 1990s, only ob-scured the problem of the political, as well as the historical dimension of this problem; thanks to this obscurity, post-modern deconstructions in the West crossed paths with some cultural constructions of eastern Asia and China (until the Asian economic crisis of the late 1990s imposed a certain discretion on that level). Economic success encouraged research into what could positively make a system where it was asserting itself most spectac-ularly.[2] Far from those delusions, researchers suggested that opening up

---

[2] That is why the *problématiques* of transition (to the market economy) have taken a culturalist turn. The Chinese performance, attributed in the mid-1980s to the highly devel-oped Confucianist culture which emphasises social discipline and the state, has asserted itself by disproving that model: it was eventually attributed to the enterpreneurial capaci-ties of the social domain, reduced to its community structures and logics alone. A good many observers cheerfully mixed up these elements, while at the same time highlighting a value system rooted in Asia; the continent's economic success encouraged creation of a

isolated and peculiar structures to the world economic system does not remove their differences, but is rather organised around them. Thus they found widely represented on the world scale—with or without 'success stories'—approaches to the market and enterprise in which the embedded modes of operation and sets of values differed from the system of collective institutions and representations prevailing in the historical emergence of capitalism.

These 'reinventions of capitalism', so far removed from the 'Washington consensus'—to quote Jean-François Bayart[3]—far from being reducible to a common system derived from their departure from the 'pure' original rationality of capitalism, are inseparable from particular historical itineraries, whose present-day unique feature is that they meet in the grand forum of the 'global' universe. In this meeting, cultural characteristics borne by history are the most visible indicators of differences, and also the elements that can be most easily instrumentalised by states and groups seeking legitimacy. So it is scarcely surprising that the remnants of the paradigm of transition have enriched the paradigm of privatisation; and that the universal trend towards privatisation is seen as blending a vision of pure economic rationality with elements linked to the social sphere, the sphere of the *imaginaire*—and the political in various cultural and historical settings.

Does this mean that the notion of privatisation is sufficiently criticised when it is related to these contexts, and that it can only be understood through particular trajectories? It seems that this criticism should also encourage us to reflect generally on the historical structuring of social action, on the social sphere (including the political, and history) as overall composition of human activity, since the movements that the privatisation concept designates in the real and imaginary structuring of the social sphere affect its basic structure and, especially, the historical and political aspects that social theories have sometimes had trouble in restoring as relevant levels of construction of the social.

Questioning the Western path: a hierarchy of social action

The fashion for the privatisation concept calls for reconsideration of what has for long been accepted as the founding parameter of modern Western societies: individualisation of the social sphere and autonomisation of

---

Chinese model (yet another!) out of characteristics that are not dominant either in China or in Asia, and which those regions share with other emerging countries. On these ideological-political constructions, cf. Y. Chevrier, 'Le génie du confucianisme?', pp. 206–24, in Jean-Luc Domenach and David Camroux (eds), *L'Asie retrouvée*, Paris: Seuil, 1997.

[3] Cf. J.-F. Bayart (ed.), *La réinvention du capitalisme*, Paris: Karthala, 1994.

differentiated areas (spheres, or fields) of activity. In the realm of Enlightenment political philosophy and political economy, the individual was thought to be the cornerstone of the social and political order. Society, in a way, was far less substantial than its individual foundations. On the other hand, perhaps in the wake of Rousseau's idea of the 'general will', the modern social sciences, especially Durkheimian sociology, developed a social paradigm of the individual in which individuality was balanced and surrounded by what I would call 'sociality'. This intellectual development reflected the socialised nature of modern society in the industrial and urbanised West. The rise of mass parties and mass democracy was the particular form achieved by the political in this historical setting.

To judge by Louis Dumont's interpretation of this change—emblematic in this respect—its guiding factor is attributed most often to the economy, individualist modernity being seen as inventing itself in substitution of the relationship of man to things for the mutual relations of human beings as the guiding paradigm of sociality (Dumont, rightly, considering sociality to be a horizon of individualised social logics). However, it is possible to argue that the modern Western form of the political was political—that is, that the social structures that fostered it were led by modern political factors as much as they were shaped by the modern capitalist economy. Modern societies were welded together in the framework of the modern nation-states, to a point that was without historical parallel even in centralised, bureaucratic premodern societies, such as Imperial China. As states and political structures became central to social life, a new hierarchy of social action was established under the prevalence not of the individual, but of the socialised political. Hence the ever open definition of modernity as a set of questions and tensions related to the real place and value of the individual in the din of the modern social setting.

That the phenomena of privatisation, in their widest sense, are seen as something new and recent could mean not a deepening or perfection of the individualist structures of society related to new progress in the market economy, but the rise of a different social logic moving from a paradigm of individualised sociality that was political to an economic paradigm of the social, falling back this time on individuality and particular identities, so that the social is forgotten as society exists no longer ideologically, doctrinally, theoretically or existentially (in the intimacy of the private sphere), as it has been in the first age of modernity—the age of sociality—but socially, that is by the social actors as the ultimate, meaningful horizon of their being and interacting together. The overlapping and fragmentation of the spheres of social activity and power in a context of the rise of the economic blur the normative and functional borders of the political and account for the current failure to observe the social dynamics of its constructions, which are no less macro-ensembles in the present than they were in the recent past, when, following the historical paths of the Western societies, the paradigm of sociality resulted in broad categories of social identification for individuals.

In this configuration, the centrality of the political did not always mean that collective social action prevailed against the social patterns and norms that were not primarily related to or aimed towards political action. The interplay of actions and norms structured an open field (the modern political) which ordered the interactions of the specialised social spheres (including that of politics). The articulation and hierarchy of the various social spheres were an essential subject of debate and conflict and hence a vital motive force in the first history of modernity. The individualisation and autonomisation of private social activity were established as a legitimate space only in relation to a demand for public action. The hierarchisation of the social spheres that ordered society was linked to processes of institutionalisation that do not stop with today's privatisation of the political, but take new forms.

The institutionalisation of society and its forms

The distinguishing feature of the classic moment of modernity, in the West, is that it associated the modern recasting of the social with a definition (though not the practice) of political links that was abstract—desubstantialising or 'formal', in the sense that the abstract rules of the institution were set against the human fullness of ritual, action, individual life, particularistic ties, ethnic and religious affiliations, etc.—because it sought to be universalist. That weakness was a strength: it implied absence of differentiation of institutions' capacity for recognition with respect to individuals, or even continuity of the founding principles of the political vis-à-vis the other fields of social activity. In this sense the formal is not only what is publicly instituted: the action of institutionalising the social in a political form transforms it while formalising it. The political becomes society, but under the aspect of formal constructions that mark its institutionalising character for society—but, at the same time, establish a distant as well as a distinct sphere of authority generating social alienation from the political structures which, on principles, represent society. Hegel's approach in *The Phenomenology of Mind* was emblematic in this respect.

If the shaping of societies is based on forms defining the place of the public sphere in lives and values of their actors, if this shaping depends also on social structures—community cells stretching the link between the state and individuals, or broad basic founding profiles of industrial sociality which have given rise to differentiation of fields of action and at the same time its individualisation in the urbanised world of the modern industrial economy—the first age of modernity was specific in the sense that it was characterised by the sealing-off effect which gave sense to the whole for the actors thanks to the constitution of a higher horizon of formality for their actions: the social sphere separated, confronted, coalesced or united, acting on itself according to formally legitimate rules, which constitutes the modern political. The state belongs to this horizon, of which it is the model in a certain sense, but the first age of modernity is precisely when the political is socialised and no longer a state monopoly. So it is best to talk of the political and its construction in a broad sense, and to fit the state in the strict sense and state building into it according to the special features of historical moments and historical trajectories.

The Western trajectories bring out a (rudimentary) table of elements of the political, classified according to institutionalising processes. The public horizon was instituting before it was institutionalising. Political actors did carve a specialised sphere of action, but the political had to negotiate its 'privilege' of representing the public at the highest normative and symbolic level with other (religious) authorities and defend its power against other powers or subversive forces. In short, the autonomisation of the political, not of the individual, paved the way for modernity. With the first and classical age of modernity, the political autonomy of the social highlights what I have called the centrality of the political. From then on, it is the social that dominates the political, that socialises it, but in the name of the *res publica* and in accordance with its forms. As a result, the political becomes the institutionalising authority.

This delicate and ever-shifting balance was upset in totalitarian configurations. In the name of a further socialisation, the political regained its former autonomy, augmented by the efficacy of modern power techniques and social discipline, and crushed (politically, this time) the private person, the possibility of autonomous social action and any competing or complementary normative order. The totalitarian institution of the social monopolises the field of values, of accomplishment, of meaning: the political is absolutely instituting in the name of the social, among other things by exclusion and elimination of segments of the social which it does not institute.

This far too sketchy historical chart of institutionalising processes in the Western paths shows that our era is characterised not only by the rise in power of economic power centres at the national and world level, regardless of political and social regimes, but also by an economic and no longer 'social' way of being socially: beyond the privatisation of the state, the privatisation of the political. This transformation is reflected in the ideology that views the market as the place of all powers and all social energies, abolishing by exchange and negotiation the opaque aspects and the conflicts of the social domain which have generated a political sphere not conducive to economic activity and to the full emancipation of the 'true' individuals as opposed to the formalised citizens of the institutionalised democracies. In the name of a fuller socialisation now indexed on individuals, the political technostructure and technology are criticised and the political is recast as a technique whose most adequate forum would be the art of governance.

Let us now examine whether these phenomena could not mean not the utter demise of the political (including the state) relatively to the economic, but a changing logic in the processes of social institutionalisation. It should be noted that our approach to institutions differs noticeably from those that define it as a rule, possibly combined with informal constraints, or else as a compromise. Not every form given to relations among men in society, nor every rule of their interaction is an institution in the sense adopted here. What distinguishes an institution among the guides for activity or the compromises in action described in the literature is, precisely, its institutionalising character: the element of recognition that it contains and implies, as well as its efficacy in guiding and harmonisation. The fact that institutions relate to different times of the social experience is linked to this function of a collective recognition as well as to mere social efficacy. The French sociologist Montuclard analyses institutions as relating to what is 'important'. That 'importance' relates to the relationship between the hierarchy of social values and the institutional organisation of modern societies mentioned above.

During the first age of modernity, when the political became the modern horizon for institutionalising of the social, this institutionalising capacity involved not only the recognition of the collective form of the social as the legitimate wielder of sovereignty—the politicised form of the 'public' domain constituted by civil society (or the 'public sphere') alongside the state—but also the recognition that society was more, and more valuable, than its individual parts: as participants in the societies organised according to the principles of sociality, individuals could overcome the limits of creative individual activity—work, production, profit and enterprise, even artistic expression and religious salvation. Even though these activities were viewed by many as legitimate aspirations to master the world and the meaning of existence in connection with private beliefs, social action loomed as something more important. The present privatisation of social action involves returning, in the domain supposed to be that of sociality and the political, to activities and powers of a special sort—like the *labour command* considered by Adam Smith to be the basis of economic activity, not only as more efficient tools, but also as more important for founding the collective being. It does not involve emptying those domains of their substance, but re-working them on the basis of a demand for meaning that no longer places them at the pinnacle of social life.

Where the autonomised social domain in citizens' political action would operate according to the operational character of state organisation, as well as social rituals modelled by the instituted authority of the state, the state is called upon to break away from its centralising and authoritarian habits, its inclination to organise the social side in a pyramidal and concentric fashion. The state and social action should back up the private activities of individuals and groups, and find their limits there. If public action goes beyond those limits, it seems legitimate for it to do so following the model of the private sphere's modes of activity. Ideas follow the movement; specialists speak of a 'political market' and 'democracy of opinion': corruption, even 'market corruption', is not the only aspect of privatisation. What changes, within this change, is specifically the form in which the social takes shape. In contrast to the relationship of the social with the public, there appears the figure of the institutionalising private sphere: the autonomy of the social not within the political but outside it, and the claim to recast the political without it. Can the institutionalising of the social proceed on the basis of the social sphere itself, not in the sense of sociality, but starting out from individuality? So what remains of the political and its aim to transcend particular differences? The question asked, through the *problématiques* of privatisation of the state, is that of the future progress of this significant horizon.

From the viewpoint of institutionalising processes, the basic question is not that of technique; it could be put like this: if the 'private' becomes institutionalising, is that 'private' the market? Can an autonomous economic sphere, in the sense of a universal system of exchange, found the social? As is well known, the neo-liberal view has been undermined from 'within' by a growing scepticism as to the self-regulatory capacity of the market. We have already noted that, according to the Western histories of the institutionalising processes and forms, the modern institutionalisation of society was achieved as a strong (albeit unstable) collective compromise between the two utopian limits of the modern political: the limiting of the social sphere by the private (the market and nothing but the market) or the public sphere (the state and nothing but the state). Outside the ideological debates about social relationships linked with political institutions, economists see in the necessity of institutionalising the market an essential question for their discipline. In the 'subjectivist' perspective adopted by Hayek, for example, individual actors are unable to master their environment. Failing such mastery—which alone would make them totally efficient economic agents of a perfect market—the free market can only operate through institutions establishing stable and predictable conditions for exchange that are out of actors' control. From this viewpoint institutions are regulators that arise from the subjective limits of actors in the face of the objectivity of their activity, that is, their interaction.[4]

However, this view once again deprives the political of its normative essence—the ordering of society on the basis of open interplay of social actors—because it is recast as a mere technique, while in today's world, the political perspective is not lost. The assumption is that society still needs to be founded socially, not economically, if the political is to be cleansed of its original sins: elements of authority derived from former command powers and logics of exclusion absorbed in the legitimate monopoly of violence. In a macro-sociological perspective, this change underlines a structural evolution towards a society that is not less differentiated but divided into more numerous and fragmented social fields, while the social world of the political appears distant, alien ('politics'). In this configuration of a social sphere that is at once more specialised and less hierarchised and collectively oriented, political action is judged by the standard of political expectations, and an all-important development is that the standard is becoming the individual's own realm.

Commentators like Marcel Gauchet speak of disenchantment with the political, linked to unlimited assertion of individuals at the expense of the social body as a whole—that is, of the inability of the political to occupy the centre of social life or, as Dominique Schnapper put it, the end of transcendent features that structured the sociality of the first modern world and, more concretely, the erosion of norms of authority, discrediting of actors in the political sphere and the need to establish 'proximity' between the political and society.[5] The challenge for democratic constructions is that they must be totally transparent to what the individuals feel they are and need privately and socially, or else they are perceived as distant and opaque and deserted by the citizenry. Rights become interests. The con-

---

[4] These themes have been abundantly developed on the basis of Keynes (*A Treatise of Probability*, 1927) and Hayek ('Economics and Knowledge', 1937, reproduced in *Individualism and Economic Order*, 1949). The works of D. C. North (*Institutions, Institutional Change and Economic Performance*, Cambridge University Press, 1990) illustrate a different but no less critical approach to the individualist and un-institutional postulates of classical theory. It can be recalled in this connection that Adam Smith himself sought the form of universal exchange not in the hidden hand but in aesthetics, and in particular in music (cf. Bruno Nassim-Aboudrar, 'L'esthétique d'un économiste', *Critique* 617, October 1998, pp. 603–16); and that in Kant's thought aesthetic judgment is precisely what reconciles the separate worlds of (subjective) freedom and the (objective) law for the founding of society.

[5] Cf. M. Gauchet, *La démocratie contre elle-même*, Paris: Gallimard, 2002; and D. Schnapper, *La démocratie providentielle*, Paris: Gallimard, 2002. Pierre Rosanvallon has analysed these tensions in terms of a modern history of the political in his inaugural lecture at the Collège de France, 28 March 2002.

temporary political debate in Western democracies is fed by these hesitations and expectations. To go back to the French example (which, in truth, would need a detailed analysis of the French historical path), some of the authors just mentioned were, in 2002, actors in a debate that divided French intellectuals on the foundations, transformations and history of democracy.

Indeed, what the progress of the notion of privatisation shows—in a hazy way—is the continued specific character of political claims which are no longer constitutive of a legitimate political sphere. The political, then, continues not as a utopia leading to its taking over the collective fate—the 'illusion of the political' (as Furet put it) linked to modern sociality; rather, like Eliot's 'heap of broken images', it is the dream of the citizen who, a collectivised individual in the classic age of modernity, now claims to bring to society (and to the resolution of social problems) the benefit of the full richness of his or her identity. What this signifies is that we are not in the world that we call post-modern, but in a historical development of the *res publica*'s first modernity, that is in a history of the modernity of the political that is fed by the crossing of various historical trajectories with the trajectory of globalisation (including the long-term effects of decolonisation in the former imperial centres).

Privatisation, in the broad sense, is therefore neither an unmitigated triumph for the private sphere, nor its exclusive domain. We can say that it corresponds to a state of society where the orientation of social action and the production of meaning pass from the state and state-dominated social and normative patterns to the social—a social which claims to be 'pure', without taint of any state, not by a simple effect of ideology, but because, historically, the modern social sphere has been 'socialised', given density, ramified and structured, so much so that the social actors feel society has no need of the framework of the state any more. That was the conviction of Auguste Comte, and the ambition of sociology in his thought, whereas according to Montesquieu no society could exist without government.[6] What seems significant is that the production of social rationality, like the production of legitimate forms of social ties, is becoming (or returning to being) a multiple-entry process, from the point of view of both actors and factors. In this process the possessor of the most official mark of collective recognition—the state—no longer has a privileged position. Its legitimacy is redefined, authority loses its one-dimensional strength. Rather than expressing the development in terms of a retreat of the public before the private, it is preferable to say that the state is losing the monopoly of institutionalisation of the social.

[6] Cf. Pierre Lantz, 'Dépolitisation et sciences sociales', *Journal des Anthropologues* 92–93, 2003.

We should not view this change as one set of social and normative structures replacing another one. The social and normative patterns conducive to the first modernity did not obliterate former ones (e.g. communal identities), which were embedded in the new contexts of modernity, where they retained some specific significance while they became building blocks of the new social order. Similarly, the new, socially structuring power of individuality privatising the political does not stem from a completely and globally transformed world. State structures and state authority are still valid organisational and normative standards in many parts of the world, even in those parts where the new paradigm is strongest. Although the very substance of political claims and action is being changed, the lingering past of the state still contributes to the twists and turns in the paths of the political. And we should not overlook the fact that state actors do capture the new trends of privatisation in order to strengthen ('modernise', 'privatise') state structures which depart from the standard model of the nation-state.

While the changing structures of the states in the old democracies may lead some to conclude that the political is undermined there, it does exemplify the differentiation between the state and the political that has been the very hallmark of their modernity. Because they recognise the supremacy of economic rationality, at the same time as a large number of authorities and legitimacies different from their own, these states, in the (in fact variable) contexts where phenomena of privatisation appear, seem like ordinary actors in a generalised negotiation of norms and authority, just like economic powers and interests. Certainly the sovereign function remains; but, in at least some parts of the world, the state now exercises it only at the limits of legitimacy, and has to give way—even in its monopoly of use of legitimate violence—to the social norms that cross its path. A telling example was a statement made by a Geneva official in the first days of the Iraq war in March 2003, concerning the Convention barring the photographing or filming of POWs. Since the Convention was a treaty signed by states and concerning states, it could only be hoped that journalists would comply with it.

Other historical processes

The historical dynamics in which the real and theoretical perspectives of privatisation are situated are not more likely to lead to the disappearance of the political than to the triumph of an immediate and universalised form of exchange, which would place every individual at the centre of all possible networks, his or her strength enhanced thanks to limitless technological advances. Advancing the idea of renegotiating the institutionalisation of the social involves breaking with the common idea of the end of the state and the political by and through privatisation spilling beyond its technical domain (economic and legal) to reach the universal perimeter of globalisation. Nonetheless it does challenge a form of institutionalising social differentiations and autonomies that constituted modern Western societies. From the moment when, at the root of the logic of privatisation, the problem of the specific character of the political and the institutionalising of the social is raised, it is right to recognise the full importance not only of historical depth within a historical trajectory—that of Western modernity, as has just been outlined—but also of widening of the framework of analysis beyond the Western route. That means that on the non-Western historical routes, as on that taken by Western societies, the analysis encounters episodes of state formation—that is, institutional and informal reshaping of the state structure—which, as Béatrice Hibou has shown, are on the horizon of logics of privatisation.[7] However, when the phenomenon of privatisation is examined, in the broad sense, it is seen that the movement of history, in the societies that were the crucible of modernity of the political, displaces the shaping of the social.

The broader criticism of the notion of privatisation that is sketched here leads us to reflect not only on the continued formation of the social sphere and the state, in accordance with changing and historically rooted configurations, but also on the forms of the social and the political deployed across those separate itineraries: not on institutions, but on what institutionalises. Studying the continuous path of state formation does not remove the basic difficulty of the notion of privatisation: it mixes the idea of the social formation of the state and that of forms of the social, without distinguishing social forms from specific political forms of the social. Overcoming this difficulty involves returning to the founding processes of the social through various historical worlds.[8]

It may seem paradoxical to seek to escape from the essentialism of current ideas by invoking something so 'essential' as the shaping of a form. Yet it is at the 'deep' level of the forms of institutionalising processes that one may differentiate not only between historical periods (for example, the two different phases in the Western history of modernity), but also between different historical paths of the political. That the *problématique* of privatisation is being globalised today does not take anything away from the special historical character of the processes that built it. Conversely,

---

[7] B. Hibou, 'Retrait ou redéploiement de l'Etat?', *Critique Internationale*, 1, autumn 1998, pp. 151–68.

[8] On the Chinese trajectory, see Y. Chevrier, 'L'empire distendu. Esquisse du politique en Chine des Qing à Deng Xiaoping', pp. 262–395 in J.-F. Bayart (ed.), *La Greffe de l'Etat*, Paris: Karthala, 1996.

that special character does not mean that other historical processes owe their other-ness to an absence of formalisation of the social sphere—not even if cultural traditions and the general set of norms suggest it, especially as such suggestions owe less to old traditions than to relatively recent ideological-political reactions in the face of Western domination. 'Making society', and doing so in the political sense of the term, is not the monopoly of a particular tradition of formation of the social and the state—that is, our own, which has rooted production of social sense in the institutionalising processes constructing a formalised form of the political. What is involved is not a characteristic or a privilege of history, peculiar to a civilisation, which became central in its first modernity and then challenged in its second modernity, but a general mechanism of ordering and hierarchical arrangement of societies, whose modes of operating can be discerned and differentiated in space and time. The history of the political moves away from a general comparison, which can only raise anew the never-ending issue of the terms to be compared and by which the comparisons are made (that is, the ever-open question of the language of the social sciences in Area Studies). It becomes a matter of situating contexts and reciprocal contextualisations between historical trajectories in terms of time and spatial scales. These scales of history may thus do away with the teleology of the Western path to modernity while retaining the universalistic claims of modernity.

Historical analysis shows that it is not on the basis of the figures of the private and public spheres as presented in Western modernity that a way should be sought to differentiate the forms of political construction of the social. Those differences appear more clearly in the establishment of recognised hierarchical relations among genres of social activity as founding the institutionalising of society. This supposes that forms of the political are empirically discerned and theoretically assigned, avoiding a twofold trap: the trap of institutional description, and the symmetrical trap of reducing institutionalising forms to social forces, economic positions, powers, or mechanisms (networks of overlapping, privatisation of the state) which they institutionalise. If we examine the changes that occur in ways of institutionalising the social, the criterion of comparison must not be the more or less formal register of these operations (the legal, administrative, ritual or ethical 'form'), but rather what they signify: it is the structured, interrelated social whole that, through those operations, attains a form which—in view of the possible variety for ordering of significant factors, as shown in history—we shall say is political. Care must be taken, however, not to make it a nature of the political, but rather to relate this sort of shaping to historical trajectories of the political, as was suggested at the beginning of this Postface.

Implicit or explicit hierarchies of social action do not depend on differentiation of specialised social fields, which would confine them to modern Western societies and make them a characteristic of Europe's first modernity (which, indeed, refers to a structuring link between the politically constructed emancipation of individuals and a social form whose operation and effect have formalised the forms of the social). They are inherent in all forms of social organisation, even if their significant factors vary and are more or less formalised in the political. In the historical trajectory of Western societies, formalisation of sociality in the political was the effect of a long history of reciprocal building of the state and the social: Giddens's perspective—a capitalist society is only a society (a modern society) because it is a nation-state—corresponds, basically, with de Tocqueville's perspective on the Ancien Régime and the Revolution.

Why should this genesis of modernity not be à special case of those hierarchy-creating configurations, of which a general historical analysis would reveal other figures, like so many dispositions ordering social action and structuring the socio-political order? This hypothesis should not be formulated in relation to the specific features of the political but more widely, in comparison with the specific character of the political in other spaces of civilisation and history. Hence the fundamental question would be: the reality of the political is 'substantial', relatively to civilisations and historical moments under consideration, because it proceeds from dynamics of hierarchisation of social activity, not only in power but also in dignity, as the foundation of institutionalising action of societies. Other configurations and other histories were possible, from which many specific paths to the present day have emerged. These crowd and mingle together on the interactive, but falsely uniformised, scene of globalisation.

INDEX

The CERI Series in Comparative Politics and International Studies

Series editor CHRISTOPHE JAFFRELOT

This series consists of translations of noteworthy publications in the social sciences emanating from the foremost French research centre in international studies, the Paris-based Centre d'Etudes et de Recherches Internationales (CERI), part of Sciences Po and associated with the CNRS (Centre National de la Recherche Scientifique)

The focus of the series is the transformation of politics and society by transnational and domestic factors—globalisation, migration, and the post-bipolar balance of power on the one hand, and ethnicity and religion on the other. States are more permeable to external influence than ever before and this phenomenon is accelerating processes of social and political change the world over. In seeking to understand and interpret these transformations, this series give priority to social trends from below as much as the interventions of state and non-state actors.

Founded in 1952, CERI has forty full-time fellows drawn from different disciplines conducting research on comparative political analysis, international relations, regionalism, transnational flows, political sociology, political economy and on individual states.